PEEL

Norman Gash

Longman
London and New York

LONGMAN GROUP LIMITED London and New York

Associated companies, branches and representatives
throughout the world
Published in the United States of America by
Longman Inc., New York

© Longman Group Limited 1976

First published 1976

Library of Congress Cataloging in Publication Data
Gash, Norman.
    Peel.
    "A condensed version of Mr. Secretary Peel (1961)
and Sir Robert Peel (1972)."
    Bibliography: p.
    Includes index.
    1.   Peel, Robert, Sir, bart., 1788–1850.
DA536.P3G315   941.081'092'4 [B]   75-25695
ISBN 0-582-48083-3

Set in 10 point Baskerville
and printed in Great Britain
by Lowe & Brydone (Printers) Ltd, Thetford, Norfolk

Contents

Illustrations

Foreword

This single-volume life of Peel is a condensed version of *Mr Secretary Peel* (1961) and *Sir Robert Peel* (1972). It seemed unnecessary therefore to include acknowledgements, footnotes, references, or bibliography, all of which may be found in the original volumes. For those who are interested a brief list of books and articles on Peel for further reading is given at the end of the text.

St Salvator's College,
St Andrews

Norman
Gash

January 1975

Chronological Table

1788	birth of Robert Peel	*1789 French Revolution*
		1793 war with France
1796	Drayton Manor purchased	
1800–04	at Harrow School	
1805–09	at Oxford University	*1805 Trafalgar*
1809	enters parliament	*Perceval prime minister*
1810	under-secretary for War & Colonies	
1812	Chief Secretary for Ireland	*Liverpool prime minister*
1814	dissolution of Catholic Board	*Insurrection & Peace Preservation Acts*
1815	O'Connell affair	*Waterloo*
1817	M.P. Oxford University	*Catholic debates*
1818	resigns Irish Secretaryship	
1819	Bullion Committee: Currency Act	*Peterloo: Six Acts*
1820	marries Julia Floyd	*accession of George IV*
1822	Home Secretary	*death of Castlereagh*
1827	resigns office	*Canning prime minister*
1828	Home Secretary	*Wellington prime minister*
1829	resigns seat for Oxford: formation Metropolitan Police	*Catholic Emancipation Act*
1830	death of his father: M.P. for Tamworth: resignation of ministry	*accession of William IV: general election: Grey becomes prime minister*
1831	reform bills defeated	*general election*
1832	refuses office	*Reform Act: general election*
1834	recalled from Italy to become prime minister: *Tamworth Manifesto*	*resignation of Grey: Melbourne becomes prime minister: dismissal of Whig ministry*
1835	Ecclesiastical Commission: resignation of government	*general election: English Municipal Corporations Act*
1836	elected Rector of Glasgow University	*Irish Corporations and Irish Church bills abandoned:*
1837	Glasgow speeches	*accession of Queen Victoria*
1838	Merchant Taylor's Hall speech	*Irish Poor Law & Tithes Acts*
1839	Bedchamber crisis	*Melbourne resigns*

1840	failure of no-confidence motion	*Irish Corporations & Canada Acts*
1841	negotiations with Prince Albert: becomes prime minister	*Whigs defeated on sugar: general election*
1842	corn bill, budget and income tax: accompanies queen to Scotland	*Ellenborough goes to India: Webster-Ashburton treaty*
1843	Drummond's assassination arrest of O'Connell Devon Commission	*Repeal movement in Ireland: Annexation of Scinde: 1st Chateau d'Eu meeting*
1844	cabinet discussions on Ireland: defeat on factory & sugar bills: Tahiti incident	*Bank Charter Act: Ellenborough recalled from India: Heytesbury Lord-Lieutenant*
1845	second free-trade budget: Maynooth bill debates: potato disease in Ireland: cabinet discussions on corn	*government rearmament programme 2nd Chateau d'Eu meeting: Russell's Edinburgh Letter: Russell fails to form ministry*
1846	Canning episode: resignation of government	*repeal of Corn Laws: defeat on Irish protection of life bill general election*
1847	financial discussions with Wood	
1849	speeches on Free Trade and Ireland	*repeal of Navigation Acts*
1850	Peel's accident and death	*Don Pacifico debate*

The Peel Family

Ròbert Peele (purchased Peel Fold 1731)

William Peele (1682–1757)

Robert (Parsley) Peel (1723–95)

Children: William · Edmund · Jonathan · Lawrence · Joseph · John · Anne · Harriet (m. Robert Eden, Lord Henley)

Robert Peel (1750–1830) m. Ellen Yates (1766–1803), cr. Bt. 1800

- Mary — m. George Dawson M.P.
- Elizabeth — m. Rev. Wm. Cockburn, later Dean of York
- ROBERT PEEL, 2nd. Bt., b. 5 Feb. 1788, d. 2 July 1850, Prime Minister 1834–35, 1841–46
- William Yates — m. Jane, d. of E. of Mountcashel
- Edmund — m. Emily Swinfen
- John — m. Augusta Swinfen
- Jonathan — m. Alice, d. of M. of Ailsa
- Lawrence — m. Jane, d. of D. of Richmond

ROBERT PEEL m. Julia d. of General Sir John Floyd, b. 1795

- Julia, b. 1821, m. Vt. Villiers, later E. of Jersey
- Robert, b. 1822, 3rd. Bt., m. Lady Emily Hay, d. of M. of Tweeddale, M.P., P.C., G.C.B., Chief Secretary for Ireland 1861–65
- Frederick, b. 1823, M.P., barrister, P.C., K.C.M.G., financial secretary to Treasury, 1859–65
- William, b. 1824, capt. R.N., K.C.B., V.C., served in Crimean War and Indian Mutiny, d. on active service in India 1858
- John Floyd, b. 1827, capt. Scots Fusilier Guards
- Arthur Wellesley, b. 1829, M.P., secretary Poor Law Board, Board of Trade, and Treasury. Speaker of the House of Commons 1884–95, cr. Vt. Peel 1895
- Eliza, b. 1832, m. Hon. Francis Stonor s. of Lord Camoys

Introduction

Peel, born in 1788 in the world of Gibbon and Joshua Reynolds, of stage-coaches, highwaymen and the judicial burning of women, died in 1850 in the age of Faraday and Darwin, of *Punch*, railway excursions, trade unions, and income tax. Between these terminal dates lay a period of revolutionary change and quasirevolutionary violence. In the first half of the nineteenth century British society was remodelled into recognisably modern shape. But the process, logical and successful as it seems in retrospect, was for the people of the time a confused and painful experience. The crashing of ancient landmarks was more obvious, and to many seemed more significant, than the tentative approaches to a new society, more united, more contented, and more orderly, which in the latter part of the century was able to work out the problems of democratic government, industrial regulation, public health, and popular education, at greater leisure and with greater stability. Peel grew up in the shadow of the Revolutionary and Napoleonic Wars. He was a child of five when the struggle began. Sixteen years later, when he entered parliament, the British effort against Napoleon was entering its last, and for the first time victorious, stage. When the crowning news of Waterloo reached an expectant London, he already had five years experience of office. The events and memories of the Napoleonic wars, slowly diminishing into nostalgic perspective, captured the imagination of many Victorians in the peaceful, sunny decades later in the century. For Peel, however, it was the first great formative experience of his career; and when peace came at last, the country swept on, unprepared and untutored by any historical precedent, to grapple with problems which were the direct social and economic consequences of the greatest and most expensive war it had ever fought.

But this was only the overture to the nineteenth century. The real body of the drama was the development that had been going on before and during the war: the unparalleled growth of industry, mechanical power, population, and urban communities which historians were to call the Industrial Revolution, and the social changes, political struggles, wars of classes, institutions and ideas, to which it gave rise. It is true no doubt that the Industrial Revolution has never finished, or more accurately, that it was the first of a series of industrial revolutions. But what gave unique importance to the initial wave of industrialisation was that it struck what was essentially a decentralised and rural community, governed by a landed aristocracy under the narrow parliamentary and Anglican constitution laid down at the Revolution of 1688. Not until fundamental alterations had been made in that historic fabric was the way clear for later Victorian developments. These were difficulties enough; but outside and menacing was the problem of Ireland, where the complex of ills represented by the sister island was harsh and alien to the point of despair. Pitt's Act of Union in 1800 had done nothing to solve Ireland's basic troubles—the problem of poverty and the problem of disorder—and as long as those evils continued to fester, Irish nationalism and Irish separatism possessed an ever-welling source of popular support.

It was in this world that Peel's political career was cast; and it was to these problems that his mind was turned in the forty years in which he was engaged in public affairs. That by the end of his life he dominated the British political scene as no one since Pitt had done, was a measure of the impress which his character and statesmanship had made on the national consciousness. But that position was only secured through a succession of achievements, crises and bitter controversies. Two great 'betrayals' of his followers, over Catholic emancipation in 1829 and the Corn Laws in 1846, marked the abnormal strain to which his sense of administrative duty and national necessity was subjected. His career therefore was controversial, both in his own lifetime and afterwards, and his own personality did little to assist comprehension. To his public work he brought a fine apparatus of personal qualities: complete integrity, a high standard of duty, a lucid and powerful intellect, an immense capacity for hard work. But behind these visible characteristics lay his own essential temperament, usually held in check, not always appreciated by the casual observer, but exercising a profound influence on his actions. He had pleasure in achievement, an instinct for leadership, a quick pride and a hot temper, a courage that sometimes became stubbornness, an intense mental and physical sensitivity which was both a strength and a weakness in the rough school of politics; and finally, concealed in the recesses of his nature, a curious self-consciousness and lack of assurance which formed the one great flaw in his emotional equipment. It was a flaw which betrayed itself in time of strain and injury, and it had disagreeable secondary effects which won him many enemies. In Peel's complex nature jarring forces were at work; and though his strong mind and character dominated his life, it was at the cost of conflict and bitterness that left scars on his soul and made him to many people a cold and unattractive figure.

To succeeding Victorian generations, whose outlook was conditioned by the ordered warfare of a more modern parliamentary system, it seemed a natural conclusion that Peel had 'chosen the wrong party'. But by the late nineteenth century the age of Peel had already passed into the limbo between the remembered present and the historically recorded past. Most late-Victorian verdicts on Peel were intrinsically unsound because they projected back into his time the conventions and images of their own. To judge Peel by subsequent standards of parties and programmes is a patent anachronism. His lifework was to fashion a compromise between the system he inherited and the necessities of a changing world. Too often posterity judged him as though that compromise was already in existence; or at least, as though the machinery for contriving that compromise lay already to hand. The political tradition to which Peel was heir, however, though not without its virtues, did not include a balanced rivalry of parties and policies through which all necessary political and social adjustments could be made. Though Peel can claim to be the founder of the Conservative Party, he was in a fundamental sense never a party politician. Son of a cotton-spinner though he was, he carried on the aristocratic tradition of 'the king's ministers' and the 'king's government'. He looked first, not to party, but to the state; not to programmes, but to national expediency. His conservatism was not a party label, still less a class interest. It was an instinct for continuity and the preservation of order and good government in a society which was confronted with the choice between adaptation or upheaval. If he 'broke' the Conservative Party, which he had created, that was of secondary importance compared with the fact that by insisting on changes in the national interest, and on concessions to national demands, he helped to preserve the flexibility of the parliamentary constitution and the survival of aristocratic influence in a period of distress and challenge.

To the next generation, entering the political vineyard after the heat and burden of the day, that was not always obvious. Rarely can such a clever character sketch by such an intelligent man have been based on such false premisses as, for example, the famous essay on Peel by Walter Bagehot. But such a misunderstanding, common enough in any generation which succeeds a great historical career, is doubly comprehensible in this case. Later Victorian Liberals could feel with justification that, however liberal in his policies, Peel was never one of them. Later Victorian Conservatives, looking to the disruptions of 1829 and 1846, and influenced more than they realised by the brilliant political pamphlet which Disraeli wrote under the title of *Lord George Bentinck*, found it equally hard to recognise in Peel one of the principal architects of the modern Conservative tradition. Romantic Tory historians, following the pseudohistorical inspiration of those two great men of literature, Bolingbroke and Disraeli, could pass him over almost without mention in the genealogy of titled families and broad acres that constitutes for them the history of the 'Tory Party'. But though the myth of Conservatism has been more often Disraelian, its practice has been almost uniformly Peelite. With that Peel would have been content; he preferred facts to phrases.

Chapter 1

Father and son

In 1790, the year after the outbreak of the French Revolution, the Marquess of Bath sold a large part of his Staffordshire estates, including the manor of Drayton, to two north country cotton manufacturers, Joseph Wilkes of Measham in Leicestershire, and Robert Peel of Bury in Lancashire. The two partners, who had taken a mortgage to assist in raising the purchase price, sold part of the estate and divided the rest between them. By a separate and simultaneous transaction Peel also bought from Lord Bath a big block of land and house property in nearby Tamworth. Some years later, in 1796, he acquired at a reduced price the manor of Drayton which had originally been part of Wilkes's share of the purchase. It is probable that from the start Peel was bent on securing a permanent position in the country. His Tamworth property enabled him to succeed to the share in the parliamentary representation formerly enjoyed by the Marquess of Bath's family; and the year of the sale saw the new proprietor returned as M.P. for the borough. The final step was the removal of his family from Bury and the establishment of a new home at Drayton Bassett. The dilapidated Tudor manor-house was pulled down and before the end of the century a large modern building, Old Drayton Hall, solid, rectangular and unpretentious, rose in its place. But if the house lacked distinction, the combination of the Drayton estate, industrial wealth, and a parliamentary seat was enough to secure for Robert Peel a position of influence in the county and make him the object of respectful, if curious attention, from the Staffordshire gentry among whom he had chosen to settle.

The new owner of Drayton Manor came of a Lancashire family, settled at Peel Fold near Oswaldtwistle since the beginning of George II's reign. Like many other farmers and cottagers the Peels had intermittently combined agriculture and wool-weaving; but it was his father, the first Robert Peel, who had taken advantage of the little pocket of expanding textile manufacture and piecemeal mechanical invention in his neighbourhood to lift himself and his family into a new sphere of life. Along with his brother-in-law, Jonathan Haworth, who had learned the technique of calico-printing with a Dutch firm in Spitalfields, and William Yates, son of a Blackburn innkeeper, who supplied some of the capital, he set up about 1760 a factory at Brookside, not far from Peel Fold. The three men lacked neither inventive skill nor commercial enterprise; and along with the Claytons of Bamber, the firm of Haworth, Peel and Yates could claim the honour of being the founders of the great Lancashire calico-printing industry. After some years the partners disbanded. Haworth and Yates moved to Bury; but though Peel remained at Brookside, he had his own difficulties to face. Following an outbreak of rioting and machine-breaking in the Blackburn area in 1779, he migrated to Burton in Staffordshire and built new cotton mills on the banks of the river Trent. There he carried on a flourishing business until about 1792 he relinquished direct control, leaving his extensive interests in Lancashire and Staffordshire in charge of some of his sons.

'Parsley' Peel, as he was known (the nickname derived from one of his favourite calico patterns), was like many later Peels a big, reserved man. He possessed other family characteristics: a singleminded application to his work, considerable business acumen, and a marked independence of character. Barring accidents, he used to say, a man could be what he chose. Certainly he had come a long way himself and at Burton upon Trent he was something of a celebrity. The inhabitants called him 'the philosopher' and the stooping, silent old man in bushy wig and dark coat was one of the sights of the town as he paced slowly through the streets with his gold-headed stick, gazing abstractedly at the cobbles. Much had happened since the days when he had gone about his farm work at Fish Lane, burly and erect in woollen apron, calf-skin waistcoat, and wooden clogs. It was a touch of pride in his achievement, perhaps, that made him in 1792 obtain a coat of arms for his family. The arms, with their bundle of arrows symbolising family unity, the bee and shuttle as emblems of industry and manufacture, and the motto *Industria*, fitted the man himself and the family which inherited them.

Of his seven surviving sons (the Peels were prolific as well as prosperous), it was the third, Robert born in 1750, who most resembled his father. Educated at Blackburn Grammar School, he was sent to London for a time before returning to the family business at Brookside. Ambitious and self-confident, however, he did not easily reconcile himself to the position of a younger son. At the age of eighteen he told his father that they were 'too thick on the ground' and offered to go elsewhere if he were given £500 with which to start himself. The offer was not immediately accepted but about 1773 it was arranged that he should become a partner of his father's old associates, Messrs Haworth and Yates at Bury. There, by his energy and assiduity, the younger man soon became the dominant personality in the firm. Though the profits steadily increased, most of the money was ploughed back into the business; and his own life was frugal and temperate. For many years he lived as a lodger with his partner and when at the age of thirty-three he allowed himself the luxury of marriage, it was on the eldest daughter of the house, Ellen Yates, a pretty affectionate girl of eighteen, that his choice fell.

By that date he was already a wealthy man and virtual head of a prosperous business. Ten years of unremitting effort had put him abreast, if not ahead, of his father, and by the start of the new century he was one of the richest cotton manufacturers in the kingdom, employing some 15,000 people and paying over £40,000 annually to the government in duty on his printed goods. There was a dark side to this upward progress. Like most factory-owners in the pioneer days of the Industrial Revolution he made extensive use of child labour and as his personal supervision relaxed, ill-health and malnutrition became increasingly evident among them. One of his mills near Manchester was involved in a fever epidemic in 1784 which provoked one of the first public enquiries into factory conditions. But if Robert Peel was one of many mill-owners with reason to be ashamed of the conditions which produced their wealth, he was the first to move in parliament for intervention by the legislature on behalf of factory children. In 1802 he carried through the Health and Morals of Apprentices Act which limited hours of labour, forbade night-work, and made provision for clothing, education and conditions of work. Over a decade later he acted as the parliamentary spokesman for Robert Owen in securing the committee of 1816 which resulted in an act of 1819 laying down similar provisions for all factory children. In the absence of statutory inspectors neither act was very effective. But public attention had been drawn to the problem, certain principles were on the statute book, and in Peel's factories at least there was reasonable observance of the regulations. After 1802 he was able to pride himself with some justice on the state of his mill-hands.

By then he had fully realised his youthful ambition to raise himself and his descendants to 'rank and consequence' in society. When he entered parliament in 1790, only two years remained before the European monarchies went to war with the French Revolution; only three before Britain began the exhausting and costly struggle with the Republic and Empire which with one brief interval was to last for twenty-two years. Against such a background it was natural that the new member for Tamworth should take his place as a supporter of the government. In the first peaceful decade Pitt had shown himself the friend and patron of the great commercial and manufacturing interests of the kingdom. With the outbreak of war he became something even more symbolic: the leader of Christian and monarchical Britain in its duel with the regicide and radical republic across the Channel. Robert Peel, Anglican and conservative, shared that innate feeling for order, piety and patriotism which George III and Pitt were able to rally to the side of authority when the conflict not only with the power but the ideas of Jacobin France commenced in 1793. He was early prominent among those who came forward in defence of liberty, stability, and property against the propaganda of native and foreign republicans. In 1792 he spoke at the foundation meeting in Manchester of an Association for Preserving Constitutional Order; between 1796 and 1798 he took an active part in raising and commanding volunteer forces for Pitt's supplementary militia in his own localities of Lancashire and Staffordshire; and the firm of Yates and Peel subscribed £10,000 in response to Pitt's appeal in 1797 for free-will tax contributions from persons of substantial wealth. This patriotic effort did not pass unnoticed. A little later the Prime Minister offered him a baronetcy. Peel accepted and the patent appeared in November 1800.

It was as Sir Robert Peel therefore that the owner of Drayton Bassett settled down in the new manor-house. The children of this marriage with Ellen Yates were already growing tall around him. Mary, the eldest, born in 1785, had been followed by another girl in 1786. Then, on 5 February 1788, came the first son, blue-eyed and reddish-haired like many of his family and christened Robert after his father and grandfather. He was born at Chamber Hall, Bury, where the Peels had moved after their marriage, 'in the old ivied room at the back, overlooking the court'. William was born in 1789 and Edmund in 1791. Two more girls followed, both of whom died in infancy. Then came three boys, John, Jonathan and Lawrence. The quiverful was completed by Harriet Eleonora, born in 1803 at 16 Upper Grosvenor Street, the house her father had taken as his London residence. Before the end of the year the family of nine children were left motherless. Ellen Yates was a lively energetic woman, with a happy temperament and high spirits. It was from her perhaps that the children inherited their love of sport and their strong, active physique. Two years later Sir Robert married again. His second wife was Susanna Clerke, sister to the rector of Bury. But the marriage was not a success and in the end there was a separation. For all practical purposes the younger Peel children grew up without the warmth and care that a mother, or even in happier circumstances a stepmother, might have given them. Of their father's affection there could be no doubt. Plain in manner and blunt of speech as he appeared to outsiders, he had a strong vein of kindliness and humour. But he was not a man who could easily express his emotions; and his love for his family issued as often as not in rough, half-joking exhortations and admonition. He placed high standards before them and the Peel boys grew up in the gospel of hard work and achievement as the proper duty of man.

The transfer from Bury to Drayton and the acquisition of a London home was the first loosening of the tight provincial circle of Peels which had grown up in Lancashire and Staffordshire. Robert, the eldest boy, received his early education from his father and his own reading. His father made him, even as a child, repeat the substance of the Sunday sermons and recite from Goldsmith, Pope and other poets. 'His eldest son, a youth of the most promising talents,' wrote an admirer of Sir Robert in 1804, 'has been so much in the habit of exercising the retentiveness of his memory, conformably to this method, that very few indeed of his age can carry with them more of the sentiments of an author than himself.' The older children were also instructed by the local curate who came daily to Chamber Hall for a couple of hours. In those early days Robert was a quiet, well-mannered and disciplined boy, much praised by his elders, not over-popular with the young, and already showing a certain selfconsciousness that kept him aloof from the society of other children. At Bury the Peels were in a position of eminence which exposed the younger members to some ridicule and jealousy by the urchins of the neighbourhood. Lawrence Peel, a cousin, later recorded that Robert 'would walk a mile round rather than encounter the rude jests of the Bury lads'. Yet from other childhood incidents it is clear that he had all the activity, fearlessness and quick temper of his family.

After the move to Drayton he was sent to a small school for sons of neighbouring gentry kept by the vicar of Tamworth where he extended his classical studies and was soon recognised as the best scholar of his years among his school companions. Drayton had other advantages. With its broad park and surrounding countryside it fostered the love of outdoor life and field sports which marked several of his family in later life. Robert early took up shooting, a passion shared by his second brother William; and Jonathan, their junior by ten years, was subsequently to win fame as a racehorse owner. Though their father made little effort to preserve game, there was plenty of rough shooting in the flat waterlogged meadows and spinneys round Drayton, wild duck on the park lake, pigeons, partridges, hares, and an occasional bittern. As a matter of course he rode both for exercise and utility, and later in Ireland tried his hand at driving. But his favourite exercise for the rest of his life was on foot with a gun. A good eye and constant practice made him an excellent shot, and at more than one country-house party wagers were subsequently to be laid and won on his unusual skill in the field. Partly perhaps as a result of this early love of sport, he grew up strong and active, a good walker and capable of great physical endurance.

Years later legends began to circulate about his boyhood which various proud but embarrassing parental utterances seemed to confirm. There was a story, for example, that at his birth the elder Peel fell on his knees and dedicated his firstborn son to the service of his country; and that at the christening he expressed the hope that he would walk in the footsteps of his hero Pitt. The origin of the tale is more likely to have been words uttered by his father many years afterward in the House of Commons. In a debate on cash payments in 1819, which found him in opposition to his son, or as he termed him 'a very near and dear relation', Sir Robert went on to speak of Pitt.

He well remembered, when that near and dear relation was only a child, he observed to some friends who were standing near him, that the man who discharged his duty to the country in the manner in which Mr Pitt had, did most to be admired, and was most to be imitated; and he thought at that moment, if his own life and that of his dear relation should be spared, he would one day present him to his country, to follow in the same path.

It would have shown more consideration to his son if this silent thought had never been communicated, even twenty years later, to such a ribald audience as the House of Commons.

Sir Robert was ambitious for all his children. He had been helped to a successful career by his father and he in turn placed his sons in positions where nothing was beyond their reach. If his thoughts centred on his eldest, it would only have been natural; and since that son won fame and the others did not, it was remembered what had been said and done on his behalf. But Sir Robert was paternally active for them all. When the eldest was well launched on his political career, his father more than once solicited from the prime minister some equally promising opening for his second son, William. Nor was it clear in the early years that Robert was the ablest of the family. His two nearest brothers, William and Edmund, showed externally at least greater liveliness and initiative; and his uncle Joseph thought William by nature had the quicker mind. It was of his second, not his first son, that Sir Robert was speaking when he asked his clerical tutor whether he would be a William Pitt. 'I hope so,' came the answer, 'but Robert will be Robert Peel.'

The phrase, authentic or not, had insight as well as neatness. Many characteristics of his father, and indeed of his grandfather, reappeared in the Robert of the third generation. Perhaps for that reason there always seemed a bond between them; and even when they disagreed, there was never any quarrel or estrangement. If the younger man was ever restive under his father's clumsily expressed feelings, he never betrayed it. In later life he would good-humouredly relate to friends some of the remarks his father made when he was a boy. He told Sam Rogers, for instance, that Sir Robert used to say to him, 'Bob, you dog, if you are not prime minister some day, I'll disinherit you.' The elder Peel is not the only father to have addressed his young in such terms; but perhaps, as the younger Robert's life fell more and more into the pattern his father wanted to see, the high aims constantly held out to him were not without effect in stimulating his ambitions. Prime ministers in the early nineteenth century, however, were not likely to be produced by the schools of Tamworth or any other small industrial town. Sir Robert Peel was too shrewd not to see the advantages of coming into contact at an impressionable age and on equal terms with the future governing class of England. So Robert and William were in due course despatched to Harrow, and later John, Jonathan and Lawrence to Rugby. For Robert, who in February 1800 at the age of twelve, was the first to leave home, public school meant the first real separation from his family and the first upward step from his father's social environment.

II

At the start of the nineteenth century Harrow was already established as one of the leading public schools of the country. Under its eminent headmaster, Dr Joseph Drury, its numbers were flourishing as never before and no fewer than four future prime ministers sat on its benches during his twenty years of rule from 1785 to 1805. Peel was placed in the fourth form and found himself with fifteen companions of similar age, one of them another Staffordshire boy, George Chetwynd, later M.P. and second baronet. Among the others were Murray, son of the Bishop of St Davids who left in 1803 to enter the Bengal civil service and was dead within five years; Williams of Glamorgan, who went on to Cambridge and became an expert in Bardic literature; and Dawkins who joined the Guards in 1804, served in the Peninsula and at Waterloo, and survived to become M.P. for Boroughbridge. In the upper third was William Lowther, the future second Earl of Lonsdale; in the Shell George Granville, later second Duke of Sutherland. George Dawson, who was to be Peel's private secretary, brother-in-law and political follower, did not arrive until a year later. But Sir Thomas Acland, the great west country member who sat for Devonshire almost continuously from 1812 to 1857, was already at school and became one of Peel's friends. With Palmerston, who left the year Peel arrived and was in a different house, he could scarcely have become acquainted; but a year later a new boy called Byron joined the school.

Like other schools of the time, it was a hard and unruly society. Swearing and drinking were fashionable; the monitors were autocratic and sometimes tyrannical; there were rough customs and rougher sports, including nocturnal paper-chases and fights behind the schoolhouse. Organised compulsory games were something for the future; but cricket and football were played, and there were cross country runs, and in summer swimming in the school pool known as Duck Puddle. Lack of supervision made it easy for boys to wander over the open countryside which still separated the school from the brick and mortar tide of the metropolis ten miles away. Enjoyment of liberty, individual initiative, and respect for physical courage (or in the language of the day 'bottom') were the main virtues of the public school system before Arnold's day.

Peel's most unpleasant recorded experience at Harrow came early on. The fourth form in which he had been put required a knowledge of Latin versification which he had not been taught at Tamworth. He was therefore kept back for a time for special instruction and consequently, in the eyes of some of the senior boys, he could not claim the exemption from fagging which was the privilege of the upper school. Having been told by his tutor that he would be placed in a form which would free him from that obligation, Peel was bold enough to refuse when ordered to carry out some fagging duty and was duly thrashed by his aggrieved senior. Once he had mastered his deficiency in verse, however, he soon made his mark as a scholar. For years afterwards his tutor, Mark Drury, kept many of his exercises to show to other pupils as examples of terseness and clarity in both English and Latin. A fellow Harrovian

7

recalled in later years the picture of a smiling goodnatured boy 'surrounded, while the school bell was yet ringing, with boys who had neglected their exercises, calling upon him to supply them, which he did, writing now Latin, now Greek, with as much facility as though it were his mother-tongue'. Though not gregarious in his habits, his generosity and kindness, together with his strength and courage, made him popular with his fellows; and his intellectual powers evoked from his tutor a prophecy which Sir Robert would have rejoiced to hear, that 'you boys will one day see Peel Prime Minister'. The steadiness of his character kept him from the more impulsive escapades of his companions and he was hardly ever in trouble with authority.

Nevertheless, he was not without some private and illicit amusements of his own. It was noticed in his early years at school that he rarely joined in the conventional sports of cricket, football, and hare-and-hounds, but preferred to go off into the countryside, occasionally returning with a bird or two which his more ingenuous fellows thought he had knocked down with a stone. In fact he had secretly arranged, with a close friend, Robert Anstruther, for his guns to be kept during term at a nearby cottage. When the two boys were assumed to be peacefully rambling abroad, communing with nature, they were actually beating distant hedgerows and coverts for small game. In his last years at Harrow, however, he took a greater interest in football and according to his brother, William Peel, he was 'one of the best players in the school'.

Clearly his Harrow days were far from being absorbed in bookish studies and many years later he disparagingly referred to the school as being 'better conducted now than it was when I misspent my time there'. Yet if there was some relaxation or dissipation of energy during his Harrovian period, it may not have been without advantages. For a young boy unduly influenced, however subconsciously, by his father's constant supervision and his position as eldest son, public school provided a different and less inhibited atmosphere. More important than any subsequent depreciation is the fact that his life at Harrow was happy and successful. It lasted only five years. In 1803 he reached the upper fifth; in 1804 he was a monitor; and speechday on 5 July of that year, when he declaimed as Turnus, with Byron, sitting to hide his lameness, as Latinus, crowned his school career. He went back for one more term but at Christmas came the final departure.

Oxford was the next step, but he had nine months at his disposal before going into residence in October 1805. The winter of 1804-05 he spent at the Peel town house in Grosvenor Street, attending scientific lectures at the Royal Institution but more often to be found under the gallery of the House of Commons, listening to debates. A little incident of which he was reminded long afterwards, may have referred to this or an even earlier period. One day, while still a schoolboy, he was standing at the entrance to the House with his father and Samuel Oldknow, another great cotton manufacturer, when Pitt came up. He asked who the boy was, and when told he was Sir Robert's son, took him by the hand and led him into the chamber. The session of 1805 was the last when anyone was to see Pitt on the floor of the assembly he had dominated so long. The months from January to July witnessed the final bout in the classic duel between Pitt and Fox which had lasted since 1783. Yet it was not Pitt but his unsuccessful rival who left the indelible memory in the young Peel's mind. Over twenty years later he recalled in the same place the Catholic debates of May 1805: an occasion 'he should never forget. . . . He never heard a speech which made a greater impression on his mind than that delivered by Mr Fox during that debate.' Eight months later Pitt was dying at Putney and in the autumn his old antagonist followed him to the grave.

Returning to Drayton at the end of the session Robert settled down in earnest to repair the gaps in his Harrow education and prepare for Oxford. A Cambridge senior wrangler had been engaged by his father in response to his son's request for some preliminary tuition in mathematics, a subject still ignored by the Harrow curriculum. During the summer months of 1805, while the *grande armée* stood at Boulogne and the British ships of the line cruised monotonously off Brest and Cadiz, waiting for Villeneuve, the Rev. R. Bridge coached his young pupil in the rural tranquillity of Drayton Park. Autumn came and on 21 October, when Peel in his gentleman-commoner's cap and gown was being inducted as a matriculated member of Oxford University, a thousand miles away the last great fleet action of the war was being fought off Cape Trafalgar.

III

At the time Peel went to Oxford the university was already extricating itself from the political and academic torpor which had characterised it in the middle decades of the previous century. From about 1780 a new spirit had begun to make itself felt. Eveleigh of Oriel, Parsons of Balliol and Jackson of Christ Church led the movement for a reform of the antiquated degree system; and in the year Peel arrived at Harrow, the new examination statutes finally received the assent of Congregation. If the standards of the examination were pitched too high at the outset, the quality of college tutors was steadily improving. Under the autocratic rule of Cyril Jackson, who became Dean of Christ Church in 1783, that college had reached a peak of intellectual reputation unmatched before or since; and it was to Christ Church that Peel went. Lord Dudley's disapproving remark in 1818 that the college had secured 'an almost exclusive connection with Oxford-going nobility and great gentry' was equally true ten years earlier. In the period just before Peel's arrival, there had passed through Jackson's hands Canning, Jenkinson (later Lord Liverpool and Peel's first departmental chief), Sturges Bourne, Granville Leveson Gower (later first Earl

9

Granville), Morpeth (later Earl of Carlisle), Henry Fox (third and most famous Lord Holland), and Nicholas Vansittart. It was a company such as the Dean delighted in. A scholar, a disciplinarian, and something of a snob, he loved his young men, entertained them hospitably, followed their careers, and kept in touch with them when they went down. It was this formidable figure, one of the great university characters of his day, who remarked with satisfaction some time afterwards that 'Harrow has sent us up at least one good scholar in Mr Peel'.

For Oxford undergraduates who wanted amusement as well as scholarship, there was as always no lack of opportunity. Peel acquired a moderate taste for sport; it is hard to believe that he always left his guns behind him in Staffordshire; and Lawrence Peel has recorded that he was a boater and a cricketer. 'The hen,' his cousin went so far as to say, 'was a good deal off the nest.' One of his own college friends endorsed this account. Peel, he said, 'was fond of athletic exercises. He took great delight in cricket and in boat-racing and exercise on the river.' Handsome, tall, his strong physique masked by his height, Peel blossomed in the congenial atmosphere of Oxford as something of a dandy. For company there were plenty of former schoolfellows in the college, though one of his closest friends, as it happened, was not a Harrovian. This was Henry Vane, son and heir of Lord Darlington and later Earl of Cleveland, who came up to Christ Church in 1806. Not having been to a public school he had few acquaintances, and, as he later expressed it, Peel took him by the hand and they lived together on terms of closest intimacy for three years. At the time of Lord Melville's impeachment in 1806 Peel and Vane posted together in a hack chaise from Oxford to be present at the trial. With him and others Peel passed his lighter hours; and an anecdote of a practical joke played on an Irish and reputedly unclassical freshman, in which Peel dressed up as the Vice-Chancellor conducted an impromptu examination in the Greek Testament, showed a characteristic taste for the ludicrous which was never far below the surface in those youthful days.

In the Christ Church of Cyril Jackson, however, there was work to be done. Peel's first tutor was Gaisford, later Professor of Greek, the best scholar though perhaps not the best teacher in the college. He then passed to Lloyd, later Regius Professor and Bishop of Oxford, an excellent tutor though inclined to be timid and irresolute in more worldly matters. A close friendship developed between the two which lasted until Lloyd's premature death in 1829. Like the Dean, he was something of a college character. His eccentric dress, his constant snuff-taking, his habit of kicking the shins and pulling the ears of his students, were oddities which apparently did little to detract from the affection which he inspired; and in Peel he found his most brilliant pupil. Since 1800 further changes had been made in the degree statutes which established it on a recognisably modern basis. The unwieldy list of subjects had been divided into two separate schools; *Literae Humaniores*, which included classical literature and philosophy; and Mathematics.

Two annual examination periods were appointed; and the successful candidates were arranged into first and second classes and a pass list. Though split into two, the examinations were held at the same time, and it was clear that a candidate who offered himself for both was virtually submitting himself to two degree examinations simultaneously.

Peel made up his mind nevertheless to try for the double achievement. The effort involved was a prodigious one. Most candidates who sat the joint examination concentrated on the classical at the expense of the mathematical school. But Peel, tenacious as his father and grandfather, determined to make a bid for the highest honours in both. 'I doubt', wrote his brother afterwards, 'whether anyone ever read harder than Robert for two or three terms before he passed his examinations. He assured me that he had read eighteen hours in the day and night.' Before the date of the examination finally arrived, from lack of sleep and exercise he had brought himself to such a nervous state that he wrote to his father, suggesting that he should not present himself, since he was convinced that he would achieve nothing. The old baronet, more experienced than his highly-strung son, returned him sound advice mixed with timely encouragement. Robert recovered his self-control and with it his judgement. The day before he was due to appear before his examiners, a friend was astonished to find him nonchalantly engaged in a vigorous game of tennis. In the event he gained a resounding success which became something of a legend in the university.

> Previous to it [George Dawson wrote to their old Harrow tutor Mark Drury] he could not but have been aware that the knowledge of his great abilities had excited considerable expectations not only in his own college, but throughout the whole university. . . . The crowd that went to hear him resembled more the assembly of a public Theatre than that attending a scholastic examination.

In these remarkable circumstances, as trying perhaps to the examiners as to the examined, Peel showed a becoming modesty of manner, a clarity of language and a strength of reasoning which surpassed the hopes even of his friends. At the end of the ordeal the examining Masters separately thanked him for the pleasure they had received. In the mathematical examination, according to Gaisford, Peel's answers to the questions on Robertson's *Conic Sections* evoked the admiration of all who heard him. In both schools he was placed in the first class, and so became not only the one candidate in November 1808 to be awarded that honour but also the first to be given the double distinction since the schools were divided in 1807.

By contemporary standards it was a feat of unusual brilliance. To compare it with the later Oxford system is not easy. The mathematical side was less developed and less formidably contested; and on the classical side translation and construing of difficult passages played a larger, philosophy and ancient history a smaller part than in Jowett's generation half a century later. There is too the difference between an examination conducted orally as in Peel's day, and one, as later became the mode, conducted principally on paper. Both systems have their merits, though the qualities elicited are not the same. Oral examination needs a quick mind, an instant memory, and a power of verbal expression. A good man would probably have got a first class in either, but he would have been trained in different ways. For a parliamentary career there can be little doubt which was the more valuable preparation.

Peel took his bachelor's degree at the end of term and after Christmas returned to Christ Church for a final period of residence. It is possible that he started to read law, for later in 1809 he put his name down on the books of Lincoln's Inn. Of more importance was the fact that on 5 February of that year he came of age. For Sir Robert, to whom his son's Oxford triumph must have come as a crowning joy, it was a significant date. The following month negotiations were started to bring Robert into the House of Commons. There was a vacancy at Cashel, a corrupt Irish borough where money was the best persuader; though the baronet did not omit to use his personal influence with the government. Sir Arthur Wellesley, not long back from Portugal, dealt with this among other items of business at the Irish Office before going off to Spain the following month. On 25 March he sent to Ireland a laconic request that Mr Peel ('I will let you know his Christian name by express tomorrow') should be elected. 'We wish to have him returned by the meeting of Parlt. after the Recess.' The transference of the Oxford double-first from the quadrangles of Christ Church to the halls of Westminster was smoothly effected. The House of Commons assembled after Easter on 11 April. Three days later Robert Peele, as his name was still spelt on the parliamentary roll, was returned for Cashel City in the county of Tipperary.

There is no record that he took part in any of the debates of that year, an unedifying session dominated by the opposition attacks on alleged scandals and instances of corruption in army and Indian administration. After a solitary holiday in the Highlands with a hired horse in the summer (the first of many excursions north of the Border), Peel returned to London in November and settled down in chambers at Lincoln's Inn to his legal studies. It was not clear even then whether he had decided between politics and law as a career.

> You are engaging in a profession that will render your attainments at school and college of much use [wrote his father approvingly soon after he had taken his residence at Lincoln's Inn] . . . You have hitherto afforded me unspeakable pleasure in the manner in which you have conducted yourself, and I have no fears for the future. . . . By reading men and books you will not fail to rise to eminence in the profession of the law.

Clearly this letter in itself is enough to discount the legend of the single-minded and undeviating training of his eldest son from earliest years for high political office. What Robert thought is not known. But that summer and autumn, even while he was exploring the lonely mountains and glens of Badenoch, events were taking place in the higher reaches of parliamentary life which were to launch him irretrievably into a political career.

Chapter 2

Political overture

The death of Pitt left the country leaderless at the height of the war against the most redoubtable opponent in its history. Apart from the small rump of Foxite Whigs, nearly all the leading politicians had been at one time followers or adherents of the dead statesman; and his departure left a group of rival claimants to his inheritance. The predominantly Whig ministry of Lord Grenville fell in March 1807, having quarrelled unnecessarily with the king on a question of Catholic disabilities. The Portland administration which followed broke down in 1809 under the double strain of political jealousies at home and military disasters abroad. With Portland dying, the two antagonistic secretaries of state, Canning and Castlereagh, resigned office and subsequently fought a duel. The old king, now over seventy and almost blind, chose Spencer Perceval as his new minister. Unable to obtain the services of the leading Whigs, unwilling to admit Lord Sidmouth, the weakened cabinet limped on with what secondary reinforcements it could scratch together. Lord Liverpool took over War and Colonies in succession to Castlereagh, Lord Wellesley (Wellington's brother) was brought into the Foreign Office, and for lack of a suitable replacement Perceval retained his old post of Chancellor of the Exchequer. It was not an impressive array of talent; but as the prime minister observed, since they were abandoned by so many of the old Pittite connection, they were obliged to look for assistance in new quarters and bring forward young men.

The 1810 session opened in January. To move and second the reply to the king's speech in the House of Commons, the prime minister selected two untried members, Viscount Bernard and Robert Peel, aged twenty-four and twenty-two respectively. The invitation was a mild compliment; acceptance indicated political allegiance. This, at the start of a session which there could be no confidence the ministry would survive, argued that Peel had made up his mind. Bernard, also making his maiden speech, was a failure. Peel on the other hand was an undoubted success. Speaking with youthful fire and eloquence he defended the government's conduct of the war, looked hopefully to the future of the little British expeditionary force in Spain, and urged united resistance to the tyranny of Napoleon. He was on his feet for forty minutes without showing any sign of nerves, and when he sat down received an acclamation. The Speaker and other leading politicians assured the delighted Sir Robert that it was the best first speech since Pitt's; and old Cyril Jackson, now retired, wrote a benign letter of congratulation. 'If I had you here I would feed you with ling and cranberry tart.' In default of that delicacy, he urged Peel to give a final polish to his mind by the continual study of Homer.

But for all the flutter of pride in the Peel household, the government still had its difficulties in front of it; and others besides Perceval were casting a speculative eye on promising young men in the Commons. Canning, roving as a formidable freelance between government and opposition, had hopes of attaching Peel to his following; and Creevey the Whig diarist noted with satisfaction any small signs of independence he manifested. Whatever he felt about Canning, there was little likelihood that Peel could have entertained much sympathy for the small and isolated group of Foxite Whigs. A feature of their conduct that session was a spiteful campaign against not only the whole strategy of the war but the professional competence of the commander-in-chief in the Peninsula. For Peel on the other hand, as for most of the British public, the paramount national objective was the war; and it could scarcely have been a coincidence that the refrain of his first two speeches was the need for a vigorous prosecution of the struggle against Napoleon. The second speech had come in March, when he spoke in defence of the government's decision to send the abortive expedition to the Scheldt the previous year. The speech was well received and one of Cyril Jackson's correspondents told him that it was even better than the first. The old Dean concluded therefore that Peel had been studying Homer and dispatched another instalment of practical advice.

> Work very hard and unremittingly. Work, as I used to say sometimes, like a tiger, or like a dragon, if dragons work more and harder than tigers. Don't be afraid of killing yourself. Only retain, which is essential, your former temperance and exercise, and your aversion to mere lounge, and then you will have abundant time both for hard work and company, which last is as necessary to your future situation as even the hard work. . . . I trust and hope you will not be tempted to take employment too early, nor any, at any time, but what is really efficient and of high consideration.

For all his cautionary words Jackson obviously assumed that Peel would be ready to take office under Perceval if asked.

Perhaps it was not so much an assumption as self-evident. Any legends to the contrary, it is clear that Peel from the start was a government man. His family background had given him a colour and bias even before he entered parliament. The outlook of his father and grandfather was that of middle-class Pittite Anglican Toryism, not far removed from that of Perceval himself. It is unlikely that Harrow or Oxford had done anything to weaken those emotional and intellectual ties. When as a young M.P. Peel visited the more liberal household of his uncle Joseph in London, this fact was recognised and deplored. After one conversation with his nephew, in which Peel with a detachment rare among Englishmen had praised Napoleon's military and administrative genius, Joseph Peel observed with a sigh that he wished 'Robert were as liberal in his home as in his foreign politics'. To Whig satirists he seemed for many years no more than a chip off the old block.

> What is young Peel made of, made of,
> What is young Peel made of?
> Ginger hair
> And Sir Robert's stare,
> Such is young Peel made of.

Whatever the future held, in 1810 there was little doubt where his political sympathies lay. Proof of this was not long in coming.

In the summer of 1810 a vacancy occurred in one of the under-secretaryships at the Department of War and Colonies and Lord Liverpool offered it to the young member of his own college who had made so promising a debut at the start of the year. Sir Robert was overjoyed and old William Yates congratulated his grandson with a letter and brace of moor game. Robert's reply from Downing Street, the earliest surviving letter in a career which was to be full of letters, still showed something of the round unhurried hand of a schoolboy. He spoke of his regret at being unable to accompany his uncle, Colonel Yates, to shoot on Church Moor, promised sport for them both at Drayton in the autumn, and told his grandfather that 'your simple assurance that anything I have done gives you pleasure and satis-faction is the dearest and proudest reward I can receive'. Meanwhile, on 14 June, a week before the end of session, he had signed his first official letter. He was then only a few months past his twenty-second birthday and it was just fourteen months since he had been elected for Cashel.

As an introduction to administration the post in which he found himself was not without its salutary aspects. It involved much writing and even more reading. Most of the work was detailed and routine, requiring neither urgency in performance nor responsibility for policy. It had little in the way of heroics and was of a highly miscellaneous nature. Nevertheless, it placed him, however junior and unimportant, on the fringe of great affairs. He was working under the eye of a senior cabinet minister and occasionally he came in touch with the tide of events in Europe. Liverpool naturally devoted himself to the military side of his department and conducted the major correspondence with the commander-in-chief in Spain. The other under-secretary, Colonel Bunbury, handled the routine military matters while to Peel was delegated the colonial side of the office—'an ample field . . .' as he later wrote, 'extending from Botany Bay to Prince Edward Island'—together with the administration of the secret service money. Most of his work was unexciting, though Liverpool must have noted the manner in which his fledgling junior was dealing with it and made his own estimate of his ability. Moreover, as the only member of the department in the House of Commons, he had the responsibility of answering there on its behalf. In a debate on war policy in March 1811, for example, Plumer Ward reported that Fremantle, an inveterate and violent critic of the war in Spain, 'was answered and pulled to pieces in one of the most beautiful as well as argumentative speeches ever delivered in the House, by young Peel'.

He was in fact enjoying the reputation, harder to maintain than achieve, of being a coming man. In private even the Whigs, as Ward later noted when discussing the rising generation of politicians, 'seemed disposed to allow, what Tierney once allowed to me before, that we had the best in Peel'. It was probably not in his disfavour that he was taking Jackson's advice to find time for company as well as work. Lord Liverpool had given him a small residence, part of Fife House (Liverpool's town mansion), with its own entrance in Little Scotland Yard near Whitehall Stairs. He furnished it at considerable expense and frequently entertained there. Some of his visitors were old college friends, like John Mills, now in the Coldstream Guards; more often they were other young politicians on the government side, Croker, Goulburn, Vesey Fitzgerald, Lord Desart, Manners Sutton and Palmerston. He dined out, once at least at the prime minister's table, and he joined his first London Club, the Alfred, a junior establishment which had been founded only a year or two earlier. He was still very much the Oxonian in society, attentive to dress and following the fashion. It was still modish to wear powder in the evening and this custom, which concealed the reddish colour of his hair, became him very well. With good features, a pleasant smile and occasional animation in his expression, he was a presentable young man, even if not so handsome as his brother William. To his physical qualities was added a lively conversation, a sense of fun, an eye for the absurd and a quiet, slightly malicious pleasure in exposing it.

But while Peel, socially and officially, was making a promising start in London society, the government was still plagued by weakness and fatality. In the autumn of 1810 the king's mind once more gave way, and this time permanently. The prolonged crisis created by the Regency undermined the administration for almost two years until the Regent finally confirmed Perceval in office. The reconstructed ministry, with Castlereagh and Sidmouth back in the cabinet, had hardly settled down when Bellingham, a mentally unbalanced bankrupt with a grievance against the government, in May 1812 shot the prime minister dead in the lobby of the House of Commons. Even to neutrals it seemed as if the headless cabinet could not possibly carry on without assistance from Canning, Wellesley, Grey and Grenville. While Peel's chief, Lord Liverpool, took over temporary leadership of the government, the Prince Regent embarked on yet another attempt to construct a more impressive administration than the one he actually possessed. But as in 1810–11, the fresh round of negotiations failed to discover any common ground between the men in office and the group of jealous and ambitious politicians outside. In the end there was nothing to be done but patch up the old Perceval cabinet and set it going once more. In June Liverpool was confirmed as prime minister; Vansittart took Perceval's place as Chancellor of the Exchequer; and Lord Bathurst moved from the Board of Trade to succeed Liverpool at War and Colonies. It was a shaky start for an administration that was to last for the next fifteen years. When one final effort to bring in Canning broke down on his unreasonable refusal to concede any superiority to Castlereagh, the new prime minister faced the future in much the same spirit as Perceval had done in 1810. He had, he wrote to Wellington in Spain,

> no resource but to bring forward the most promising of the young men, and the fate of the government in the House of Commons in another session will depend very much on their exertions. I should be most happy if I could see a second Pitt arise amongst them.

With only three cabinet members in the Commons—Castlereagh who was a poor debater, the genial but unimpressive Vansittart, and Sidmouth's insignificant protégé Bragge Bathurst—the prospects for young men of talent were clearly not going to be obscured by a phalanx of able and experienced seniors on the front bench.

II

One minor consequence of the political crisis of 1812 was the resignation of Wellesley Pole, Chief Secretary to the Lord-Lieutenant of Ireland, the Duke of Richmond. A younger brother of the Marquess Wellesley, he felt committed both by the latter's own resignation earlier in the year and by his private conviction that Perceval's death had reopened the question of Catholic disabilities. Much as he disagreed with Pole's views on emancipation, Richmond was apprehensive about fighting the unending battle with Irish politicians and Irish jobbery with an inexperienced secretary fresh from England. 'Pray don't let them send me a Catholic or a timid Man', he wrote to Bathurst in June. Had the negotiations with Canning succeeded, Wellesley would have gone as Lord-Lieutenant to Ireland with Huskisson as his Chief Secretary. When by July it was obvious that all negotiation was fruitless, Liverpool decided to offer the secretaryship to his former junior at the Colonial Department, Robert Peel. Of his administrative ability the prime minister could judge better than anybody; of his sound Protestant opinions there had been proof in an Irish debate earlier in the session. Though Peel took time to consider the proposal, he told Liverpool immediately that if the Canning negotiations were resumed, he would not be prepared to stay on in Ireland under Lord Wellesley.

His simultaneous vote against Canning's motion to take Catholic claims into consideration the following session demonstrated once more his attitude on this fundamental domestic issue.

Comforted by this, Richmond was further reassured by a letter from the prime minister.

> I can speak with more confidence of Mr Peel than I could of most persons to whom such an office might be offered. He has been under me in the Secretary of State's office for two years, and has acquired all the necessary habits of official business. He has a particularly good temper, and great frankness and openness of manners, which I know are particularly desirable on your side of the water. He acquired great reputation, as you must have heard, as a scholar at Oxford, and he has distinguished himself in the House of Commons on every occasion on which he has had an opportunity of speaking.

By that date Peel had resolved his doubts and accepted the post. A second letter to Richmond left London the same day from the young secretary-designate, written (to judge from the heavily scored and emended draft preserved by Peel among his papers) with some degree of nervousness. Its tone was modest. Conscious of his many disqualifications, he told Richmond, all he could oppose to them was 'a most anxious desire to acquit myself to the satisfaction of those under whom I am to be employed and to prove myself not unworthy of their confidence'.

The next few weeks were full of correspondence, congratulations and preparations. Peel cleared up his files and handed over to his friend Henry Goulburn who was to be his successor in the Colonial Department. Meanwhile his postbag was already providing evidence of his rise in the official hierarchy with the first of a rapidly swelling stream of letters seeking patronage, pressing claims, and quoting promises, which was to beset him for the next six years. On 28 August he left London and though he probably stayed a night at Drayton to take leave of his father and his more bantering schoolboy brothers, Holyhead and the Irish Channel loomed up at last. On 1 September he set foot in Dublin. Neither his appointment nor his arrival attracted much attention in the Irish capital. Vesey Fitzgerald who had been simultaneously appointed Chancellor of the Irish Exchequer, as an Irish landowner naturally possessed greater interest for the Irish press; and the continued political gossip that Wellesley would succeed Richmond as Lord-Lieutenant gave to the appointment of 'Mr Peele' an air of impermanence and unimportance. In the narrow circle of the Castle the first reaction to the two newcomers had been one of disapproval at their youth. Both were under thirty and Peel indeed was still short of his twenty-fifth birthday. Fortunately he struck up from the start a friendly relationship with the Lord-Lieutenant. Soldier, politician, cricketer, duellist and patron of the prize ring, Richmond had the easy tolerant attitude of his class. Though somewhat addicted to the wine bottle, he was a good and kindly superior; and his stout Protestantism endeared him to the equally stout Protestants who surrounded him at the Castle. Whatever their private views, official society at Dublin showed Peel traditional Irish hospitality. In the first few weeks after his arrival he found himself dining out night after night. His Dublin hosts were mildly surprised by his preference for port, and that as little as possible, instead of repeated bumpers of claret; and the Governor of the Bank of Ireland told him with horror that he was clearly not impressed with the necessity of toasting the glorious memory of William III. Peel at that date was not 'Orange Peel' in Protestant eyes; nor ever, perhaps, except in the journalistic abuse of Catholic agitators.

Before Peel left England he knew that the cabinet was meditating a dissolution of parliament, and his first letter from the prime minister warned him to start preparations for a general election. It seemed a propitious moment to go to the country. The news from Spain was good; at home the harvest was abundant and Ireland quiet. Politically all chance of a reconciliation with Canning and Wellesley seemed to have disappeared. As Bathurst idiomatically expressed it, everything was now afloat, and they must fight on their own bottoms. At the end of September the dissolution, kept secret until the last minute, was announced in a proclamation from the Prince Regent. Within a month of landing in Dublin, therefore, Peel was not only facing his first general election but, as far as Ireland was concerned, he was in charge of it. Without much helpful advice on how to achieve those desirable ends, it was made clear that his duty was to get as many ministerial supporters elected as he could, without exposing himself to detection in any illegal operation—'bound', as he light-heartedly expressed it to his friend Croker, 'to secure the Government interests if possible from dilapidation, but still more bound to faint with horror at the mention of money transactions'.

Fortunately, in view of his inexperience in those delicate matters, there was less to be done in the way of management than he had feared. In the counties it was mainly a question of stimulating the exertions of friendly landowners. In the boroughs there were few constituencies where arrangements had not already been made. For the most part Peel found himself playing an ancillary role in the bewildering medley of negotiations, bargains, compromises and foregone conclusions which constituted the bulk of an Irish general election at this period. He was able to observe at close quarters the rapacity and ingratitude of magnates such as Lord Charleville and Lord Waterford, and more gratifyingly the peremptory refusal of the prime minister to barter peerages for political support. For himself, to avoid the risk of compromising his official position by any dubious electoral transactions in Ireland, he abandoned Cashel and his father found a seat for him at Chippenham, Wiltshire, after a hardheaded cash negotiation with one of the proprietors. When the election was over the government had clearly strengthened their position. In Ireland their hope had simply been not to lose ground and this modest ambition had been more than achieved. In October Peel was able to report a gain of five seats, a loss of three, and of the contests still to be decided, a possible further net gain of two. Goulburn wrote flatteringly to say that 'you have gained much honour, and I only wish that Arbuthnot had done half as well in England'.

But even in England the government had not done badly. If, as many thought, the main purpose of the snap election was to weaken the Canning–Wellesley party, this had been achieved. There was a gratifying rally to the government in some of the larger constituencies, and Peel himself shared the general feeling that Canning had over-reached himself. Writing to Croker, who was something of a Canningite despite being in office as secretary to the Admiralty, Peel made no secret of his opinions.

> There never was a time when I felt more determined to do all I could to support the Government on its present footing and on the principles on which it will meet Parliament. If I understand, as I believe I did, the offers made to Canning, I think they were fair ones.

Whatever likelihood existed in 1810 that Canning could have seduced Peel from his allegiance to the government, it was obvious by 1812 that a wide gap had opened up between them. Nevertheless, as the prime minister himself confessed to Peel,

> Our danger is not from Opposition, but evidently from the third parties headed by Lord Wellesley and Canning, who will represent themselves as holding the same opinions as we do on all popular topics, who will say that they have as much right to be considered as the successors of Mr Pitt's party as ourselves, and whose object will consequently be to detach as many of our friends as possible.

A great deal therefore depended on the parliamentary manoeuvres of the new session. When Peel, rather reluctantly, went across at the end of November for a brief attendance at the opening of parliament, he detected a considerable feeling in favour of Canning and told the Lord-Lieutenant that he anticipated a strong effort by the Catholic party as soon as the session got under way.

III

With a general election, a parliamentary meeting, and three channel crossings, Peel had compressed a considerable amount of experience into his first five months as Chief Secretary. He was now able to settle to the routine of work and travel which was to be his lot for the next six years.

The structure of the Irish government in the early nineteenth century was relatively simple. The Lord-Lieutenant governed, assisted by a Privy Council. Under him was the Chief Secretary and through him were controlled the armed forces in Ireland, the revenue departments, and the other offices and boards which supervised the standing civil service of the country. The simplicity of the administration was the key to its outstanding feature: the concentration of power in the Viceroy. Not only was all ordinary administration and the bulk of Irish patronage, including legal and ecclesiastical appointments, in his hands, but through his control of the armed forces and the financial departments, he enjoyed a combination of authority scarcely paralleled by any formal office in Britain. He was in fact the immediate source of sovereign power in Ireland; the legal, and not infrequently the political mainspring of governmental action. But if the Lord-Lieutenant was an Irish constitutional monarch in miniature, his Chief Secretary was the equivalent of prime minister, Home Secretary, First Lord of the Treasury, President of the Board of Trade, and Secretary for War rolled into one. Even allowing for the smaller scale of Irish affairs and the ultimate control of the cabinet in London, it was an extraordinarily varied and testing office. Goulburn in 1821 called it 'one of the most difficult and laborious offices under the Government'. Though his remark was prompted by the circumstance that he was about to take it himself, it remained true that the Irish secretaryship was an effective device for making or breaking the career of a young politician.

Certainly the Union in 1800 had ended the Chief Secretary's role as manager of an independent legislature. But in recompense he had become the expounder and defender of Irish policy in the House of Commons at a time when Ireland was steadily moving into the front line of British domestic problems. It was inevitable therefore that in the eyes of the cabinet the office should increasingly rank as possessing an importance equal to that of the resident Lord-Lieutenant who never left the country. Only the rapid changes in personnel—nine Secretaries in the twelve years from 1800 to 1812—had prevented it from assuming greater weight. Peel had succeeded to a post of considerable potentialities; but its potentialities had scarcely been realised by his predecessors.

As he soon realised, attendance at Westminster was a substantial ingredient in the multifarious duties of his office. At least once, often twice a year, he had to abandon his spacious office in Dublin Castle and his elegant Secretary's Lodge in Phoenix Park to make the tedious journey to London. Holyhead, nominally seven hours sailing from Dublin, in winter took sometimes fourteen hours to reach; and the lack of a pier at Dunleary (not commenced till 1817), foul roads in Wales, and frequent accidents to horses and carriages, added to the miseries of travel. Once arrived in London, however, his life became more orderly and comfortable. His house in Little Scotland Yard had been given up when he left the Colonial Office, and for a while he rented Vansittart's house in Great George Street. In 1814 he moved to 12 Stanhope Street which remained his home for the next decade. With his election to White's Club in 1813 his London *ménage* was as well organised, though not quite so formal, as that in Dublin. The purely mechanical part of his official correspondence was facilitated by the existence of the Irish Office in Queen Street, though it was some time before he could instil into his staff on either side of the water the accuracy and punctuality demanded by his own high standards of public business. Fortunately he had in Dublin as under-secretary a first-class subordinate in William Gregory, the younger son of a Galway landowner, educated at Harrow and Trinity College, Cambridge. With his support the new Chief Secretary's brisk reforming temper gradually made its influence felt on the indolent habits of the Irish clerks. Despite the twenty-two years difference in their ages a close friendship developed between Gregory and Peel which lasted long after the latter left Ireland.

Outside his own department he found that little could be done in the sphere of Irish affairs unless he personally saw to its execution. Sidmouth, the Home Secretary, who was officially responsible for Ireland, maintained a routine correspondence with the Chief Secretary but showed little desire to control or initiate policy. It was from Liverpool that Peel secured as a rule most support in time of need; though immersed in more pressing affairs, the prime minister could only give intermittent attention to his problems. Irish legislation was necessary; but the House of Commons was already beginning to find Irish business tedious and incomprehensible. Apart from the inflammable topic of Catholic emancipation it was not easy for the Chief Secretary to interest his more senior colleagues, still less the government whips, in the details of Irish administration. Peel was constantly frustrated by having his proposals shelved until the dogdays at the end of session when he would be left to his own devices to whip up attendance in a thin and jaded House. In July 1814 he made the rueful remark that people were accusing him of bringing in more bills than a hundred other members and choosing the last possible moment to introduce them.

The House of Commons, it was true, possessed a hundred Irish members, most of them supporters of the government. But they were not always present, and when present not always prepared to display the discipline which constitutes nine-tenths of effective parliamentary effort. Ordinary members would clutch at any excuse for absence and delay, and even the office-holders among them were singularly lax in their performance. Support for Irish measures from Irish M.P.s was therefore spasmodic and incalculable. 'Receiving ten times as many favours as the English members,' wrote Peel severely in 1813, '[they] do not give us one-tenth of their support.' In theory the government controlled a mass of patronage which could be put to political use. In practice the amount actually at the disposal of the Castle for this purpose was very small. The old eighteenth-century habit of regarding patronage as a social perquisite rather than as a political bargain still persisted; and favours that had been clamorously demanded produced little sense of reciprocal obligation once they had been bestowed. Open defiance could be punished; blatant attempts to corrupt or menace government officials could be peremptorily rejected. But sloth, indifference, fits of independence, fair promises and sluggish execution, were not so easily open to suitable penalties.

In England growing wealth and changing political habits had emancipated society from undue dependence on court and administration. In Ireland the Protestant caste had been permanently conditioned to look to the state for support and nourishment. This Irish tendency made an early impression on Peel's mind.

> There is a disposition in Ireland [he wrote in 1814] which I will do all in my power to check, to refer everything to 'Government'. I think the majority have the same idea of the Government which the natives are said to have of the East India Company. They attach to the Government all the attributes of omnipotence which it is peculiarly disposed to exert in every species of job, and fraud and peculation.

For posts of any administrative importance he insisted, as far as he could, on the appointment of candidates who, in his own disarming phrase, had 'no other claims than those of merit'. But with the whole host of Irish suitors on his back, Peel could do no more with the minor situations than reject corrupt bargains, punish fraud, and ensure that local patronage was channelled through those Irish M.P.s who had earned it by their votes in parliament. He did so with a satiric humour that at least added flavour to an otherwise flat and tedious traffic. 'I do not think your son can make a more inefficient member of the Board of Stamps than Mr T. has done,' he wrote to Gregory in 1816. 'I am perfectly ready therefore to acquiesce in the exchange.' On a recommendation of somebody described as an honest man: 'Pray reward him then—*rari nantes in gurgite vasto*.'* On a letter from an Irish judge: 'I would rather give Judge Smith five gaugers' places than receive one letter from him.' But this flippancy merely masked his complete antipathy to what he once called 'the vortex of local patronage'. 'I am quite tired and disgusted', he wrote to the Lord-Lieutenant in 1817, when pressing for disciplinary action against a defaulting government official, 'with the shameful corruption which every Irish enquiry brings to light.' Irish patronage and Irish administration formed a school of human nature in which the youngest official rapidly matured. The

---

*Virgil. 'Here and there in the ocean a swimmer or two.'

constant canvassing, the bluster and deceit, the tendency of Irish applicants to claim silence as assent and a friendly remark as a promise, taught Peel precocious habits of official caution and reserve. 'I had experience in early life in that country,' he remarked long afterwards, 'of the danger of saying a civil word, and of the utter uselessness of attempting to coax people out of disappointment at not getting what they wanted.'

The efficiency of Irish administration depended therefore on the quality of the men at the top; and at that level everything turned on the relationship between the Lord-Lieutenant and his Chief Secretary. Without harmony between them there could be no unity in government; without unity, little strength. The Lord-Lieutenant was no cypher. His office was largely what he made it; and that varied with experience and temperament. A Viceroy of three or four years standing, a Viceroy of sagacity or strong character, could easily outweigh a Secretary newly appointed, or lacking either administrative skill or political talent. The relationship between the young Peel and the middle-aged Richmond in 1812-13, one beginning and the other ending his Irish service, was one in which the balance of authority lay with the older and more experienced man. It was true that an easy confidence soon grew up between them and Richmond was always mindful of the need to delegate responsibility to the official who toiled at 'the labouring oar' at Westminster. Nevertheless, despite this happy relationship, it represented a decided enhancement of Peel's position when the Duke of Richmond laid down his office in August 1813. It was the Chief Secretary now who was armed with knowledge and experience and the new Viceroy who had his Irish apprenticeship to serve.

Lord Whitworth, who took Richmond's place, was an elderly professional diplomat who had represented his country in Poland, Russia and France. Even before his arrival in Dublin Peel had formed a favourable impression of his future chief. 'All that I see of Lord Whitworth', he wrote to Richmond from London in June 1813, 'convinces me that his appointment is a good one.' In September he was telling Goulburn that though he missed the society of the Duke of Richmond and his daughters, Lord Whitworth would do admirably and a better successor could not have been found. At the outset the new Lord-Lieutenant was clearly feeling his way in the labyrinth of Irish politics and personalities. But as time went by, his early scepticism and tolerance gave way to a closer apprehension of the inherent difficulties and dangers of the Irish situation. With less knowledge of Ireland than Richmond, he had the better mind and his correspondence reveals a cool and acute intellect. Under his firm and urbane exterior, however, there was perhaps a need for warmth and friendship which was not satisfied elsewhere and from the start his relationship with Peel was unusually affectionate. When they were separated he kept up a constant correspondence irrespective of official requirements and conventions. He had no news, he wrote in December 1813, but 'I have a gratification in scribbling to you and you must indulge me'. Again in 1816: 'I have a pleasure in talking with you which I cannot resist, so you must bear with me.' In such circumstances it was natural that Lord-Lieutenant and Chief Secretary soon looked on Irish matters with a single eye. 'You estimate so purely the state of this country,' Whitworth observed in July 1814, 'and are so anxious to provide the best means of preserving its tranquillity, that I can have nothing to do but approve as I do most cordially of all your proceedings.'

In February 1815, when Whitworth was anxious to take his duchess to England to recover from the shock of her son's recent death in the hunting-field, Peel saw the prime minister and Home Secretary to get permission for him to leave the country. The timing of his absence proved unfortunate. The viceregal couple were met at Holyhead by the news of Napoleon's escape from Elba and at every stage of their journey to London they received, in Whitworth's trenchant words, 'formidable accounts of the Ruffian's progress'. Even more disquietingly, reports from all over Ireland spoke of the general joy of the poorer classes at Napoleon's reappearance in France and the renewal of political excitement and disaffection. With Ireland promptly stripped of 5,000 regular troops to reinforce the small British army in Flanders, it was a critical time for both Whitworth and Peel to be absent. At one point it was decided that Peel should return to Dublin for a while, to be relieved by Whitworth as soon as possible. But by May the Lord-Lieutenant was back at his post in the Castle, writing cheerfully to Peel that 'everything is going on so smoothly here, barring Murder, Rape and Robbery, that there can be no necessity for hurrying you away from London'. Waterloo was fought on 18 June and two days later Peel was able to send off the first unconfirmed reports of a great allied victory. The official confirmation of the news was celebrated in Dublin with an illumination, fireworks and a salute of guns; and the police were ordered to clap into the watch-house what Whitworth described as 'blackguards running about the streets in the night, denying the Victory and asserting that Bonaparte was the conqueror'. It was the end of a long period stretching back to the Battle of the Boyne in which Ireland had not only been England's weakness but France's opportunity; and, what was more the concern of most English people, the end of the war with which they had lived for nearly quarter of a century.

Peel profited from the general festive spirit to obtain leave to visit France before returning to his duties in Dublin. Together with Fitzgerald and Croker he set out at the end of the session. On 11 July they reached Paris where their eyes were gladdened by the sight of the Life Guards patrolling the boulevards just as they were accustomed to do at Charing Cross in time of riot. They saw most of the notabilities, including Wellington, Castlereagh, Talleyrand, Fouché, the King of France, the Emperors of Austria and Russia and a bevy of French marshalls. On 19 July they dined with Wellington, when Peel had the honour of sitting next to the duke and hearing from the victor the details of the battle. Returning through Belgium they called on the Duke and Duchess of Richmond in Brussels and drove out in pouring rain to inspect the field of Waterloo. They found the ground still littered with the untidy melancholy debris of war: scraps of clothing, helmets, torn papers, empty cartridges and bits of cannon-wadding, with here and there the raw mounds of mass graves. People were still searching for mementoes, but there was little left on the actual battle-field. The Belgian peasants had been over the ground like harvest gleaners and were offering their plunder at steadily mounting prices. Peel bought a French cuirass for two napoleons and Croker a cross of the Legion of Honour. Early in August he was back in Dublin after a miserable passage of thirty-three hours in the teeth of a westerly gale with a shipload of passengers, the men all sick and the women and children moaning and screaming; 'ludicrous enough for half an hour,' he wrote dryly to Croker, 'but, like other good things, wearied by constant repetition.' It was by then his thirteenth crossing of the Irish Sea.

Chapter 3

Problems of a Chief Secretary

In the litany of Irish problems which any early nineteenth-century Chief Secretary could recite by heart, the most obvious and politically the most embarrassing was Catholic emancipation. Legislation in the tolerant early decades of George III's reign had removed nearly all the repressive anti-Catholic laws of previous generations and Roman Catholics were no longer penalised as subjects for professing their religion. Nevertheless they were still largely excluded from the service of the state in its institutional aspect. In Ireland as in England Catholics could not, for example, become judges or county sheriffs, generals or admirals, members of parliament or ministers of the Crown. In Britain, with its small ingrown Catholic community, this was not a matter of great political significance. In Ireland however the question of Catholic disabilities provoked fierce political controversy, since only in Ireland did the great majority of the population belong to the Roman Catholic Church. Pitt's inability to follow his Act of Union with the expected measure of emancipation transferred the issue from Irish to English politics; and for the next thirty years it remained the most harassing of all domestic problems. Politicians, parties, parliaments, even cabinets were divided on the issue; the professed followers of Pitt showed no more agreement than the rest. Inevitably therefore Liverpool's cabinet of 1812 had to be based on the principle of neutrality towards Catholic claims. Ministers were left free as individuals to follow their own convictions and, officially at any rate, the government whips were not put on for Catholic debates. Without government support it was improbable that the question could be carried through both Houses of Parliament; but the known sympathies of leading members of the government and the absence of organised government opposition, invited an almost annual trial of strength. Consequently Catholic emancipation proved an irritant in every ministry up to 1830, dividing men who might otherwise have worked amicably together, and clogging all leading politicians with a record of public commitment on an unresolved controversy.

For the Irish executive the neutrality of the government was a peculiar embarrassment. Though a few of its members favoured emancipation, the central core of officials from the Lord-Lieutenant downward was composed of supporters of the Irish establishment. In a direct sense they were the guardians of that establishment. It was not merely through the law but through their dominance of the executive that the Protestant party upheld the Anglo-Irish ascendancy. There was a marked contrast therefore between the preponderance of

Protestant feeling in the official corps at Dublin Castle and the neutrality of the cabinet, between the Protestant administration of the law in Ireland and the divided opinions of the House of Commons at Westminster. Discussing the proposed grant to the Catholic seminary at Maynooth in 1813, Peel wrote to Richmond with youthful severity that

> All this difficulty arises out of the unfortunate state of the Govt. as far as the Catholic question is concerned. I always thought that to throw open a question of that kind, perhaps the most important one that concerns the domestic policy of the country, and to leave each individual to take his own course upon it, was a very impolitic measure, and one which would involve the whole Govt. and particularly the Irish Govt. in daily embarrassment.

Embarrassing it clearly was. Nevertheless, neither Liverpool nor any other prime minister could have kept an efficient cabinet together except on the principle of neutrality. The Irish executive was therefore obliged to administer a system which was under constant attack in parliament and on which cabinet ministers notoriously disagreed.

Ireland of course was a country not of one but of three religions; and Peel was not an uncritical supporter of any of them. He commented with irreverent freedom on the extent to which the bishoprics of the Church of Ireland were monopolised by Anglo-Irish aristocratic families; he was conscious of the dangers to government from the unbending Presbyterians of Ulster with their traditions of democratic republicanism; and he found the strident support of the Orange Lodges for 'the Protestant establishment in Church and State' almost as objectionable as the attacks of its enemies.

> The more I think upon the subject [he wrote to Gregory in July 1814], the more am I convinced that even the most loyal associations in Ireland for political purposes are dangerous engines. . . . Regiments and Colonels and Captains, etc. do not sound well to my ear when applied to societies not under the control of Government.

Nevertheless the prevailing sympathies in both the Irish and English executives made it impossible even to consider the dissolution of the Orange Society. All that could be done was to follow a policy of studied official neutrality which at least had the merit of making it difficult for the parliamentary opposition to fix responsibility for Orange excesses on the Irish government.

The political difficulties caused by ultra-Protestant activities in Ireland, however, were slight compared with the rising tide of Catholic agitation. With the Catholic Church in Ireland the government had hardly any direct contact. The Roman hierarchy, with its four archbishops and twenty-two bishops, stood aloof and independent. Their only connection with the state was through the parliamentary grant to Maynooth College which dated back to the time when the spread of the French Revolution had denied the Irish Church access to the established Roman seminaries in Europe. In 1813 the Irish government had, with some misgiving, supported a request from the college for an increase in its grant. The proposal was sponsored by Fitzgerald and backed by Manners, the Lord Chancellor. Richmond was decidedly hostile and Peel himself felt no enthusiasm. He agreed with the Lord-Lieutenant that if the object in acceding to the request was to conciliate the Catholics, 'there is not a hope, not the most distant one of attaining it'. But he found the cabinet as usual divided and he was conscious of the embarrassment of a parliamentary clash between himself and Fitzgerald. Further than this however he was not prepared to go. When the Catholic bishop of Cashel asked for an annual grant of £1,000 to enable ten young priests from Maynooth to teach the lower orders in Ireland their moral and religious duties and enjoin obedience to the law, he advised the Lord-Lieutenant to reject the request. Even apart from the difficulty of establishing the requisite machinery for such an ingenuous scheme, the character of the Maynooth seminarists offered little expectation of profit to the government from their apostolic labours. All observers agreed on the profound change made in the Irish clergy by the substitution of Maynooth for the continental seminaries. In the old days the colleges of Douai, St Omer, Coimbra and Salamanca had produced a recognisable type of Catholic priest—well-educated, urbane, royalist and authoritarian. The raw youths of Maynooth, drawn almost exclusively from the poorer classes of Irish society, imperfectly and spartanly educated, knowing nothing of society outside Ireland, went back to their parishes, as one Lord-Lieutenant expressed it, 'with the bitterest feelings of the Partizan and the grossest habits of a Peasant'. The Catholic bishops of Peel's day were of the old school; but the growing nationalism of the younger parochial clergy was not the least important element in the ultimate success of the Catholic movement.

Of education in the wider sense Peel was always a firm advocate. At the time of his appointment in 1812 the Irish Commissioners of Education prepared a report recommending the creation of a new board to supervise a national system of education which was to include Catholic children. One of Peel's first tasks as Chief Secretary was to discover whether the cabinet would approve a form of general education in Ireland without distinction of religion, or one indeed in which Protestantism would not necessarily have any place. He was anxious that the Anglican parochial schools should continue to educate their own children, but he argued cogently that new establishments were needed for the poorer classes, on as liberal a scale as possible, and that Catholics should be admitted to membership of the National Board. But though he repeatedly urged the importance of education in Ireland, the time was hardly propitious for such a controversial proposal. He passed a limited bill creating a new board for the endowed schools, but the wider issue of national schooling foundered on innumerable obstacles. The growth of organised Catholic agitation put it out of the question even to begin the fundamental task of Irish elementary education.

In 1813 the House of Commons, in accordance with the pledge secured by Canning the previous year, took Catholic claims into consideration and after much preliminary work in committee a bill prepared by Grattan received its second reading in May. It was finally defeated towards the end of the month by four votes in one of the fullest divisions ever recorded. In these proceedings, lasting from February to May, the Chief Secretary both from his public position and his private convictions felt impelled to take an active part. If he needed further incentive, he found it in the weakness and lack of spirit on the Protestant side. He told Richmond disgustedly that there was no *esprit de corps* among the Protestants; and what irked him as much as the steady succession of early defeats was the half-heartedness evident among them. On the second reading of Grattan's bill on 13 May, for example, nobody except Patrick Duigenan, a notoriously militant Irish Protestant M.P., seemed inclined to speak against the measure. In the end he and Ryder, the former Home Secretary, made up their minds to intervene if only to prevent the indignity of an un-opposed passage of the bill. In his own two contributions to the debates he put his main emphasis on the omission of adequate safeguards to compensate for the admission of Catholics to complete political equality. As long as Catholics recognised the supremacy of the Pope, he wrote to Richmond, and would not give voluntarily those securities which nearly every crowned head in Europe had by agreement with the Pope himself, 'I will not consent to admit they are excluded from privileges for which they will not pay the price that all other subjects pay, and that all other Catholics in Europe but themselves consent to pay'.

The emphasis on securities was sound tactics. It was precisely this issue which roused most concern in the House of Commons, and after the second reading Canning added various amendments to the bill, including one giving the Crown a power of veto on the appointment of Catholic bishops. The more, however, the English liberals sought to disarm opposition by providing safeguards, the more they alienated opinion on both sides. The English Protestants recoiled instinctively from a settlement that for the first time since the Reformation would bring the state into constitutional relationship with the Papacy. The Irish Catholics reacted equally strongly against legislation that would subject their Church to erastian and Anglican control. In fact the Catholic hierarchy in Ireland rejected the ecclesiastical clauses of the bill before they knew that it had been finally defeated in the Commons.

Gratified as he was by the victory, Peel was sensible enough to realise that Protestant rejoicing on the one hand and Catholic disappointment on the other might simply exacerbate religious tension. The Catholics in Ireland, picking their way astutely through the legal entanglements that hampered any unofficial representative body organised for political purposes, had formed a committee known as the Catholic Board; and Peel immediately instructed Gregory to spare no expense in getting inside information on its activities. The danger, from the point of view of the Irish executive, was that the old-fashioned aristocratic element on the Board which exercised a moderating influence on its policy, would now be overborne by the more violent middle-class group of lawyers and journalists headed by Scully and O'Connell. Indeed the Irish government seriously considered the possibility of suppressing the Board altogether. But such a drastic step raised a number of legal difficulties which would certainly be exploited by the ingenuity of the Catholic barristers, backed as they would be by the partisan votes of a Dublin jury. For the time being therefore the executive contented itself with a warning prosecution of Magee, editor of the *Dublin Evening Post*, the principal organ of the Board, for a libel on the Lord-Lieutenant.

By 1814 hopes that the Board would expire of its own folly and fanaticism were steadily diminishing and the Irish government grew increasingly restive at the continued agitation of which the Board was the focus. Early in May Peel raised with the prime minister the possibility of strengthening the law against illegal political conventions so as to bring the Catholic Board more clearly within its scope. Liverpool and Sidmouth, however, after the narrow escape of the previous summer, refused to sanction any change in the law which would involve another Irish debate at Westminster; and the cautious law officers in Dublin were disinclined to advise any action on the basis of the existing statute without the backing of the cabinet. The new Lord-Lieutenant himself was clearly perturbed by Liverpool's non-committal attitude. His energetic Chief Secretary in London was not prepared to give in so easily. He assured Whitworth that the cabinet had no desire to discourage the Irish executive and would be happy to leave the decision, time and manner to them. After much hesitation and delay a proclamation dissolving the Board was signed by the Lord-Lieutenant on 3 June.

Despite all the misgivings in official circles which had preceded it, the proclamation achieved a complete success. The long forbearance of the Irish government had in fact served to rally opinion to its side and even the parliamentary supporters of emancipation made no protest. The timing of the stroke was excellent, coming as it did soon after the intervention by the Vatican in the form of a rescript enjoining Irish Catholics to receive Grattan's bill with gratitude. Weakened by internal disagreements and discouraged by the Quarantotti letter, as the rescript was known, the Board made no effort to resist. For the remainder of Peel's secretaryship the organised Catholic movement ceased to be a force in Irish politics. For Peel it was almost a personal triumph. Of all the members of the Irish government he had shown the greatest constancy and resolution, first in waiting until the time was ripe, then in guiding the Lord-Lieutenant past the doubting of his own legal advisers and the discouraging neutrality of the cabinet. To Gregory he wrote with engaging candour that the proclamation of peace with France the previous month had not given him a tenth of the satisfaction which the proclamation of war against the Catholic Board had done.

The success had one unpleasant consequence for Peel personally in the start of a hostile relationship with O'Connell which was to last until the latter's death. The debate on Grattan's bill in 1813 had brought Peel for the first time to the notice of the rising Irish agitator. In May O'Connell had held the Chief Secretary up to ridicule as

> that ludicrous enemy of ours . . . 'Orange Peel'. A raw youth, squeezed out of the workings of I know not what factory in England . . . sent over here before he got rid of the foppery of perfumed handkerchiefs and thin shoes . . . a lad ready to vindicate anything, everything.

In August, when Peel was cited as a witness in an earlier prosecution of Magee, he saw O'Connell for the first time in action as counsel for the defence; and he found the experience an interesting one. O'Connell, whom he thought 'an eloquent and vulgar speaker', used the court as a platform for scurrilous abuse of the Attorney-General and was more libellous as counsel than his client had ever been in print. The encounter could only have strengthened Peel's conviction of the need to suppress a Board in which O'Connell was already the moving spirit. In an Irish debate in 1815, a year after the dissolution of the Board, Peel quoted from O'Connell's speeches there to illustrate his argument that the Irish Catholics had themselves been opposed to Grattan's bill of 1813. Though the reference to O'Connell was completely factual and contained no personal criticism, the Irish leader took umbrage and at a Catholic meeting in July made the offensive observation that Peel was too prudent to abuse him in his presence. This was a different and more personal matter; and O'Connell followed up the initial insult at a meeting in August. Calling on the reporters present to record his words, he observed with studied emphasis: 'Mr Peel would not dare, in my presence, or in any place where he was liable to personal account, use a single expression derogatory to my interest or my honour.' In the wider society to which Peel and O'Connell both belonged, this was a challenge to which there was only one answer. O'Connell's language could only have been intended either to browbeat Peel into silence or to bring on, as the phrase went, an affair of honour. Coming from O'Connell the insult was peculiarly venomous since he was an excellent shot and in February of that very year had killed an opponent in a duel which had itself grown out of political controversy.

After ineffectual attempts by Peel's representative, Colonel Saxton, to obtain an apology, which got into the press and provoked from O'Connell the complaint that Peel 'preferred a paper war', a meeting was arranged at Ostend. But the delay and the newspaper comments had by this time aroused the authorities. Though the Home Office failed to intercept Peel, O'Connell was arrested in London on his slow and conspicuous passage to the continent. The possibility of a duel between the two principals soon collapsed in an atmosphere of recrimination and publicity which began to border on the absurd; though, as not infrequently happened in such situations, the two seconds got themselves into a quarrel which led to a belated meeting between them at Calais in November. Peel, who had taken offence himself at some words uttered by Lidwill, O'Connell's second, also went across in a vain attempt to obtain the kind of satisfaction denied to him on the first occasion. In this he allowed his pride and exasperation to carry him far beyond the point which good sense and official duty could justify. Though his earlier coolness and courage had won the approval of such eminent critics as the Lord-Lieutenant, the prime minister, and the Home Secretary, his later stubbornness made even his closest friends feel that he was acting with little sense of what was owing to himself and his position.

Peel himself chafed miserably at the outcome and was left with an immediate feeling of dislike and contempt for O'Connell which was revived by a curious sequel several years later. In 1825 O'Connell conveyed to Peel through intermediaries an apology for his remarks in 1815. Peel returned a handsome reply, saying that if he had not long ago ceased to have any feelings of hostility or resentment, O'Connell's message would have completely removed them. The news of this *amende honorable* later became public and O'Connell was taunted with having 'crouched' to Peel. His explanation was that he had only made the apology to propitiate Peel on the Catholic question then being debated in parliament. This was something Peel could neither understand nor forgive. For his own part O'Connell retained an inveterate dislike of Peel. Politically they were always opposed; temperamentally they were antipathetic; and O'Connell, the older man, had twice been put in the wrong on a personal matter.

II

The Catholic campaign which had been halted in 1814 was a political movement to secure the second half of Pitt's Irish programme of which the Union in 1800 had been only the first instalment. Beneath this publicised campaign was another Ireland whose problems were less easily defined and for which remedies were less easily discernible. No Chief Secretary could be in office for more than a few weeks without realising that Ireland was a country of endemic lawlessness and violence. England and Ireland were not only two societies but different to a degree which few Englishmen without personal experience of Ireland could comprehend. Pouring into the Castle, month after month, from county after county, the teeming correspondence on the 'state of the country' afforded evidence of conditions which were not only absent in England but would scarcely be credited there. From peers, magistrates, landowners, clergy, police officers and military commanders came a steady stream of reports whose content seemed endless and unvarying: robbery, arson, cattle-maiming, assaults, rape, mutilation, murder, attacks on revenue officers, tithe collectors and stragglers on the line of march, intimidation of juries and the assassination of witnesses. It is not surprising that Peel remarked ironically to his friend Goulburn in 1814 that if he stayed much longer in Ireland, he would never get used to an uninterrupted state of tranquillity.

Among the Castle correspondents there were of course liars and alarmists. The experienced Dublin officials looked with scepticism on all unsupported allegations, especially the wilder rumours of French agents and conspiratorial priests. The absence of reports of disorder on the other hand did not in the peculiar atmosphere of Ireland indicate necessarily that all was well. As Lord Desart, a Kilkenny landowner and friend of Peel, wrote to him a trifle cynically in the winter of 1813–14, 'matters are . . . sometimes represented as worse than they are in order to call for assistance, and sometimes as better than they are to excuse inactivity'. But even with exaggerations reduced and alarms ignored, the state of the Irish countryside was still a sombre spectacle for the Chief Secretary. From time to time during his period of office came reports of singularly barbarous incidents, verified by irrefutable evidence, which made a profound impression on his mind. One of them took such a hold of his imagination that seventeen years later he was able to quote it from memory in the House of Commons. A man called Dillon had given evidence against persons charged with Whiteboy offences on which they were found guilty and hanged. For a time he sought safety with his family in Dublin but eventually, ignoring all warnings, he returned to his home in Co. Limerick. One night a dozen men broke into his house, dragged him from his bed and killed him with pitchforks outside the door. His wife, knowing that her turn would come next, threw a piece of dry turf on the fire and told her eldest daughter, a girl of fourteen, to remember the faces of the men when they came in to fetch her. When they entered she struggled as long as she could while the child watched in the firelight. Then they forced her out and killed her over the body of her husband. Through the efforts of a local clergyman, a number of men were subsequently arrested and, mainly on the evidence of the daughter, nine of them were convicted and hanged. Four others offered to plead guilty on condition of having their sentences commuted to transportation. But the Dillon case was one of many. Peel, as he told the Commons in 1833, remained haunted by such 'scenes of atrocity and suffering'.

The root of this violence and brutality was not crime in the ordinary sense but a species of intermittent social warfare that had existed for over a generation in Irish rural society. One of its features was the existence of innumerable secret societies and confederations among the peasants, of which the Whiteboys were only one example, though the name was often used generically to indicate the whole system. Whatever their name or locality, their objectives were the same: to wage war on landlords and tithe-collectors, to intimidate any who aided their opponents, and to revenge any action taken against their members. To the average Englishman this endemic lawlessness and the silent refusal of the mass of the population to offer any support to the authorities in suppressing it, presented an incomprehensible problem. Reporting to the prime minister the results of a special commission sent down in 1816 to deal with an outburst of crime in Tipperary, Peel added

> you can have no idea of the moral depravation of the lower orders in that county. In fidelity towards each other they are unexampled, as they are in their sanguinary disposition and fearlessness of the consequences.

Liverpool replied sympathetically but helplessly. 'In truth, Ireland is a political phenomenon—not influenced by the same feelings as appear to affect mankind in other countries.'

From the start of his secretaryship the state of the country in Peel's view was one that called for immediate attention. Returning to Ireland after the 1813 session he wrote in strong terms to the Home Office asking for military reinforcements; and in the succeeding weeks he turned his mind to the possibility of new legislation to deal with the problem of disorder. His most constructive idea, that of enlarging the police forces in Ireland, needed time to work out in detail. It was not until January 1814 that the Lord-Lieutenant was able to give formal notice to the Home Office of his intention to recommend legislation to strengthen the legal powers of the Irish executive and magistracy. When Peel returned to England at the end of March he began preparations for two measures. The first was for the renewal of the old Insurrection Act which armed the executive with extraordinary powers in time of emergency. The second was for the establishment of a special police force to act in disturbed districts as a reinforcement for the magistracy and local police. The latter, the old baronial constables known as 'Barneys' were in practice as inefficient and despised as their counterparts, the parochial constables or 'Charleys' in England. The Lord-Lieutenant had given a cordial support for these proposals; the cabinet was less enthusiastic. They were reluctant to sanction the re-enactment of the Insurrection Act repealed in 1810 and the mere word 'police' was sufficiently novel and odious to English ears for Liverpool and some of his colleagues to shrink from such an unpopular innovation.

Peel picked his way cautiously through the doubts and hesitations of the English government. Early in June he told Gregory that he was going to postpone the police bill in order to see the effects of the fall of Napoleon and later he decided that in view of the cabinet's objections he would drop the Insurrection bill and incorporate its more useful clauses in his police bill. On 23 June he introduced his Peace Preservation bill as his police measure was innocuously entitled. He drew a graphic picture of the disturbed state of Ireland, emphasised the need for magistrates to be able to repress disorders without calling on the military, and expressed a wish to have his bill regarded as a permanent part of the peace-keeping machinery in Ireland. In the House of Commons there was a gratifying and ready acceptance of the measure. Thus encouraged Peel made another request to the cabinet, backed by further evidence sent over from Ireland, for the Insurrection Act. The prime minister remained doubtful and the otherwise sympathetic Castlereagh was concerned for the effect on British diplomatic prestige at the forthcoming peace conference in Vienna. Nevertheless the energetic Chief Secretary, with the strong backing of Lord Sidmouth, in the end secured permission to attempt to secure a renewal of the act on his own statement of the case in the Commons, avoiding as far as possible any reference to the existence of general disaffection in Ireland.

This was not quite the method Peel would have preferred, but he characteristically chose the course of boldness. Early in July he rose once more in the House to propose a renewal for three years of the old Insurrection Act of 1807–10. As foreseen there was more opposition to this than to his first bill; but with the loyal support of Castlereagh, Fitzgerald and other Irish members, Peel overrode all criticisms. 'I feel strongly inclined', he wrote confidently to Whitworth on 13 July, 'to resist any innovation whatever, however plausible, and to keep the screw as tight as we can.' To Gregory he had already described the salutary effect of the evidence he had laid in front of the House of Commons. 'Though I fear', he added dryly, 'that it will not encourage them to settle with their families in Ireland.' The screw-tightening tactics were successful and both bills went through without amendment. By the end of July the Peace Preservation and the Insurrection Acts were safely on the statute book. It was Peel's first essay in major legislation and he was pardonably gratified at the result. It had been almost entirely his battle and the bold decision to proceed with the Insurrection Bill completely so.

Peel's new police, designed not as a standing provincial force but as a central organisation with units detached locally in time of emergency, came into action for the first time in Tipperary in the autumn of 1814. It is clear that he had in mind the ultimate introduction of a general police force in Ireland with fixed stations in every county. But such an organisation could not be created overnight. The chief difficulty was shortage of suitable men. 'I frequently considered the possibility of introducing a general system of Police,' he told the Marquess Wellesley in 1822, 'and was more dissuaded from it by the fears of not being able to procure proper instruments than by any conviction that such a system was not highly desirable.' This was not just an afterthought. He told the House of Commons as early as 1816 that while he regretted the imperfect nature of the Irish police and was convinced of the need for further improvements in it, he would always prefer an army of police to an army of soldiers. But such an extensive force would have taken a long time to create, even if he had won consent for such a costly and un-English innovation. As it was, the first years of the Irish Constabulary were marked by a certain amateurishness scarcely avoidable in an age which was only gradually evolving the distinction between professional soldiers and an armed civil police. Efficient organisation and discipline, even a common uniform, were all lacking in the early stages. The original constabulary appeared in a variety of military costumes, some in long scarlet cloaks with brass helmets, some in hussar uniform, others attired as mounted riflemen, commanded by officers equally splendid and heterogeneous.

The organisation of the Constabulary on a national basis was not carried out until 1822 when Peel was at the Home Office and Goulburn Chief Secretary; and when the great consolidating act of 1836 was passed, Peel's statute of 1814 was repealed along with most of the earlier peace enforcement legislation. Its work had been done, however, and subsequent legislation was merely an enlargement of the narrow foundations of 1814 and a rectification of defects disclosed by experience. The term 'Peelers', by which the Irish Constabulary soon became known, was a proper recognition of their true founder. Even before he left Ireland his new police had begun to play an integral role in reducing the dependence of the Irish executive on the regular army.

III

The alternation of duties between Dublin and Westminster left little leisure for the Chief Secretary. Except for his continental trip in 1815 Peel took no real holiday at all during these years. Brief visits to family and friends in England were all that could be spared from his parliamentary and administrative duties. In Ireland, however, almost every winter he was able to get away from his desk for a week or two, usually to join a shooting party at the country house of one of his many Irish landowning friends. In this way he saw something of at least three of Ireland's four provinces and it is unlikely that he failed to make his own observations on the state of the Irish rural classes. The poverty; the over-population; the dangerous reliance on one staple crop, the potato; the desperate struggle for land; the pathetic division and subdivision of holdings; landlord neglect on the one hand and on the other the silent social resistance of the peasantry which defeated all the efforts of improving landlords; these were phenomena which did not take long to impress themselves on any close observer of the Irish scene.

The coming of peace in 1815 made it inevitable that parliamentary scrutiny should be turned at regular intervals to the affairs of the sister island. A government which asked for a Peace Preservation Act, a renewal of the Insurrection Act, a new type of police, and a peace establishment of 25,000 troops, was bound to be asked occasionally some awkward and searching questions. If the Commons were not the best qualified tribunal to deal with the subject, this was simply a penalty of the Union. 'I believe', Peel wrote to Gregory in 1816, 'an honest despotic government would be by far the fittest government for Ireland.' But since despotic government, honest or otherwise, was out of the question, he fully accepted that Irish affairs would have to be debated at length in parliament even though most of its members, as he once satirically remarked, knew as much about Ireland as they did of Kamchatka.

In 1816, when the start of the postwar depression had exposed Lord Liverpool's government to the redoubled attacks of its enemies and the disappointed criticisms of its friends, a motion was introduced into both Houses of Parliament calling for a general enquiry into the state of Ireland. Peel's instinct, like that of some of his more militant colleagues in Dublin, was to resist the motion pointblank. He was convinced that no certain good and much probable harm would come from a full-scale discussion which would be bound among other topics to raise the question of Catholic disabilities. But his growing political sense made him realise the need for a more prudent line of defence. When writing to Lord Whitworth he suggested that they should try to limit enquiry to the disorders which had led to the application of the Insurrection Act. The cabinet in any case offered no encouragement for a heroic policy and though Peel tried to impress on the Prime Minister the danger of a purely political inquest, he soon realised that some enquiry there would have to be, however profitless. He turned his mind therefore to the framing of a counter-motion which would guard against any attempt by the opposition to drag in the disruptive issue of Catholic emancipation. Meanwhile, mobilising with practised skill the resources of his office, he prepared a massive dossier on conditions in Ireland to lay before the House. It was armed and prepared at all foreseeable points that he rose on 26 April to move his carefully worded amendment expressing regret at the disturbed state of Ireland and calling for information on recent disturbances and the measures taken to deal with them. His speech was a general survey designed to identify problems rather than to suggest any sovereign remedy. 'The difficulties and evils which encompassed Ireland', he told the Commons, 'formed a Gordian knot which could not be cut and which only the gradual lapse of time could unravel.' His sober tone was reflected in the ensuing debate and his amendment was carried by 187 votes to 103. Though he was not entirely satisfied by the division, he could take comfort in the thought that members had been given the opportunity to fire off their views and would be unlikely to want another major Irish debate that session.

As he had anticipated, there was little real demand in the House for the information it had agreed to request. It was the more political and clearcut issue of Catholic emancipation that aroused the greater interest. Less than a month later Grattan moved once more the familiar formula that the House should take the Catholic question into consideration the following session. The motion was lost, though only by a narrow margin; and the debate made Peel acutely conscious once more of the intellectual poverty of his own side. It was characteristic that this, so far from discouraging him, only spurred him to fresh effort.

> The Protestant cause [he wrote to Whitworth] has fallen into the hands of the lukewarm or timid or incompetent men. . . . Our friends proposed that we should not divide, fancying we should be in a small minority. . . . Not a single Protestant had said a word, and I determined therefore to take a part which others with more weight might have taken, and to divide the House at any rate. . . . The result was a majority of thirty, to our great surprise and satisfaction.

The debate on Grattan's motion in 1816 was of little importance in the history of Catholic emancipation; for Peel's own career it had much greater significance. The combination of courage, pride and tenacity which induced him to come forward on this occasion made it now almost unavoidable that at the next trial of strength he would be regarded as a pillar of the Protestant cause.

In 1817 a great attempt, the first since 1813, was made by the emancipationist party in the House of Commons to reopen the central question of Catholic disabilities. As always, it was impossible to tell what the outcome would be; though the little group of leading Protestant Irish members with whom Peel usually worked thought that Grattan would succeed in carrying his motion for a final settlement of the laws affecting Roman Catholics. Nevertheless they were determined not to go down without a fight and before the debate came on, they consulted together on tactics and speakers. Their preparations were important since in the event it was on this small Anglo-Irish group, together with Bathurst, that the entire burden of the Protestant cause in the House of Commons fell.

The debate on Grattan's motion took place on 9 May 1817 and to Peel was allotted the crucial place of last speaker on the Protestant side. His speech was not only one of his outstanding parliamentary performances but in its indirect consequences one of the most fateful for his political future. As a contribution to the debate it owed much of its powerful effect to the precision with which he related his arguments to the detailed proposals for a settlement put forward by the supporters of emancipation. He took his main stand on Ireland and his efforts were directed to proving that the proposals were unwelcome to the Catholics on whose behalf they were being made and calculated only to undermine the recent Union with Ireland and the Protestant establishment which was essential to its survival. Emancipation would not bring peace to Ireland since it would do nothing to solve the problem of the impoverished Irish peasantry. Emancipation would only weaken the ability of the Irish executive to govern effectively. It was a telling line of attack since the differences between Peel and his opponents was not that they looked to separate ends but that they disagreed on the means to the same end. They thought that their proposals would save the Union; he did not. Yet in elaborating his arguments he was led on to the expression of opinions which were opposed to emancipation in any form and at any time. He achieved the dangerous feat of both discrediting his opponents' policy and suggesting that no policy they could offer would be likely to succeed. In winning this dialectical battle he denied to his own side, and to himself, any room for manoeuvre.

This was a consequence for the future. What was of immediate significance was that his speech was an oratorical and political triumph which won him for the first time a national reputation. Canning, the most brilliant parliamentary speaker of his age, spoke generously of its 'consummate ability'; and people told Peel that it had changed the votes of over a dozen members. If so, it had been decisive, since Grattan's motion, against all expectation, was defeated by a majority of twenty-four. Congratulations poured in from his friends; the Corporation of Dublin asked him to sit for a portrait; and Gregory wrote for printed copies of the speech to be distributed in Ireland.

Less than a month later he received the final accolade. He was invited to stand for election as M.P. for Oxford University. The vacancy was created by the retirement of Charles Abbot, the Speaker, and until the spring of 1817 the obvious successor to him was Canning. Not only did he wish to change his costly and irksome seat at Liverpool for a cheaper and less onerous constituency, but he had been carefully preparing the ground at Oxford for several years. Like Abbot he was a Christ Church man and if the convention was maintained whereby that college claimed one of the two university seats, the choice of Christ Church was likely to be decisive. But at the crucial college meeting at the end of May feeling swung against Canning and in favour of his younger rival. On 30 May his old tutor Lloyd posted up through the night to bring Peel the college's invitation to accept nomination. The subsequent election in June was uncontested but it is probable that Peel's newly won position as head of the parliamentary Protestant party would have secured him victory even against Canning. Nevertheless, the cardinal decision had been that of the Christ Church common room. There the significant fact was that Canning had been proposed and rejected; and only after that rejection had the meeting gone on to consider whether to put up another Christ Church man. Writing to Peel some years later Lloyd denied that Canning's Catholic advocacy had been the main cause of his failure to win the support of his own college. The real reason was that 'they did not believe in the sincerity, the consistency, the honesty of the man. . . . The Catholic Question had nothing to do with it.' It was in fact round Canning, not Peel, that the issue had revolved. Peel came in, rather fortuitously, on his rival's unpopularity rather than on his own sudden reputation as Protestant champion.

He had, as more than one observer noted, been very fortunate. Before he had reached the age of thirty he had gained one of the prized honours of the electoral world. He himself not only showed extreme gratification but seemed momentarily overwhelmed by the compliment paid to him. He even at one point mentioned the possibility to Lloyd of abandoning office if he were elected: a quixotic gesture which would scarcely have pleased his new constituents or satisfied in the long run his own deeper if unconscious ambitions.

> If I succeed [he wrote effusively to old Dean Jackson], I shall have attained the paramount object of my ambition, one to which I should have looked forward as the ample reward of a long political life. And I trust in God that my success, though it may make me undervalue the usual objects to which political men aspire, will stimulate me to those exertions by which alone I can prove myself worthy of the confidence which the most distinguished body on earth has been pleased to confer on me.

Whether many people would have shared this exalted opinion of Oxford University is perhaps beside the point. But an older, more prescient man might have weighed more objectively the price of accepting a seat normally reserved for independent M.P.s and, once obtained, held for life. It was, oddly enough, left for the unworldly Lloyd to raise delicately and fleetingly the question whether a professional politician almost at the start of his career could guarantee to hold permanently the opinions which in 1817 recommended him to his electors. In assuming the representation of Oxford Peel had put his political future under bond; but to him, even less than to Lloyd, such a mortgage on the future seemed to offer little risk.

IV

Life as Chief Secretary however left Peel little leisure in which to speculate on his future. It was to the realities of the cottar's cabin rather than those of college common rooms that his mind was turned in the summer of 1817. The year of the great Catholic debate and the university by-election brought as urgent and serious a problem as any he encountered during his six years in Ireland: the threat of famine. Bad weather the previous autumn had spoilt the wheat crop and gravely affected the size and quality of the potatoes. The danger period began in the late spring of 1817 when the diminished supplies of the previous year were being eaten up and the new crops not yet harvested. Peel had left Ireland in January and by the beginning of March was anxiously waiting for detailed evidence of the anticipated scarcity which he could lay before the cabinet. Though he obtained a special meeting of the departmental ministers most concerned to consider the threat of famine, their decisions were hampered by lack of adequate information. The failure of the Castle to produce anything more than expressions of alarm and requests for such time-honoured but delusive expedients as prohibiting distilleries and banning food exports, provoked Peel to exasperation.

> I must beg of you [he wrote sharply to Gregory] to consider the peculiar difficulties of my situation. I am here between three and four hundred miles from the seat of the Government for which I am acting. If I receive a letter from Ireland upon any subject of importance that requires immediate decision, I must act . . . I cannot call for explanation or wait for authentic documents, as men in public situations in this country can do.

Gradually, however, under the impact of his brisk despatches and searching questions, the officials in Dublin began to take hold of the situation and by the beginning of April a flow of information began to arrive in London.

The crisis came in June, in the last weeks before the start of the harvest. The distress was particularly severe in the west and north-west and in the districts around Dublin. With near-famine conditions prevailing in some areas, there were outbreaks of rioting, looting of shops and bakeries, attacks on food transports, and an influx of destitute and beggars into the capital bringing with them disease and infection. Peel, who had already authorised Gregory to take £2,000 from the civil contingencies fund for general relief purposes, redoubled his efforts from London. He had secured permission to draw on the Treasury for further relief and he suggested to the Lord-Lieutenant that the money should be put in the hands of parish clergy and Roman Catholic priests. For relief in kind he proposed the establishment of soup kitchens and the purchase of biscuit in bulk from Bristol and Liverpool. For the supervision of these activities he recommended the appointment of a government commission to collect information, supplement local relief funds, and distribute food. With all this went the familiar and necessary warning that no suspicion of jobbery should attach itself to the commission. 'Put a Quaker or two, a Catholic or two, let it be quite clear there is no party, no government view in the appointments.' The executive government in Dublin, which had produced from its own wisdom nothing more helpful than a proclamation calling on the wealthier classes to discontinue eating potatoes and reduce their horses' rations, hastened to put these practical suggestions into effect. By the end of the month £14,000 had been spent in direct assistance; and in the course of the relief work it became obvious that the real trouble was not so much an absolute shortage of food as lack of money, among peasants living on a subsistence economy, with which to purchase it.

In contrast to the negative policy of the Castle, Peel's insistence on positive relief measures—the distribution of money (amounting in the end to £37,000) and the procurement of food—marked him out as the one member of the Irish government who had penetrated any distance into the heart of the problem. The relief measures undertaken at his instance, combined with precautions against disorder and a welcome return of fine weather at the end of June, enabled the Irish authorities to control the situation until the danger had passed away. Before the onset of winter there were heartening signs that adequate supplies of food and fuel were becoming available once more, and there was less disorder than had been known for many years. Though Peel admitted to the prime minister in the autumn that 'people attributed their relief in a much greater degree to the intervention of Government than they ought to have done', the prominent part played by the Castle authorities in alleviating the famine earned them one of their rare moments of popularity. Nevertheless, 1817 was a portent. It was the first substantial failure of the potato harvest since Ireland had become dependent on that one vulnerable crop; and after the famine had come typhus fever, from which perhaps as many as 50,000 people died. Faced with this new danger, Peel called for an immediate report on the nature and causes of the disease and the following spring was active in extending the enquiry and obtaining more money to improve the fever hospitals in Ireland. All through 1818 the Irish government was combating this sinister aftermath of the famine; and only in 1819 did it die down.

The 1817 famine showed Peel at the height of his powers as Chief Secretary. With equal knowledge and sharper imagination than his permanent officials, he was nearer to grasping the realities of the Irish social problem than perhaps any other man in public life. His foresight, energy and brisk readiness to override conventional policy and government regulations, made him even three hundred miles away the mainspring of the Irish executive. He had learnt the art of harrying his subordinates in private while defending them in public; and he extracted from the limited machinery of government at his disposal its maximum efficiency. By 1817 he had evolved his own style of administration: the eliciting of specific information by means of detailed questionnaires to the men most likely to have access to the knowledge he needed; the checking of generalities and opinions by reference to the facts; prudent choice of agents; caution in coming to a conclusion and energetic action once a decision had been reached. Few things are more striking in his dealings with his Irish subordinates than his insistence on precise, factual information, a commodity not easy to obtain in Ireland. Facts to Peel were the basis of sound administration; facts were the best arguments to lay before the legislature. 'There is nothing like a fact,' he observed when writing to Gregory in June 1814 about his Peace Preservation Bill; and again in April 1816—'facts are ten times more valuable than declamations'. In administration this was an admirable attitude; in politics, where much depends on appearances, it was not always to be so infallible a guide.

The time was coming, however, when the end of his Irish labours was in sight. In the end his secretaryship overlapped three vice-royalties; but in a personal sense his own Lord-Lieutenant was Whitworth. The close relationship which had grown up between them made the Irish administration of 1813–17 an example of unity and efficiency rare in the history of nineteenth-century Irish government. From Peel's point of view therefore it seemed appropriate that they should leave Ireland together. To the cabinet it seemed otherwise and Liverpool was clearly regretful at seeing him go at all. He was not alone in his regret. In June 1817 Peel received an unusual compliment in the shape of a letter signed by fifty-nine Irish M.P.s paying tribute to his conduct of Irish administration and expressing the hope that he would remain in office under the new Lord-Lieutenant. In the end he yielded to this flattering pressure and agreed to stay for one more year to initiate the new Viceroy, Lord Talbot, and to supervise the Irish part of the general election in 1818. It was a different Peel now from the young inexperienced Chief Secretary of 1812 who had written pleadingly to Arbuthnot, the patronage secretary in London, for any advice he could spare on the delicate art of electoral management. With the ease born of a wide circle of Irish connections and long familiarity with the Irish scene, he embarked on the task of recommending individuals, canvassing borough patrons, appealing to county magnates, composing differences and suggesting compromises. When he rendered up his electoral account he could look with satisfaction on this final act of his political stewardship. Of the hundred Irish members, seventy-one were marked down after the election as government supporters.

In contrast to his inconspicuous arrival in 1812, there was hardly an Irish newspaper of any note which did not take the occasion of his departure in 1818 to publish articles on his character and policy. Whatever else he had done, he had put a personal stamp on the Irish administration equalled by perhaps no previous Chief Secretary and certainly none since the Union. He had six years intensive experience of government; he had acquired a deep knowledge of Ireland; he was now a rising politician with not only a future but a record and a reputation. Among Irish M.P.s he even had something of a personal following. There were rumours that he was to be promoted to the cabinet; but his friends knew better. He was tired of the secretaryship; tired of Ireland; and anxious for a respite. To Croker who conveyed to him some of the more extravagant gossip about his political prospects, he replied, 'Fudge! I am thinking of anything but office and am just as anxious to be emancipated from office as the Papists are to be emancipated into it.' He continued with a burst of his old youthful liveliness,

> A fortnight hence I shall be as free as the air—free from ten thousand engagements which I cannot fulfil; free from the anxiety of having more to do than it is possible to do well; free from the acknowledgements of that gratitude which consists in a lively sense of future favours; free from the necessity of abstaining from private intimacy that will certainly interfere with public duty; free from Orangemen; free from Ribbonmen; . . . free from perpetual converse about the Harbour of Howth and Dublin Bay haddock; and lastly, free of the Company of Carvers and Gilders which I became this day in reward of my public services.

On 3 August 1818 came his final departure from Ireland. He never went back; it is unlikely that he ever wanted to. Perhaps there was no need; for the rest of his life Ireland was rarely far away.

Chapter 4

Interlude

Peel's six years in Ireland had been long enough. He had been in no danger of killing himself but the incessant energy he had displayed during his term of office could not be continued indefinitely. Palmerston, his contemporary, who had been made Secretary at War in 1908, was content to saunter along in that junior and routine office for nineteen years. Peel's temperament was different. Work and responsibility attracted him like a magnet. Given the challenge and the opportunity he was ready to exert his intellectual and physical resources to the limit. As a result his career tended to fall into stretches of great creative activity followed by temporary lulls. In 1818, at the comparatively youthful age of thirty, he only needed a brief fallow period in which to recruit his energies. In the autumn of that year he took a long holiday in the Highlands with a party of friends and followed that by visits to Oxford and Paris. When the parliamentary session started he was regular in his attendance and several times proved an effective speaker on the government side; though Arbuthnot, the Treasury Secretary, noted with some sourness that he gave too many dinners and rarely stayed late in the House.

In his more leisurely hours he tried to improve his debating powers by studying the formal art of ratiocination. It was typical that it was on reasoning rather than on rhetoric that he laid most emphasis.

> Pray tell me [he wrote to his old mentor Lloyd] what you consider the best specimen, not exactly of reasoning, but of that part of reasoning which is occupied in confutation of your adversary's argument. I want, as I have often told you, from reading much of polemics, to form some general principle of arguing and reply . . . I do not want to read for information on the subject; at least that is not my chief object. What I want is subtle reasoning in reply. I care not if the book is on alchemy. There is not half reasoning enough in politics—not half.

To attach prime importance to the role of reason in politics was perhaps a slightly dangerous proclivity. But a man who was prepared to read alchemy to improve his powers of debate was clearly not without ideas on his own future.

Meanwhile he kept his administrative talents from growing rusty by becoming chairman of the important Commons committee on the resumption of cash payments appointed in 1819. Determined to break out at last from the postwar stagnation created by commercial depression, stringent economy and inadequate revenue, the cabinet was beginning to evolve a more constructive economic policy. The teaching of the classical economists pointed clearly to a return to sound budgeting, greater freedom from commercial restrictions, and (despite the caution of the Bank of England) the stabilisation of the currency on a metallic basis. The committee included all the leading ministers in the Commons—Castlereagh, Canning, Vansittart, Robinson and Huskisson—and Peel expressed a wish to Arbuthnot also to serve. After consultation between Arbuthnot and the Prime Minister it was decided not only to put Peel on the committee but to make him chairman. Though his general political support could be counted on, he would at least give the appearance of independence in the chair and it was a neat way of harnessing his talents to the service of the government. There was from the start little doubt what the recommendations of the committee would be; but Peel approached his task with an open mind. In 1811 as a young member he had voted with Vansittart for a continuation of paper currency as against the recommendation of Horner's committee for an early resumption of cash payments. But he did not profess any special knowledge of the subject and was determined to form his own judgement in the light of the evidence submitted to the committee. Indeed, he stipulated, before accepting the invitation to take the chair, that he must reserve his right to take a course unfettered either by his vote in 1811 or the views of the ministerial members of the committee.

> I conceive [he wrote to Lloyd] my chief, perhaps my only qualification . . . is that I have not prejudged the question, am committed to no opinion upon it, and shall be therefore at least disinterested in the result of our investigation.

Nevertheless, listening to a long train of distinguished witnesses—directors of the Bank of England, private bankers, merchants, and economists—he was soon convinced that the wartime system of paper money had resulted in a depreciation of the currency, an increase in bullion prices, and an unfavourable rate of foreign exchange.

In May he introduced the committee's report, which he himself had written, in a speech which in length and detail was perhaps the most difficult he had yet delivered. There was little opposition to the principles of the report. The real issue was not the return to gold. Liverpool and Huskisson, the chief economic experts in the government, and the repeated sense of parliament, were all united on that point. The question was more the technical one of when and how to put the principle into effect. Before the end of the month the Commons had approved a series of resolutions embodying the main recommendations of the report and a bill giving them force went rapidly through both Houses. It was a singularly quiet passage for an act which settled an issue of so much controversy in the past and which was to raise so much controversy in the future. For Peel however it had brought enhanced reputation and much personal satisfaction. He had learnt a great deal about an important but highly technical subject; and the settled views he had formed, together with his role as chairman and introducer of the report, firmly identified him with the government's new financial policy. It was not long in fact before the act of 1819, enforcing the return of British currency to the gold standard, became known as 'Peel's Act'.

The remainder of the session gave him less cause for pleasure. He found no opportunity of speaking in a brief, untidy debate on Grattan's Catholic motion in May and the result (the defeat of the motion by only two votes) made him pessimistic about the ultimate chances of successful resistance. In June his ill-timed and clumsy attack on Brougham's education committee in the role of defender of public schools and the ancient universities exposed him to some rough handling by the greatest master of invective in the Commons. In the summer, when Peel was once more on a shooting party in the High-lands, occurred the mismanagement and bloodshed at a radical reform meeting at Manchester which added the word 'Peterloo' to the nation's political vocabulary. Though, at the emergency meeting in parliament in November, he supported the ministers and their notorious Six Acts to deal with disorder and sedition (not all as unreasonable as their notoriety might suggest), he was struck by the widening gap that seemed to exist between the government and the nation. He had no fears for the political stability of the ministry, but the larger problems of British society remained in his mind during the rest of the winter.

> Do you not think [he wrote to Croker in March 1820] that the tone of England—of that great compound of folly, weakness, prejudice, wrong feeling, right feeling, obstinacy, and newspaper paragraphs, which is called public opinion—is more liberal, to use an odious but intelligible phrase, than the policy of the government?

A curious and dangerous situation, in his opinion, had developed in which public opinion, exercising more influence on government than it had ever done in the past, was never more dissatisfied with the share of influence it possessed. 'It is growing too large for the channels that it has been accustomed to run through.' Moderate reform of some sort seemed unavoidable; and in that case he thought it better that Whigs and Tories should combine to carry it out rather than allow the radicals to dictate the course of events.

It was the instinctive voice of the conservative politician; but there seemed little opportunity to put the doctrine into practice. The year 1820 was a depressing time in English politics. In January the old for-gotten King died at Windsor and the accession of the Regent to full regal powers brought to a head the long estrangement between him and his foolish, vulgar, ill-treated wife. The strain of the 'Queen's divorce' proceedings not only forced a postponement of the government's programme of financial and trade reform, but dragged their political reputation through the dirt. Though, with the cabinet's prestige at its lowest ebb, some ministerial changes were confidently expected, it was hardly an auspicious season for recruitment. Peel, moreover, who was one of the obvious candidates for office, had acquired an even stronger motive for holding aloof.

II

In February 1820 he had reached his thirty-second birthday, wealthy, successful and still unmarried. He was one of the more eligible bachelors in London society, but so far no woman's name had been linked with his, nor indeed had there been any breath of scandal about his private life. His father had not married until he was well past thirty and the pattern was repeated in the son. From the time he left Oxford he had put all his energies and emotions into his work. Too busy to think of marriage, too fastidious to be a rake, he remained one of the steadily declining number of bachelors in his own particular circle. For that reason perhaps he was an object of interest to women and the more leisurely life he was leading after 1818 gave at least one of them the opportunity to satisfy her curiosity.

Pretty feather-headed Lady Shelley was introduced to him for the first time in January 1819. Attracted by the enthusiasm with which his friends spoke of him, but slightly repelled by his plebeian origins, she looked forward with interest to the meeting, though womanlike made up her mind to dislike him. At the outset she found him something of an enigma among the hard-drinking, hard-spoken aristocrats whom her husband usually brought to the house. 'At first sight he displeased me. He spoke of shooting and country pursuits in a condescending manner; and his parade of good breeding and attention, a parade to which an Englishwoman is unaccustomed in a man of talent, disappointed me.' However his attentiveness had its effect. With serene assurance she soon decided that he was the English Metternich. 'He has a foreign *tournure de phrases* which I delight in, and yet in an Englishman it had at first displeased me.' They discussed literature, including the identity of *Junius* and the authorship of the Waverley novels; and Peel described some of the Irish atrocities that had occurred while he was Chief Secretary, including the Dillon murders. He obviously felt at ease with his hostess for at breakfast he entertained the table with an anecdote of Sir Frederick Flood, the Irish member for Wexford, at the time of the 1815 Corn Law riots in London. Having been roughly handled by the crowd outside, Flood made his way into the House of Commons to complain swelling with anger and importance. 'Mr. Speaker, I appear before you, literally torn into four quarters. (Shouts of Hear! Hear!) I have been seized by the mob. They wanted to know my name. Mr Speaker, I *scorned* to equivocate. I told them my name was Waters.' 'I wish,' added Lady Shelley enthusiastically, 'I could render justice to the humour with which Mr Peel told this story.'

Mr Peel in fact had made a conquest and since he was also approved by the great ladies who ruled Almacks, it was not long before they met again at that smart and exclusive assembly. 'Wednesday's Almack's was very pleasant,' recorded Lady Shelley on 17 March. 'I talked a great deal to Mr Peel, who came to me with the greatest *empressement*. He is a most delightful person.' In November she dined at Peel's house, the only woman present in a company that comprised Vesey Fitzgerald, Grant, Huskisson, Beckett, Lord Westmorland, and Sir George Warrender. The conversation was mainly political; and with six chaperons Peel was in no danger of compromising his own or his fair visitor's reputation. In any case, Almacks and dinner parties notwithstanding, his affections were already committed elsewhere. Ireland, which had done so much to mould his political career, had been fateful for his private life also.

When he first went to Ireland in 1812, the second-in-command of the military forces had been a General John Floyd, a veteran soldier who had fought as a boy in the Seven Years War and later with Arthur Wellesley in India. He had been made a baronet in 1816 and died at the age of seventy shortly before Peel retired from the Irish Secretaryship. When in India he had married a daughter of Charles Darke, a merchant of Madras, by whom he had four children: a son Henry who entered his father's profession, and three daughters, Miranda, Julia and Flavia. His wife and youngest daughter died of scarlet fever in 1802 and three years later he married again. His second wife was the widowed Lady Denny of Tralee, a handsome worldly Irishwoman who took charge of her two stepdaughters with a brisk competent hand. In 1815 Miranda married Major-General Fuller of the Coldstream Guards and there only remained Julia to be provided for. By 1817 Lady Floyd was on terms of close friendship with Peel's sister, Mary, who had married George Dawson, M.P. for Co. Kerry and formerly Peel's private secretary. Lady Floyd and her stepdaughter were both entertained at the Secretary's Lodge in Phoenix Park and the acquaintanceship ripened. When the Floyds moved to London in 1817 the two ladies undertook to find some Dresden china ice-pails to match Peel's dinner service; and Peel was unusually attentive to them on their departure from Dublin. After 1818 the relationship between Julia Floyd and himself deepened, though it was characteristic of his reticence over personal matters that the progress of his courtship left no trace in his correspondence and went unrecorded by his friends.

Julia Floyd was born in India in 1795 and at the age of twenty-five had experience of a wider social life than that provided by regimental balls and provincial garrison towns. With her oval face, dark ringlets, and fine neck and shoulder, admirably set off by the low-cut, high-waisted Regency fashion, she was one of the society beauties of her day. The future Tsar Nicholas enrolled himself among her admirers when he visited England at the end of 1816; and another of her followers was the dashing and popular Hughes Ball, known from his great wealth as the 'Golden Ball'. But it was Robert Peel in the end to whom she gave her heart. Early in March 1820, when less fortunate politicians were intent on the approaching general election, they became engaged. At one point, according to family tradition, Peel had misgivings whether she would be able to abandon her gay fashionable world for the severer climate of a professional politician's wife. 'You are my world,' she replied disarmingly. It was a love match; and probably the first time either had been in love. Even apart from the coincidence that each had been motherless from childhood, they had certain temperamental traits in common. Both were outwardly cool and self-contained; both capable of passionate, singleminded devotion. But strong feeling does not necessarily produce smooth relationships and they had much to learn about each other. Peel perhaps had even more to discover than Julia.

In the interval before the wedding, the strict, old-fashioned proprieties were observed. Julia took up residence with her aunt in Berkeley Square while Peel went off in self-imposed exile to Bognor with his sister Mary. His first letter from the seaside began with the unwise premise that having no news, he would not supply the deficiency with 'impassioned declarations' of love and admiration, as such declarations, he added slightingly, were easily made and often insincere, and in any case 'so unnecessary to convince you of the ardour and constancy of my attachment to you, that I purposely avoid them'. The ethics of engagement and perhaps a feminine obliquity in Miss Floyd deprived him of anything more than a few brief and unsatisfactory lines in reply. Perhaps Julia had found his letter equally unsatisfactory. Another love-letter he devoted largely to aesthetics in a somewhat Wordsworthian vein.

> I hope you take delight in the wildness and magnificence of Nature, as well as in the calmer beauties of cultivated scenery. . . . I do not want you quite to agree with me in having a particular admiration for the sterility and solitude of a rocky, uninhabited wilderness; I will be content if you will think a very high mountain, with a rude craggy outline, a splendid and awful sight, but I am sure you have much too pure a taste not to think so.

Though his family highly approved of the match, a malicious story was conveyed to Julia that old Sir Robert did not like his son's choice. The mixture of indignation and lofty pride with which Peel assured Julia of its falsehood led him into a somewhat selfrighteous and involved expression of feeling.

> If the iniquity of our enemies had been half so great as their malice, surely they might have invented something more plausible. . . . All

they have fabricated is not only without foundation, not only at variance with but in direct contradiction to the truth. We wish to take no revenge but it would be inconsistent with candour and fair dealing to pretend to be on terms of friendship or even intimacy with them. I forgive them, for they have afforded me a proof of your generous confidence in me which without their artifice I never could have had. I do not mean that I ever could have doubted it but without them it never would have been put to the test of a serious trial.

In other respects he showed himself a more natural and human lover, teaching his little nephew to pronounce the name Julia and forgetting in the absorption of his letters to London that he was temporarily disqualified from using a parliamentary frank in lieu of postage.

The wedding took place on 8 June in the drawing-room of 45 Upper (West) Seymour Street where Lady Floyd had taken up residence after the death of her husband. The honeymoon was spent at a country house that Peel had rented at Mickleham in Surrey. From there the young couple sent their first letter to Lady Floyd, writing together on one sheet of paper.

My dear Mamma, [ran Julia's contribution]
My Robert says truly that I am well but he does not add what I do, which is that I believe myself to be the very happiest of all human beings. I am thank God united to a thoroughly amiable Man and one *whom I adore, for whom* I would willingly risk existence itself. I can not write more at present. Give my love, my best love to my dear Henry, my Aunt, etc. etc., and Believe me ever,
Your very affectionate,
Julia Peel
I was going to write Floyd

Later that summer they went down to Drayton where Julia charmed Sir Robert and demonstrated a not total inaptitude for country life by making her first essay in gardening. At other times, to his father's mild alarm, her husband drove her round the countryside in a tilbury behind a high-spirited hunter. When they took up residence in London for the parliamentary session all their friends could see the pride and affection he felt for his young bride.

One cloud on their early married life was Julia's stepmother, known to the Peels as the Dowager. Talkative, unabashed, gossipy and mischievous, with an Irish expectation of favours from her influential son-in-law, she hovered on the fringe of the Peels' circle in a manner which caused him peculiar annoyance and provoked sharp-tongued remarks from Julia. Lady Floyd fortunately inspired in them a common sentiment. More difficult to endure were the little hurts that arose between themselves. Julia was jealous and possessive; he was sensitive and, for all his seven years advantage of age, inexperienced in women's ways. When he resumed the more normal pattern of his life he was necessarily or by choice often absent from her. She could not refrain from an occasional tart remark about his social activities. He at a distance could not prevent himself from an exaggerated pain over trifles. Writing from Sudbourne, Lord Hertford's country house in Suffolk in December 1823, he assured her that 'if I could love you more, the sight of others and their odious ways would make me do so'. Yet he mixed with no apparent objection in sometimes questionable society and not all their ways were found odious. It was on this visit that Henry Baring bet Lord Hertford that Peel could not kill in the course of a day a pheasant, a red-legged partridge, a common partridge, a snipe, a jack-snipe, a woodcock, a wild duck, a rabbit and a hare. Peel backed himself to the tune of three hundred guineas, began shooting at ten and had won the bet before one o'clock. The following year he was back at Sudbourne in a party which included the Duke of York, Wellington, Croker, Arbuthnot, and various of their wives. The shooting was good, but that over, 'my pleasure is at an end'. Moreover, Lord Hertford being a notorious libertine whose current mistress was Lady Strachan, Peel was shocked to find Admiral Strachan arrive at the house in the role of complacent husband. 'I must say I am pleased with the compliment which Lord Hertford paid to you', he wrote to Julia, 'by not asking you to this house. . . . He paid homage to your virtue and good name.'

Julia was less appreciative of the homage than piqued by her husband's readiness to remain in a house from which propriety excluded her. 'I do not understand', she wrote with understandable coolness, 'how the house at Sudburn which you used to describe to me as small and uncomfortable in bedroom furniture can accommodate such a very large party as the one now assembled within its adulterous walls.' Back came his reply with a shade of pain. 'My dearest Julia, I have just received your letter, and I presume, as you consider the party here so perfect and fashionable, that my letter of yesterday may have surprised you.' But Julia could not resist another barb. 'How will you bear to think of *one*, compared to *fifteen*. *I know it is nothing in the scale*.' Her husband was hurt and showed it in a ponderous masculine way.

> I should have but little satisfaction in the thought that anyone but myself had seen a letter from you to me, during my separation from you, in which there is such a sentence. . . . I will only remark upon this that I would suffer much rather than write such a sentence to you. . . . Kiss my children for me. I hope they will always justly estimate my affection for them.

And to add point to the last sentence, he signed himself with unusual distance, 'I am, dearest Julia, your attached husband, R.P.'

But these were mere spots on the sun which did not so much obscure as arise out of the intensity of their affection. Most of his letters to Julia flowed naturally and happily, and nowhere else did he write in such a pleasant, easy style, free from official jargon and political reserve, and full of little sketches of people and places in his gently humorous, mildly malicious vein.

From Apethorpe, the country house of the Earl of Westmorland, for example, he wrote in January 1833.

> The house is exactly like a small college in Oxford. It is a building about two hundred years old, built round a tolerably sized quadrangle which is large enough to be entirely of grass, a little field. Its equal in discomfort cannot be produced.

The whole party except for Peel and Croker consisted of relatives— 'Fanes and Chaplins with a gruff general of the name of Fisher'. The weather was wet; there was no shooting; and to avoid the solid family group of Fanes playing whist in the drawing-room, Peel took refuge in the billiard-room where Croker was playing with Lord Westmorland. The establishment included, to Peel's amusement, a domestic chaplain of the eighteenth-century type: a Dr Bunney 'who performs all the duties of the Groom of the Chambers and some of those of the housemaid. His civility in showing *little conveniences* to the guests is amazing.' Peel's bedroom, dark and rat-infested, was in a distant wing of the house. Having reached it at the second attempt, his candle having blown out halfway, he discovered that the servants, in obedience to Lord Westmorland's caution against large fires, had raked out all the coals and left both windows wide open, with the result that his candle promptly went out once more as soon as he entered. His vignette of country life, which could not have been greatly improved upon by the creator of Jorrocks, was rounded off by a description of the dinner— with one side-dish consisting of two whole infant pigs, with their trotters resting beside them, and another composed of pickled herring and apples—and the sporting side of the establishment—'louts that are called gamekeepers' and some remarkable spaniels, each with a muzzle to prevent it from eating the game and one leg tied up to prevent it from running too fast.

When they were separated, he wrote almost daily to his wife and all his letters told the same story. 'I find it very lonely without you, my own Julia,' he wrote from Stanhope Street in August 1823, 'and believe me, I sleep no better when I am away from you.' And from Sudbourne at the end of the year,

> You know my darling that I wish you were with me and with what delight I shall clasp you to my arms on Sunday next. It would be difficult for me to say when I do not think of you. You are always present to my thoughts.

She for her part was equally constant and affectionate. While at Stratfield Saye in 1827 Peel wrote that he was depressed at being without a letter from her for two days running. 'It never happened before', he added; and that was after nearly seven years of marriage.

Politics entered little into their correspondence and when he some-times passed on little confidential items, it was usually with an injunc-tion to mention them to nobody. What he needed from her was a respite from the world and the refuge of warmth and love. Julia Peel was not a *femme politique* like Lady Palmerston or Princess Lieven, nor did she even pretend to a knowledge of affairs like Lady Shelley. She had no in-fluence over her husband's public life nor did she try to exercise any. 'She is not a clever woman,' the Duke of Wellington once observed. 'Peel had no wish to marry a clever woman.' Instead she was content with the other half of her husband's life; home, family, children, friends, holidays, house and garden. His letters to her seemed deliberately to shut away everything else. Apart from his amusing little descriptions of country house life, the only activities he described were his shooting, which she encouraged him to write about, and little shopping com-missions he undertook for her in London. For the rest he wrote almost too critically of the boredom and unpleasantness of the society in which he passed much of his time, the buffoonery of some, the loose-living of others. He had a special dislike of men who neglected their wives for other women and was one of the few who were moved to any sympathy for the poor, foolish, short-sighted Duchess of Wellington, so openly abandoned by the great Duke for the attractions of sprightly ladies like Mrs Arbuthnot or Lady Jersey. Perhaps he dwelt on these things to reassure Julia; but he was also expressing a side of his own nature. Happy in his own marriage, totally uninterested in other women, he took a severe view of the vagaries of less fortunate men. 'What wicked-ness and what folly to underestimate and to be insensible to the affection of a wife,' he wrote to Julia on one occasion.

Yet Peel was no outward purist, as his friendship with the Marquess of Hertford demonstrated. A man of pleasure, separated from his wife, Lord Hertford in the 1820s was a peer of some influence on the Tory side, a leading figure in society, and a man of wit and charm. Peel probably met him through Croker, who had constituted himself a kind of unpaid manager of Hertford's estates, and he clearly enjoyed not only his shooting-parties but his personal company. 'I like him,' he wrote to Croker in 1822. 'He is a gentleman and not an everyday one.' The references to Hertford in his letters to Julia were unusually gentle. In 1823 he sent her one of Hertford's notes. 'I have just got the enclosed from Lord Hertford, which is as usual very civil and kind. He never wishes to separate us. I have just told him we cannot be of his party.' At Hertford's death in 1842, despite the sordid last years which made his life a European scandal, Peel paid the debt of old friendship and earned the disapproval of the puritanical by sending his carriage to the funeral. Yet though many men took their wives to Sudbourne, Peel would never allow Julia to go.

Considerations of propriety apart, Julia's social activities were limited by the burden of a steadily growing family. Their first child, Julia the second, was born in April 1821, eleven months after the wedding. A year later, in May 1822, came the first boy, Robert. Then followed four more boys in quick succession: Frederick, named after his godparent, the Duke of York, in 1823; William in 1824; John in 1827; and Arthur Wellesley, for whom the Duke stood godfather, in 1829. The house in Stanhope Street was too small for this growing brood of children and in 1823 Peel bought the expiring lease of an old building belonging to the Crown Commissioners only a quarter of a mile from the House of Commons. A fresh lease was obtained, the old house pulled down, and under the superintendence of Robert Smirke, the fashionable architect of the day, Peel's new town residence no. 4 (renumbered no. 3) Whitehall Gardens was finally completed in 1825. An elegant building, in style halfway between the classic Regency and the more florid Victorian manner, its most notable feature was the great gallery on the first floor. A small garden at the back went down to the Thames, whose broad waters still rose and fell where the Victoria Embankment now stands. From the bay window at the end of the gallery the visitor could look across the river to the arches of Westminster Bridge or north-east over the rooftops to the great dome of St Paul's floating like a bubble in the London haze. The house cost Peel £14,000, or so it was said; and the figure is not improbable. This was more than his official salary could bear and it seems likely, as Greville the diarist recorded in 1831, that his father came to his assistance. Even so Peel had outrun his resources so much by the summer of 1825 that he was obliged to borrow £5,000 from his brother William.

The long gallery was not an empty embellishment. At the date of the move from Stanhope Street Peel had already started the great collection of pictures which was to be one of the private pleasures of his life. His first recorded purchase was a Rembrandt which he bought at a sale in Dublin for the moderate sum of fifty-nine guineas. After his marriage he began systematically to collect paintings, mainly of the Dutch and Flemish schools, which the upheaval of the Napoleonic Wars were increasingly bringing on the London market. Among them were two famous paintings by Hobbema, the 'Château de Brederode' and 'The Avenue, Middleharnis'; though the outstanding, certainly the most expensive, item was Rubens's 'Chapeau de Paille'. For this he paid £2,725 in 1824, almost a record price for a half-length portrait, the money (according to the usually well-informed Greville) being advanced by his father. A more dominating canvas, though less costly purchase, was Rubens's 'Triumph of Silenus'. Dr Waagen, the head of the Berlin Royal Picture Gallery, who saw it at Peel's house in 1835, thought it almost too massive for the delicate seascapes and interiors by which it was surrounded. Nevertheless, he was impressed by the taste and skill which had gone into Peel's collection. By that date Peel had already made his reputation as art patron and connoisseur. In 1827 he had become a trustee of the National Gallery where, long after his death, the best of his collection found their permanent home; and it was to Peel that the great art dealer J. M. Smith dedicated in 1829 his *Catalogue Raisonné of the Works of the Most Eminent Dutch, Flemish and French Painters*.

Peel's interests were not confined to the classical school. He soon began to commission works by contemporary British artists, among them Sir Thomas Lawrence, William Collins, Haydon and Wilkie. His greatest patronage went to Lawrence, who between 1820 and 1830 produced no fewer than fifteen paintings for Peel, more than for any other single person except George IV himself. They were all portraits, many being of Peel's political colleagues: Liverpool, Aberdeen, Huskisson, Canning and Wellington. Others were of the Peel family: Julia (twice), old Sir Robert, and one of Peel himself, exhibited at the Royal Academy in 1825. This, the most famous of all the Peel portraits, depicted him standing at a table with his left hand on his hip in an orator's pose. Though photographic likenesses are hardly to be expected from the brush of a successful court painter, the picture shows the elegant clothes characteristic of Peel's early manhood, and the growing maturity of the face with the strong slightly curved nose and determined chin beneath the curling auburn hair. The main series of Lawrence paintings were transferred to Drayton after his father's death and the feature of the Whitehall Gardens gallery remained the Dutch and Flemish paintings. In its final form the London collection comprised about a hundred pictures, half of which were hung in the long gallery and the remainder (including five by Reynolds) elsewhere in the larger public rooms. From about 1830 the fame of his collection began to spread and Peel took pleasure in showing visitors round his gallery, pointing out the features of the different canvasses. Though he profited by the advice of artists and art dealers, he clearly had a keen appreciation of certain aspects, at any rate, of the painter's craft. He made himself something of an expert on the Dutch and Flemish schools. His purchases were never indiscriminate. He knew what he wanted and was always ready to discard minor pieces for something better.

Of the deep satisfaction he found in his collection there can be no doubt. One of the few personal documents he left behind was a manuscript notebook written in his own hand and containing a list of his pictures, with prices, dates of purchase, and various other details concerning them. He had other aesthetic tastes. He attended concerts and formed the tolerably good library which a man of his education and wealth might have been expected to have. But his paintings touched a more private side. For a man whose business in life involved so much reading and writing, it was perhaps natural to find greater relaxation in the visual stimulus of pictorial art than in literature. There had been little in his upbringing to encourage any interest in art. It was a spontaneous and personal development; and for that reason more revealing. The artistic strain in the third Robert Peel seemed a departure from the utilitarian tradition of his father and grandfather. Yet it would be a misconception of the puritan strain in the English social character to deny any hereditary influence. An appreciation of artistic achievement that had colour and form was only one remove from the ingenuity and effort that had produced calico patterns and mechanical improvements. It was significant too that Peel preferred the classical Dutch-school with its robust realism and solid landscapes, mirroring nature rather than swathing it in romantic imagination or seeking to pierce through it to ineffable depths of allegory and passion. If it is true that within every art collector is an imprisoned artist, Peel's rigorous classical and mathematical training, followed without a break by entry into politics and administration, had possibly prevented an even more surprising breach with family tradition. Instead, the mainstream of his emotions and energies was to be directed into the supreme art of all, politics. The medium was to be life itself; the canvas, contemporary society. What kept him irresistibly in public life, despite its animosities and sordidness, was a deep pleasure in political creativity.

Chapter 5

Back in harness

The affair of the 'queen's trial' in 1820, which for Peel acted as a deterrent to office, for the ministry made his presence in the cabinet even more desirable than ever. At the end of the year, deserted by Canning and forced to abandon the bill of Pains and Penalties, the government could only look forward with gloom to the January meeting of parliament. Before Christmas Croker had an interview with George IV who told him of Canning's resignation and of the king's wish that Peel should fill the vacancy. Peel showed little enthusiasm at the news and when the following week the prime minister duly offered him Canning's post of President of the Board of Control with a seat in the cabinet, he declined. He did so in a friendly way but he told Liverpool that he thought the government had been wrong in denying the queen the customary honours on her return to England, thereby prejudging her case, when it was already intended to proceed against her in a semi-judicial manner by means of the Pains and Penalties bill. He felt he could not place himself in a position in which he would be officially bound to defend all the previous actions of the cabinet. He added that he was in any case not anxious for office and that if a sense of duty should induce him at a later date to enter the ministry, he was indifferent what post he took.

The cabinet, not unfairly, took this rather high-flown expression of sentiment as indicating a prospect of ultimate union. Other politicians, who merely knew the bare fact of his refusal, wondered whether he preferred the company of his pretty young wife or whether he thought that the ministry would not survive the forthcoming parliamentary attack on its handling of the queen's case. In fact there is no evidence that he shared Canning's pessimism about the government and he was certainly not inclined to remain neutral while its fate was being decided in the new session. He spoke against a Whig motion in February which condemned the whole course of action against the queen; and politicians searching for straws noted at the same time that he shifted his seat in the House from the upper isolated benches he had previously been occupying to his former place in the rear of the Treasury Bench. Within a few weeks moreover his influential position in the Commons was further demonstrated by a renewal of the interminable Catholic question. It was not an issue which involved the existence of the government but it was one to which Peel was more committed than any other leading Protestant in the lower House. Public support for his side was clearly waning but his past record and his duty to his Oxford University constituents thrust him into the leadership. Though he took his place once more in the Protestant van, it was with less immediate hope and a more profound conviction of ultimate defeat than ever before.

On 28 February Plunket introduced a motion for a committee of the whole House to examine Catholic claims. His speech was to a large extent an analysis of Peel's arguments four years earlier and was directed at him personally. It had the perhaps intended effect of bringing Peel promptly to his feet in reply. Yet it was noticeable that his language was unusually restrained and some at least of his supporters thought he betrayed his consciousness of the defensive position into which the opponents of emancipation were now forced. Early in his speech he admitted that 'he had never viewed the question but as a choice of evils; nor had he been ever satisfied with the alternative proposed; but it had grown out of the anomalous state of society which he found pre-existing'. He emphasised the vulnerable position of the established Church of Ireland; he argued that the troubles in Ireland were not caused by Catholic disabilities; but he admitted that no result of the debate would bring him unqualified satisfaction.

It was a personal confession rather than a trumpet call to his party. Not surprisingly there was some disappointment among his followers. Plunket's motion was carried by six votes and though Peel continued to lead the opposition to the bill, the little knot of Protestant speakers seemed a frail defence against the galaxy of 'Catholics' headed by Plunket, Canning, Castlereagh, Grant and Mackintosh. On the third reading Peel made one final effort. He pointed out that emancipation would create a predominantly Catholic parliamentary representation for Ireland and that it would be necessary to consider seriously the future relationship between the state and the Roman Church. The securities in the bill had already been rejected by the Irish Catholic clergy and he prophesied that they could never be put into execution. The bill in fact would neither unite British subjects nor consolidate the Union. It was a good and effective speech but it came too late. Plunket's bill passed the Commons by nineteen votes and though it was later defeated in the Lords, it was now an open question whether the veto of the upper House could long delay the seemingly irresistible movement of parliamentary opinion in favour of Catholic emancipation.

Meanwhile the separate problem of the intrinsic weakness of the government in the House of Commons had still not been solved. Plans in the spring for a general reshuffle of offices that would put Vansittart at the Board of Control, Canning at the Admiralty, Melville at the Home Office, and Peel at the Exchequer, broke down on the curious. objection by Castlereagh that the appointment of Peel to such an important post would weaken Castlereagh's authority as Leader of the House. It was evident that Castlereagh was disturbed by talk of changes, and perhaps the real explanation of his otherwise incomprehensible hostility to Peel's promotion was that he was already suffering from the psychopathic distrust and persecution mania that was to bring tragedy only a year later. The prime minister's primary object was to secure the return of Canning; but faced with the open hostility of the king and a marked lack of enthusiasm among the rest of the cabinet to welcome back their brilliant but erratic colleague, Liverpool was in a position of some embarrassment. He had an interview with Peel at the end of May in which he made an offer of a cabinet post in what Peel described as 'a strange, shuffling, hesitating sort of way', leaving it to his visitor to infer that he intended the Board of Control. Peel, not best pleased, refused in terms equally vague and non-committal. He told Liverpool that he was well disposed towards the government, but from the state of his health he had no great desire for office. However, he said he would like to know what office was contemplated for him, and what other changes were planned, before he decided. Finally, early in June he saw the prime minister once more and made a clear verbal refusal of the India Board. When Liverpool asked him if his refusal applied to any other post, Peel said a trifle coldly that there would be time enough to decide that when an offer was made. He thought Liverpool peevish and embarrassed, and was inclined to think that he was not being very straightforward.

Liverpool's uncharacteristic obliquity is in fact comprehensible. He had strong grounds for thinking that the king would press for Peel's immediate inclusion in the cabinet as a means of excluding Canning. On the other hand, since Canning had made it clear that the one post to which he would not return was the India Board, it was difficult to offer Peel anything else until Canning had made up his mind. Finally, to fill the Prime Minister's cup of troubles to the brim, Castlereagh suspected that the failure to mention the Board of Control at the first meeting with Peel indicated that Liverpool was harking back to the original plan of reconstruction which would put Peel at the Exchequer. What Peel's motives were in rejecting the renewed offer can only be guessed. The plea of ill-health was not just a diplomatic excuse. He had been having trouble with inflammation of the eyes and he told Liverpool that he could not read at all by artificial light and very little during the day. But he was ruffled at Liverpool's devious behaviour and he probably had no great liking for the Board of Control, which merely supervised Indian affairs and provided little scope for creative work. His friends regretted his refusal of the post even though some were ready to accept his view of its unattractiveness. Croker went round telling people that Peel's objection was solely to the India Board and that he would be perfectly ready to take the Home Office or the Exchequer. This may not have been wide of the mark; but Liverpool was not prepared at that stage to take any step that would exclude Canning or alienate Castlereagh.

In the end the Prime Minister gave way to the pressures all round him. George IV built a bridge for his adversary by offering to send Canning to India; Castlereagh and others used their influence with the king to get his consent to a grand new scheme of ministerial reconstruction. By November it was all settled. A coalition was at last made

with the more than willing Grenvillites, and one of their House of
Commons men, Charles Wynn, went to the vacant India Board. Canning was appointed Governor-General of India; Sidmouth resigned
from the Home Office. For his successor there could only be one man.
On 28 November came the expected summons and this time there was
no hesitation.

> I will not prove myself unworthy [Peel wrote back] of that signal
> confidence with which the King has honoured me, by either yield-
> ing to the fears of my own unworthiness, or by taking that course
> which if I consulted merely my private inclinations, I might
> probably have preferred.

After three and a half years out of office, he was back in the saddle once
more.

The reconstructed cabinet in which he found himself, however,
only lasted intact one session. In August the king made a state visit to
Scotland and the new Home Secretary as in duty bound travelled north
to be in attendance. The first appearance of a Hanoverian king north
of the Border had its attractive and sometimes its comic side. On 17
August there was a *levée* at which George IV appeared in tartan and
kilt. 'I had some doubts on this point,' Peel dryly reported to Liverpool,
'but I dare say it has greatly pleased the Highlanders.' The weather
was vile, but what depressed Peel more than the constant rain and fog
was the letter he received from the prime minister on the day of the
king's arrival announcing Castlereagh's suicide two days earlier.
Personal feeling apart, it was obvious that this at once raised the
question of Canning and the cabinet vacancy. The king informed Peel
that he had written to Liverpool instructing him that the arrangement
for Canning to go to India was to remain unchanged; and he tried to
elicit an expression of approval from the Home Secretary. But Peel
refused to commit himself either to the king or to Croker, who wrote
from London that Canning would be ready to take Castlereagh's
position as Foreign Secretary and Leader of the House but would not
accept anything less. Peel declined to comment. 'There are some subjects on which one does injustice to one's feelings by saying anything,'
he wrote back, 'and our departed friend's death is one of them. I
bitterly deplore it.'

On 29 August the king departed in the royal yacht and Peel made
his way south as expeditiously as possible. In the interval Liverpool had
been discussing the situation with Wellington and Bathurst; he had
allowed talks to take place between Arbuthnot and Huskisson, Canning's friend and confidant; and his instinct to keep Canning in
England had been reinforced by a hint from the Duke of Buckingham
that the Grenville party would withdraw their support if Canning were
not given office. It was essential, however, first to see Peel and learn his
views. Castlereagh's death had left him as the ablest representative of

the government in the Commons and he might well object to being passed over in favour of Canning as Leader of the House. Peel also had been given time to reflect. On arrival in London he wrote to his friend Manners Sutton, the Speaker.

> The question may be put to me, what I think and feel with respect to Canning's accession to the government. I intend to answer that I should be ashamed of myself if I personally threw a difficulty in the way of it. . . . As to his being leader of the House of Commons, I must fairly own that he being so would be no personal disappointment to me; and if it were, I should think it quite unworthy of me not to submit to it.

To Liverpool, when he saw him, he spoke in the same strain. He would do what his colleagues thought was in the best interests of the government; he had no wish for the leadership of the House, nor would he decline if it was thought that he ought to undertake it.

Of the latter offer the prime minister made no mention to the king. Instead he proposed, with the backing of some of his senior colleagues, that Canning should succeed to the whole of Castlereagh's political inheritance. The king was not to be overridden so easily and consulted other members of the cabinet. Sidmouth stoutly advised him to make Peel Leader of the House and fill the Foreign Office with someone other than Canning. Eldon, the Lord Chancellor, probably expressed himself even more strongly against Canning. This attitude on the part of the Protestant old brigade in the ministry was not unexpected. But when Peel had his audience he merely repeated his readiness to do as his colleagues thought best; and added, according to one account, that he was indifferent to ambitions for office and preferred the pleasures of private and family life. The last sentiment was not uncharacteristic. Peel never thought of himself as ambitious; and in a superficial sense perhaps he never was. Tired, ill and depressed after his Scottish visit, he probably felt more distaste than usual for the intrigues and rivalries of political life.

In the end the king yielded and as soon as Liverpool received the grudging royal assent to the new arrangements, he wrote to inform Peel even before communicating with Canning. 'I think it due to you on every account and not the less so, from your handsome and disinterested conduct throughout the whole business.' The compliment was not undeserved; Peel had it in his power if not to prevent at least to make Canning's succession to Castlereagh difficult and embarrassing. But in the circumstances his attitude of total passivity had been the safe and wise course. To have objected to Canning would have precipitated a crisis which might have split the government. Though his only overt disagreement with Canning was over Catholic emancipation, that in itself was a formidable division; and the rivalry of two political careers could easily supply more. There were some politicians who, from dislike of Canning rather than love of Peel, were prepared to set the two men up as personal opponents. Sidmouth in fact told the king that Peel and Canning could not go on together indefinitely; and that when Liverpool retired, he would have to choose between them. Neither man, however, lent himself to this game. Only the preceding April Canning had told Croker that 'to Peel especially I feel it quite impossible to do justice, for a frankness and straightforwardness beyond example, and for feelings for which I own I did not before give him credit but which I hope I know how to value and to return'.

Yet no amount of straightforwardness could bridge the separation over the Catholic question; and with every prospect that it would be brought up in Parliament the following session, Peel was faced with the embarrassment of working under a man who was a more active and influential leader of the Catholic party in the Commons than Castlereagh had ever been. Writing in September from his holiday home at Lulworth in Dorset, he disclosed his inner thoughts to the faithful Goulburn.

> I never had a doubt as to what I *ought* to do . . . I therefore was spared the pain of any consideration, being perfectly satisfied that what is right, must inevitably be politic. I think with you, that that which has been done, is the best that could be done, but even the best, is not unmixed good. I should conceive that in the *Vox Stellarum** for March next there might be a safe general prophecy of much perplexity and debate in Parliament.

But March was six months ahead and in the meantime he had congenial work on hand in his own department.

II

At the time when Peel took the Home Office, the state of English criminal law had been attracting the attention of reformers for over a generation. In theory England had one of the severest penal systems in Europe; in practice it was lenient, defective and haphazard. The eighteenth-century legislature had tried to meet the problem of law enforcement by increasing the severity of judicial penalties. By George IV's reign some two hundred offences (nobody knew exactly) were punishable by death. But the absence of an efficient police, the tortuous technicalities of an antiquated judicial procedure, the sympathies of jurymen and a growing humanitarianism among judges and crown advisers, had produced what Romilly described as a 'lottery of justice'. In the House of Commons, where the Whigs Mackintosh and Buxton

---

*The title of Francis Moore's, better known as Old Moore's, *Almanac*.

were carrying on the campaign initiated by such pioneer reformers as Eden, Howard, and Romilly, there was a general agreement in principle on the need for reform. Only in the House of Lords, where Eldon and Sidmouth added ministerial weight to the innate conservatism of the peers, was there substantial legislative resistance to change. Mackintosh in 1819 had obtained a parliamentary committee of enquiry which drew up a comprehensive list of reforms. But virtually all attempts to translate the recommendations into law had failed. The arrival of Peel at the Home Office offered some hope that the government would now lend its authority to the movement for penal reform.

In fact Peel made it clear in a debate in June 1822 not only that he was in sympathy with Mackintosh's reform programme but that his department already had under consideration bills dealing with police and prisons. This choice of priorities was of significance since it reflected a certain divergence of opinion between Peel and his officials on the one hand and the Romilly–Mackintosh school of thought on the other. The Whig legal reformers believed that to humanise the law was the surest method of getting it enforced. It was because the law was so brutal, they argued, that it had become so inefficient and uncertain. To the question of effectual secondary punishment they had devoted little consideration and to the idea that the law might be better enforced if there was an efficient police they showed a marked distaste. In this they were reflecting a deepseated popular prejudice. An efficient police force seemed inconceivable to early nineteenth-century Englishmen, except as an arbitrary and oppressive instrument of executive tyranny. The very word 'police' seemed un-English and the parallel most likely to spring to the insular mind of John Bull was the *gendarmerie* of the Bourbon kings and all they connoted as the agents of centralised autocracy. The tradition of English liberty that was the boast of the natives and the admiration of the foreigner was in some respects a dangerous tradition of public and private behaviour free (in Paley's words) from 'inspection, scrutiny and control', and subject only to the operation of the law after an offence had been committed. The ferocious paper clauses of the old English criminal law had been an answer in fact to the excesses of a remarkably disorderly as well as brutal society.

Nevertheless it was the settled conviction of most Englishmen that this was the price of liberty and that the price was not too high. Patrick Colquhoun in a classic book published in 1795 had argued the case for a central police authority separate from the judiciary and the need for prevention rather than punishment of crime. But though he gained the support of the Benthamites and his concept of a 'preventive police' had entered the vocabulary of the experts, he failed to command a wider audience. Peel by temperament was more likely to be on the side of the experts than of the common man and as author of the Peace Preservation Act in Ireland was unlikely to share the prejudices of ordinary politicians. Recent events in London had underlined the need for some corrective to the excesses of the mob. The rioting at the time of the

Robert Peel, aetat. 23. From the painting by William Owen R.A.

Julia, Lady Peel. From the painting by Sir Thomas Lawrence P.R.A.

queen's trial, the unseemly but successful intervention of the crowd at her funeral, and some ominous signs of unrest among the troops stationed in the capital, were all fresh in the minds of the cabinet.

It was not surprising therefore that the subject of police reform was one of the first to which the new Home Secretary turned his attention. In March 1822, in a brief and carefully moderated speech, he moved for a committee to enquire into the police of the metropolis. He obtained his enquiry but not his reform. The result merely emphasised once more the immense weight of prejudice against any effective police system. His committee elicited much useful information, made a few suggestions for minor improvements, but on the only issue which mattered recorded a flat negative.

> It is difficult [ran the salient passage of its report] to reconcile an effective system of police, with that perfect freedom of action and exemption from interference, which are the great privileges and blessings of society in this country; and Your Committee think that the forfeiture or curtailment of such advantages would be too great a sacrifice for improvements in police, or facilities in detecting crime, however desirable in themselves.

Disappointing as the outcome was to Peel, it was clear to him that the question would have to be shelved until the times were more propitious.

Reform of the criminal law offered a better prospect of success. A bill to consolidate laws relating to prisons and improve prison discipline had been accepted by the government in Sidmouth's last year as Home Secretary and despite Eldon's cantankerous objections Peel's tactful handling steered it through to the statute book in 1823. Though in so doing he was acting more as midwife than parent, it was nevertheless a landmark in the history of penal legislation. For the first time the government had taken responsibility for a national measure of prison reform; and its dual character, as a consolidating as well as a reforming statute, formed a precedent for much of Peel's later work. Two further acts in 1823 and 1824 demonstrated his continuing interest in the problem. Some uniformity was imposed on the medley of different institutions and jurisdictions in which a prisoner might find himself; most of the larger prisons were brought under the direct supervision of the Home Office; and a set of general regulations was prescribed for their administration. The outstanding difficulty remained that of secondary punishment. As capital sentences decreased, the problem of suitable treatment for the convicted offender increased. Transportation was not in itself a deterrent; solitary confinement had sometimes disastrous psychological results; whipping and the treadmill aroused humanitarian compassion; hard labour involved nice calculations of work and diet. Writing to Sydney Smith in March 1826 Peel half-humorously expatiated on the dilemmas of prison administration. On normal diet the life of prisoners, during the winter season at least, so far from acting as a deterrent was 'thought by people outside to be rather an enviable one'. If the diet was reduced, the usual result was an outbreak of fever which emptied the prisons either by the death of the inhabitants or by their hasty evacuation to more salubrious establishments.

> The real truth is [he continued more seriously], the number of convicts is too overwhelming for the means of proper and effectual punishment. I despair of any remedy but that which I wish I could hope for—a great reduction in the amount of crime.

There remained however the more publicised, more controversial, but more manageable task of legal reform. As early as October 1822 Peel outlined to the prime minister the way in which, after a nine months' experience of his new department, he proposed to deal with the opposition campaign for a more humane system. It was important, he wrote,

> not to argue as if there was some Criminal Code which must be maintained in all its integrity, but to look at all the offences which are now punishable by death, to select those (if there be any) which can be safely visited with a mitigated Punishment, and to be prepared to assign our reasons for maintaining the Punishment of Death, in each case where it ought to be maintained.

He did not, he added optimistically, think that between reasonable advocates of change and reasonable defenders of the existing system there was any irreconcilable difference on points of real importance. Some aspects of the campaign for law reform, such as improvements in Scottish legal procedure and an acceleration of the cumbrous procedures of the Court of Chancery, he was able to delegate to specialist bodies. The great field of English criminal law amendment he kept in his own hands and early in 1823 he let Mackintosh know that the government was ready to bring forward its own measures. When in May the Whig reformer introduced a list of nine resolutions founded on the report of his 1819 committee, it was made clear that the government approved of the greater part of them and that the Home Office would take the lead in producing the necessary legislation.

If there was any residue of doubt in the minds of the Whig legal reformers, it was removed by the passage of five acts in the two remaining months of the session. Two features were noteworthy in this early batch of legislation. One was the inclusion, following the systematic scrutiny of the Home Office, among crimes for which the death penalty was abolished of some not previously included in any opposition proposals; the other was the speed and silence with which these reforms, some of them demanded for years, passed through the barrier of the House of Lords. With Peel as Home Secretary the citadel of legislative inertia had finally been outflanked. It required more than mere executive initiative however to produce such gratifying results. The 1819 committee had tried to take the government and the judiciary by storm; Peel saw his task as one of persuasion. The tranquil passage of his bills was the reward of hard work behind the scenes. What the Whig reformers had lacked was tact, influence and organisation; it was this which Peel made it his business to supply. In Hobhouse, his under-secretary, and Gregson, a barrister who was his chief legal adviser and draftsman, he had invaluable assistants. But he also took care to secure the approval and support of the judicial authorities themselves. Drafts of his bills were circulated among the judges for comment and from the Lord Chief Justice, Lord Tenterden, he secured both technical and practical assistance in piloting his measures through the House of Lords.

For this there was a price to pay. The legal profession and judges in particular are not as a rule in the van of legal reform; and Peel's proposals did not go as far as some of his critics would have liked. To Peel's administrative mind, cautious and sure, it was more important to obtain maximum consent over a wide field of legal reforms than to risk defeat or delay by trying to press forward immediately to the furthest visible objective. Though at certain points he stopped short of what he might have achieved, the methods to which he owed his success imposed their own limitations. But the very confidence which he inspired helped to disarm opposition. The great Jeremy Bentham himself, before the end of his long life, bestowed a jocular word of praise on the Home Secretary, despite his own doctrinaire preference for a complete recasting of the law on logical first principles.

> What is this I see? [he wrote to Peel in 1830]. One of his Majesty's Principal Secretaries of State become a Reformist? a Law Reformer in good earnest? . . . Sir, you have passed the Rubicon. Your foot in on the career that leads to the ends of justice. . . . You Sir, even you are fallen into the same pit with me.

His earlier correspondence with Peel had not been so approving. Unlike Bentham, the Home Secretary approached the work of law reform in the spirit of Francis Bacon, whose words he once quoted to the House of Commons: 'the work which I propound tendeth to pruning and grafting the law, and not to ploughing up and planting it again.' But it was a mark of his thoroughness that he sought the advice of the foremost legal theorist of the day as well as of more practical exponents like W. O. Russell whose well-known *Treatise on Crimes* had appeared in 1819.

Meanwhile the flow of legislation continued. The Jury Act of 1825 was his first great legal consolidating statute. This was followed in 1826 and 1827 by a group of measures to consolidate and amend the whole body of criminal law. In all these reforms Peel had three objects in view: simplification, consolidation, and mitigation. What was achieved under the first two headings alone constituted a massive reform. It involved not only the mechanical process of collecting under one heading a confused mass of statutes and parts of statutes dealing with crime and criminal jurisdiction, but the more difficult task of simplifying, pruning, discarding and amending the accumulated legislation of centuries, some of it dating from the thirteenth century. What he accomplished represented in scope and thoroughness a fresh point of departure in the history of English criminal law. His work under the third heading was necessarily more cautious and more provisional, since it involved the central problem of the period: the extent to which it was safe to abolish capital punishment. Much was done even here, either by direct repeal or by various technical alterations in the law. What he achieved did not satisfy all the demands of the humanitarian reformers; but Peel was reluctant to proceed too rapidly. There had already been a marked decrease in executions during his Home Secretaryship compared to the years 1810–17 and he preferred to retain a relatively severe penal system combined with wide administrative use of reprieve, rather than propose immediately a sweeping reduction in the number of offences which technically carried the death penalty.

In this he was influenced not only by the practical argument for a gradual, almost experimental, relaxation in the severity of the law but also by the startling increase in crime since he had commenced his reforms in 1823. In a speech of March 1826 he emphasised the unsatisfactory trend of criminal statistics. In the seven years ending December 1825 criminal commitments in England and Wales had almost doubled compared with the seven years ending December 1816. Convictions had more than doubled; capital sentences had almost doubled; though it was a mark of the more merciful administration of justice that there was hardly any increase in the number of actual executions. Even allowing for such factors as growth of population, improvement in crime detection, and greater readiness to prosecute and convict, it was difficult to avoid the conclusion that law-breaking was on the increase. Faced in the country with every appearance of a rising tide of crime and in the Commons with a legislature that refused to sanction any radical reform of the police system, Peel deliberately set himself against any further reduction in the number of offences that carried the death penalty. As it was, he rarely lost an opportunity of reminding parliament of the interdependence of the three topics of crime, police and penal reform. At the end of 1826 he again gave notice of an enquiry into the police of the metropolis. With the reform legislation of 1827 he felt he had gone far enough down the road of purely legal improvements. If five years of penal reform had merely resulted in an increase of secondary crime, it was time to make another effort to secure a 'preventive police'.

Chapter 6

Public discontents

Since its creation in 1782 the Home Office had been primarily an agency for preserving law and order. Peel turned it into an instrument of social policy. His great series of legal reforms not only enhanced his own reputation but raised immeasurably the status of what had been previously a somewhat small and inferior department of government. As the Irish Lord Chancellor Manners wrote to him in 1826,

> You have made the office of Secretary of State for the Home Department of infinitely more consequence than it has ever been in the hands of any of your predecessors. The well managing of our foreign affairs and interests may be more striking and brilliant; it is by no means more substantial or more important.

Yet law and order remained a central responsibility of the Home Secretary for which no amount of liberal reform legislation could be a substitute.

Under Sidmouth the Home Office had borne the burden and unpopularity of dealing with the social disorders created by the post-war depression. Peel was fortunate in succeeding him just as the country was returning to more stable and prosperous conditions. From 1822 to 1825 his department enjoyed a halcyon period of freedom from the kind of acute industrial distress which necessitated direct intervention by the central authorities. Apart from a little unrest in the early months of 1822, there was little call for unusual activity by the Home Secretary in the industrial sphere until the second half of 1824; and even then it was of a fortuitous nature. In the parliamentary session of that year a campaign led by the radical Joseph Hume in the Commons and by McCulloch the economist in the press, aided by Francis Place, the radical tailor of London and (in his own eyes at least) the uncrowned king of the working-class movement, had with the sympathetic approval of the Board of Trade secured an act abolishing the old Combination Laws. Workmen were now free to combine over questions of wages, hours and conditions of employment and to persuade others to join them, subject only to minor penalties for intimidation and violence.

The Benthamite argument was that the Combination Acts had produced the combinations and that in a free society workmen would once more act as individuals, ready to accept a free market in labour governed by the same iron laws of economics which regulated other commodities. This doctrinaire illusion was immediately shattered once the Combination Acts were repealed. Between August 1824 and

January 1825 there was an outbreak of trade disputes and strikes all over the country. Workmen openly organised as never before; and the general demand for higher wages was accompanied by others which struck contemporary observers as novel and tyrannical: a closed shop for union men, dismissal of unpopular foremen, restrictions on the use of machinery, limitations on the number of hands employed. The wave of strikes and industrial disputes were marked by a number of murders and other brutalities, mainly directed against non-unionists and blackleg labour imported by employers. Before the end of the year it became obvious that the situation could not be left as it was. The problem of trade unions, previously dealt with by Huskisson and the Board of Trade as an aspect of industry, would have to be considered by Peel and the Home Office as an aspect of social disorder.

In March 1825 Huskisson moved for a new committee of enquiry, confessing at the same time that he had not examined the 1824 bill with sufficient care when it passed through the House. Peel supported the motion in a brief speech giving examples of what he called 'an excessive and infamous tyranny' exercised by the unions in the exhilaration of their newly won freedom. He had already taken soundings with the law officers and it was the Home Office which drew up the bill to amend the 1824 act. In the new committee neither Place nor Hume were able to rig the proceedings as they had done the previous year. Both were displeased and not inclined to credit Huskisson and Peel with any motive except a desire to serve the interests of the employers. Nevertheless the amendments to the 1824 act which resulted from the 1825 enquiry were strikingly moderate. No fundamental alteration was made to the principle of the legality of trade unions; but stiffer penalties were fixed for intimidation and the procedure for obtaining convictions was simplified. Peel's object was not to weaken the unions or collective bargaining but simply to prevent abuse of union power and protect individual workers and employers.

> I think the law [he wrote] . . . is founded upon just principles and I believe it will ultimately be as effectual as law can be. Men who . . . have no property except their manual skill and strength, ought to be allowed to confer together, if they think fit, for the purpose of determining at what rate they will sell their property. But . . . such a privilege justifies, while it renders it more necessary, the severe punishment of any attempt to control the free will of others.

It was impeccable liberal doctrine and there was nothing in either his public or private expressions of opinion that contradicted the claim he made when replying to Hume in June, that 'ministers had never felt the slightest inclination to attend to the interests of the master, and to neglect those of the workmen'.

Indeed he could have cited his administration of the existing Factory Acts as proof of his official impartiality in the thorny field of industrial relations. From the commencement of his secretaryship the Home Office was unusually active in securing information from magistrates on the extent to which the provisions of the 1819 act were being observed. Many J.P.s in the industrial districts, themselves often factory-owners, were palpably lukewarm in enforcing the statutory regulations. But the detailed returns demanded by the Home Office on such matters as hours of work, meals, ages of children, and cleanliness of factories, provided at least one form of pressure to secure better attention to the law; and in cases of flagrant neglect of duty the Home Secretary was quick to exert the full weight of his authority. A particularly unsatisfactory town was Wigan where the acting magistrates in the borough were all mill-owners. When complaints both from the county magistrates and from John Doherty, the secretary of the cotton-spinners union, made it clear that previous Home Office reprimands had failed to have effect, Peel reacted sharply. He warned the Wigan J.P.s that if any further breaches of the law were reported, he would introduce legislation to give the county magistrates jurisdiction within the borough. Doherty was informed of this letter and asked to communicate with the Home Office if he became aware of any further offences.

Without a paid inspectorate early industrial legislation was extremely difficult to enforce. But it is evident from the Home Office correspondence that after Peel's arrival a decided improvement began to show itself. Though Peel was in principle against state intervention in the ordinary economic life of the society, he was no doctrinaire. He had argued as early as 1818, for example, when supporting his father's factory bill, that the question of individual economic choice had no relevance to child labour. What he wished to foster in the raw industrial society of his day was both greater liberty and greater order. What was doubtful was whether the growing working-class movement would, or even could, be built up on voluntary and humane principles; or whether combinations of employers would not always continue to be confronted by combinations of workmen. Peel was sufficiently imbued with the teaching of contemporary political economists to dislike all forms of direction and restraint. But, as he pointed out to the Commons in 1825, what was allowed to workmen could not be denied to masters. Combinations in industry, however, inevitably produced conflict and disorder in periods of economic difficulty; and any disorder was a matter of concern for the Home Secretary.

The sudden trade depression of 1826 called into operation these more fundamental responsibilities of his office. Preceded by the financial crisis of the previous autumn, the industrial slump brought its usual grim concomitants: short-time working, lower wages, unemployment, hunger, riot and crime. The trouble started with scattered outbreaks of disorder in Wales, the midlands and the north-east. By April the wave of unrest was spreading rapidly through the great industrial district of Lancashire and spilling over into the West Riding. In the Blackburn and Manchester areas large armed mobs assembled at the end of the month and despite the efforts of the military went round for several days attacking mills and smashing machinery. At Blackburn it was reported that not a single power-loom was left standing within a six-mile radius of the town. The first task of the Home Department was to stiffen the morale of magistrates and local inhabitants and encourage local initiative in defending property and prosecuting offenders. While advising magistrates not to depend solely on the assistance of the military, Peel at the same time steadily strengthened the forces available for keeping order. At the start of the disturbances an additional regiment was stationed in Lancashire and further reinforcements were despatched at the end of April. More troops were sent north from London in May and others ordered across from Ireland.

Prevention rather than repression was Peel's main object. He made enquiries about the temper of the working classes in a number of previous danger-spots that had not so far been affected and he took precautionary measures in South Wales as soon as he received reports of disputes there between the iron-masters and their men. One perennial handicap for both central and local authorities was lack of precise information. Peel sanctioned the use of spies by military commanders in the northern districts and told Foster, one of the leading Manchester magistrates, that the Home Office would reimburse any expense incurred in securing private intelligence on disaffected individuals in his neighbourhood. But he issued a warning against provocative action, treated all reports that came to the Home Office from such sources with considerable scepticism, and refused to sanction any prosecutions based on their statements. What he did not do was to confuse symptoms with causes. The disorders arose from unemployment, poverty and starvation. Though his duty was to repress disorder, he knew that there could be no permanent social security until the economic causes of the unrest were removed. 'The great cause of apprehension', he wrote to Goulburn in July, 'is not in the disaffection but in the real distress of the manufacturing districts. There is as much forbearance as it is possible to expect from so much suffering.'

The only short-term palliative was direct relief and in this he took an active part. From April onward sums of £500 or £1,000 at a time from the Royal Bounty were sent to supplement local funds in severely distressed areas. By June all the money at his disposal was used up, the balance having been given to a national relief committee set up in London with whom he was in constant touch. In the second half of July the committee was distributing £5,000 weekly in relief. Even so, Liverpool, Robinson and Peel advised them to continue until the remaining £57,000 in the fund was exhausted and assured them that the government would support a further appeal for money. To direct encouragement of industry by means of government subsidies, a suggestion which Peel bluntly described as 'quackery', he was opposed both by theory and instinct. His main hope was to tide over the bad months until the economy righted itself once more.

In May the government proposed to parliament that bonded wheat lying at the ports should be allowed to come on the market at a low rate of duty, and asked for discretionary power to admit foreign corn during the recess. Both proposals, though eventually carried, were opposed by the outraged agriculturalists. The government was accused both of wishing to undermine the Corn Laws and of tamely surrendering to the rioters. As in previous economic debates the front bench encountered bitter resistance from its usual supporters aided, not disinterestedly, by many of its usual opponents. The small knot of cabinet ministers in the Commons had to work tenaciously against a divided and angry House. When Peel made his major contribution to the debate on 5 May, he sharply contradicted the charge of dangerous concessions to destructive mobs. 'There are two sorts of courage which may be displayed in respect of them,' he said in a characteristic passage.

> There is the courage of refusing to accede to such demands at all; and there is another kind of courage—the courage to do that which in our conscience we may believe to be just and right, disregarding all the clamour with which these demands may be accompanied.

There was never to be any doubt which kind of courage Peel preferred.

The cabinet's foresight in asking for emergency powers was soon justified. To unemployment, distress and riot in the summer of 1826 was added in the autumn the culminating disaster of a bad harvest. At the beginning of September the government opened the ports for oats, rye, peas and beans and called a special session of parliament before Christmas to obtain indemnity for their action. By the time parliament met the disorders in the country had passed their peak, though distress, especially in Lancashire and Scotland, continued throughout the winter and a steady trickle of reports came in from all over the country of illegal union activities, strikes and rioting. It had been the most difficult and harassing year for Liverpool's cabinet since 1819; but at least there had been no Peterloo, no Six Acts, no widening of the gulf between the state and the industrial proletariat. Though much damage had been done and some lives lost, the situation had never got out of hand. By its nature military force was a repressive rather than a preventive agency and it was the only force at the Home Secretary's disposal. Yet what was remarkable was the restraint with which that force had been used; the absence of wanton bloodshed; and the successful cooperation between central local authorities in containing the worst excesses. Above all the attitude of the Home Office throughout had been shaped by the realisation that the problem with which it was faced was fundamentally one of human suffering.

II

In Ireland, the other large but indirect sphere of the Home Secretary's responsibility, there had been troubles of a different nature. At the end of 1821, shortly before Peel's entry into the cabinet, the Marquess Wellesley had been appointed Lord-Lieutenant. He was not an ideal choice, but he possessed a residual if fading political prestige and he was on close terms with the Grenvillites. His defects as an administrator, however, were notorious and in order to inject a modicum of business-like habits into his viceroyalty, a slightly reluctant Goulburn had been sent out with him as Chief Secretary. There was a certain political calculation in this odd coupling which was underlined by the additional appointment of Plunket as Irish Attorney-General. Wellesley and Plunket were 'Catholic' (in the sense in which politicians were becoming labelled according to their attitude on the great controversy of the day), while Peel and Goulburn were 'Protestant'. In effect the Irish executive had been reconstructed to reflect more closely than in the past the divided state of the British government on the issue of Catholic emancipation. Whether this would improve efficiency was another matter. Though it was no business of the Lord-Lieutenant to promote any alteration in the law, the significance of the first 'Catholic' appointment to the Lord-Lieutenancy since the Grenville administration in 1806 was not lost on observers.

In the interval since 1818 Peel had not lost his interest in Irish affairs. In 1820 he had commissioned the secretary of the Irish Records Commission to collect for him a representative set of over a hundred books on Ireland. As Home Secretary he read the Irish newspapers. Indeed he sometimes seemed to be keeping a closer watch on the Irish press than the Chief Secretary himself; and he instructed Gregory in 1823 to send him over all publications bearing on Irish affairs. From the start it was obvious that the new Home Secretary was going to play his full part in the direction of Irish policy and his early letters to Lord Wellesley were clearly designed to encourage a constant and confidential exchange of views between them. Energy and informality, however, were the last qualities likely to appeal to the former Governor-General of India. A long despatch from Peel in April 1822, covering eleven sheets of paper and every important aspect of Irish business, was briefly acknowledged by Wellesley's private secretary who explained that the Lord-Lieutenant was ill, concurred with his views, and would write later. As time passed it became evident that Wellesley's habit of 'writing later' was almost a disease. When in November 1824 Peel told Goulburn privately that it was some months since he had heard from the Lord-Lieutenant, the Chief Secretary replied mordantly that Wellesley's misfortune was to have the reputation of an able writer and a great statesman. 'To preserve this he considers and reconsiders every point until the moment is past when a knowledge of his sentiments would have been useful.' When he did bring himself to write, he was apt to do so without consulting either Goulburn or Gregory. Both men in consequence felt deliberately excluded from his confidence. Even Goulburn's mild temper began to show signs of strain and the more hot-tempered Gregory had to be dissuaded more than once from resignation.

Throughout his period of office the Lord-Lieutenant, like an ageing and jealous actress, continued to inflict his temperament on all around him. He brought over his illegitimate and intriguing son Edward Johnston to act as his private secretary; and after Wellesley's indiscreet marriage in 1825 to a beautiful widow who suffered from the double disqualification as vicereine of being both an American and a Roman Catholic, Johnston began to make trouble not only in official circles but between the viceregal couple. Dublin gossip was regaled with reports of violent domestic quarrels; Lady Wellesley was clearly unhappy; her husband was always being announced as indisposed and was undoubtedly ill and excitable. That this disjointed Irish executive hung together for six years can only be attributed to the political necessities of Liverpool's cabinet on the one hand and on the other to the steadiness and efficiency of Peel, Goulburn, and Gregory. The long-standing friendship between the Home Secretary and the two officials in Dublin was one of the few stabilising features of Irish government between 1822 and 1827. It offered some guarantee that the more important part of the executive machinery would function adequately and it enabled Peel to guide the inexperienced Goulburn to an extent which would have hardly been practicable with another man. Out of his own store of Irish knowledge the Home Secretary was able not only to answer questions when put to him but also to offer advice, make suggestions, and initiate action. Goulburn, a sound but not brilliant administrator, lacked neither energy nor intelligence. But dealing with a difficult country and an almost as difficult Lord-Lieutenant, he stood in need of all the encouragement Peel could supply; and there were times when his spirits perceptibly flagged. Indeed, in April 1827 he wrote that it would be impossible for him to remain in Ireland if Peel abandoned the Home Office.

In his very first year of office Goulburn was confronted with a partial famine over most of Ireland as a result of the failure of the potato crop the previous autumn. With the precedents of Peel's policy in 1816–17 to follow the Irish government was able to cope with the emergency and it was not until the generally disastrous year of 1826 that anything in the nature of a social and economic crisis occurred. The commercial panic of that year in Britain affected trade and manufacture in Dublin and the economic difficulties were further complicated by a severe outbreak of typhus and a partial failure of cereal crops. Preoccupied as he was by more serious troubles at home, Peel still did not forget Ireland. Thinking with justice that Goulburn would need 'a little oil', he arranged in July for a subsidy of £7,000 to be made to meet the fever epidemic and relieve distress. In August he called for a special meeting of the cabinet in view of the discouraging reports of the potato harvest and discussed with Wellington ways and means of meeting the crisis. In the event the worst anticipations were not realised. Though the early potatoes were scarce, the main crop held out. Some relief was necessary but Peel was anxious not to commit the government to a general and, in his view, demoralising policy of interference which would allow the Irish landlords to escape responsibility for the welfare of their own tenants.

Questions affecting the rights and duties of the Anglo-Irish governing class had for some time been engaging his attention. In his first long despatch to Wellesley in 1822 he had raised two matters which were to loom large in all Irish discussions for the next twenty years, tithe and magistracy. Both issues, though technical and complicated, had political implications. One affected the rights and property of the established church; the other the problem of maintaining law and order in the most lawless part of the British Isles. In the summer of 1822 a start was made on plans for reforming the magistracy but the Irish government, perhaps understandably, showed little sign of evolving a solution of the tithe problem. Nevertheless, it was ominously clear that if the property basis of the Church of Ireland was not altered by the government, an attempt to do so would be made by the opposition; and Liverpool was anxious to be prepared against attack on an exceedingly vulnerable flank. A tentative plan for tithe commutation was submitted by Wellesley in the autumn of 1822 but Peel, not satisfied that the subject had received a thorough examination at the hands of the Dublin officials, started an exhaustive correspondence with Goulburn on every conceivable aspect of the question which carried on till Christmas. When the amended bill for tithe commutation was introduced into the Commons in the following session, the clause providing for arbitration in case of dispute aroused considerable criticism and was finally dropped in committee. Peel himself was unhappy at any form of compulsion and it was probable that, as M.P. for Oxford, he was particularly sensitive to the implications of tithe reform for the whole position of the Established Church. At least one opposition spokesman attributed the dropping of the compulsory clause entirely to the Home Secretary's position as university member.

By then, however, more immediate religious and political quarrels were claiming the attention of the Irish government. Wellesley's ineffectual attempts to hold the balance between Catholic and Protestant in Ireland merely exacerbated feeling on all sides. It was not long before the Irish executive was falling back on a series of ill-timed and unsuccessful prosecutions against both parties. The Lord-Lieutenant, who during 1822 had combined suggestions for damping down Orange activities with exaggerated expressions of alarm over the alleged existence of secret Catholic committees, pressed for legislative action against treasonable and seditious societies. Peel viewed this proposal with little favour, particularly as it seemed as if any new powers would be used solely against the Orange Lodges. However, with the parliamentary opposition calling for action, Peel obtained authority to announce in the Commons in March 1823 that legislation would be introduced at an early date. The difficulty was to know what kind of legislation. With Goulburn tied to London during the session, the constant embarrassment was lack of any communication from Wellesley. In June, anticipating a renewed discussion of Irish affairs in parliament, Peel was obliged to send over a special messenger to request a report on the state of the country. It was then four weeks since he had last heard from the Lord-Lieutenant.

Worse was yet to come. From 1824 onward the apprehensions of the Irish government, previously diffused over a miscellany of Irish discontents, were increasingly focused on one specific point: the startling growth of the Catholic Association founded in 1823 by Sheil and O'Connell. The turn in its fortunes came in 1824 with the successful institution of a scheme for raising subscriptions, known as the Catholic Rent', by means of a nationwide organisation. With the powerful assistance of the parochial clergy, supported by several of the Catholic bishops, O'Connell soon found himself at the head of one of the most formidable instruments for constitutional agitation that had ever been known in British history. Peel, Goulburn and Gregory took care to inform themselves from the start of all the details of the Association's membership and activities; and Gregory was noticeably more pessimistic about the state of Ireland than he had been at any earlier period. But Wellesley, hesitant and evasive as usual, refused to give any clear guidance on policy. Though there was desultory discussion of legislation to suppress the Catholic Association, Peel did not get the impression that the Irish government was convinced of its immediate necessity.

When Goulburn returned to Ireland after the 1824 session he became gravely concerned at the gathering momentum of the Association's activities and the prospect that it would be in a position to challenge the leadership of the Anglo-Irish gentry at the next general election. At the end of October he sent Peel a long despatch, covering fourteen sides of quarto, giving a gloomy catalogue of the political dangers to which Ireland was exposed but confessing his hopelessness at finding remedies for the evils it cited. Peel, who had not been unprepared for this communication, was now convinced that the time had come for action. Whether it would be successful was another matter. But he did not think that passivity in the face of danger was a particularly statesmanlike attitude and mere expressions of disapproval by ministers were worse than useless: 'the Association would beat us at a scolding match'. Even if legal prosecutions failed (as Irish prosecutions usually did) and new laws were evaded (as in Ireland they usually were), at least they would demonstrate the concern of the government and force the problem to the notice of parliament. He was not alone in thinking that something ought to be done. The Duke of Wellington prophesied civil war if the Association was not put down and later in November the king wrote a stiff letter to Peel referring to the activities of the Association as 'intended rebellion'.

The stumbling-block was the Lord-Lieutenant, who at first sulkily declared that as the cabinet had rejected his previous advice responsibility did not rest on his shoulders; argued next that the division of the opinion among his legal advisers made it impossible for him to act; and finally recommended that the whole question should be referred to a parliamentary committee. Nettled by Wellesley's evasiveness and misrepresentations, Peel argued strongly in the cabinet that action should be taken by the government on its own initiative without any preliminary parliamentary enquiry. With this the cabinet concurred and, after detailed consultations, a bill to deal generally with unlawful societies in Ireland was introduced early the following session.

The decision to keep the measure in government hands and the care devoted to its preparation were more than justified by the hostile reception it received in the Commons. The concern of the opposition, however, was less for the details of the bill than for the general cause of emancipation; and a further diversion of interest was created by attacks on Canning and the Grenvillites for having deserted the Catholic cause as the price of their admission to the ministry. When Canning came to make his contribution to the debate, he devoted the last part of his speech to an eloquent vindication of his consistency. Referring to his lost hopes of representing Oxford University he pointed to Peel sitting beside him, a living symbol of one sacrifice he had made for the sake of emancipation. 'He laid hold of Peel's shoulder awkwardly,' related an amused Whig, 'and wished him "a long possession of the mistress he had lost". Peel, who was apparently not prepared for the familiar wishes of his colleague, shrugged his shoulder and looked uncomfortable'. Complimentary as Canning no doubt meant to be, the metaphor was probably not one that Peel had relished. In the event the bill passed, the Catholic Association was formally disbanded, and the collection of the 'rent' for a time discontinued. The effect however was transitory. Soon after the close of the session the New Catholic Association was set up, with the proclaimed and ingeniously insolent programme of not acting in any way inconsistent with the recent statute, while in fact continuing much as before. Given the constitutional framework within which both sides were acting, it was impossible to prevent the subtle Irish barristers of the emancipation movement from contriving ostensibly legal methods of carrying on their agitation. Without arbitrary powers, which the government did not want and parliament would not have given, the Irish executive could never hope to crush O'Connell's national movement by mere legislation.

Nevertheless, the act of 1825 was not without some hampering effect and the government was satisfied with what it had done. The event to which it looked forward with greater apprehension was the general election due in 1826. When it took place their worst fears were realised. It was not the first time that the Catholic clergy had intervened in elections; but what was new and significant in 1826 was the extent to which they exerted their influence with the electorate and the striking successes they obtained. Though the boroughs with their small Protestant oligarchies were virtually immune to popular or clerical pressures, in the counties it was a different story. Catholic support was instrumental in returning candidates for County Dublin, and Roscommon. In Waterford, Louth, Monaghan, and Westmeath the freeholders deserted their landlords in droves to return emancipation members. The priests in some constituencies not only preached from the pulpit against government candidates but took up their stand at the polling stations to supervise the voting of their flocks. To Goulburn, as to many other of Peel's Irish correspondents, the outlook after the election seemed black and foreboding. Peel in his replies tried to extract what grains of comfort were discernible in the general scene of Protestant discomfiture and alarm; but even he admitted that the crucial question was whether these ominous developments were due solely to the existence of Catholic disabilities or arose from something deeper and more ineradicable in Irish society. 'It would be a greater relief to my mind than I ever hope to enjoy,' he confessed to one correspondent, 'to be persuaded that the removal of the present disqualifications will be a cure for the present evils, and at the same time leave Ireland under a Protestant government.' It was because he felt unable to arrive at that optimistic conviction that he stubbornly continued his opposition to Catholic emancipation, however inevitable it now seemed.

The illness of the prime minister the following year broke up for ever the uneasy team of ministers and officials which had ruled Ireland since 1822. For Peel personally it had been an unsatisfactory five years. In the triangular relationship between himself, Wellesley and Goulburn, he could only guide and stimulate policy, not initiate or enforce it. The unpleasant truth remained that Ireland had been more efficiently and peacefully governed between 1812 and 1818 when he had been Chief Secretary than between 1822 and 1827 when he was Home Secretary. That was not his fault, but compared with England, where he could bring his direct authority to bear, the Irish pages of his Home Office administration formed a largely barren chapter. More significant still, Catholic emancipation had made more headway in the five years since 1822 than in the first twenty years after the Union. For a politician who was a committed opponent of that cause, it was an uncomfortable reflection.

Chapter 7

The end of Lord Liverpool's administration

The reconstruction of the administration after 1821 gave it a renewed lease of political life. With the loss of Castlereagh made good by the retention of Canning, Peel installed in the Home Office, Robinson replacing Vansittart as Chancellor of the Exchequer in January 1823, and Huskisson appointed President of the Board of Trade the following April, the government took on an increasingly workmanlike appearance. The additional number of cabinet ministers in the Commons redressed the balance of executive authority which had become dangerously uneven after Canning's resignation in 1820 and there was a greater air of government activity. More things were being attempted by ministers than were thought possible or prudent in the immediate postwar years; and the liberal, reforming, free trade tendencies always latent in Liverpool's cabinet were being given wider scope. Though the king was sulky and resentful over the old grievances and the new liberalism, the recruitment of the Grenvillites ensured that there was not even the semblance of a third party to whom he could turn for an alternative government. The Whigs, after the collapse of the queen's 'affair', were left frustrated and impotent in the face of returning prosperity and ministerial reforms. Indeed the main danger to the government came not from the official opposition but from the back-bench country M.P.s who were unhappy with a deflationary money policy, complained of low farm prices, and distrusted the government's steady advance towards economic liberalism.

Yet for all that there was among the ministers themselves a feeling of looseness and disunity. Part of it was due to the effects on the prime minister of the strains of the preceding years; part to the unsettling presence of Canning; part to the consciousness that the Catholic question was more open than it had been for many years. It was a change of atmosphere rather than of policy. Canning, like the Grenvillites, had entered the ministry on the old principle of neutrality. If there was an impression of change, it was because the movement for emancipation was stronger than ever and the inclusion of so many 'Catholics' in the government had aroused the expectation of partisans. One thing at least seemed constant in politics; the agitation for Catholic emancipation. In 1825 the issue was once again brought before the Commons. It was not one which Peel enjoyed meeting. 'There is little feeling, I think, in this country', he wrote to Gregory in March 1825, 'upon the question. People are tired of it and tired of the trouble of opposing it, or thinking about it.' But he could not accept the

general apathy as a reason for abandoning his own attitude and prepared, though without enthusiasm, for a renewal of the struggle.

The tactics of the emancipationists were now more subtle. Three
distinct measures were proposed: the relief of Catholic disabilities, the
assumption by the state of responsibility for the stipends of the Irish
Catholic clergy, and the abolition of the Irish forty-shilling freeholder
franchise. These last two provisions, the so-called 'wings', were offered
as securities to set Protestant fears at rest. On 1 March Burdett moved
for a committee of the whole House to consider the laws affecting
Roman Catholics in a speech which sought to prove that no danger
need be expected from liberated Catholicism or from the political
changes which would result. To the massed oratory of Canning, Plunket
and Brougham, Peel could only oppose an unimpressive team composed
of such men as the Protestant Irish member Leslie Foster and the ultra-
Tory Wetherell. For himself he asked whether emancipation could be
safely granted and if granted whether it would bring tranquillity to
Ireland. 'I am not afraid of the Pope, nor of the Pretender; but I am
afraid of a powerful internal party in this country, of whom great
numbers are dissatisfied, as they must be, with our principles of
religion.' And he quoted from a pamphlet by Bishop Doyle of Kildare
and Leighlin in which that great Catholic controversialist had admitted
that 'emancipation would only lead a passage to ulterior measures'. But
the tide was running against him and Burdett's motion was carried by
thirteen votes.

While the consequent bills were being prepared, Peel consulted
friends and advisers in Ireland on the value of the proffered securities
in limiting the political effects of emancipation. Gregory, while admitting the desirability on general grounds of raising the Irish county
franchise, thought that payment of the Roman clergy would increase
their power without decreasing their independence. But his tone was
pessimistic and he could do little more than reaffirm a melancholy
trust in Peel as the 'ablest and most uncompromising defender' of their
dying cause. How far that cause seemed already dead was shown by a
rumour which went round London, and even appeared in the press, to
the effect that the cabinet had decided to make emancipation a government measure and that the Home Secretary had resigned. When the
debate on the bill took place Peel argued once more his inability to
believe in either the efficacy or the practicability of the proposed
securities. Indeed, he said that if the bill passed, he would prefer to
place his trust in a 'principle of generous confidence' rather than in a
'jealous and ineffectual system of restrictions'. But he mustered even
less support for his attack on the 'wings' than on the main measure; and
in May the third reading was carried by 284 to 227.

The triumphal procession of Burdett's bill was accompanied behind
the scenes by a protracted cabinet crisis. At the start of April the prime
minister had raised with Wellington the question of his own retirement
if, as he anticipated, the bill passed the Commons. Part of his anxieties

concerned Peel; and in the next few weeks they seemed more than justified. Faced with the opposition of all four of his cabinet colleagues in the Commons— Canning, Robinson, Huskisson and Wynn— and encountering one defeat after another on every aspect of the bill, Peel in the end came to the conclusion that his position was an embarrasssment both to himself and to the government. At the end of April he tendered his resignation. The crisis which Liverpool had foreseen was now imminent and on 1 May the Protestant members of the cabinet—Liverpool, Peel, Bathurst, and Wellington—met to consider their future. Though the last two argued for delay, the Prime Minister and the Home Secretary were not to be dissuaded; and it was virtually settled that they would both resign as soon as the bill met its expected defeat in the Lords. The assumption was that the king would then send for Canning. Whether the rest of the cabinet would accept him as leader was a different matter; and the entire disintegration of the ministry seemed more than probable. The key to the situation lay with Peel; for the prime minister admitted privately that he would stay if Peel would. Bathurst therefore added his entreaties to the personal arguments earlier employed by Wellington; and under this renewed solicitation Peel's resolution began to waver. What was made supremely clear to him was that if he resigned he would bring down the government, and that the only possible successor was a ministry headed by Canning pledged to bring in Catholic emancipation.

The crisis then took an unexpected turn. Immediately after the anticipated defeat of the measure in the House of Lords in the middle of May, Canning asked for a special meeting of the cabinet to consider the Catholic question and told Liverpool privately that he thought the ministry could no longer remain neutral on the question. The harassed prime minister once more consulted his Protestant colleagues. Bathurst was prepared to let Canning resign and stand the consequences. But Liverpool, whose partiality to Canning was notorious, was as loth to lose Canning as he was Peel. Nevertheless, the cabinet could only preserve its neutrality on the Catholic question if all its members agreed to do so. If any of them chose to make it a cabinet matter, it was hard to see how the ministry could continue. In the event, however, a split was avoided. When the cabinet met, Canning's Catholic colleagues displayed no desire to follow his lead and he finally consented not to press the issue. Liverpool and Peel contented themselves by saying that if the majority in the Lords had been smaller, they would have felt obliged to resign. With that the danger was over for the time being. With no resignations and still agreeing to disagree, the Liverpool ministry had survived once more.

The crisis had been more severe than the public had realised; and in the last analysis it had only been the indispensability of the prime minister that had prevented an open breach. Even so, it was little more than a respite. Though the Lords had killed Burdett's measure, another majority in the Commons for another bill would almost certainly force the cabinet out of its precarious neutrality. Even if Canning had mistimed his initiative, the logic of his argument was undeniable. For the moment, however, there was by common consent a temporary truce. Neither in the short session of 1826 nor in the general election which followed was emancipation made a central issue. Nevertheless, within the cabinet there were many dissatisfactions and animosities only needing an occasion to make their presence felt. Wellington disliked Canning's foreign policy, his systematic attempts to curry favour with the king, and the unusual hold which he seemed to possess over the prime minister. Glad as he would have been to see Lord Liverpool settle the Catholic question, he would certainly have retired if Canning had become Prime Minister in 1825. Peel himself shared something of the suspicion and distrust which surrounded the Foreign Secretary. He too noted and disliked Liverpool's undue reliance on Canning's opinion even when Peel raised with the prime minister purely departmental matters. Insensibly therefore he began to gravitate towards the Duke of Wellington. But while receptive to the emotional feeling against Canning prevalent in Wellington's circle, he wisely refrained from any speculative commitments. He had no quarrel with Canning over his foreign policy; and on the Catholic issue his *alter ego* in the cabinet was not the duke but Lord Liverpool. Indeed in February 1827 the duke's confidante, Mrs Arbuthnot, complained that 'he and Mr Peel talk together upon the Catholic question till they persuade each other they must be driven out by it. Mr Peel is perfectly sincere and moreover would be very glad to go.'

II

Though the general election of 1826 had brought some accession of strength to the government, the first full session of the new parliament in 1827 seemed certain to test its resources to the utmost. For over a year the Prime Minister had been in poor health and had talked more than once of resignation; the new ministerial corn bill, proposing the first significant reduction of the prohibitive tariff imposed in 1815, was likely to meet considerable cross-bench opposition from the agriculturalists; and the Catholic party, after their victory in the Commons in 1825, were resolved on an early trial of strength in the new House. Parliament had scarcely begun the work of the session, however, before the ministry received a mortal blow.

On the morning of Saturday 17 February Lord Liverpool was found unconscious on the floor of his breakfast-room. He had evidently had a stroke and though he recovered under medical treatment, his right side remained paralysed and his speech was inarticulate. To some observers it seemed already that his political career was over. For the cabinet the fatality was made even worse by the fact that Canning was ill. Throughout February he was confined at Brighton, suffering from a cold and rheumatic fever. A third invalid, the king, was also there, nursing a sharp attack of gout. In the circumstances the practical direction of the government fell on Peel. After a hasty ministerial meeting he went down to Brighton on the afternoon of the 17th. With Canning agreement was easily reached on the expediency of proceeding with government business in the ordinary way, saying nothing publicly to suggest any doubt of Liverpool's ultimate recovery. With the king, who had a fit of agitation and panic over the weekend, the task of persuasion was more difficult. In the end, however, he consented to do nothing until more information was available on Liverpool's medical condition. On the Monday Peel returned to London to report to the rest of the cabinet. In private discussion with Wellington a few days later the two men agreed that it was not their business to offer advice to the king on the choice of a successor to Liverpool and that no step should be taken until the king had made that choice.

As temporary Leader of the House Peel was able to secure postponement both of the government's corn bill and of Burdett's resolution on Catholic disabilities; and only when Canning returned at the beginning of March was the interrupted programme of the session resumed. The corn bill had a relatively easy passage. Though agriculturalists objected to any tampering with the absolute prohibition of corn imports when the price was under eighty shillings a quarter, others thought the ministerial modifications too small. Between extremists on both sides the majority in the House was inclined to think that the government was following a safe middle course, and by April the bill had passed all its stages. The Catholic debate took a more surprising turn. The result of the 1826 election in Ireland and the activities of the Catholic Association had led emancipationists to believe that another triumph like that of 1825 was within their grasp; and the issue of the debate was awaited with greater expectation than the fate of the corn bill. Moved by Burdett in March the Catholic resolutions were debated for two nights and no fewer than 548 members voted in the final division. After twenty years of discussion it was beyond the wit even of politicians to produce new arguments; the only interest was in the result. When it came it was both unexpected and, to Peel, gratifying: for the motion 272, against 276. The victory, narrow as it was, proved decisive. Parallel motions to be moved by Lord Lansdowne in the Upper House were abandoned without a discussion.

Nevertheless the political situation remained as uneasy as ever. Peel told Arbuthnot on 9 March that the defeat of Burdett's motion had merely left Canning free to postpone any solution of the Catholic question and take over the ministry on the old principle of neutrality. He added that he would need to talk to the duke on the line they should follow. Nettled by Peel's evident assumption that Canning was bound to succeed to the premiership, Arbuthnot wrote to him next day describing Wellington's attitude and begging him, when they met, to discuss the duke's own claims to the succession as well as those of

Canning and Peel. On 12 March Peel and Wellington met to consider their position. The duke said frankly that he did not think he could remain in a cabinet led by Canning and suggested putting a Protestant peer at the head of the administration. Peel was sceptical of some of the names he mentioned but said he would be ready to serve under Bathurst or the duke. He added (a trifle optimistically if he was correctly reported) that Canning would probably not object to serving under the duke; but he insisted that they would not be acting fairly by the king if, by abandoning him, they forced him into the arms of the Whigs.

Meanwhile the cabinet crisis dragged on. Towards the end of March Liverpool showed signs of recovering some political awareness but made it clear to his wife that there could be no prospect of his immediate return to work. When Wellington approached the king, he was told that the matter must be left until after the Easter recess. The anxious cabinet urged that at least some communication should be made to Lady Liverpool and eventually the king received from her on her husband's behalf a formal resignation of office. Other politicians were less restrained in their activities. Lord Lowther, backed by the Duke of Newcastle, advised the king to form a Protestant administration under Wellington, with Peel as Leader of the Commons. The Whigs for their part had already had a meeting and agreed to support Canning should he become prime minister. Fortified by this news Canning assured Knighton that he could manage both the corn and the Catholic question if his hands were left free; which was the equivalent of saying, if the king refrained from demanding any pledges from him. In terms of age, seniority and parliamentary experience Canning clearly had better claims than any to succeed Liverpool. But everything depended on the king; and the one point to which George IV still clung was his consistency as a Protestant monarch.

On 28 March Canning and Wellington had separate interviews with the king at Windsor. The duke told him that he must choose between Peel, Canning or some third person under whom both would serve. With Canning there was a more delicate fencing-match. Canning's ironic advice that the king should consult his own feelings and form a purely Protestant ministry was, as both knew, an impossibility. But while offering assurances, Canning refused to give pledges on his own course of action if he became prime minister. The king was equally reluctant to commit himself unreservedly to a ministry headed by a 'Catholic' and expressed a wish to see Peel. On his return to town Canning told Peel of what had passed and there was a frank exchange of views between the two potential rivals. Peel made it clear that he wished the government to remain on its old footing and was perfectly ready in those circumstances to serve under Canning in the Commons. But there was an insuperable obstacle, he pointed out, to his remaining Home Secretary under a 'Catholic' prime minister because of the close connection between the two offices. In all the speculation and intrigue of the preceding month Peel had been given ample opportunity to decide on his attitude; but this was the first time he had revealed to anyone what he had decided. Now that the time for decision had come, he left no doubt as to his standpoint. 'I will tell you without reserve what are my feelings as to my particular situation; they dictate to me retirement from office, if His Majesty should select you to form an administration.' Though disappointed, Canning appreciated his candour. 'What his ultimate decisions may be—or *might* be—', he wrote to Knighton, 'I cannot say. But it is impossible to do more than justice, by any expression of mine, to the frankness and generosity, and *self-denial* of his declarations.'

Next day Peel travelled up to Windsor for his own audience. To the king's unorthodox notion of asking the cabinet to choose its new head, he raised constitutional objections; and George finally agreed that, if Canning shared those objections, the proposal should be dropped. They then discussed Peel's position and it was probably now that Peel formally told the king that if Canning became prime minister, he himself would feel bound to retire. The king was still looking for a way out of his dilemma, however, and though he had perhaps already made up his mind to appoint Canning, he hoped to preserve the balanced composition of the ministry that had characterised it under Liverpool. In a letter sent to Peel the following day he said he could do nothing until some progress had been made in the talks between Peel and Canning and he pointed out with emphatic underlinings that on the Catholic question the king would act as a guarantee to Peel just as Peel would be a guarantee to the king. 'So that no means, let the Government be formed as it may, can ever be practised with a view of *carrying* the Catholic question or of *injuring* the Protestant Constitution of the country.' George IV was not conspicuous for political sagacity, nor did his assurances usually inspire his hearers with much confidence. Yet by a quirk of fate which neither could foresee, it might have been better for Peel had the royal advice been followed. Certainly Peel's career would have been very different and he himself would have been spared much pain and difficulty had he become second-in-command to Canning in 1827.

Once he had made up his mind, however, Peel was not a man to be easily shifted. Two considerations seemed to him paramount. He could not sanction the great political advance of the Catholic cause which would result from the appointment of the first 'Catholic' prime minister for twenty years. He could not remain in an office which would make him for many purposes the instrument for the actions of that prime minister. All Irish affairs passed through the hands of the Home Secretary; every warrant for a peerage, appointments to every political and ecclesiastical office in the gift of the Crown were signed by him. Unless there was agreement between himself and Canning on the Catholic issue, his position in the new government would be intolerable. Canning did all he could to cajole him. He offered him a peerage with the leadership of the House of Lords or alternatively a transfer to the Foreign Office. He mentioned his own failing health and the probability of Peel's early succession to the premiership. But Peel remained adamant. He told the king early in April that he could neither advise nor support a purely Protestant administration and that Canning in view of his seniority could not reasonably be expected to acquiesce in Peel's accession to the premiership. The only acceptable solution therefore was a continuation of the old mixed ministry with Canning as Leader of the House of Commons. In a written statement to the king a few days later he added that it was only the Catholic question which prevented his cooperation and that if the ministry as a whole stayed in office, he would give it a general support.

The practical difficulty, as he realised, was to find a Protestant peer of sufficient weight to take over the leadership. There was in fact only one possible candidate; and when at the king's request he had one more interview with Canning, he formally proposed that their differences should be resolved by the appointment of the Duke of Wellington. This for Canning was no solution at all; and on 10 April the king bowed to the inevitable by asking Canning to prepare a plan for the reconstruction of the government. The phrase was vague but the meaning was clear. Two days later, when Canning was officially installed as First Lord of the Treasury and Chancellor of the Exchequer, Peel sent in his resignation. It was one of many; Wellington, Eldon, Westmorland, Bathurst and Melville from the cabinet, Goulburn in Ireland, and dozens of minor office-holders and Household officials. Some of these Canning had expected; but he could scarcely have been prepared for the shoal of resignations which greeted the announcement of his appointment as prime minister. To many of his supporters it looked like a concerted attempt to wreck his administration before it had even started.

There had been no cabal. Wellington disliked and distrusted Canning but he had made no attempt to exclude him from the premiership; and there was no predetermined plan of resignation by the Protestant members of the cabinet. In fact there was a singular absence of discussion between them on what their course of action should be. What plotting against Canning had taken place was by great Tory peers like Rutland and Newcastle, not by the professional politicians. Nevertheless the combination of those intrigues with the prompt withdrawal of half the cabinet; Wellington's resignation not only from the cabinet but from the command of the Army; the decision of Melville, though a 'Catholic', to go out with his Protestant colleagues: all these circumstances added to the bitterness of the secession. At bottom it was not merely Protestant feeling but a deep distrust of Canning himself that was responsible for the split. Deprived of Liverpool's protection Canning had at last been exposed to the full force of the unpopularity and suspicion with which for twenty years he had contrived to surround his extraordinary career. The party which

Liverpool had held together since 1812 had broken at last; and, ironically, the cause of the disruption was Liverpool's favourite colleague.

Peel, who resigned on the single and understandable issue of Catholic emancipation, escaped almost entirely from the angry charges levelled at many of the seceders. When on 1 May he gave an explanation of his conduct to the House of Commons, he based it entirely on the disagreement between himself and Canning over the Catholic question and the incompatibility of that disagreement with his position as Home Secretary. He denied any personal hostility, mentioned his proffered resignation in 1825 as proof of his consistency, and defended himself and his outgoing colleagues from the insinuation of 'concert and cabal'. He ended with an expression of regret at terminating his public services and a reference to his own record in office. 'I may be a Tory, I may be an illiberal,' he said ironically, but, he continued, the fact was undeniable that the legislation connected with his name had all been directed to an improvement, mitigation and reform in the law; and that in the industrial disorders of the previous two years he had preserved public order without once applying to parliament for repressive powers.

This self-advertisement was not to everyone's taste but the feeling which prompted it was perhaps something more than mere pride. Conscious of the growing unpopularity of his uncompromising opposition to Catholic emancipation, conscious too of the reactionary prejudices which moved many of Canning's enemies, he wished to remind his audience that Whigs and Canningites had no monopoly of 'liberalism' and that to be unyielding on Catholic claims did not necessarily imply a negative attitude on other questions. If a 'Tory' label was to be fixed on the seceding section of the old Liverpool administration, he at least would wear his with a difference. Though the public at large perhaps only half-understood this reminder, others behind the scenes appreciated his position. The king, despite his disappointment, was generous in his remarks and Canning, the figure round whom the controversy had raged, was equally friendly and understanding.

While many politicians would have been glad to set Peel up as the leader of an anti-Canning party, there had in fact been nothing in their previous relationship to suggest that Peel was influenced by any motive except political principle in resigning office. In the cabinet he and Canning had been on cordial if not intimate terms and their correspondence had been markedly unreserved. Peel passed on Goulburn's confidential communications and Canning in return regularly submitted to him current diplomatic documents. When they disagreed they did so openly; but in fact on foreign affairs there was little at issue between them. To the outstanding measures of Canning's foreign policy—the recognition of the South American colonies and the Portuguese expedition of 1826—Peel, much to Wellington's disgust, had given full approval. Only a short time before Lord Liverpool's stroke Peel had told a relative that when he went into a cabinet meeting he usually found that Canning had come to the same conclusions and would advance the same arguments as had occurred to himself but express them in better language than he could have done.

The reasons Peel had given to the king, to Canning, and to the House of Commons were convincing as public explanations for his retirement. But there were aspects of those arguments which in greater privacy were equally decisive in shaping his conduct. If he had acted as an individual in the crisis, it was because he felt an individual in the cabinet. He headed no group, he neither led nor wished to lead the ultra-Tory members in parliament. Had he consented to be put forward by them, he would have been the figurehead of a faction rather than the leader of a party. Equally so, had he joined Canning, he would still have been an individual with no power in the cabinet beyond his personal influence. He could not predict what Canning would do about the Catholics; and he did not trust him to maintain indefinitely the balanced inactivity of Lord Liverpool's cabinet. Indeed it might be impossible for Canning to do so; and if another Catholic crisis arose, Peel would be obliged to retire in circumstances more painful than those of 1827. Estranged from his old colleagues, severed from his new, he would then be open to the charge of having clung to office for its own sake and failing to foresee the inevitable outcome of a Canningite ministry.

It was a natural consequence that Canning, deprived of half of the old cabinet, made up his ministry by taking in Whigs. It was equally natural that Peel should regard that action as a justification for what he himself had done. 'Thank God, I never had a doubt as to what course I individually ought to pursue, and never have had a moment's repentance that I did pursue it,' he confided to his old tutor Lloyd on 20 April. And to Gregory he wrote the same day; 'My answer to Canning contains the general grounds on which I retired from office but it gives a very imperfect view of the difficulties with which I should have had to contend in remaining'. In the circumstances it is difficult to see how Peel could have come to any other decision. As he told Lloyd, all his subsequent reflection merely confirmed his first instinctive impulse. It was a crucial decision for himself, the most crucial since he had accepted junior office under Perceval seventeen years earlier; but only hindsight can describe it as an error of judgement. Nevertheless by leaving Canning, with whom he agreed on all matters save one, he found himself associated with men with whom he disagreed on almost all matters save one. Above all, by his virtual acceptance of the leadership of the Duke of Wellington, he, a professional politician, placed himself under the most unpolitical of all the members of Liverpool's old cabinet.

The remainder of the 1827 session brought little clarity to the confused political situation. In private it was marked by an unpleasant disagreement between Peel and Croker and an interruption to their friendship which lasted for several months and from which perhaps it never completely recovered. Croker had busied himself in procuring support for Canning and giving him advice. Peel thought that as an intimate friend, with confidential knowledge of Peel's views, he should have abstained from such activity. The puritanical rigidity of Peel, the Irish indiscretion and tortuousness of Croker, created a breach for which there was possibly no real justification though it vividly revealed two contrasting characters. In public the insinuations of the government supporters as to the real motives of the seceders, together with the unwonted irritability of the prime minister himself, produced some angry bickering in the Commons into which Peel was momentarily drawn. But in May he went out of his way to declare himself satisfied with the proclaimed policy of the ministry and contented himself with criticising the Whigs for abandoning their principles for the sake of office.

By July 1827 Canning's ministry had barely begun to gather momentum. The corn bill, as a result of an amendment moved by Wellington in the Lords, had been withdrawn and that issue, like the Catholic question, was postponed to the following session. How long Canning could resist the pressures of his new allies for such measures as parliamentary reform and the repeal of the Test and Corporations Acts was a question for the future. It was one that was never answered. The prime minister was already a sick and tired man and in July his health rapidly deteriorated. He died at Chiswick on 8 August 1827.

Chapter 8

The duke's cabinet

On the death of Canning many observers expected that the coalition he had constructed would fall apart and that the king would revert to the alternative which had faced him in the spring. But the events since Liverpool's illness had created a logic of their own. The men who were scarcely warm in office had no desire to vacate. The king, having secured a ministry, was not anxious to expose himself again to the fatigues of cabinet-making. His lingering resentment against the seceders of April made him relish rather than otherwise the prospect of leaving them a little longer in the cold. Canning's colleague Robinson (now Viscount Goderich) was promptly offered the premiership and the old cabinet continued in power on the understanding that Catholic emancipation remained an open question and that there was no intention of bringing forward a measure of parliamentary reform. Of these events Peel was a rural and only mildly interested spectator. He approved Wellington's acceptance of the king's invitation to resume command of the Army but for himself he was inclined a trifle cynically to believe that the king had made his exclusion from office a *sine qua non* when appointing Goderich. 'It is very natural in a man,' he wrote to Arbuthnot, 'and particularly when that man is a king, to hate another who declines to trust him.'

The rickety structure of the government collapsed at the beginning of the new year. Goderich had inherited Canning's ministry but not the wit or character which might have enabled him to dominate the discordant factions of which it was composed. On 8 January he told the king that he wished to resign and was at once instructed to summon the Lord Chancellor. He in turn was told to send for Wellington. When the duke arrived at Windsor the king informed him that he wished him to head a new ministry. The same evening Wellington wrote to Peel asking him to come up to town and assist him in executing 'this interesting commission'. The only stipulations the king had made were that Catholic emancipation was not to be a cabinet question, that the Lord-Lieutenant and Irish Lord Chancellor were to be 'Protestants', and that Lord Grey was not to have office. This letter reached Maresfield at midnight on 9 January and with a heavy heart Peel left his family and travelled up to London in the small hours of the morning. He had no illusions about the difficulties ahead. To rely simply on a Tory following in the Commons was for him neither politically practicable nor personally acceptable. Yet the task of piecing together the broken fragments of the old Liverpool party after the events of the spring and summer was not one that could be approached with any confidence. When he arrived at Apsley House he told Wellington that he would be content to serve under him and that it would be an advantage to have at the head of government a man whose name and reputation might exercise a conciliatory influence; though he hinted that it would be proper in those circumstances for the duke to resign his command of the Army. He made it clear however that he was opposed to any attempt to form an exclusively Protestant, still more an ultra-Tory administration.

> My view is [he confided to Julia the same day] to re-unite the old Party which was in existence when Lord Liverpool's calamity befell him. I cannot undertake the business in the House of Commons without more assistance than the mere Tory Party, as it is called, would afford me.

The discussions of the next few days showed that what he proposed was not going to be a simple enterprise. The seceders of April made it clear that they expected to return *en masse* under the banner of Wellington and Peel; and the hope that some from age or tact would withdraw their claims soon waned. To construct an administration of anti-Canning politicians alone, however, was simply to invite disaster. In a phrase of Peel's, which Wellington quoted approvingly to Croker, it would mean going into the House of Commons with half a party to fight a party and a half. Peel's plan was to recruit the more efficient of Liverpool's ministers and reinforce them with any other men of ability they could find who would be prepared to throw their lot in with the duke. For the cabinet he suggested the addition of Aberdeen and Ellenborough from the Lords, Goulburn and Herries from the Commons.

> I care not [he wrote to Gregory on 18 January] for the dissatisfaction of the ultra-tories. The country ought not, and cannot, be governed on any other principles than those of firmness, no doubt, but of firmness combined with moderation.

and again on 1 February to the same correspondent:

> What must have been the inevitable fate of a government composed of Goulburn, Sir John Beckett, Wetherell and myself? Supported by very warm friends no doubt, but no more than warm friends—being prosperous country gentlemen, fox-hunters, etc. etc., most excellent men, who will attend one night, but who will not leave their favourite pursuits to sit up till two or three o'clock fighting questions of detail on which, however, a Government must have a majority. We could not have stood creditably a fortnight.

If the attempt to recreate the Liverpool party failed, he was ready to make a fight of it in the House of Commons with what material was available. But his satiric comments showed what he thought the chances of success for such a venture.

The chief obstacle to reunion was Huskisson, whose quarrel with Herries over the Chairmanship of the Finance Committee had precipitated Goderich's resignation. One of Liverpool's chief economic survivors, friend and protégé of Canning, his undoubted talents were marred by shyness, irresolution and pique; and he was unpopular with the country gentlemen. Nevertheless he was an acknowledged expert on trade and finance and he was the leader, if one could be said to exist at all, of the Canningites.

Largely through Peel's patient persuasions he finally overcame his doubts and expressed himself ready to enter the cabinet provided Herries was not appointed Chancellor of the Exchequer. Ten days of negotiation gave Peel his reward at last and the rest of the ministry quickly fell into place. For Peel there could be no question of anything but the Home Office and the Leadership of the House of Commons. Goulburn became Chancellor of the Exchequer; Bathurst returned as President of the Council; Ellenborough came in as Lord Privy Seal; and Aberdeen as Chancellor of the Duchy of Lancaster. Of Goderich's old cabinet Lyndhurst remained as Lord Chancellor, Dudley at the Foreign Office, Huskisson in the Colonial Department, Charles Grant at the Board of Trade, and Palmerston as Secretary at War.

Though the king had been anxious to retain some of the Whigs, in the event none of them would take office; and of the old Tories Eldon, Vansittart and Westmorland were deliberately discarded. In Ireland Lord Anglesey, under a previous arrangement, succeeded Wellesley as Lord-Lieutenant and William Lamb (the future Lord Melbourne and a 'Catholic') stayed on as Chief Secretary. Despite the partisan criticisms of the excluded Whigs, the new team offered on paper at least a reasonable combination of central, moderate elements. While some of its adherents, like Bishop Lloyd, were uneasy at the spectacle of a professional soldier at the head of the civil government, other right wing supporters thought his presence a welcome curb on the liberal propensities of his second-in-command. They were not alone in their suspicions of the Home Secretary. When Peel had his official audience with the king, he was treated to what George complacently described to Knighton as 'a very strong lecture respecting his conduct both as to the past, as well as to the future'.

The composition of the cabinet in fact bore the strong imprint of Peel's influence and as such it was both a mixture and a compromise. Every cabinet since 1812 had been of this character. In the independent and indisciplined early nineteenth-century House of Commons only a central coalition could hope to survive. Peel's insistence on a reconstruction of the Liverpool system was therefore sound political instinct. Yet the prospects for such a coalition were less promising than under Liverpool; and not only because Liverpool was gone. When the

new cabinet dined together for the first time on 22 January, Ellenborough noted that 'the courtesy was that of men who had just fought a
duel'. Four prime ministers in less than twelve months had destroyed all
sense of continuity and stability; the secession under Canning and the
quarrels under Goderich had created enmity and distrust; and the
Whigs after twenty years had been given a taste of office. Equally dis-
quieting was the fact that despite the political upheavals of 1827 none
of the outstanding problems had been brought nearer a solution.
Canning had not settled emancipation; Huskisson had not settled corn;
and moving up in the rear was the question of parliamentary reform.

Conscious of all these difficulties, the cabinet approached the work
of the session in a mood of studied agreement. Once the parliamentary
inquest on the dissolution of the Goderich ministry commenced, the
unfortunate Huskisson found himself the centre of a bitter public and
personal controversy. The Whigs professed their amazement at seeing
the great follower of Canning in a Wellingtonian government and raked
over the quarrel with Herries for evidence of court intrigues. There was
open disagreement between Wellington and Huskisson on whether the
latter had received 'guarantees' or merely general assurances on entering the cabinet; and simultaneously Huskisson was assailed by savage
reproaches from Canning's family. In all this unpleasantness Peel stood
out as one of the few cool and conciliatory figures. Not only was he the
principal link between the Canningites and the rest of the cabinet but
his position of authority in the government helped to provide some
semblance of unity and direction. But though in matters of general
policy, such as foreign affairs and finance, he soon made his influence
felt, the fact remained that he was not head of the government nor
could he provide the numbers in the division lobby necessary to control
the House of Commons.

The parliamentary weakness of the government was sharply
illustrated before the session was a month old. At the end of February a
long and carefully organised campaign by the united English Dissenters
culminated in a successful motion by Lord John Russell for the repeal
of the Test and Corporations Acts. The theoretical effect of these old
statutes in excluding Dissenters from offices in municipal corporations
and under the Crown had long been removed in practice by annual
Indemnity Acts. Nevertheless they remained on the statute book as
historic symbols of the political monopoly of the Anglican Church; and
in private correspondence with the Home Secretary Bishop Lloyd
urged the need to preserve the distinction between religious toleration
and maintaining the privileges of the Establishment. But Peel was not
impressed by the usefulness, for House of Commons purposes at least,
of an argument which depended on the fine distinction between Anglicanism as a test of fitness and Anglicanism as a qualification for
office. His own view, accepted by the cabinet, was that they should
defend the existing law on the modest ground that the relationship
between Church and Dissent had markedly improved and that this

improvement might actually have been fostered by a system which gave Nonconformists practical enjoyment of political rights while recognising the titular predominance of the Established Church. There was the further consideration that a repeal of the acts might prejudice the Catholic question. It was a very English, very pragmatic attitude but it failed to commend itself to the House of Commons and the ministers lost the division by forty-four votes.

The narrow and unemotional grounds adopted by the government caused some disappointment in Peel's university constituency. But Oxford was not England and even at Oxford there was no strong feeling against repeal. The Home Secretary himself was not disposed to be apologetic. He thought that a more rigid line would have met with equal failure and done more damage to the Church. It was certainly not an issue on which the ministry was prepared to stake its existence. Instead Peel concentrated his efforts on finding a formula acceptable to the Church leaders in which to embody the principle agreed on by the Commons. While a bill founded on Russell's resolutions received its first and second readings, Peel consulted with the two archbishops and a number of other bishops. At a conference at Lambeth on 15 March a form of declaration was drawn up for new office-holders under the bill, binding the declarer not to use his influence to injure the interests of the Church; and in a conciliatory speech in committee three days later, Peel secured its insertion in the bill. When it went up to the Lords, it had become for all practical purposes a ministerial measure, and eighteen bishops voted with the government on the crucial issue of the declaration. After their initial reverse the ministers had clearly conducted a neat rearguard action and the compromise of the declaration had saved the credit of both Church and cabinet. Nevertheless, it remained indisputable that a measure which Liverpool had resisted and Canning pledged himself to oppose, had been yielded almost without a fight by Wellington's administration in the first few months of its existence. It was a portent for the future.

In the meantime tempers in the cabinet were strained on a separate issue. In the second week of March they discussed the postponed corn bill. Wellington wished to incorporate his amendment of the previous session and also have a higher scale of duties. Huskisson while offering minor concessions, adhered to the main provision of the original bill, which in fact was the creation not so much of Canning as of Lord Liverpool. In the end the entire cabinet, with the regrettable exception of the prime minister himself, was ready to approve it. For a time there was stalemate and Huskisson seemed prepared to resign rather than abandon his tariff scale. Finally, however, he gave way and in deference to the duke accepted a slightly higher rate. It was then Grant's turn to make difficulties. He declared he could not support the compromise in the Commons and Huskisson in consequence showed signs of retracting from his earlier concessions. For nearly a fortnight the cabinet was on the brink of collapse, since Huskisson insisted that he could not continue without Grant's support. The difference between the original bill and the compromise was slight, but with the obstinacy of a weak man Grant clung to his position against all the pleadings of his colleagues. He began to absent himself from ministerial meetings and at one point a letter of resignation from him was actually read out in cabinet. Only at the eleventh hour, when Huskisson had actually gone to the king to offer his own resignation, did Grant finally agree on a modified scale which Peel had put forward in an attempt to bridge the gap between the cabinet's compromise and Grant's own proposed scale of duties.

The crisis was over but, like another of the duke's battles, it had been a near thing. Wellington himself was intensely irritated by the whole episode. He felt that he was alone in the cabinet; that nobody was ready to make any concessions to him; and that the Canningites were personally hostile. He was sorry in fact that the affair had not ended with their resignations. It was Peel who in and out of cabinet had acted as the great conciliator. Theoretically he preferred the original bill to the subsequent compromise; but he attached greater importance to cabinet unity and harmony. He had worked wholeheartedly for an amicable compromise and as a result enjoyed the confidence of Huskisson and his followers to a much greater extent than any other member of the cabinet. 'Peel is so rightheaded and liberal,' wrote Palmerston to his brother on 25 March, 'and so up to the opinions and feelings of the times, that he smooths difficulties which might otherwise be unsurmountable.'

Long before the corn bill reached the statute book, yet another crisis had occurred in Wellington's uncomfortable cabinet. Early in the session a bill had been introduced to deal with two rotten boroughs, Penryn and East Retford, previously declared by the House of Commons to be corrupt and meriting disfranchisement. Peel brought the matter up in cabinet in mid-March. The duke and Bathurst favoured the conservative course of enlarging the boroughs by incorporating them in the neighbouring hundreds. The Canningites wished to conciliate the advocates of parliamentary reform by transferring the seats to some of the large unrepresented towns. Peel's only doubt was whether the abolition of both boroughs would not set a precedent for a regular process of transference in future. He proposed therefore to give the Penryn seats to Manchester or Birmingham and enlarge East Retford. Huskisson agreed with this in principle though he wished to reverse the procedure. Dudley alone wanted to take advantage of the situation by enfranchising both Birmingham and Manchester. If only one of the offending boroughs was to be disfranchised, the case against Penryn was overwhelming. It had the worst record of corruption and Cornwall was already grossly over-represented. The cabinet came down on the side of Peel's proposal and he put it forward in the Commons on the assumption that the two constituencies were to be considered in conjunction. In the Lords the proposal to transfer the Penryn seats to

Robert Peel, aetat. 37. From the painting by Sir Thomas Lawrence P.R.A.

A Metropolitan Police Man.

A radical caricature published when the Metropolitan Police Act was passed in 1829.

Manchester met with such opposition that Lord Carnarvon, who was in charge of the bill, announced that he would seek its withdrawal. In this unexpected situation the cabinet on 19 May agreed with some hesitation to adhere to its proclaimed policy over Retford until a final decision was reached in the Lords about Penryn. There was a general feeling that if the Lords proved obstinate over the first borough, the government would have to reconsider its position on the second: but Peel was primarily concerned with the task of getting immediate cabinet agreement on the Retford bill which was to be debated that same day.

In the debate the government was charged with inconsistency in continuing to press for the inclusion of Retford in the hundreds when the bill transferring Penryn to Manchester had virtually been killed in the Lords. Peel, who had never pledged himself on what was to be done if there was only one constituency to dispose of, was able to reject the accusation with ease. Huskisson, on the other hand, who at an earlier stage in the Commons, had said that if only one constituency was available, he would favour transferring it to a town, was made to feel distinctly uncomfortable. When the division finally took place, he and Palmerston voted in the minority against the government. Peel who had no suspicion of his colleagues' defection until the vote was taken, felt a natural annoyance but said nothing. Huskisson, who was sharply reproached by Planta, the government chief whip, went home in an agitated state and sat down in the small hours of the morning to write a letter of resignation. There is little doubt that he intended, by placing his office at the duke's disposal, to offer an apology and make amends for his conduct. But the letter read like an unconditional resignation; Wellington took it as such; and Peel, to whom he immediately showed it, was of the same opinion. That afternoon the letter was placed before the king. Though in the next few days several of the Canningites tried to bring about a reconciliation, the breach proved irreparable. The duke hinted that if Huskisson had not really wished to resign, his proper course was to withdraw the letter. Huskissson insisted that though the letter had not been meant as an unconditional resignation, it would be a personal humiliation to withdraw it. After waiting five days Wellington informed him that arrangements had been made to fill his office and the resignation of other Canningites— Palmerston and Dudley from the cabinet, Lamb from the Chief Secretaryship and a few others from minor office—promptly followed. It was the final break-up of the old Liverpool party after only four troubled months of temporary reunion.

In this second crisis Peel made no attempt to intervene on Huskisson's behalf, though consistency and interest might both have pointed to some effort at mediation. But patience with Peel was more a product of training than of temperament; and perhaps the point had been reached when he was weary of well-doing on behalf of the Canningites. He did not attach much importance to the East Retford issue in itself;

but the fact was undeniable that the cabinet had agreed to support the line he had taken as Leader of the House and he was vexed at Huskisson's failure to give him the slightest hint of what he intended to do. Palmerston, who saw Peel the day after found him 'evidently hurt and angry, though his manner to me was perfectly kind and conciliatory'. He had some reason to feel resentment. He had been the chief advocate for the inclusion of the Canningites in the ministry; he had sided with them against the prime minister on most of the cabinet controversies that had arisen: Greece, corn, parliamentary reform. But his new allies had scarcely made things easy for him. Grant's obstinacy had tried everybody's temper and Huskisson's letter of 20 May was the third resignation to come from the Canningite group in two months. It was doubtful in any case whether Peel could have intervened with success; and had he come forward once more as the defender of Huskisson and his awkward squad, his relationship with the duke might have been put under a severe and useless strain.

The departure of the Canningites, however, was more acutely felt by Peel than by any other member of the cabinet. This was not entirely on account of policy, for the liberal tendencies of the government did not depend solely on Huskisson and his three immediate associates. Still less was it on account of the resultant decrease in voting strength, for not all Canning's followers recognised Huskisson as their leader and not all ranged themselves in opposition after May 1828. But the loss of ministerial talent and debating strength was a decided blow; and one that directly affected Peel's position as Leader of the House. On him rested the responsibilities of government in the Commons; but he did not command a majority there and even the nominal ministerial party did not give him the support he would have liked. He pressed the duke to take as many of the new ministers as possible from the Lower House but the result only demonstrated the poverty of resources at the government's disposal. Sir George Murray, Wellington's quartermaster-general in the Peninsula, became Colonial Secretary and another Peninsular veteran, Sir Henry Hardinge, was made Secretary at War. Vesey Fitzgerald, in a fateful move, took the Board of Trade and among other appointments Aberdeen was promoted to the Foreign Office and Leveson-Gower replaced Lamb as Chief Secretary in Ireland. Though the governmental strength in the Commons was only marginally worse in the face of an opposition itself divided into miscellaneous groups, the quality of the front bench there had markedly deteriorated and a greater burden in consequence placed on Peel's shoulders.

II

If quarrels and resignations seemed an inevitable accompaniment of office, Peel's return to the Home Department at least enabled him to resume his interrupted programme of legal reform. Two bills, prepared in the Department during his absence but forming part of his general consolidation of criminal law, went through parliament in the 1828 session: one relating to offences against the person and the other dealing with the law of evidence. As a result of all his consolidating measures since 1825, 278 acts had been repealed and their remaining provisions summarised in eight statutes. Nevertheless, his appetite for reform was not yet sated. In making a survey of the whole field of legal reform in February 1830 he gave notice of his intention to bring in more consolidating bills relating to the magistracy, the coinage, and forgery, which, if passed, would mean that nine-tenths of the cases coming before the courts would· have been brought within the scope of his reforming activities since 1825.

Of these new topics, the controversial one was forgery. The commonest type related to currency and bills of exchange; and because of the effect on public revenue and commercial credit, and the difficulty of catching the skilled forger as distinct from those employed to pass the false notes or coin, the law had always regarded it as a particularly heinous crime. The 1819 Committee had recommended the retention of the death penalty only for forgery of Bank of England notes or for a second offence of uttering ordinary notes. But no reforms had followed and liberal opinion continued to press for a relaxation of the wider penalties for forgery. In 1828 the case of Hunton, a Quaker who had committed multiple forgeries involving at least £5,000, demonstrated the growing gap between public opinion and the existing law. Despite a massive agitation on Hunton's behalf Peel, after consulting the Lord Chancellor and the Lord Chief Justice, refused to advise a reprieve. The last two forgers convicted on capital charges had been respited but Hunton's guilt was clear and his offence aggravated. 'It would be very difficult', Peel wrote to the king, 'hereafter to enforce the capital sentence of the law in any case of forgery, if mercy be extended in this case.' Given the law as it stood, the decision was justifiable. The fact remained that increasingly the chances of life and death in such cases depended less on judicial sentence than on executive policy. And the decisions of ministers were influenced as in Hunton's case, not merely by the gravity of the individual offence but also by the number and circumstance of similar crimes committed at the same period.

The remedy lay in fresh legislation, and in the course of the succeeding year Peel made preparations for a change in the forgery laws. The history of this particular reform was a characteristic instance of Peel's administrative technique. In the early summer he had discussions with Scarlett, the Attorney-General, who at his request produced a sketch of a bill embodying the changes which the Home Secretary had indicated. This document was studied by Peel and his two Home Office advisers, Hobhouse and Gregson. The Attorney-General suggested making a distinction between forgeries immediately convertible into cash and those which needed time, preparation and connivance to achieve their object. Gregson thought this was an impracticable distinction which would not only increase their difficulties but actually make some forgeries felonies which were not so under existing law. One major complication was that there were not only general laws against forgery but a mass of particular acts (360 for the Customs alone) relating to specific departments of state. Gregson's solution was a bill covering all statutory forgeries except those affecting public departments which were to be dealt with separately in bills drafted by the departments themselves. Peel adopted this plan in preference to Scarlett's and by the end of the year a draft bill was ready. Its principal effect was to bring under one act all capital forgeries and consolidate all remaining forgery provisions other than those relating to departments. The draft was then sent to Lord Tenterden, the Lord Chief Justice, with an accompanying note in which Peel asked once more for 'the cheerful and most valuable aid which I have uniformly received from you throughout my labours on the consolidation of the criminal law'. Other drafts were circulated among the Lord Chancellor, the Attorney-General and the Solicitor-General; and discussions and alterations went on until March. The Lord Chief Justice again offered to take charge of the bill in the House of Lords while Peel made himself responsible for it in the Commons. From the Attorney-General came criticisms which were perhaps not unconnected with the fact that his own scheme had been rejected. Nevertheless his comments were duly passed on to Gregson for consideration. It was clearly on Gregson rather than on his more eminent legal colleague that Peel was disposed to rely; and for what was probably the last conclusive interview with the Lord Chief Justice, Gregson briefed the Home Secretary with a long memorandum.

As presented to the Commons in April 1830, after nine months of continuous discussion and examination, the bill made no sweeping changes in the penalties prescribed by existing statutes. Capital punishment was retained for forgery of bank notes, negotiable securities, wills involving personal property, and public stock; but Peel accepted the recommendations of the 1819 Committee to abolish the death penalty for a variety of other types of forgery. A strong party in the Commons, headed by Mackintosh, Buxton, Brougham and Russell, fought for greater relaxation of penalties on the grounds that public dislike of capital punishment for forgery resulted in a general reluctance of injured parties to prosecute and of juries to convict. Peel argued in reply that fear of trouble and expense was a greater deterrent than any inherent dislike of the death penalty. Nevertheless, the great public controversy aroused by his bill showed that the bulk of the professional middle classes, including the bankers themselves, were convinced that a more lenient system of penalties would result in a more effective legal protection. Peel, as usual, clung stubbornly to a decision which he had reached after long consideration and consultation. But all his debating skill was needed to preserve the slender government majority in committee; and on the third reading, in a thin House, Mackintosh secured a majority of thirteen on an amendment to substitute imprisonment or transportation up to fourteen years as the penalty for all cases of forgery except those of wills. Peel was piqued by his defeat and thoroughly dissatisfied at the general weakness of the government in the Commons. Nevertheless he accepted that it would now be almost impossible to secure a capital conviction for forgery and in cabinet it was agreed to leave the bill as amended. In the Lords the Lord Chancellor and Lord Tenterden succeeded in removing the Mackintosh clause and when the bill came back to the Commons in July it was clear that because of the lateness of the session it would have to be accepted as it stood or abandoned. The House preferred the first course and four days before prorogation the bill passed into law in substantially the same form as that in which Peel had introduced it. Nevertheless, as Peel realised, Mackintosh had in fact decided the issue; after 1830 no one in England was executed for forgery.

More strikingly than any other of his legal reforms, the 1830 forgery bill demonstrated that public opinion was increasingly on the side of the Romilly–Mackintosh school. Yet Peel was not as inflexible as he appeared. At the outset of his work at the Home Office he had favoured a decrease in the severity of the law; and despite all he had accomplished since 1823, he continued to move, deliberately but un- mistakably, in that direction. In private he told Buxton that he was on his side in the matter of capital punishment but 'you must give me time'. His own administration of the Home Department in fact had seen a notable continuation of the progressive fall in the number of executions which marked the postwar period. In the seven years that followed the close of the American War in 1783, the average annual number of executions in London and Middlesex was fifty-six; in the 1816–22 period it had fallen to twenty-seven; between 1822 and 1829 (almost the exact period of Peel's Home Secretaryship) to only seven- teen. His preference for a gradual relaxation of the law had as its object not the rigid enforcement of the death penalty but the retention of discretionary power until the full effects of his legal reforms were apparent. 'He looked forward', he told the Commons in May 1830, 'to the time when the criminal law, after the consolidation of its different parts had been carried into effect, should be again brought under con- sideration.' By 1830 that work of consolidation was almost complete. Behind him lay an impressive range of reforming statutes; the Juries Act of 1825, the Criminal Justice Act of 1826, the Larceny Act and Malicious Injury to Property Acts of 1827, the Offences against the Person Act of 1828, and the Forgery Act of 1830. A mass of obsolete legislation, the debris of centuries of English legal history, had been reduced to a handful of intelligible statutes. In criminal law alone more than three-quarters of all offences were now covered by Peel's reforms. Between the law books of George III and those of William IV there was now a great divide.

III

There remained one sphere of administrative reform at the Home Office in which Peel had already shown himself more anxious for bold innovations than either the public or the majority of politicians. It was to this he now returned. London in the third decade of the century had a population rising to one and a half million, as great as the total of the fifteen next largest towns in the British Isles. This vast conglomeration of people and buildings was still regulated and policed under an inefficient and chaotic set of institutions inherited from the past. The City, with 108 parishes and 125,000 inhabitants crammed into its six hundred acres, had its own separate force of about a thousand watchmen and constables, together with some fifty regular City police. The other London boroughs, Westminster, with a population greater than that of Dublin, and Southwark, larger than Bristol, were controlled by seven separate police offices set up in 1792, each staffed by three stipendiary magistrates, a couple of clerks, and eight to twelve constables. In addition there were the Thames River Police, established in 1800, and the old Bow Street Office, dating from the middle of the eighteenth century, which had a general jurisdiction over the whole metropolitan area outside the City. Beneath these specialised agencies was a motley and incompetent collection of constables and watchmen employed by parishes and other miscellaneous public and private authorities.

> Just conceive [Peel wrote to the Duke of Wellington] the state of one parish, in which there are eighteen different local boards for the management of the watch, each acting without concert with the others! . . . Think of the state of Brentford and Deptford, with no sort of police by night! I really think I need trouble you with no further proof of the necessity of putting an end to such a state of things.

It was not the professional soldier but the public and the professional politicians whom he had to persuade.

By 1826 Peel had determined to make a fresh effort to reform the London police. He invited suggestions from the police magistrates, and procured statistics of crime abroad, especially in the great European cities. There was a general feeling in the Home Office during the winter of 1826–27 that the work of legal reform was at last going to be flanked by a reorganisation of the metropolitan police. The events of 1827 postponed his plans for a twelvemonth but no sooner was he back in office than he set to work. In February 1828, in a carefully moderated speech weighted with uncomfortable statistics, he moved for a committee to enquire into the state of the police and the increase of crime in the metropolis. From the deceptively mild and disarming nature of his observations there seemed to be little to fear, if little to hope, from an

enquiry and he obtained his committee without difficulty. The committee sat between March and May, examining written evidence and
interviewing a specialised body of witnesses. In July its report was presented to the Commons. It came in two parts, corresponding to the
double nature of its remit. The first part demonstrated from Home
Office returns the steady increase of all forms of crime except coining
and forgery. The crucial section however was the second part which
dealt with the police of the metropolis. Here, for the first time in the
history of parliamentary police enquiries, the committee declared itself
in favour of a radical change. Its principal recommendations were the
establishment of a general police office under the immediate direction
of the Home Secretary, on which should devolve the control of all the
police establishments in the metropolitan area and its environs; the
exemption of the magistrates in charge of that office from ordinary
judicial duties; and the defrayment of the cost of the establishment
partly from public funds, partly from a rate to be levied on the parishes
within the area.

To have secured such a report was an achievement; it remained to
translate its recommendations into law. No more could be done that
session but the following April Peel introduced his Metropolitan Police
Improvement bill. The main objects were briefly stated but the details
were left to a select committee; for which purpose he asked for the
reappointment of the committee of enquiry. With a remarkable
absence of opposition or even comment the bill passed through the Commons and went up to the Lords in May. The deliberate omission of detail,
the neat stratagem of reappointing the old police committee, and the
absorption of public and parliamentary interest in the Catholic
emancipation crisis, all helped to screen the measure from vexatious
criticism and delay. As it went into the statute book in June 1829 the
act set up a single new police organisation under two magistrates for an
area virtually corresponding to a ten-mile radius from central London,
excluding the City. It was to be financed by a special police rate and a
third post, that of Receiver for the Metropolitan Police District, was
established with responsibility for money, property and legal contracts.
The outstanding feature of the act was the wide power given to the
Secretary of State to constitute the new force. The act made the
Metropolitan Police possible; it was left to the Home Secretary to
establish its character.

The first and crucial task was the selection of the men who would
have to organise and lead the new force. For the senior of his two
directing magistrates, who became known almost at once as Commissioners, Peel after careful enquiry chose Colonel Charles Rowan, a
retired officer of forty-six who had served in the Peninsula and at
Waterloo. He was a product of Sir John Moore's enlightened training
methods and as colonel of the 52nd had brought his regiment to the
highest pitch of efficiency. As his civilian colleague he appointed
Richard Mayne, a young Irish barrister thirteen years his junior. The

two Commissioners, deliberately selected for their complementary qualities, proved an admirable team. Rowan's tact, imperturbability, and professional competence was the foundation of the partnership; but in Mayne he had a colleague of marked intellectual powers and business skill. Within a fortnight Rowan and Mayne produced a draft establishment for a body of over 1,000 men and during the summer the details of the organisation were worked out with the Home Secretary. It was decided to enforce the wearing of uniform and a handbook of general instructions was drawn up for Peel's scrutiny. The first instruction, 'that a principal object to be attained is the prevention of crime', embodied Colquhoun's classic doctrine; and constables were further enjoined to be 'civil and attentive' in all their dealings with the public. In Peel's new police the tests of efficiency were from the start the prevention of wrongdoing and good public relations.

On the evening of 29 September 1829 Londoners saw the new Metropolitan Police, in their blue uniforms and iron-framed top hats, on their beats for the first time. They were inevitably objects of interest and, with some sections of the public, of outright hostility. But a month's experience of their conduct drew a gratifying compliment from that iron disciplinarian, the Duke of Wellington. 'I congratulate you', he wrote to Peel on 3 November, 'upon the entire success of the police in London. It is impossible to see anything more respectable than they are.' Though Peel was unable to carry out the national plan of police reform which he clearly had in view, the Metropolitan Police he created at least served as a model and a recruiting ground for the borough and county police forces gradually built up in the next quarter of a century. Once the early difficulties and unpopularity were over, the respect and trust which the London police won from the public was proof of the value of the 'preventive' principle just as the nickname of 'Bobby' or 'Peeler' was a tribute to the man who was the founder of the force. From being a hated and 'un-English' importation, the Bobby on the beat by the early Victorian period had been accepted half-humorously, half-affectionately, as a British institution, an instantly identifiable figure in the mythology of popular jokes, cartoons, and street ballads. Peel himself had by this time become a cartoonist's subject, frequently and inevitably depicted during the next few years wearing policeman's uniform with belt and truncheon. By 1830 the Home Secretary had emerged as a public figure in his own right, a central character in innumerable political sketches and caricatures familiar to a wider cross-section of the population than that which read the columns of *Hansard* or *The Times*, and almost always portrayed as 'gay, handsome and likeable'.

Chapter 9

Catholic emancipation

The Irish executive at the start of Peel's second term of office as Home Secretary was largely a legacy from Canning's short ministry. Anglesey the Lord-Lieutenant, Lamb the Chief Secretary, Doherty the Solicitor-General, were all 'liberals' and their retention in office could hardly have been a better advertisement for the intention of the Wellington ministry to pursue a balanced and moderate policy. Anglesey, a professional soldier of sixty who had been Master-General of the Ordnance under Canning and Goderich, was almost as sympathetic to Catholic claims as Wellesley, though in politics he was as impetuous and naive as his predecessor had been cautious and irresolute. Lamb, besides being a 'Catholic', had Whig as well as Tory connections. Of his young, aristocratic, easy-going Chief Secretary, Peel was inclined to think well. Anglesey was a more difficult colleague. He found it hard to think of the ministry as a party to which he himself belonged; he was conscious of a large gap between his attitude to Irish affairs and that of Peel and Wellington. From the start he tended to regard Ireland as a kind of separate command which he had to protect against the distant civilians in London.

On the advice of the Irish government the act of 1825, which had been unsuccessful in its principal object of suppressing the Catholic Association, was allowed to lapse, and in May 1828 Anglesey wrote to Peel that 'Ireland is, I believe, now in a state of balance and a very little bad or a very little good management may turn it either way'.

The proposals he put forward were the not unfamiliar devices of an extensive programme of public works and direct assistance to industry. Peel replied temperately and even authorised an immediate grant of £10,000 for road-building in Tipperary. But he pointed out the problems involved in any large-scale intervention which involved expenditure of public money, and he detailed the considerable efforts already made by government to assist the Irish economy. Anglesey, like some other governors of Ireland, was apt to assume that until his arrival no one had properly understood or tried to solve Ireland's multifarious problems. Part of the Home Secretary's business was to preserve some kind of balance in the handling of Irish affairs. England might have done more for Ireland; it was patently untrue that she had done nothing.

While this correspondence was going on events at Westminster had already put Anglesey's relations with the ministry under strain. In May the indefatigable Burdett once more moved for a final and conciliatory adjustment of the laws affecting Roman Catholics. After a debate in which speakers could do no more, as Peel observed when making his own contribution, than repeat 'to a reluctant audience topics and arguments which had been argued almost to satiety', the motion passed the Commons by six votes, thus narrowly reversing the equally narrow defeat of the previous year. In the House of Lords a similar motion was lost by forty-four votes; but more important than the division figures was the speech made by Wellington. It was the first time he had spoken at length on the subject as prime minister and he based his opposition to the motion entirely on grounds of expediency. If concessions were to be made, he said, he would wish to see real securities. Though the kind of concordat with the Pope secured by many European heads of state was out of the question for a British government, perhaps other kinds of safeguard could be devised. If the difficulties of the question were not aggravated by public discussion, it might prove possible to do something. Though the division in the Lords recorded a technical victory for the Protestants, after the prime minister's words it needed no special perspicacity to believe it would be the last.

Wellington's speech was given in June, a fortnight after the retirement of Huskisson and his followers. These were not the only resignations which had been meditated. When the House of Commons early in May had carried Burdett's motion, Peel's instinct, as in 1825, was to abandon office. Now that he was Leader of the House, he had even more reason to regard his position as untenable. Not only numbers but talent and most of the younger generation in the Commons were against him. In little over a week, however, the cabinet was unexpectedly plunged into the East Retford crisis. For Peel to have insisted on resignation, when the Canningites were walking out on a totally different issue, would have been both egotistic and irresponsible. It might have brought about the collapse of the government at a time when it was immensely difficult to form any ministry at all; and at best it would have left Wellington's administration crippled and ineffective. Nevertheless, in the interval between the Catholic debates in the Lower and Upper Houses, he made it clear to the prime minister that his retirement could not be indefinitely delayed; and in those circumstances he urged the duke, who was less committed than himself on the issue, not to say anything in his speech which would prevent him from trying during the summer recess to find a final solution to the Catholic problem. This advice Wellington had clearly followed when he came to make his own statement in the Lords. It was the first step on the road to Catholic emancipation; and it followed logically that Peel's tenure of office was now only provisional. For himself, as minister if not as private politician, he regarded the battle as already lost. With the waning year after year of the Protestant cause, with the new parliament now committed, the cabinet divided, and Ireland a prey to agitators, Peel had come to the conclusion that it was no longer in the interests of the country for the stalemate to continue.

Meanwhile there was the short-term policy to be considered. The

Huskissonite secession had cracked not only the cabinet but, in his own special sphere of responsibility, the structure of the Irish executive. To fill the post of Chief Secretary left vacant by Lamb's resignation, the prime minister chose Francis Leveson-Gower, a son of the Marquess of Stafford. Though, like his predecessor, he was a 'Catholic', Anglesey would have preferred an older and more experienced man; and he accepted the new appointment with a minimum of grace. His real objection perhaps was that Leveson-Gower was a follower of Wellington. The sudden exit of the Canningites had made Anglesey suspect a plot by the prime minister to get rid of all his unwelcome liberal colleagues and he felt in consequence more isolated than ever from his official masters in London. Not unnaturally but highly unwisely, he turned to friends outside the government. In the last week of May he was asking Lord Holland to advise him whether he could remain at his post with satisfaction to himself and advantage to Ireland. Since the government had assured him that no change in Irish policy was contemplated, Anglesey had no tangible excuse for giving up the Lord-Lieutenancy. Nevertheless the events of May had destroyed his last remnant of confidence in the ministers and led him into a relationship with members of the opposition which steadily eroded his sense of responsibility to the cabinet of which he was the political servant. From June 1828 Anglesey's real views were contained less in his despatches to the government than in the secret and extraordinary confidential correspondence he carried on with Lord Holland, one of the most influential members of the Whig party.

If from folly rather than knavery Anglesey was thus something less than a reliable agent of government, the new Chief Secretary himself was not among the more distinguished holders of that difficult office. A well-connected, pleasant young man with mild literary pretensions, Francis Leveson-Gower had a great deal to learn and little time in which to do so. Even with Goulburn, an older and more experienced man, Peel had gone to great pains to give encouragement and support. With Leveson-Gower he redoubled his care and consideration. The new Chief Secretary was at least a diligent writer and the two men remained in close contact all through the disturbed autumn of 1828. Even when Leveson-Gower, with a year's experience of office behind him, returned to Dublin at the end of the 1829 session, a voluminous correspondence was carried on between them. Peel himself was conscious of the unusual degree of supervision he was giving to his junior. No amount of supervision, however, could disguise the fact that the cabinet was unable to lean with much confidence on the judgement of their colleagues in Ireland. Wellington had to face the critical summer of 1828 with an inexperienced Chief Secretary, an alienated Lord-Lieutenant, and a Home Secretary who was contemplating an early departure from office.

II

Under the friendly administrations of Canning and Goderich, the Catholic leaders in Ireland had been content to lie on their oars and await events. The appointment of Wellington acted as an immediate spur to action. January 1828 saw meetings in two-thirds of the Irish parishes and O'Connell's claim to be master of the Irish peasantry seemed not far short of the truth. Though in private he was sometimes uneasy at the forces he had conjured up from the depth of Irish society, he could not resist the temptation of brandishing the threat of physical violence against an English government headed by a professional soldier. The known sympathies of the Lord-Lieutenant, the success of Burdett's motion in the House of Commons, the expiry of the 1825 act, all encouraged him to drive forward while popular feeling and clerical support were at their height.

From this situation came the desperate decision to stand himself as candidate against Vesey Fitzgerald, whose appointment as President of the Board of Trade in place of Grant had necessitated a by-election in his constituency of co.Clare. As a good landlord, a 'Catholic' and a friend of the Roman hierarchy, Fitzgerald against any other opponent would have carried the election with ease. Against the great agitator he collected less than a third of the votes, and was amazed he did so well. He polled the gentry, the more important freeholders, and his own tenants. The mass of the peasantry, in a striking display of order, discipline and loyalty, voted for O'Connell. 'The organisation exhibited is so complete and so formidable,' wrote Fitzgerald to Peel, 'that no man can contemplate without alarm what is to follow in this wretched country.' It was not merely that the Anglo-Irish landowners had once more been defeated by the political alliance of the Catholic Church and the Catholic Association; or that a popular, resident, emancipationist candidate had been beaten by a Catholic lawyer from co.Kerry who could not even take his seat in parliament if elected. The very strength of Fitzgerald's position had prompted the Association to a feat which until then had never come within range of its ambition. From using the representative system to secure the return of candidates favourable to emancipation, it had passed almost without design to an attack on the actual system itself. What had been done in co.Clare could be repeated at the next election on a national scale. English laws prevented Roman Catholics from sitting in parliament; Irish agitation could now ensure that in a score of counties only Roman Catholics could be elected. Within the legal structure of the constitution there was to be a revolutionary clash of wills; and it could not be assumed that the consequences would remain entirely legal.

For Peel the result of the Clare election meant that the government had come to the cross-road of decision. One way led to deepening disorder with no likelihood that the House of Commons would sanction effective means of repression; the other to concession. In Ireland the Lord-Lieutenant had come to the same conclusion. Though he realised that he had over-estimated his influence with the Catholic party and that O'Connell represented a more formidable danger than he had been prepared to admit, he felt that a solution of the Catholic question had now been brought a stage nearer. In a letter to his Chief Secretary in London he emphasised the enormous power in the hands of the agitators—'I am quite certain they could lead on the people to open rebellion at a moment's notice'—the impossibility of suppressing the movement, and the consequent necessity of conceding Catholic emancipation. The embarrassed Leveson-Gower was charged with the responsibility of transmitting these views to the cabinet. It was clearly impossible for them, however, to give any reply to this clumsy incursion of the Lord-Lieutenant into the realms of high policy. No decision of the kind Anglesey wanted could be taken before the end of the session and for the moment the cabinet preferred even to leave O'Connell's parliamentary status undecided rather than raise the issue in the House of Commons.

Immediately after the close of session Wellington and Peel had a number of private discussions on the course to be adopted. By this time Peel had made up his mind not only to resign, but to place on record before leaving office his deliberate conviction that the cabinet should take the Catholic question into consideration during the summer and offer its advice to the Crown as on any other important matter. He also resolved to state his firm view that there would be less danger in attempting to solve the problem by way of concession than in continuing to resist a settlement. When he went off to Brighton with Julia early in August it was agreed that the prime minister should send him a copy of a memorandum he was preparing for the king on the subject and that Peel should put his own views into writing in reply.

Wellington's memorandum to the king, dated 1 August, was brutally explicit. He said that rebellion was pending in Ireland; that in England the government was faced with a House of Commons it dared not dissolve which contained a majority who believed the only solution was Catholic emancipation; and finally that he wished to have permission to consult Peel and the Lord Chancellor. On 9 August he sent Peel copies of his correspondence with the king and the Lord Chancellor, together with a memorandum of his own, outlining a scheme of settlement. Two days later Peel sent back a formal statement of his own views contained in two documents. The first dealt with general principles. While Peel had not changed fundamentally his conviction of the danger of emancipation, he argued now that it was a choice of evils. Given the divided state of the legislature and the menacing situation in Ireland, there seemed a balance of advantage for the government in endeavouring to find a solution of the problem rather than letting it continue as an open question. He did not think it would be conducive to a settlement for the conduct of the measure to be in his own hands but he was prepared to assist out of office in conciliating Protestant opinion and ensuring a good majority for the government's proposals. He would therefore retire as soon as a time was suitable.

His second memorandum dealt with the specific plan that had been put forward by the prime minister. The three principal suggestions made by Wellington were that the laws excluding Roman Catholics from parliament should not be repealed but annually suspended; that the Irish county franchise should be raised; and that the Irish Roman clergy should be paid by the state and debarred from exercising their spiritual functions without royal licence. On the first Peel's comment was that any settlement put forward by the government must be final and comprehensive; partial concession would merely give Roman Catholics power without satisfaction. He argued therefore for full equality of political rights, with perhaps exclusion from certain specified offices or a limitation on the total number of Roman Catholics in parliament. He approved a limitation of the franchise, though he wanted a more accurate assessment of the actual effect of any technical alteration. He criticised strongly, however, the proposals for the clergy. To pay their stipends would arouse the jealousy and opposition of Protestant dissenters and British tax-payers; a licensing system might easily degenerate into a mere formality, offering no real control. Both devices would in effect recognise the authority, not merely of the Roman Church in Ireland, but of the Papal See.

There for the time being the matter rested. It was not until September that he was able to have any private discussion with Wellington and Lyndhurst; and even then the talk revolved mainly round Peel's personal position. Wellington wanted him to tell the king that he advised a settlement even though he could not be an official party to it. Peel, on the other hand, extracted a promise from his colleagues not to reveal in advance that he would support the measure in parliament. In October he went off for a semi-public visit to Lancashire during which, with an irony of which he could scarcely have been unconscious, he was dined and toasted by the Lancashire gentry and manufacturers as the great Protestant minister. All this time no progress was made in the grand design. The chief obstacle was the king, since nothing could be said in cabinet until his permission had been received. George, ill with gout, deadened with laudanum, and besieged with stout Protestant letters from his brother the Duke of Cumberland, was in no state to make a decision. On 10 October the prime minister at last had an interview with him, but one in which the king did all the talking. Among other propositions he put forward were the recall of Anglesey from Ireland, the return of Lord Eldon to the cabinet, the dissolution of parliament and an appeal to the Protestant feeling of the country. Unable to get a hearing for his own views, the Duke subsequently put them down in writing. But apart from countering the king's proposals, all he could do was to repeat the arguments of August. The autumn months of 1828, which Peel had hoped would bring a decision, ran to waste in the presence of a sick, uneasy and querulous monarch.

Meanwhile the situation in Ireland steadily deteriorated. The Association had continued to hold mass meetings during the summer and by the autumn the peasants themselves were coming together in great assemblages, organised in semi-military fashion, with banners, music, green sashes and cockades. Though the actual disorder was relatively slight, there was a growing sense of insecurity among the Irish Protestants and mounting anger in Ulster, where the agitation of the Association was answered by the formation of Brunswick Clubs led by the Protestant gentry and clergy. The continued maintenance of peace and order in Ireland seemed to depend less on the normal controls of government than on a dangerous tension of social, religious and political forces which could hardly be sustained indefinitely. The passivity of the Irish executive merely heightened the widespread feeling of crisis.

In this highly charged atmosphere the Lord-Lieutenant was caught between two impulses which a far more skilful politician would have found difficult to reconcile. He wanted to persuade the cabinet that the dangerous state of Ireland made a settlement imperative; he also wished to avoid any repressive action which would appear to be aimed at the Catholic movement. In consequence his letters had an ambiguity which further discredited his influence. Though his Chief Secretary took a more direct view of the dangers of the situation, it was evident that Anglesey was not disposed to interfere. For Peel the policy of non-intervention had few attractions and in September he conveyed to Anglesey his strong conviction that the government ought to put a stop to the mass meetings. Belatedly coming to the same conclusion, the Lord-Lieutenant made up his mind to ban further meetings by proclamation and asked simultaneously for immediate military reinforcements. To a certain extent the edge was taken off his action by the tactics of the Catholic Association which called for an end to the disturbances and invoked the aid of O'Connell and the Catholic priesthood in preserving order. But Peel was not prepared to leave the responsibility for the peace of Ireland in the hands of agitators and throughout the autumn he continued to urge strong, impartial and unflagging action on the part of the Irish executive.

The Lord-Lieutenant concurred only half-heartedly in the spirited policy forced on him and did what he could to minimise its effects. In private he complained to Lord Holland that the ministers were keeping him in utter ignorance of their intentions and lacked the courage either to approve or disapprove his actions. In view of the delicate position with the king, however, it was not possible for Wellington and Peel to take him into their confidence even if they had felt able to trust in his discretion. 'Under any circumstances', Peel wrote dryly to the duke in September, 'I should doubt the policy of communicating now to Lord Anglesey the resolution of the Government, supposing a resolution to have been formed.' As autumn turned into winter, relations between the Lord-Lieutenant and his government came under increasing strain. All they asked, all they wanted, was that he should preserve order. But Anglesey, convinced of his ability to settle Irish troubles, could not refrain from gestures of sympathy with the Catholic cause which to the ministers and to many Irish Protestants were incompatible with executive impartiality. At the end of December the cabinet came to the conclusion that he must be relieved of his office.

Before Anglesey left Ireland he and Wellington were involved in one final piece of publicity which must have raised serious doubts in Peel's mind of the aptitude of the military mind for the conduct of politics. Earlier in the month Wellington had written to Dr Curtis, the Roman Catholic Archbishop of Armagh, an old friend and correspondent since his Peninsular days, giving his views on the Catholic question. Curtis passed the letter round his domestic circle and inevitably a copy found its way into the Irish press. In it the prime minister said no more than he had stated publicly in the House of Lords; the significance lay in the recipient. Wellington had a right to complain of violation of confidence; but only a very guileless politician would have assumed that such a letter in Ireland would remain secret. Anglesey then took a hand in this disastrous epistolary game with the Roman ecclesiastics. Having obtained a copy of the duke's letter from Curtis, he returned it to the Archbishop with an expression of regret that the issue was not to be settled in the forthcoming parliamentary session; but added that he was glad that the duke was not wholly against a solution and advised the Catholics in Ireland to propitiate him by every means in their power and throw no obstacles in his path. When rumours of the Lord-Lieutenant's recall began to circulate, Anglesey, allegedly to allay any uneasiness at his sudden departure, authorised the publication of his letter in the Dublin press. Informed by Leveson-Gower of this final indiscretion, the Home Secretary replied with pardonable irony.

> I was surprised, I confess, by Lord A's letter to Dr Curtis but I should not be justly repaying the confidence with which you have written to me respecting it, if I did not add that I was almost as much surprised when I read for the first time in its printed form the Duke's letter to the same Reverend Divine.

The effect on the cabinet was decisive. On 10 January Peel despatched a letter to the Lord-Lieutenant instructing him to quit Ireland immediately.

III

By January 1829 the margin of time for the government was rapidly disappearing. The king, in response to a request by Wellington in November, had allowed him to confer with the heads of the Church of England on the emancipation issue but showed no sign of being converted himself. The bishops themselves, led by the Archbishop of Canterbury, were almost without exception against concession; and the dismissal of Anglesey made it obvious to the public that there had been a serious divergence of opinion within the government. What Peel feared was that the king, encouraged by the bishops' intransigence, would make some public utterance which would commit him to total resistance. Even the duke began to despair of success and he was not a man who easily envisaged defeat. In Peel's view, however, if the Catholic question was to be settled, only the duke could do it. With Canning dead and Goderich discredited, the only conceivable alternative minister was Grey; and it would have taken a prolonged and bitter political battle to force him into office against the known personal hostility of the king. Even if he became prime minister Peel did not believe that Grey could succeed where Wellington had failed. The choice was Wellington or nothing; and, as at Waterloo fourteen years earlier, the duke was in need of all the reinforcements which could be brought to the field of action.

With these considerations in mind Peel came to one of the crucial decisions of his career. On 12 January he wrote to Wellington that if his resignation would, in the duke's opinion, make it impossible to carry emancipation, he was prepared to stay in office. With the letter he enclosed a long memorandum on the Catholic question to be laid before the king. The whole position was now unblocked. The duke presented Peel's memorandum to George on 14 January. The following day all those members of the cabinet who had previously opposed emancipation had separate interviews with the king at Windsor. All of them expressed the opinion that the government must take the Catholic question into consideration. The last resistance in Peel's mind to his own participation in the settlement was destroyed, unexpectedly and curiously, by George himself. The king, forced now towards a decision from which he inwardly recoiled, turned the tables on his Home Secretary by demanding why, if he approved the measure, he would not make the same sacrifice which he wished the king to make by remaining in office to carry out the policy which he himself advised. To this there could be only one answer.

Following this demonstration of cabinet solidarity, the king reluctantly gave permission for them to consider the question though he insisted that he would not necessarily feel bound to act on their advice. There remained only the question of Peel's future and this was settled at an oddly formal interview on 17 January. On that day Wellington came to Whitehall Gardens bringing with him a letter in which he stated that he saw no chance of overcoming his difficulties unless Peel remained in office. Peel read it in his presence and told him at once that he was ready to stay and bring forward the government's proposals in parliament. His decision was cordially received by the cabinet and some at least of its members were impressed by the courage it displayed. Two of them, Bathurst and Ellenborough, wrote to Peel afterwards to express their admiration. For Peel himself, now that his personal Rubicon had been crossed, the decision brought its own form of relief. He always preferred the role of actor to that of spectator; and the new responsibilities and dangers involved aroused all his native spirit and resolution.

His proposal to resign had been serious. As late as 12 January he had renewed his offer and repeated his conviction that he was not the person to whom the conduct of the Catholic bill should be entrusted. But the five months' delay had itself become an ingredient in the situation. He had shared all Wellington's problems; he had given prolonged thought to the technical problems involved in settling Catholic claims; and he agreed with the prime minister that a solution must be found. From being a consenting colleague he had become almost a committed partner. His final decision must have been reached after a long period of reflection; and in the last resort the personal appeal for his support from a prime minister whom he deeply respected was one which a man of Peel's temperament must have found peculiarly hard to resist. In the hard game of politics, where actions are more easily understood than motives, this strong strain of loyalty in Peel's nature was not always an advantage. Nevertheless, the die was cast and there was little opportunity for afterthoughts. Much had to be done; and they did not have much time in which to do it.

To be exact, they had eighteen days. In that time they had to prepare the king's speech, decide in principle on a measure to end the Catholic question, and secure the king's consent. Of the extent to which the prime minister was relying on Peel's intellectual preparedness there was immediate proof. On 17 January, the first occasion on which the cabinet formally discussed the problem, Peel drew up a memorandum for his colleagues defining and analysing the issues involved. From 18 to 26 January there were almost daily meetings to work out both policy and detail. Some aspects, such as the county franchise, were referred to specialist committees; but it was in the cabinet that the crucial decisions had to be taken. The main differences of opinion came over Wellington's proposals for the Irish clergy. It was clear that Peel's attitude had hardened since the summer and it was significant that he put forward no draft to the cabinet on this aspect of the question. Instead he strongly advised his colleagues not to risk failure on the main measures of relief and disfranchisement by adding to them legislation to regulate relations with the Roman Church or the Irish clergy. In fact, the more closely the cabinet examined the technicalities of such legislation, the more they were impressed by its difficulties. In the end Wellington and Ellenborough, his chief supporter, yielded to the majority. On this, as on every important feature of the proposed measure, Peel's view prevailed.

Meanwhile the last days of the great secret were running out. On 4 February Peel gave the customary eve of session dinner to the principal government supporters in the House of Commons at which the king's speech was read out. It was not a lively occasion. Croker was told that some of them had refused to believe in Peel's 'conversion' until they actually heard him read the speech. A similar atmosphere of stunned shock was detectable next day in the Commons. There was a full House which quickly thinned and the applause came mainly from the opposition. Ellenborough had advised Peel to speak early in the debate and to take a high line. Certainly there was nothing lacking in either frankness or firmness in what he said. Even so, he had to meet the reproaches of some of his former supporters and his own circle of friends was already giving him a foretaste of the public reaction. His old mentor Lloyd, now Bishop of Oxford, though aware in general terms of the government's policy, was distressed and anxious at Peel's decision to remain in office. Croker told Peel that the greatest surprise would be not that Catholic emancipation was to be conceded at last but that he was to be its prime mover. Gregory, whom Peel had told privately in advance, wrote back in shock and dismay. 'Your letter has overwhelmed me.' His father, though sympathetic and affectionate, warned him that concession would only encourage resistance. From his relative and fellow-sportsman, Colonel Jonathan Peel, he learned of the astonishment and indignation occasioned in Bolton and Manchester. Meanwhile in newspapers and clubs the wits were getting to work. A new festival, it was reported, had been inserted in the calendar by the Pope: the Feast of St Peel. The Home Secretary, it was said, was now regarded so sourly by his former supporters that instead of Orange he had become Lemon Peel. The cartoonists showed Wellington and Peel with rosaries in their hands, kissing the Pope's toe. Even the Whigs, bound in consistency to support the government's measure, had reservations about Peel's personal position. Lord John Russell and others were inclined to believe that Peel must have held similar views on the need for concession when he made the Catholic question his ostensible reason for separating from Canning in 1827. More ominous still were early signs of disaffection among government members. Some resigned at once; others declared they could no longer give the ministry their confidence; and there was unusual difficulty in finding candidates for minor vacancies.

In the middle of this gathering storm came the first great measure foreshadowed in the king's speech, the bill to suppress the Catholic Association. There was little interest in the bill itself. The ultra-Tories could not oppose and the emancipationists accepted it as a necessary preliminary to relief. But the debate brought up the wider issue and more personal attacks were launched on Peel from his own side of the House. By 5 March, when the bill became law, he had suffered another blow; he had ceased to be member for Oxford University. At the end of January he had informed the Dean of Christ Church of his decision to remain in office and bring forward a bill for Catholic relief, and offered to tender his resignation if the feeling in the university required it. The conditional offer merely embarrassed the college and on 5 February, therefore, Peel sent a formal letter of resignation to the Vice-Chancellor, merely asking when it would be convenient for his resignation to take effect. Opinion in Oxford was divided and in any case it was not clear whether Peel wished to stand for re-election. Outwardly he professed indifference. 'In very homely phrase,' he wrote to Lloyd, 'I say to you (what I could not say to anyone else) I care very little about the matter.' But he allowed his name to go forward and it is hard to doubt that he would have been glad to receive a mark of confidence which his pride prevented him from soliciting. Lloyd, through delay and timidity, failed to mobilise the undoubted feeling of Christ Church in favour of renomination; and a powerful opposition party emerged elsewhere in the university in support of a rival candidate, Sir Robert Inglis. Though a liberal committee was eventually formed under the Warden of Merton College to promote Peel's election, the effort came too late. At the poll which took place at the end of February, Peel was beaten by 609 votes to 755. His supporters included the cream of the university: a majority of men with first-class degrees, professors, prizemen, M.P.s, noblemen and fellows of the more distinguished colleges. But a phalanx of lesser voters, including what Greville described as an immense number of parsons, made up in numbers what they lacked in quality.

It was clear to observers that the election had been mismanaged from start to finish. Peel's pride and Lloyd's irresolution between them had thrown away an excellent chance of securing an unopposed return. But whatever his private feelings, Peel took his defeat with outward calm. Ellenborough, who was not an uncritical colleague, wrote in his diary that 'really I must confess that he has shown himself *a great man* by his equanimity in all that has taken place'. Since he could not afford to be out of parliament a day longer than was necessary, a seat was obtained for him, through the agency of the party managers, from Sir Manasseh Lopez, a Spanish Jew of doubtful electoral antecedents, who vacated his pocket borough of Westbury. It was not an edifying transaction and was made worse by the rowdy scenes on election day in the normally sleepy little Wiltshire town where Protestant feeling had been roused to a pitch of violence.

In the interval the cabinet had proceeded with its preparation of the two main Catholic bills and as soon as Peel resumed his place in the Commons, he gave notice of the government measure to remove Catholic disabilities. At this point opposition from the king threatened to destroy the whole programme. Influenced partly by the Duke of Cumberland, who had returned to England to stiffen his volatile and irresolute brother, George at the beginning of March showed alarming signs of returning to his previous uncompromising Protestant standpoint. After hearing reports from Wellington and Lyndhurst the cabinet concluded that it was impossible for them to continue without written authority. A note was therefore drafted by Peel to the effect that the ministers could not advise the king to consent to the bill for suppressing the Catholic Association unless he continued to approve their general policy and was prepared to give them his full confidence and support. Two days later Wellington, Peel and Lyndhurst were summoned to Windsor to explain the emancipation bill in detail. In the course of a four-hour interview the king, nervous, anxious and continuously imbibing brandy and water, informed them that he could not agree to a change in the ancient Oath of Supremacy (which was one of the provisions in the bill) and his consent to the measure must therefore be withdrawn. He asked what their attitude would be in those circumstances. Headed by Peel the three ministers answered in turn that their only course must be immediate resignation. Arriving back late at night they broke in on a cabinet dinner at Lord Bathurst's house and told their colleagues that they were all out. The cabinet was annoyed rather than distressed since it was obvious that the king would be unable to find an alternative ministry. In fact at that moment George was already writing to Wellington to say that he had decided to give way. The crisis was over; and a letter carefully concocted by Peel and Wellington defined the king's consent in a way which made it impossible for him to retreat once more.

A few hours later, on 5 March, Peel rose in the Commons to move for a committee of the whole House to consider Roman Catholic disabilities. The chamber was packed. It was by common consent a great parliamentary occasion and Peel rose to it superbly, making what was generally acknowledged to be one of the best speeches he had ever delivered. He made it clear at the outset that he was yielding to a 'moral necessity'. In both government and parliament the Catholic questions had created a long-standing schism that had its origin as far back as 1794. The inability to sustain the Protestant cause was not personal but public: a failure of will on the part of both parliament and people. In Ireland the passage of one repressive law after another had shown that the agitation for emancipation could not be solved by statutory means. If coercion was out of the question, there remained only one alternative, concession It was a question not of right but of expediency; not of what was desirable, but what was possible. What he demonstrated was that the government was in a position from which there was no escape. After dealing with the details of the bill—the admission of Catholics to parliament and to all but a handful of public offices, the new oath of loyalty, the deliberate omission of any form of control over Roman Catholic ecclesiastical appointments—he ended with an appeal for charity and conciliation. The settlement would give as much security to the Protestant establishment and interest as was possible in existing circumstances. If it failed to end agitation, the contest would be 'for other objects and with other arms. The struggle will be, not for the abolition of civil distinctions, but for the predominance of an intolerant religion.'

The speech took over four hours to deliver and was listened to with deep attention punctuated only by bursts of applause. When he sat down a long roll of cheering went up that was heard as far away as Westminster Bridge It was a parliamentary triumph and within forty-eight hours, when the press had brought the text to towns and villages all over England, it was a national triumph as well. At Drayton Manor Peel's brother-in-law, Dean Cockburn, read the speech aloud after dinner and as the old baronet listened he interrupted with characteristic ejaculations—'Robin's the lad after all', 'no administration can stand in this country without him', 'the Duke could do nothing without him', 'those gentlemen, the Whigs, have no chance of getting in while Robert lives'. But though Sir Robert could allow his fatherly pride to carry him away, others had different feelings. As they listened to the lucid and powerful flow of his argument in the Commons or read the speech next day in the columns of *The Times*, men had almost forcibly to remind themselves that this was Peel, the great Protestant champion, who was speaking. The immediate impact of the speech soon diminished; and as it did, the memory of his previous attitude returned with increasing force. Peel's triumph was achieved at a price; and the price had still to be paid. In one sense he went on paying it for the rest of his life.

When the House by a two to one majority voted to go into committee, over thirty usual government supporters were found in the minority; and in the debate on the bill proper some of the ultra-Tory members launched personal attacks on the ministers. Sadler repeated the sneer that the men who had deserted Canning in 1827, and joined in hunting him to death, had been moved by anything but principle. Wetherell, though still holding office as Attorney-General, delivered a coarse and savage attack on his colleagues for their 'miserable, contemptible apostacy'. Peel answered Wetherell himself and though in a temper, controlled his feelings admirably. After dealing with his opponents, he ended with a generous ascription to others of the credit for emancipation; to Fox, Grattan, Plunket and Canning, that 'illustrious and right hon. friend of mine who is now no more'. Despite the rancorous passions exhibited in the Commons, the solid voting strength of the House was with the government. At the end of March both the emancipation and the disfranchisement bill passed their third readings with massive majorities.

To the end the Protestant party fought desperately and bitterly for their lost cause; and their savage denunciations in the Commons only reflected the equally violent feeling without. The ultra-Protestants who had feared the worst seemed vindicated; those who had trusted Wellington and Peel not to leave them entirely defenceless felt abandoned. Their mortification was expressed in every shade of emotion from sad elegies on the destruction of the old constitution to gross personal abuse of the two ministers chiefly responsible. Vicious as some of the passions raised by the 1829 crisis were, the intensity of Protestant feeling was understandable. Though liberals regarded emancipation as a long-delayed measure of social justice, the Protestants saw in it the overthrow of one of the principles on which the constitution rested. There at least their instinct was right. The act of 1829 was a sentence of death on the Anglican settlement made in 1689. The repeal of the Test and Corporation Acts the previous year was by comparison of secondary importance Not only were they for most purposes already obsolete, but Protestant nonconformists could be regarded in some sort as members, if dissenting members, of the Established Church. The Catholic Emancipation Act made a fundamental change and a deliberate revolution. Consciously and rightly the Protestant party felt that the country had come to an end of a long historic period; and they could only look with foreboding to the future. In whatever form emancipation had come, it would have left bitterness. That it was forced on them by their own leaders was the final insult.

Their anger and resentment was concentrated almost entirely on Peel. This was natural. Not only had he played the leading part in conducting the bill through parliament but the reputation he had won by his previous opposition made his 'recantation' even more inexplicable. The idolised champion of the Protestant party was now its betrayer. Even though some of them gave him credit for honesty of motive and unselfishness of action, they could still only regard what he had done as desertion. And desertion, on such an issue and after so many years of leadership, brought with it suspicions of Peel's character and temperament that had never occurred to any one before. Perhaps the hardest punishment for so proud a man to bear was not the bitter disappointment of his followers but the damage to his own reputation which was its permanent legacy. It was a change of feeling which he could not only hear in speeches and read in the press but encounter among his closest friends. Months passed before his change of opinion ceased to be a topic of conversation; and even when other matters drove it from men's minds, they never forgot. He had given a hostage to fortune; and it was irredeemable.

At the time the main charges against Peel were that he changed his mind when he did, and that he did not change it earlier. On the surface both are easy to refute. Yet behind the unreflecting personal rancour of dull men like Knatchbull and violent men like Wetherell, there was a real case which Greville later expressed in more temperate language. It was that for fourteen years Peel had led the Protestant party against a host of abler men, and that by his personal efforts he had prolonged a hopeless contest which by reason of its prolongation had brought the country at last to the brink of civil war. 'I do not see how he can be acquitted of insincerity,' Greville wrote long afterwards, 'save at the expense of his sagacity and foresight.' If this was the charge, it was one which the accused, with unwitting anticipation of the exact phrase used by the diarist, himself acknowledged in the account of these years which he wrote towards the end of his life.

If it had been alleged against me that the sudden adoption of a different policy had proved the want of early sagacity and foresight on my part—if the charge had been that I had adhered with too much pertinacy to a hopeless cause—that I had permitted for too long a period the engagements of party or undue deference to the wishes of constituents to outweigh the accumulating evidence of an approaching necessity—if this had been the accusation against me, I might find it more difficult to give a complete and decisive refutation.

The case against Peel was not so much lack of prescience perhaps as delay in accepting the inevitable.

But politics is not merely an exercise in prevision. A politician is a creature of his time and a combatant in the struggles which it is his duty to resolve. The cause for which Peel stood was lost in the end, but it would be a cynicism to require men to abstain from conflict unless they are on the winning side. Though Peel was finally converted to the necessity of emancipation, he was never persuaded of its desirability. It was not that he had changed his essential views, but that when weighed against the situation in 1828, those views no longer tilted the balance. The process was one of political not intellectual conversion: a not uncommon event in politics. It is probable that, despite the Anglican bias of his family, school and university, Peel would have accepted emancipation for English Catholics, as for Protestant Dissenters. The stumbling-block was Ireland. It was this which for him, as for countless others, transformed the Catholic question from an academic controversy into an issue of national importance. In essence that problem was what it had always been; a question of the unity and security of the British Isles. Since the Battle of the Boyne the Anglo-Irish connection had rested on a Protestant foundation. Pitt's Act of Union had only been a particular measure to tighten that connection at a time of great danger. What haunted Peel was the fear that concessions on religion would lead to other demands and those in the end to disruption and independence. Of the artificial nature of the Union and the abuses by Protestants to which it had led, he had no need to be persuaded. It was, as he said in 1821, a choice of evils; and if he could have convinced himself that concession would lead to peace and unity, he would have abandoned the contest. But he was not so convinced; and he was forced back on the lesser of the two evils, the continuation of the Union on a Protestant footing and the hope that by patient administration remedies could be found for the many Irish problems which had little or nothing to do with Catholic grievances. He misjudged the situation. The power of the Catholic Association advanced faster and further than he had anticipated; and divided counsels in the government made a firm, consistent Irish policy almost impossible. But he had not totally misjudged it; and in the course of the next ninety years all his ultimate fears for the Church of Ireland, the Anglo-Irish landowners, and the Union itself, were to be vindicated.

In the context of his own career it was a question not of misjudgement but of being trapped in a slowly tightening web of circumstances. Certainly he never thought he would be placed in a situation which required him to be the author and parliamentary sponsor of a bill for Catholic emancipation. But from 1819 onward, if not 1817, he realised that the tide of public opinion was turning against the Protestant party; and by 1826 he had come to the point at which he almost wished to be persuaded that Catholic relief would end Irish discontents. His task then, as he envisaged it, was to fight to the end; and when it came, to make the best terms he could for the Anglican Church. What he did not expect was that he would still be in office when that time arrived. It was here that the fatal division of the government over the Catholic question began to draw the net around him. Had a more organised and symmetrical system of party politics enabled another set of men to propose and enforce a solution, Peel could have contented himself with a moderate, critical opposition, out of office and relieved of responsibility. But such an easy escape was not possible. The Catholic question was not an issue of rival party politics but a problem calling for executive decision by government.

Three times Peel tried to escape from the gradually closing net. The first crucial year of decision was 1825 when three ministers, Liverpool, Canning, and Peel, all saw the situation clearly. All in different ways made an attempt to resolve the crisis. All three drew back under a common threat. In 1827, after Liverpool's retirement, the way seemed clear for Peel to withdraw with honour. He took it, only for that path to be blocked by Canning's death and Goderich's incompetence. In 1828 he tried once more. That he abandoned the attempt was due to three things: his sense of public responsibility, his loyalty to the duke, and his conviction that the dangers of the situation took precedence over his dislike of concession. A more prudent, a more timid, a more selfish man would have left Wellington to deal with the situation as best he could; Peel chose to remain.

Yet few could know, and even fewer appreciate, the chain of events which had put him in a situation from which in the end his pride and courage forbade him to withdraw. What men disliked was not that he had erred in his calculations but that he had confounded their expectations. And because he had disappointed so many, he became, as Greville observed, the scapegoat for the government. Though the duke had initiated the measure, fought the battle of the royal closet, and induced Peel to remain in office, he was more exempt from criticism. He had never been in the forefront of the Protestant party; his membership of the House of Lords shielded him from many of the ordinary asperities of politics; his prestige as victor of Waterloo imposed a restraint on his followers which they did not feel towards the professional politician who led them in the Commons. From start to finish, first in the cabinet and then in parliament, the passing of Catholic emancipation revolved round the position of Peel. It was his measure; and his too were the consequences. That in itself was a measure of his stature in the political world. He had reached the summit, only to find himself more isolated than he had ever been since he had entered parliament twenty years earlier.

Chapter 10

The last of the old regime

During the autumn of 1829 nothing happened to strengthen the position of the government. The passage of Catholic emancipation left the king sulky and obstructive; and his ill health, together with the extraordinary remedies he employed, made him increasingly capricious and indolent. In Ireland the new Lord-Lieutenant, the Duke of Northumberland, showed himself an unexpectedly able colleague, but the country continued to be plagued by social unrest and religious strife. At home there had been renewed trouble in the industrial north and though the immediate disorders died down in May, strikes and lockouts continued for the rest of the year. Agriculture was sharing in the general economic depression; rents were in arrears; and the country gentry dissatisfied. In the narrower world of parliamentary politics, the resentment of some of the ultra-Tories was expressed at the end of the session by the Marquess of Blandford, son of the Duke of Marlborough, who moved two resolutions against rotten and pocket boroughs on the grounds that Catholic emancipation had demonstrated the unrepresentative character of the House of Commons.

It was easy to conclude that the government needed reinforcements; difficult to see where they could be found. The Whigs were wondering whether they should wait until growing political difficulties forced the duke to take them into office or make a concerted effort to overthrow him. What seemed certain was that they would not be content with anything except office; and that if they joined the government they would want the lion's share of power. In the existing House of Commons, with Radicals in principle opposed to a Wellington ministry, the Huskissonites personally aggrieved, and a strong body of ultra-Protestants alienated, the coming session offered a dismal prospect for the cabinet. When parliament reassembled in February 1830 their depressing anticipations had not long to wait. In the Commons the king's speech was roughly handled by the agricultural Tories, headed by Sir Edward Knatchbull. There were many absentees among customary government supporters and only Whig votes saved the government from defeat. It was not an auspicious beginning; and though, as the duke was over fond of saying, the opposition was too divided to make common cause against the government, it was obvious that the Treasury bench could at any time be outnumbered and out-manoeuvred. In these circumstances their day-to-day business was likely to be increasingly obstructed and their authority steadily decline. Everything pointed to a restive and difficult session, and when the cabinet discussed the situation on 7 February Ellenborough for one already inclined to the view that the only practicable remedy was a coalition with the Whigs.

As soon as the work of the session began it became evident that Whigs and Radicals were concentrating on two lines of attack, finance and parliamentary reform. On both issues it was possible to muster a numerous if disjointed opposition in the Commons and on both the government had to endure a series of running encounters which lasted the greater part of the spring and early summer. Over parliamentary reform the attack started with a motion by the Marquess of Blandford similar to that of the previous session. Then followed the postponed East Retford bill, on which an attempt to transfer the seats to Birmingham was defeated by less than thirty votes. At the end of February Lord John Russell introduced a bill to enfranchise Leeds, Manchester and Birmingham which was supported by a composite group of Huskissonites, Whigs, Radicals and a few country gentry. Finally in May came a set of radical proposals by O'Connell for triennial parliaments, universal suffrage, and secret ballot. Blandford and O'Connell could be disregarded as irresponsible extremists. The important contests came over East Retford and Russell's carefully limited motion.

The debate on the latter elicited from Peel the first clear enunciation of his attitude towards parliamentary reform. In previous debates on the subject he had been largely a silent spectator, listening (as he told the House) 'in the spirit of a witness of the contest rather than in that of a partisan'. But if silent, he had not been incurious and he came to the debate on Russell's bill primed with reading on the question which included Burke's speech to the Bristol electors in 1780 and an analysis of the division on Fox's peace resolution of 1793. All these researches, all the teaching of such great masters as Burke and Canning, persuaded him, as he began his speech by saying, of the danger 'in tampering on slight grounds with the Constitution'. The greater part of the speech, in fact, was taken up with an exposition of fundamental principles. He denied that the British parliamentary system was based either philosophically or historically on a theory of democratic representation. He distrusted the easy prophecies of the advantages to be gained by a radical alteration of the electoral structure; he saw nothing in the composition of the House of Commons which convinced him that a change was necessary. He refused to believe that a reform of parliament was necessary to achieve reform in other branches of the state; he refused to believe that under any other system there could be a greater desire 'to promote the happiness and secure the true glory of the country'.

Descending from this elevated if somewhat negative plane of constitutional thought he argued on more conventional debating lines that the addition of six English members would be a breach of the unions with Scotland and Ireland; would form a precedent for further demands; and provoke a competition for additional seats between the industrial and landed interests. In answer to a plea by Lushington that he should emancipate himself from his supporters and appeal to the educated and intelligent classes of society, he agreed that it was wrong for a minister to be the mere instrument of party, but noted that there was equal danger in going to the other extreme. The true course was the middle way; ministers should neither be the servants of party nor, in seeking popular applause, lose sight of the true interests of the country. It was a reasoned and not unimpressive statement of the classic theory of the constitution and of Peel's view of the responsibilities of high office. But he made no attempt to consider the practical questions: whether any government could continue to be both independent of party and aloof from public opinion; or whether a defensible and workable system of representation did not cease to be so when the public had lost confidence in it. On the day the ministry gained a majority of nearly fifty. But it was not a satisfactory majority, for not more than three hundred members voted in all and Sir Edward Knatchbull, with some two dozen Tories, left the chamber before the division took place.

The question of East Retford was even more delicately balanced, since many members who did not favour a comprehensive reform of the electoral system were nevertheless anxious to see a progressive elimination of small corrupt boroughs and the transfer of their seats to the larger industrial towns. It had been decided in the cabinet to follow the line taken in 1828. Speaking in the House of Commons on 11 February, Peel said he was not against giving representation to large towns, witness his vote for transferring the Penryn seats to Manchester; but he wished the seats which might come up for disposal to be divided equally between the landed and manufacturing interests. His tone was moderate and he said he would willingly accept whatever decision the House came to on the subject. But on this occasion the high Tories voted with the government and the motion to deal with East Retford by enlargement and not by disfranchisement was carried. A bill embodying the decision went up to the Lords and though it encountered some obstruction there, Peel insisted against the wishes of most of his cabinet colleagues on pushing the bill through. He could not, he said, oppose reform in general unless the government showed itself determined to punish corruption in individual cases. It was clear that the cabinet in general did not share even this modest reforming attitude. Ellenborough, who disliked meddling with the franchise on principle, thought in fact that the Home Secretary showed himself obstinate and disagreeable on the issue. With the departure of the Huskissonites there was obviously little disposition in Wellington's ministry to respond to the growing pressure in the country and in the House of Commons for some more positive approach to the question of parliamentary reform. In the Commons a conservative, Peel in the cabinet appeared at times the only liberal. It was a position which argued some discomfort for himself and a notable degree of unrealism on the part of his colleagues.

Parliamentary reform was not as yet, however, primarily a government matter. Finance was a different and more vulnerable issue. It formed a large part of the government's business in the House of Commons. It was an area which, after the reforming rule of Lord Liverpool, offered little opportunity for further retrenchment. Yet economy was a cry to which nearly all constituencies and most M.P.s were ready to respond with alarming alacrity. From February to May the government was kept busy beating off a succession of motions for cutting down official salaries, reducing naval and military establishments, abolishing superfluous, or allegedly superfluous, offices, and revising the whole system of taxation. Only by hard work and good tactics, aided by the absurdity of some of the opposition proposals and a residuary sense of responsibility among independent members of the Commons, did the ministers come through an exhausting session with their financial measures largely intact. In this protracted warfare the mainstay of the government was Peel's parliamentary experience and tactical skill. At the outset he had determined to reduce estimates so low as to provide the smallest possible target to the opposition. He did not think that the House would yield a majority for stopping supplies and he was prepared to ignore defeats on minor issues. If necessary he was prepared to use the threat of a dissolution of parliament. In February, for example, on a motion by Sir James Graham to reduce all official salaries, Peel stated firmly that the government would make no concession simply to stay in office. They would reform where necessary, retrench where expedient; and whatever a combination of parties in the Commons might do the good sense of the country would support them. It was a clear hint that the ministers would not shrink in the last resort from the ultimate sanction of an appeal to the electorate; and the result of the debate—a withdrawal of the motion—was a complete victory for the Front Bench.

Nevertheless the universal feeling in the House for some alleviation of taxation could not be staved off indefinitely; and behind the façade of parliamentary warfare the cabinet engaged in earnest discussion of their financial policy. Reduction of taxes had already been brought to a point where the necessary services of the state were imperilled. The issue now was whether the time had not come for a revolutionary change of system. The weakness of the opposition clamour for cheap government was that it ignored the basic problem of raising revenue. The palliatives they suggested—further reduction of expenditure or currency manipulation—were equally unacceptable. Among the financial experts on both sides of the House there was a growing feeling that the only real remedy was a restoration of a tax on incomes. Arbuthnot corresponded with Peel on the subject and assured him that the Whigs, though they were unwilling to propose, would not oppose it if brought forward by the government. Peel's mind had been travelling along the same road and his influence was probably not without effect. When Goulburn submitted his budget proposals to the cabinet in

March, he included a modified property tax (as the income tax was still generally called) on income from landed and fixed property, funds and office salaries, though not on profits from trade or occupation of land. When the cabinet discussed the matter on 13 March there was a strong move by the House of Commons members in favour of tax of this nature, though Wellington and the peers were all against it. Their criticisms made Goulburn waver, but Herries remained favourable and outspoken support came from Peel. He wished, he said in a vivid phrase, to reach such people as the great banker Baring, his own father (a textile millionaire), Rothschild, and others, as well as absentees and Irish landowners; and he argued strongly in favour of aiming at the rich in order to lessen the burdens of taxation on the poor, and so to assist in reconciling the lower and upper classes. But with some of his colleagues neutral and the majority against him, he was forced to bow to the general repugnance to a revival in any form of Pitt's extraordinary wartime tax. The duke indeed was so convinced of its impropriety that he thought it would weaken the reputation of the country abroad; and he was inclined to think that Peel was actuated by a craven desire to appease the Whigs.

A motion brought forward by the Whig Poulett Thomson for a general committee on taxation certainly strengthened the hands of the financial reformers in the cabinet. Both Peel and Herries continued to argue that the Commons would accept an income tax and that it would have to be faced in the next session. Peel himself favoured Poulett Thomson's motion and was only reluctantly brought to agree with the general cabinet view that it should be resisted. In his public utterances he went as far as he could to indicate that the idea of an income tax had received and would continue to receive the attention of the government. In a debate in March he spoke in strong terms of the need to raise the standard of living of the poorer classes. One method was to find some alternative to indirect taxation. The ministers, he told the House, had carefully considered the question of a property tax and though they had decided against it for the current year, they gave no pledge one way or the other about their future policy. So the decision was left; and, as it proved, the failure to revitalise the finances of the state by bringing back the income tax at that point was a momentous one. It was the last opportunity which was to be presented to the little knot of administrative experts—Peel, Herries and Goulburn—who argued the case against their aristocratic colleagues in the spring of 1830. Their defeat, temporary as it then seemed, led to a decade of inaction. Peel was fifty-three before he was able to approach once more this fundamental problem.

II

By the spring of 1830 George IV was slowly dying. From the middle of

April bulletins on his health were being regularly issued and though to the last he fought with Hanoverian pertinacity against this final enemy, it was clear that the end might come at any time. At Drayton another old man, twelve years older than the king, was also nearing the end of his life. The first serious relapse came in April and Peel with several of his brothers and sisters went down to Tamworth. 'He was a good deal affected when I went in to him,' Peel wrote to his wife, 'cried, and kissed me two or three times.' He rallied again; and though his son had to return to his parliamentary duties, Julia went down later in the month to keep him company. At the beginning of May came news of another and more serious relapse. Taking his eldest son with him (the fourth Robert Peel in direct line), Peel went down to Drayton on 3 May. He arrived at midnight to find his father had died some six hours earlier. 'His death was so placid, so resembling sleep,' Peel wrote later to Fitzgerald, 'that perhaps I ought not to regret that he was not disturbed in his last moments by an interview which might have roused and affected him.' While Goulburn and the leaderless front bench struggled on with the business of the House, Peel remained at Drayton to supervise the details of his father's funeral and the destruction of his private papers. On Monday 17 May, now a baronet, he resumed his place in the Commons.

The previous day he had called at Windsor. He found the king huddled in an armchair, unshaven and unkempt, but still showing astonishing liveliness and intelligence. He talked kindly to Peel about his father's death and though, to avoid wearying him, Peel only stayed half an hour, George was reluctant to let him go. In the minds of both men was the thought that this might be their final meeting. Before Peel left the king asked him to push his chair to a window. He glanced out and observed that it would be the last time he would see the garden. Then he turned and said, 'You are just returned from your father's funeral; you will soon have to pay the like ceremony to me.' But he still lived on, contesting (as Croker said) every inch with death; though it was now only a question of waiting for the end It came at last in the early hours of Saturday 26 June. The event brought a rush of work for the Home Secretary in settling the formal details consequent on the demise of one sovereign and the accession of another; and Peel was among the official party that on 15 July at midnight saw the last of the Hanoverian Georges laid in his final resting-place.

The new monarch, formerly Duke of Clarence, was a simple unpolitical man, bred up in the Navy, who carried the blunt speech traditional in that Service almost to the point of uncouthness. After years of domestic but unsanctified happiness with the actress Mrs. Jordan, he had dutifully married Adelaide of Saxe-Meiningen in 1818; but no children had survived from that belated union. In that lay a problem for the ministers, since the heir-presumptive was the Princess Victoria, a girl of eleven; and next in line of succession was the unpopular and energetic Duke of Cumberland. Apart from that dis-

The House of Commons. Destroyed by fire, October 16th 1834.

"The House wot keeps bad hours" – an all-night sitting during the Reform Bill debates. The House of Commons at 7 am on the morning of Wednesday, 13th July, 1831. Wetherell is speaking, showing the famous hiatus between his waistcoat and breeches. Dozing on the front opposition bench are (left to right) Croker, Peel and Goulburn.

quieting contingency William IV promised to be a more comfortable and accommodating sovereign than his predecessor.

The same adjectives could scarcely be applied to parliament. With the start of George IV's fatal illness, the government lost their final sanction for control of the House of Commons. By the end of April it was obvious that the ministers could neither dissolve nor resign and M.P.s began to trim their political conduct to the prudent requirements of a general election During Peel's absence at Drayton discipline among government supporters had almost collapsed and even when he returned matters did not greatly improve. He himself as Leader of the House had to work harder perhaps than in any previous session. 'His single speech has, every night, supported the whole debate on our side', recorded Croker in May. Yet he could not sustain this Herculean role indefinitely and the ministers in the Lower House were convinced that some reconstruction would have to take place. It was made clear to the unwilling duke that more debating talent would have to be found to support Peel in the Commons. Hardinge indeed wished to go further. He told Ellenborough more than once that Peel's position was weakened by his subordination to Wellington and that the ministry would be more effective if Peel became Prime Minister and Chancellor of the Exchequer with Wellington as Secretary of State.

The duke himself in some moods was half-disposed to fall in with this suggestion. Eighteen months as prime minister had almost brought him to the state in which Lord Liverpool had been in 1825 after thirteen years. With all the frustrations of office and few of the qualities needed to meet them, the duke was sufficiently tired and dispirited at times to be ready to transfer his burden to the younger man. He was convinced that nobody in the cabinet paid him proper attention; he was depressed by the constant talk of the weakness of his government, which he did not think was weak; and he did not want a coalition with the various allies suggested to him whom he did not think would prove allies. In May he told the sympathetic Arbuthnots that he had made up his mind to write to Peel and resign the government into his hands. Mrs Arbuthnot used all her powers to dissuade him and won a promise not to send a letter without first showing it to her. A week later Wellington's determination was beginning to cool. He told Mrs Arbuthnot that he would simply write a memorandum for Peel pointing out the difficulties of a juncture with another party. In fact the surviving text of a letter to Peel which he did draw up reflects his earlier attitude. Writing apparently in anticipation of the death of George IV, he made it clear that he was opposed to a coalition with the Whigs and did not think that he could again preside over a cabinet which included the Huskissonites. Nevertheless he thought that the authority of the government should be placed in one person and that person should be in the House of Commons. He concluded therefore that the king's death should be made the occasion for his own retirement and Peel's accession to the premiership; and he added that he would support or serve in any government which Peel formed.

The drift of Wellington's thoughts was clear. He objected to an alliance with the Whigs; but he would accept a coalition with the Huskissonites provided Peel became prime minister. This singularly unselfish proposal would have revolutionised the position of the government at a stroke. There can be little doubt, however, that the letter was never sent. It is not impossible that he had already drafted it before he mentioned the subject to the Arbuthnots and that the subsequent discussion with them made him change his mind. When Peel returned to London after his father's funeral he further alienated the duke by proposing to reform the Scottish burghs and bring pressure on Spain to recognise the South American republics. These manifestations of liberalism were seized on by Mrs Arbuthnot to strengthen her argument that it would be folly for the duke to abdicate. In the end another way was tried. Early in July Arbuthnot wrote a flattering letter to Peel to say that the duke had greatly admired his efforts in the Commons, and would be gratified to have Peel's full and frank opinion on the apparent eagerness of Grey and Althorp to join the ministry. It is unlikely that this letter was written without the duke's knowledge; if so, it represented a complete change of attitude. It is hard to resist the conclusion that the influence of the Arbuthnots and perhaps second thoughts of his own had made the duke quietly abandon any idea of handing over to Peel the headship of the government.

Peel also in the summer of 1830 was in a state of weariness and ill-humour. The accumulated strains of the last two sessions, the increasing disorder in the Commons, lack of support from government members, continued frustration in the cabinet, had all made inroads into his physical and nervous strength. He complained sharply of his intolerable position as Leader of the House and at various meetings of ministers after George IV's death he seemed flat and listless. The general election, when it came, brought little satisfaction to him personally. His own return for Tamworth, a large part of which he now owned under the terms of his father's will, was safe enough; but two of his brothers, Edmund and Jonathan, lost their seats. Sensitive as he was to his own unpopularity, a feeling kept alive by the repeated taunts about his ratting over Catholic emancipation, he was unable to resist the conviction that his brothers' defeats were due to their family connection with him. The elections as a whole did little to clarify the confused political situation. Only about a quarter of the constituencies in England and Wales were contested and both Whigs and Tories made the customary claims to have improved their position. The truth would only emerge when parliament met. Party labels existed but there were no party programmes and candidates came to terms as best they could with their constituents. What was beyond doubt was that many electors wanted changes of various kinds—parliamentary reform, reduction of taxes, abolition of slavery, cheap bread—and that many candidates promised to support these objects if elected. In Yorkshire, in the one spectacular election of the day, Brougham was returned as a county member and at his victory dinner in September promised to bring in a grand plan of parliamentary reform.

It did not need much perspicacity to see that the new parliament would demand reforms and that if Wellington's ministry could not produce them it would have to give way to another that would. In the lull between the general election and the meeting of parliament public interest in politics was further stimulated by the news of the July Revolution in Paris, disturbances in Belgium, and renewed industrial unrest in the coal industry and among the cotton-weavers of Lancashire. Extremists on both sides tried to make capital out of the July Revolution. The Radicals hailed it as an example for the working classes in Britain, though they showed little desire to risk their own lives on the barricades. The ultra-Tories, headed by the eccentric Sir Richard Vyvyan of Cornwall, tried to identify Wellington with the discredited Bourbon ministry in France and drew lurid parallels between Peel's Metropolitan Police and the French *Gendarmerie*. That these absurd caricatures could be put forward was in itself a sign of the government's isolation. In reality, though the disturbances in Belgium brought with them the danger of French intervention, the British cabinet could scarcely have been less in the mood for spirited gestures on the Continent. At a cabinet meeting on the Belgian question early in October, for example, Peel criticised a draft despatch of Aberdeen to the British ambassador in Paris on the grounds that it might be construed as giving encouragement to intervention. His colleagues were in complete agreement and it was decided that Peel should amend the draft so as to give it a more innocuous character. It was essential, he emphasised to Aberdeen, that the government should not become involved in any European quarrel that was not demonstrably just and backed by British public opinion.

III

In the summer and autumn of 1830 the tactical question for the government was how to obtain fresh recruits without introducing fresh sources of disunity. There was reason to think that the Canningites would be open to offers; but while Palmerston and Lamb were acceptable to most of the cabinet, rather different feelings were entertained about Huskisson and Grant. On the other hand, as Peel pointed out to the duke in July, it was doubtful whether Palmerston would come back to the cabinet by himself. Nevertheless, a reconciliation with the Canningites seemed the only possible way of obtaining additional strength; and since the duke, Huskisson and Peel were all to be present at the grand opening of the Manchester–Liverpool railway in September, it was hoped that this festive occasion could be turned to some political profit. Out of this came the tragedy of Huskisson's death. On 15 September the gathering of public figures boarded a procession of trains and steamed towards Manchester at what to contemporaries was the remarkable rate of sixteen miles an hour. At Parkside, where they halted for water, many passengers stepped down on the track and Holmes, the government whip, brought Huskisson along to the duke's carriage. They had barely exchanged greetings before the *Rocket* came up at speed at the head of another train, scattering the passengers on the line and mortally injuring Huskisson as he was scrambling to safety. Peel himself was an eye-witness of the accident and wrote off accounts the same evening to his wife and the king.

In the circumstances the party which Peel had arranged at Drayton lost something of its immediate point. Nevertheless the problem remained and conceivably Huskisson's death might actually have removed an obstacle to reunion with his party. The detailed calculations of the new House made by the government whips certainly underlined the need for allies. As against 311 M.P.s classified as friends, there were reckoned to be 98 doubtfuls, 188 certain and 48 probable opponents, and 11 Huskissonites. When Wellington, the Arbuthnots, Aberdeen, Goulburn and Holmes gathered at Drayton on 22 September for a political conference, it was decided to ask Palmerston to join the government and leave further possibilities unexplored until he replied. Wellington was not happy even with this limited gesture since the man who was to be sacrificed to make room for Palmerston was Sir George Murray, one of the military politicians about whom the duke was particularly sensitive. When approached at the end of the month, however, Palmerston cautiously replied that he could not singly join the government as then constituted. This clearly suggested that he might be prepared to come in with some of his friends. Yet to create further vacancies meant asking more of Wellington's less distinguished colleagues to resign. The duke proposed that Herries should be one of them but Peel said firmly that Herries was ten times more useful in his present post than anyone else could be; and with this the prime minister was glad to agree. It left him in the agreeable position of having tried to do what his colleagues advised without, in the event, having to change a cabinet which he privately saw no reason for changing.

The autumn thus passed away with the ministry no stronger than in June. At the end of October the new parliament assembled for the swearing-in of new members, even though the session did not open until 2 November. The duke's advisers continued to press on him the need to come to terms with the Canningites and at the eleventh hour one more overture was made to Palmerston. At an interview with Wellington, who asked him to name the colleagues whom he would wish to bring in with him, Palmerston mentioned Melbourne and Grant. But he added that even so he would be disinclined to join unless the cabinet were reconstructed. The duke understood him to mean that some Whigs should also be included, and Peel agreed that this put the possibility of reunion out of the question. One final and not unimportant postscript was written to this series of desultory negotiations. On 1 November Littleton approached Arbuthnot with an offer of an alliance with Palmerston, the two Grants, and two Whigs—Sir James Graham and Stanley—provided that satisfaction was given on a number of policy matters. The most substantial of these was a measure of parliamentary reform in the minimum shape represented by Russell's bill of the previous session. If the offer was not accepted, he hinted, they would go into immediate opposition.

The effect on the prime minister of this final overture was curious and disastrous. Irritated by the Canningites and wholly averse to a coalition with the Whigs, he concluded that the best way to halt the drift towards parliamentary reform, and perhaps bring the ultra-Tories back to the side of the government, was to proclaim a policy of uncompromising opposition. Accordingly, at the meeting of parliament next day, he made his celebrated declaration that the legislature could not be improved by reform, that it was as near perfect as any legislature could be, and he would resist any change in it as long as he held any office in the government of the country.

In the Commons, where the opposition seized with glee on the prime minister's fatal pronouncement, Peel merely said that he did not see at present any prospect of a safe and moderate reform, of a kind that the government would be prepared to bring forward, which would satisfy the expectations of radical reformers. It was impossible, however, to counteract the effects of the duke's speech and attempts to do so merely gave the impression that the cabinet was divided. To several of the House of Commons ministers it seemed that the duke had succeeded in uniting all parties against them and that the fate of the ministry was now sealed. Brougham had already given notice of a motion on parliamentary reform and Hardinge told the prime minister frankly that if they were left in a minority on the issue, or even had only a small majority, he ought to resign. In this tense and incalculable situation the government threw a second bombshell.

In the late autumn of 1830 the country was sullen with unrest. The depressed agricultural labourers in the southern counties had broken out in widespread rioting and machine-breaking; and though the disorder in the industrial areas had died down, the stimulus given to radical propaganda by the continental revolutions threatened for the first time in a decade to renew the dangerous link between industrial and political agitation. While Peel was directing the work of police and military authorities in meeting the agricultural rioting, the ultra-radicals in London were holding nightly meetings at which excited crowds listened to the oratory of Cobbett, Carlile and other demagogues, pinned up tricolour cockades, and demonstrated in the streets afterwards. Menacing letters and warnings of conspiracies began to arrive at the Home Office. The new Metropolitan Police, their resources strained to the limit, were made the object of violent propaganda and physical attacks. On the night of 2 November, after the royal procession to open parliament, there were sixty-six cases of assaults on policemen. Attempts were made to rescue pickpockets arrested on the streets and the civic authorities showed a nervous desire to call in the military, despite Rowan's plea to let his men do their work alone.

Lord Mayor's Day, on 9 November, when the king and his ministers were to dine at the Guildhall, seemed likely to be the occasion for widespread disorder. There were warnings of an attack on Wellington's house at Hyde Park Gate as soon as the police were drawn off to the other end of London and thousands of printed handbills were circulated calling on Londoners to arm that day and telling them that the new police—'Peel's bloody gang'—were to be issued with cutlasses for the occasion. Hume, the cautious radical, came in person to the Home Office to show Peel an invitation he had received to head an attack on St James's Palace during the king's absence in the City. Both Peel and Wellington had received threats of assassination; and it was arranged that Hardinge and Arbuthnot, armed with pistols, should accompany the duke in his carriage to the Guildhall. The Lord Mayor-elect, Alderman Key, warned the prime minister that there was a plan to attack him and that the City authorities could not guarantee his safety. Finally, on 6 November Key and another alderman came to Peel at the Home Office to say that the City Police would not be adequate to preserve order on the following Tuesday and to ask for military aid.

Next day Peel and Wellington discussed the problem. The duke concluded that his presence in the City on the 9th would certainly provoke disorder and probably bloodshed. Peel for his part was unable to guarantee order over the whole of London that night since most of the available police and military would be needed to line the streets through which the procession passed. Whatever they decided, the credit of the government would be damaged. If they took a calculated risk, and blood was spilt, the consequences would be politically disastrous. If they chose the course of prudence, they would be accused of moral cowardice. That their decision to cancel the king's visit averted serious rioting can scarcely be doubted. On the night of 8 November a crowd of several hundreds came pouring into Westminster and received a brusque reception from the police. Next evening, the day of the cancelled visit, the crowds were out in force roaming the town, and there was much scattered rioting. At Temple Bar the mob overpowered the City Police and moved out into Westminster. But Rowan's men were made of sterner stuff and gave the rioters what Ellenborough cheerfully described as a 'terrible licking' near Southampton Row and in Piccadilly. Though troops had been kept in readiness, the civil police were completely successful in clearing the streets. There was no loss of life; and though some of the constables were severely wounded by stones, the authorities remained in control all through the night of 9 November.

Nevertheless, the very success of the government's handling of the situation made it easy for the opposition to claim that the danger had been exaggerated. In the heated political atmosphere of November 1830 the whole episode made the cabinet appear to the general public both foolish and unpopular. With their battered prestige at its lowest level the ministers now had to face their first test of parliamentary strength. Two opposition motions, to be debated on successive evenings, had been put forward. The first was to refer the Civil List to a select committee; the other was Brougham's resolution in favour of parliamentary reform. On both issues Peel had made up his mind not to surrender. The government's new Civil List showed a considerable saving on that of the previous reign and if they were now forced to the unprecedented humiliation of submitting it to a special committee, it would demonstrate that they had lost the confidence of the House. The question of reform aroused more divided feelings. It was clear that many of the government's usual supporters would vote for some measure of reform, and Ellenborough was inclined to yield a committee with the object of defeating specific proposals later on. But Peel, like most of the cabinet, was against any tactical devices. In the rigid frame of mind in which he had started the session, he argued that it was a question of reform or no reform; and he personally could not undertake such a measure. To his brother William he wrote on 12 November: 'Whatever may be the result of Tuesday next, I think it is better for the country and better for ourselves that *we* should not undertake the question.'

When the cabinet returned to the subject two days later, he went further and said that whatever the result of the division, the question was virtually carried. If the county members voted for it (and he clearly expected them to do so), it would be impossible to block them with the votes of the borough representatives. To the king, who expressed some concern on the issue and was prepared to make concessions, he argued that by opposing reform at the outset, the government would be able to make better terms afterwards. This attitude appeared to Ellenborough, with some justice, both obstinate and inexplicable. If the government objected in principle to reform, they would probably be turned out and have no power to influence a settlement; and he was tempted to attribute Peel's behaviour to an irrational reluctance to expose himself once more to a charge of ratting on previous declarations.

In a few days, however, all further argument was made unnecessary. On 15 November the goverment was left in a minority of twenty-nine on the Civil List motion. For Peel and his colleagues on the Front Bench the vote was decisive. They were convinced that even in a full House they would have been beaten. Some of their usual supporters had deserted them; so also had two dozen ultra-Tories and the Huskisson group. Most of the doubtful possibles had voted against them and most damaging of all, the majority of the English county members who were present. The only question was whether to resign at once or stay to be defeated again on Brougham's reform motion the following day. It seemed incomparably wiser to go out at once, leaving the question of reform to be handled by their successors. Next morning therefore Wellington laid his resignation before the king, followed by Peel and the other ministers. The result of the Civil List debate had taken both sides by surprise; and in their moment of victory the Whigs seemed as stunned as their opponents. But for Peel it was a welcome release. Mrs Arbuthnot, who had been at Apsley House when he went round with the news of the Civil List defeat, wrote that 'I never saw a man so delighted as Peel. He said when the opposition cheered at the division, that he did not join in it but that it was with difficulty he refrained, he was so delighted at having so good an opportunity for resigning.'

IV

Peel's relief was a mark of the increasing frustration he had felt since 1828. It was this which was responsible for his earlier stiffness and irritability, and for the unreasonable attitude over parliamentary reform which Ellenborough had noted. By November 1830, if not before, he had realised that in accepting the duke's leadership he had entered a political blind alley. With the departure of the Canningites the ministry had taken on a Wellingtonian rather than a Peelite stamp. The old carefully balanced Liverpool party was dead; and it followed that Peel, who more than any other politician after Canning's death represented the Liverpool principle, was placed in a fundamentally false position. He had done his best to construct a broad basis for Wellington's ministry in 1828; he had remained loyal to him in 1829. But all he had earned was abuse and unpopularity for Catholic emancipation. For the rest, everything seemed sterile. Outside his departmental work any attempt at constructive policy seemed to founder on the dead weight in the cabinet. The duke had made no serious attempt to reinforce his depleted administration or strengthen its crumbling support in the Commons. Peel was a prisoner in a cabinet to whose composition and outlook he was increasingly averse; and the political intransigence by which the duke brought his government to self-imposed defeat was welcome to Peel as the only means of escape from an intolerable captivity.

There were of course emotional forces underlying this rationalisation. He was tired, stale and overworked. With only one substantial break he had been in office for two decades. The strain of combining a major department of state with the leadership of the House of Commons, which killed Castlereagh, had brought Peel almost to the end of his great mental and physical resources. His colleagues in the House provided little support. Goulburn was a poor speaker; Herries, Hardinge and Murray almost mutes. On the benches behind him his ostensible supporters seemed largely indifferent to the daily needs of parliamentary business. Even minor office-holders and connections of ministers showed little sense of loyalty. In a letter to his friend Hobhouse on 24 November Peel instanced four cabinet ministers with sons in the House who never spoke and who were absent from the division which brought about their fall. 'Can I personally', he ended bitterly, 'regret the end of such a government?'

Beneath these surface reflections was a deeper rift which had opened up between himself and the duke. With all their respect for each other—and Peel was always deeply conscious of the debt owed to Wellington by his countrymen—they were never intimate. Peel had an intellectual, never a personal influence with the duke; and when his intellectual arguments failed, he tended to retreat into silence. One of the consequences of Wellington's unique national position was that very few men felt able to speak frankly to him; and the duke's obvious preference for the society of pleasant young men or adoring women increased his political isolation. Accustomed to command, Wellington found it hard to adjust to the arguments and compromises of politics; and his growing irritation was turned against his chief colleague. In the spring of 1830 Peel told Arbuthnot that the duke appeared to be changed in his manner towards him and was always dissatisfied as though something were on his mind. In fact more than once Wellington expressed himself in angry terms about his second-in-command. When the Arbuthnots tackled the duke in July on the recurrent and inflaming topic of strengthening the government in the Commons, they were treated to an alarming exhibition of bad temper.

> The Duke was very violent about it, put himself into a furious passion, said he would not meet Mr Peel about it for that it was all his fault and his own bad management, and that if he turned those people out and took whoever Mr Peel chose, he should have him coming in a fortnight's time with exactly the same complaints.

Even the sympathetic Arbuthnots found Wellington's attitude unreasonably incensed and obstinate.

The increasing coolness between himself and the duke was peculiarly painful to Peel. Though it strengthened his desire to see the end of the ministry, it increased his resentment at the way in which their political collaboration was breaking up. His suppressed emotions broke out on the fall of the ministry in a remarkable conversation with the Princess Lieven, wife of the Russian ambassador and an old friend. That the outburst was uncharacteristic was only proof of its sincerity. On 20 November the Princess dined with the Peels. She questioned her host on the reasons for the fall of the ministry. The reply was startling. For a whole year, said Peel, the government had been tottering, not progressing. They had alienated the Tories without conciliating the Whigs. The collapse of the ministry was imminent and had only been hastened by the duke's declaration against reform. No man had any influence with him; he was led by women. The foolish ones enveloped him with incense; and he had fallen victim to his own weakness and vanity. As for himself, his own course of action was settled. He was an enemy only of radicalism; and the new government was equally so. In that he would loyally support them. For the rest, he would wait for their declarations of policy before deciding whether to oppose or not.

It is hard to doubt that the Princess's account of this conversation was not substantially true. The following month Lyndhurst told Greville that he knew Peel would never again serve under Wellington, that all 'the Duke's little cabinet (the women and the toad-eaters)' hated Peel, and that there was never any real cordiality between them. The recriminations were mutual. Arbuthnot complained of Peel's reserve, his failure to encourage people in the Commons or delegate business. Other men used identical language. Hardinge spoke of Peel's cold unencouraging manner; Stuart Wortley, a recent recruit to the ministry, said that it was no pleasant task acting under Peel, his manner was cold and he required little assistance from anyone. Much of this criticism was clearly well-founded, and the reasons are not difficult to find. Peel's growing reserve, his perfectionist instincts, his underlying tiredness and nervous strain all contributed to this isolation. Nor was a working day of fifteen to eighteen hours during the parliamentary session conducive to affability. Fundamentally a shy and self-conscious man, Peel was becoming further insulated by office and reputation. Those who penetrated the outward manner, and it was not difficult to penetrate, found a modesty and kindness all the more winning because unexpected. Campbell, the Whig lawyer whom Peel had put on the Real Property Commission, dined with him for the first time in December 1828, expecting to find his host dull and formal. 'But I must own', he confessed to his brother afterwards, 'he was lively and unaffected.' Ellenborough made the same discovery. Himself a proud and unpopular figure, ambitious but frustrated in his sinecure post of Lord Privy Seal, Ellenborough had more than once bickered with Peel in the cabinet. But when at a dinner he gave in July 1828 he asked Peel to drink wine with him and showed him a few pictures, Peel responded at once with a marked warmth of manner. 'I really believe', Ellenborough recorded afterwards, 'he is only rather a proud touchy man, and that the least attempt at management would make him very cordial.'

Yet not everyone had the opportunity to take wine or talk paintings with Peel; and to ordinary men there was much they disliked in his manner, however much they respected his character and talents. His self-consciousness often gave the appearance of egoism. There was an unfortunate tendency in his speeches to dwell on personal attitudes and convictions, and the constant sneers over Catholic emancipation after 1829 strengthened his trick of self-explanation and self-justification. Though in the intimate society of Dublin Castle he had seemed a friendly and popular figure, the bitter political warfare to which he was exposed after 1827 threw him on the defensive and made him appear a cold and sometimes almost repellent personality. His cousin Lawrence Peel later remarked on the contrast between the hard surface of Peel's manner and the nervous, almost feminine qualities within. That surface was becoming harder as time went on. The need for self-protection is apt to enlist less amiable qualities, and ingrowing virtues have a trick of developing ingrowing vices. Peel's humour tended to be ironic and sometimes malicious. His integrity could degenerate into self-righteousness. The unnecessary emphasis on the purity of his motives made him on occasion sanctimonious. Though he saw much of the world, he held himself too consciously apart from it. The very ease and success of his own career distilled their own subtle poisons. He never had to struggle, and he had too much scorn for those who could not afford to be nice in the methods they used to make their way in the world. He was above temptation and had too little sympathy for the petty political dishonesty he constantly witnessed. Only a man of great humility could have held Peel's standards and retained complete humanity, and Peel was not humble. He had the contempt of the professional for the amateur, the impatience of the clever man with the fools, the dislike of the honest man for the rogues.

Yet he was clearsighted enough to be aware of his own deficiencies. As he wrote to Goulburn the following year:

I feel a want of many essential qualifications which are requisite in party leaders, among the rest personal gratification in the game of politics and patience to listen to the sentiments of individuals whom it is equally imprudent to neglect and an intolerable bore to consult.

It was a self-recognition that was given sharper edge by his reaction to the collapse of Wellington's ministry. On 17 November, just before they went out of office, there was a meeting at Peel's house of some forty House of Commons men. Granville Somerset asked Peel whether he would continue to lead them. He received a discouraging answer. Peel said he wished to retire to private life; undertake no opposition; lead no party. In effect, he would leave them to their own devices. This, to the politicians who looked to him to take them back into office one day, was both depressing and irritating.

Yet, as was clear even at the time, if there was a game, there was also a business of politics to which Peel could never be indifferent. At the age of forty-two, with a record of administration unmatched by any living contemporary and a reputation no transient unpopularity could destroy, it was unthinkable that the future would hold nothing for him. 'Peel will be the leader of a party', wrote Greville confidently in his diary in November 1830, 'to which all the conservative interest of the country will repair; and it is my firm belief that in a very short time (two or three years or less) he will be Prime Minister and will hold power long.'

Chapter 11

The crisis of reform

For Peel the year 1830, in which he reached his forty-second birthday, was like a second coming of age. It gave him, personally and politically, his final independence. The death of his father brought him a baronetcy, a large estate, a fortune in invested wealth, and the patronage of the borough of Tamworth. After twenty years of financial dependence, he was now head of the family, squire of Drayton, a leading Staffordshire landowner, and virtual owner of a parliamentary seat almost within sight of his park gates. A few months later came the great divide in his political career. When he retired from the Home Office in November he came to the end of a long homogeneous phase in his public life. Never again was he merely a departmental minister; never again did he serve under another man; never again did he hold any office as long as he had held the Irish Secretaryship or the Home Department. All but five of his first twenty-one years in politics had been spent in office; of the remaining twenty all but five were to be in opposition.

Something of this fundamental shift in his position could already be discerned at the end of 1830. In the previous few years Peel had reached that stage in a man's life when the ranks of the preceding generation suddenly give way and his own moves inexorably to the front. Castlereagh, Liverpool, Canning had all gone while still in their fifties, younger by several years than Grey was when he first became prime minister. Of Peel's other cabinet colleagues of the Liverpool era, Sidmouth and Eldon lingered into the next decade but never took office again. For Bathurst and Melville resignation in 1830 was the closing event of political careers which had started under the younger Pitt. Vansittart held his last post under Canning and Goderich in 1827, though he survived into the middle of the century, an aged and forgotten figure. Of Peel's more recent companions in Wellington's administration, Dudley's eccentricities were soon to degenerate into madness and death; Huskisson had been killed; Palmerston, Grant, Melbourne and Goderich had transferred their allegiance to Grey. Not only had Peel reached the top, but all possible rivals on his side of politics had disappeared. In the general wreckage of his political world, this was perhaps an unheeded consolation. Yet misfortune is often as deceptive as success. Peel had met many things in his career so far, but not failure and defeat. These hardening elements were now added to his political education. At least he was his own master and free to make a fresh point of departure. Where the next landfall would be, could not easily be predicted; but men of forty-two, with intelligence, experience and ambition, do not easily despair.

For the present the stage was held by the new Whig ministry. When ministers met both Houses in December, Grey announced that he intended to bring forward a plan of moderate reform and parliament was then adjourned to February to allow their measures to be concocted. Peel spent a pleasant rural Christmas at Drayton where he had already begun to plan a new mansion. Meanwhile the square unpretentious house built by his father thirty-four years earlier saw a succession of political guests. The Arbuthnots came for Christmas; Charles Ross, the assistant whip, Sir George Clerk, Croker, Murray, Herries and Holmes in January. Peel refused an invitation from Wellington to join a rather more distinguished gathering at Stratfield Saye; but it was clear that for his own part he was keeping in touch with the subalterns of the party, and as newly installed master of Drayton taking the opportunity to establish his position in his own locality. With his guests he attended the Tamworth Ball on 11 January and at the end of the month a number of neighbouring squires trundled over the snowy roads for an all male dinner at Drayton Hall.

Despite the weather, the industrial strikes, the activities of reform clubs and political unions, there seemed little cause for apprehension. Everyone remembered that Grey had promised to stand by his order and any reform bill would have to run the gauntlet of a House of Commons in which the government was far from enjoying a firm majority. It was evident that some reform must come; and probably more than the enfranchisement of Leeds, Manchester and Birmingham proposed by Lord John Russell the previous session. Many Tories thought reform was desirable; others had their constituents to consider. The real question was tactical; whether to accept a moderate reform bill because it could not be defeated and because it would serve as an inoculation against extreme radicalism; or to oppose it because it embodied a pernicious principle. But tactics needed unity and leadership. In the absence of either, the country-house conversations of January 1831 could only be discussions without decisions. What Peel would do personally was no more clear than what the party would do collectively. When Croker tried to extract from him a pledge against any parliamentary reform, Peel was not to be drawn. He was sick of eating pledges, he said goodhumouredly, and though he would oppose anything, he would pledge nothing.

The issue was one on which perhaps he found it unusually difficult to make up his mind; and part of the difficulty was that principles and tactics were inextricably mixed. It was clear that he favoured a degree of parliamentary reform; but even more clear that he did not want to take a lead in proposing it. 'Peel was for Parliamentary Reform,' wrote Wellington sourly to Mrs Arbuthnot at Christmas, 'provided it was not carried by *us* in Office.' But Peel never disclosed, and possibly never decided, what degree of reform he would be prepared to support. His whole political experience and cast of mind inhibited him from any large approach to the problem. For the historic House of Commons he had a deep respect. It was an institution in which he had grown up and to the understanding of which he had given much thought. Though he never denied the absurdities and abuses of the old electoral system, the assembly produced by its antiquated machinery had as much common sense and talent as an assembly of over six hundred men is likely to possess under any system. It was parliament and not the electorate which he regarded as the final sanction for the authority and policy of the executive; and he was instinctively opposed to any reform which might change its independent character and reduce it to a mere delegacy of the electorate. Much therefore depended in his view on the precise proposals which Grey's ministry would make.

He was not alone in his indecision. When the Tory politicians gathered in London they were still uncertain about the right tactics to employ. It is probable that Peel's preference was to oppose from the outset, or at least that he was not persuaded of the wisdom of any other course. But many of his followers, for the sake of their consciences or constituencies, were reluctant to block the mere introduction of a reform bill. A ministerial defeat on such an issue would probably mean a dissolution; and at a general election anti-reformers would be marked men. On Sunday 20 February there was a meeting of House of Commons members at Peel's house in Whitehall Gardens. While some were in favour of a bold course, the general conclusion was that the party could not rely on its followers to vote in principle against parliamentary reform. A week later there was a joint meeting of leading peers and commoners at Apsley House to settle the matter. Though the duke hankered for resistance, Peel expressed the view of the House of Commons group that opposition should be reserved until the details of the bill were known; and this became the party decision.

Two days later the bandage of ignorance and miscalculation was ripped from their eyes. Tuesday 1 March saw the staging of a great parliamentary occasion which recalled the opening night of the great Catholic debate in 1829. Now it was Lord John Russell, small, sharp-featured, thin-voiced and intellectual, who was the centre of interest. As he disclosed, section by section, the government's plan, the cheering and counter-cheering from his astonished audience grew steadily in volume and violence. All boroughs with less than 2,000 inhabitants were to be disfranchised; those with less than 4,000 to lose one member; twenty-seven new boroughs to be created; 168 M.P.s to have their seats abolished; half a million to be added to the electorate. The noise and temper of the House reached a climax when he read out the list of sixty boroughs, old and honoured (or dishonoured) in parliamentary history, which were to be swept away; and ('more yet' said Russell mockingly) a second schedule of forty-seven which were to be reduced to one member. There were screams of ironical laughter from the opposition benches as each name was pronounced and even government supporters sat appalled at the holocaust they had brought on themselves. In the early stages Peel sat listening, half-angry and half-contemptuous. But as the staggering scope of the bill was revealed, the colour came and went in his handsome florid countenance. In the end, as his colleagues beside him exulted at what seemed to be the government's suicide, he put his hands before his face. With his quick political mind perhaps he realised already that there was no room for compromise and little hope for retreat. The ministers had made a bid for public support which they could never withdraw and whatever happened now the old parliamentary constitution which he had known for twenty-one years was dead.

On the third night he rose to make his first and eagerly awaited contribution to the great reform debate. Much of what he said consisted of skilful debating arguments which were to be worn threadbare by succeeding speakers over the next eighteen months. But three points in particular stood out from the close texture of his speech. He made it clear that he was opposing, not reform in general, but this reform in particular. Second, that the ministerial proposals were so extreme that there was no alternative but total opposition. Last, that by bringing forward such a plan at such a time, the government had provoked a constitutional crisis of which it was impossible to foresee the outcome. It was a good piece of debating, able, eloquent, and measured; and he received tremendous applause when he sat down. But though it was a strong speech, it concealed a delicately balanced position. He had committed himself against the bill without joining those who were committed against reform; and he had implicitly admitted the success of Grey's appeal to the public over the heads of the politicians. Already feeling in the country was showing itself overwhelmingly behind the government and opinion at Westminster was beginning to reckon on a majority for a measure on which hardly an M.P. would have laid odds ten days earlier. As the balance of opinion swung, some of the opposition members began to look back on the fatal evening of 1 March and wonder why they had not rejected the bill when the House was still in a state of wonder and shock. That a quick parliamentary manoeuvre could have averted reform is in retrospect hardly credible. Nothing could have prevented some debate; and once the details of the measure became known, public opinion would have carried it through. No other ministry could have been formed; and if Grey had been defeated in the Commons he would have been forced to go to the country.

Nevertheless the imputation of bad tactics persisted, and in proportion as Peel's leadership was criticised, the slight tendency of the opposition to unite witnessed in January dwindled once more. That three independent meetings were called before the second reading, by Peel, by Wetherell, and by Knatchbull, was in itself a proof of the fractured state of the old Tory party. Even when the narrow victory for the bill by one vote held out hopes of defeating it in committee, Peel still showed little desire to combine with the ultras. To Herries, who conveyed to him the desire of men like Wetherell and

Stormont to come together under his leadership, he observed chillingly that 'these were the fellows who turned us out three months ago', and expressed complete indifference to office on such terms. Yet his tactical skill, which made him indispensable however exasperating to the opposition, once more supplied their immediate needs. On 13 April he raised the question of the reduction in the number of English M.P.s envisaged by the bill and obtained the promise of a division on the issue. 'I think we shall beat them on that question', he wrote to Croker, and in his confidence on the technical success, he allowed himself a moment of optimism. 'Give us another month, and there is an end of the bill, positively an end to it.' He was given not a month, but only a week. When the government was duly beaten after Easter Grey took the first of the two critical decisions which ensured the ultimate passage of his reform. On 21 April Althorp announced the withdrawal of the bill and on the 22nd the king came down in person to dissolve parliament.

When the angry and excited Commons met that afternoon, Vyvyan began a wild speech against the government in the middle of which the gunfire announcing the king's approach began to rattle through the little chamber. When he sat down Burdett, Althorp and Peel all rose at once in a clamour which prevented any of them from being heard. All semblance of order was lost; members left their seats and thronged the floor of the House; Peel, shouting at the top of his voice, was inaudible in the tumult. The Speaker, in a passion of fury, finally gained a hearing and called up Peel. Completely carried away by the tempestuous atmosphere, red-faced and shaking with temper, he plunged into an incoherent denunciation of the ministers to the accompaniment of groans, cheers, and calls to order while the guns continued to boom outside. He spoke of the despotism of journalists and demagogues, and declared violently that the government was more unfit to rule than any that had previously held office in England. But in a few minutes he was cut short by the arrival of Black Rod to summon them for the prorogation. By the time he had arrived in the House of Lords with the group of M.P.s behind the Speaker, he had recovered his self-possession. But it had been a rare and startling revelation of the depths of passion which lay beneath Peel's tightly disciplined nature.

In London the dissolution was greeted with an official illumination and mobbing in the West End. Many of the aristocracy and most of the clubs in St James's had their windows smashed, and only a strong body of Metropolitan Police prevented damage to Peel's house in Whitehall Gardens. The excitement was not confined to the populace. J. C. Hobhouse, addressing his constituents in Westminster, was reported to have described Peel's behaviour in the Commons on the day of the dissolution as 'human nature in its lowest and most debased state' and accused him of having subscribed vast sums for 'deceiving and defrauding the people of England'. Peel, reacting with unnecessary but characteristic sharpness to the insult, called his friend and ex-colleague Hardinge back from his Cornish constituency to act for him, and only the prudence of the two seconds ended the incident without pistols or publicity. On the slightly less murderous field of the hustings, the anti-reformers were unmistakably worsted. The general election of 1831 was not a landslide; the unreformed electorate was too sluggish for that. But the temper and outcome of the appeal to the nation was decisive.

> I never doubted [Peel wrote to his old Home Office friend Henry Hobhouse on 9 May] that when such an extraordinary event in the history of this country should take place, as that the King of England should be proclaimed by his ministers a Radical Reformer and that the Regal name and authority should be suddenly transferred from one scale to another. . . . Royalty and Physical strength combined must carry all before them.

He could see no hope that the king would appeal to his former ministers; nor that they could answer such an appeal. It was beyond any possibility that the new House of Commons would be content with the limited amount of reform Peel himself could approve.

For his own part he wrapped himself in studied neutrality. He excused himself from the Pitt dinner at the end of May; deprecated the holding of a Tory dinner on the eve of the new session; and refused to let his name be used in the party circular sent out to ensure early attendance. On one point at least he had made up his mind. He would not angle for the support of men with whom personally and politically he had little in common. In private, moreover, he showed considerable sensitivity to the repeated suggestions in the press that his tactics over reform were merely a disguise to ensure his early return to office. He was preoccupied with the possibility of office, but not in the sense the newspapers ascribed. With a foreboding that was in striking contrast to the simple party loyalties of Herries and Goulburn, he could not rid himself of the fear that the occasion might suddenly arise when he and Wellington would be asked to form a ministry and pass a modified reform bill as the only means of dislodging the Whigs. It was a contingency he was determined to avoid. To forfeit his public reputation once again, only to find himself permanently saddled with a ministry of Wetherells, Vyvyans and Knatchbulls, all inflationists and agriculturalists, would be to commit murder in order to put himself into gaol. With a determination that bordered on frigidity, therefore, he held aloof from any move to unite on the sole ground of opposition to the bill. 'I have no wish to *slight* the offers of *new* party adherents,' he wrote to Goulburn, '. . . but I shall be very cautious in contracting any new party engagements.'

It was not surprising, therefore, that the struggle over the second reform bill, with a diminished, divided and leaderless opposition, was in the nature of a sham battle. Peel spoke on appropriate occasions; but as the session wore on his position became increasingly isolated and at times he hardly troubled to conceal his indifference. He was prepared to move amendments on large issues but not to fight every detail in the protracted passage of the bill through committee It seemed an interminable session. On and off parliament had been sitting since the previous October, and everyone's temper was tried by the heat and the endless debates in the crowded, stuffy chamber. Peel's lassitude was increased by his physical loneliness. Julia and the children had gone off to Drayton for the summer and all his letters to her spoke of his depression at their 'unusual and unnatural separation'. By the last week of August his patience finally ran out.

> I went this morning to Charles Street [he wrote to Julia] and told the persons assembled there that I could not undertake to continue in town—that in my opinion there is very little use in protracting the debates on the Reform Bill from night to night, and that I could not undertake to remain here to conduct the battle.

Despite the dissatisfaction of men like Wetherell and Stormont, his clear intention to abandon the bill to its fate had its effect. A few days later at another meeting in Charles Street, where the party headquarters had been established after the general election, it was agreed not to divide again until the third reading. Peel promptly made his escape to find peace, pleasure and partridges in Staffordshire. Once there it was feared he would remain and on 12 September Hardinge wrote a pleading letter for his return during the last weeks of the bill's progress through the Commons. Return he did; and on 21 September delivered one last great speech against the bill. 'He cut Macaulay to ribbons', wrote Greville approvingly; and the Whig Campbell admitted to his brother that it 'would have made you hesitate about carrying *this Bill* into a law'. But speeches now meant nothing; the decision lay with the peers.

On Saturday 8 October the House of Lords rejected the bill by forty-one votes. The question now was not what the Lords would do, but what the government would do with the Lords. The adverse majority seemed too large to overcome by fresh creations, even if the king was prepared to lend his authority for coercion. But William begged his ministers to continue and with considerable misgiving they decided to remain in office and introduce a third bill, rather than hand power over to their opponents. Grey had miscalculated the peers as he had miscalculated the Commons. But after extorting a dissolution to deal with the one, he and his colleagues flinched from the only means open to them of dealing with the other. In the furious temper of the country to abandon office seemed more dangerous than to attempt another reform bill. In London there were vast demonstrations, and though the new police confined the pent-up anger of the capital to the breaking of windows, in the provinces the mood of national indignation found an outlet in riot and blood. At Derby the mob attacked the houses of anti-reformers and were only prevented from breaking into the county gaol by the arrival of troops, the resort to firearms, and the loss of several lives. At Nottingham the crowd burnt down the Castle, the property of the Tory Duke of Newcastle, and roamed round the countryside attacking the homes of anti-reform gentry. At Bristol the appearance of the Recorder, the notorious ultra-Tory Sir Charles Wetherell, was the signal for a riot which as a result of civic timidity and military incompetence led to three days of mob rule, looting and arson. Behind the movement for political reform was now raised the spectre of a social war; and for the first time since the Civil War English country houses were put in a state of armed defence. Drayton Manor, wedged in the heart of the midlands industrial area, was peculiarly open to attack; and Peel left London on 12 October to see to the safety of his family in Staffordshire. His new house was slowly rising from its foundations and he imported a stock of carbines to protect the old.

But while taking precautions against popular violence and advising his friends to do the same, Peel was now faced with a new turn in the political crisis. On the initiative of Palmerston, one of the more conservative members of Grey's cabinet, an approach was made to Lords Harrowby and Wharncliffe to explore the possibility of mutual concessions over the bill. On 21 November Wharncliffe wrote to both Wellington and Peel to sound their attitude. Peel, who had already heard what was in the wind, replied discouragingly. He said he could not commit himself until he had the opportunity to talk to others in the party and he expressed considerable doubt on the likelihood of any major concession by the government. Wellington, to whom he sent his correspondence, replied in similar vein; and Herries and Holmes in London, on behalf of the party managers, sent immediate approval. The mere talk of compromise put new heart into the opposition. Peel told Holmes to send off letters for a good attendance when parliament met in December and travelled up a few days earlier to have preliminary talks on tactics. His caution proved justified. Various concessions were made in the new draft of the bill which had been refused before, and many of the government's supporters had been sobered by the events of the autumn. But the essentials of the bill remained and the knowledge that an increasing number of waverers on his side were preparing to support it instilled a greater bitterness into his words at the opening of the debate than perhaps he realised. On the second reading of the bill he spent much of his speech in a long and unnecessary explanation of his motives for remaining in office and passing Catholic emancipation: the result perhaps of some of Macaulay's sneers but conceivably also a reaction to the suggestions of the previous summer that the opposition might bring forward a reform measure of their own.

His own attitude was clear. No reform of the limited kind he could support would be acceptable to the Commons and for the opposition to take responsibility for a larger reform would be to overwhelm them with disgrace. All that could be done was to oppose, however unsuccessfully. As he said in the House on 17 December, 'the opposition now made will oppose a bar to further concessions hereafter'. When Harrowby in February suggested to him that the best course of action in the Lords would be to give the bill a second reading and amend it in committee, Peel continued to advocate resistance. Rumours were already afloat that the king had agreed to create new peers to facilitate the passage of the bill in the Upper House, but Peel thought it better to compel the government to take this drastic action rather than yield gracefully. He doubted whether any significant concessions could be wrested in the Lords' committee where the rules of the House forebade the use of proxies. In that case all that was left was to throw on the ministers the odium of coercion. Victory could not be denied them; but it could be made a Pyrrhic victory.

Though the growing body of waverers in the Lords succeeded in giving the bill a second reading, the inevitable crisis came in May when the government was defeated in committee. On 8 May Grey told the king that the cabinet would resign unless they were empowered to make at least fifty peers. The following day the king accepted their resignations. In the famous Days of May which followed, England came nearer to national popular resistance than at any other time during the reform crisis. There were demonstrations all over the country; factories and shops closed; several large industrial towns in the north virtually suspended business; the City of London, followed by hundreds of other bodies, petitioned the Commons to stop supplies; there was an organised run on the banks; there were public declarations to withhold taxes; and lower down in the social scale talk of pikes and barricades. At the centre of this angry vortex were the twenty or thirty Tory politicians into whose hands the king had thrown the initiative. They were not intimidated by the popular violence; or if they were, they did not admit it. Divided and doubtful as most of them were, the motives which prompted them were those of loyalty, political expediency, and in some cases at least statesmanlike principle. In the last resort it was the House of Commons and not the mob to which they deferred.

On 9 May Lyndhurst on behalf of the king asked Peel whether he would take office. He had already seen Wellington, who had declared himself ready to support, in or out of office, the formation of a new government. Peel understood that he was being asked to become Prime Minister on condition of honouring the king's commitment to pass a substantial measure of parliamentary reform. There was no need to reflect on an issue which had long been present in his mind. He said at once that he could not take office on those terms. He was pledged against the bill and could not participate in any ministry designed to pass it. Next day he, Wellington, Lyndhurst and Croker discussed the situation at Apsley House. Croker asked who was intended as head of the new ministry. Lyndhurst gestured towards Peel who at once replied in a tone of 'concentrated resolution' that he would have nothing to do with a settlement of the reform question. It must be settled, and on the basis of the existing bill, but he would not go through the performance of 1829 all over again. There was some talk of finding an independent mediating minister. Croker's mention of Harrowby was not received with any enthusiasm by the duke and walking back Peel suggested to Croker the name of Manners Sutton, the Speaker. It is possible he said the same to others. He did not think the duke, even more committed against reform than himself, should attempt a ministry; but Manners Sutton was in the unique position of a Tory politician who by reason of his office, was publicly neutral on the issue.

Meanwhile the duke had received the backing of the ultra-Tory peers, and thus encouraged went on with the task of finding suitable timber for building a cabinet. He met with a discouragingly small response from the professional politicians; and the odd circumstance that it was not yet clear who was to be the Prime Minister hardly assisted his efforts. On 12 May Peel had an interview with the king who formally invited him to take office, though without specifying in what capacity. Peel shortly and firmly refused; and his example probably weighed with others, for Goulburn, Herries, Wynn, Manners Sutton and Alexander Baring all declined to serve with the duke. On the following day Wellington sent for Manners Sutton and invited him to take the unwanted premiership. The Speaker was hesitant, nervous and voluble; but he asked for a day in which to consider. When he consulted Peel and Fitzgerald on Monday 14 May, they both advised him to accept. By this time the duke and Lyndhurst were beginning to regret their offer, and it was doubtful in any case whether the ultra-Tory peers would welcome the Speaker in place of Wellington as their commander. But in a few hours the comedy ended. So far as the public was concerned, it was assumed that the duke was to be Prime Minister charged with carrying an extensive measure of reform. When the House of Commons met in the afternoon there was a torrent of bitter attacks from both Whig and Tory benches. Having briefly tried to moderate the debate, Peel left early and over dinner with a number of other party politicians, he expressed his forceful opinion that the game was up and that the return of the Whigs was infinitely preferable to a Wellington or any other anti-reform ministry which took office merely to carry reform. Through Hardinge's initiative it was arranged that Peel should call on the duke; and at midnight, he, Croker, Hardinge and Manners Sutton went to Apsley House. All idea of a Manners Sutton ministry was silently dropped; and after much argument it was agreed, on Peel's proposal, that Wellington should inform the king that it was impossible to form a Tory administration, and that to save him from painful embarrassment on the question of creating peers, the duke would withdraw his opposition to the bill.

The days of May thus ended in a day of dupes. But Peel was

pleased and relieved at the night's work. He told Ellenborough that 'the Tory Party would have been disgraced by accepting office to carry the Reform Bill after all that had been said by them against it'. Yet the fact remained that the two leaders of the party, one in the Upper and the other in the Lower House, had exhibited diametrically opposite attitudes on the matter. The duke had been ready to respond with disarming simplicity to the call from the Crown for his services. Since reform was inevitable, he thought it better done by ministers who would not have to subvert the House of Lords to carry the measure. Peel, on the other hand, thought that the constitution, and the party which stood for the conservation of the constitution, would be better served by uncompromising resistance. Coercion was better than dishonourable connivance. This cleavage of opinion came out openly in parliament. In his explanation to the peers, Wellington allowed himself an acid comparison between his own conduct and that of prudent men who had ulterior considerations in mind and looked only at consistency. Everyone naturally took this as a reference to Peel and the wounds of 1830 were laid open once more. Forced into an explanation of his own, Peel the following evening in the Commons took pains to acknowledge the honourable motives of the duke, 'that man whom I chiefly honour', but riposted by saying that Wellington's feelings of shame, had he not assisted the king in his difficulties, would have been his, had he consented to do so. In the circumstances it was impossible for either man to justify himself without reflecting on the other. But this final episode turned the coolness of November 1830 into separation. After May 1832 came a gradual freezing of relations which was to last for another two years.

Nevertheless, it was the end of the crisis. With the king at last pledging himself to make enough peers to overcome the hostile majority, and leading Tory peers abstaining from further opposition, the bill became law in June. Peel departed to Drayton early in August to amuse himself with country pastimes and the supervision of his new house. Herries, Goulburn and others who spent a week there in the autumn were surprised to find him in good spirits and in no way pessimistic about the future. He pinned his faith to the steady growth in the country of what people were beginning to call 'conservative' opinion, ready to support law, order, good government, property and public credit whenever attacked. It was to give time for this more durable feeling to develop that he had wished the battle over reform to be fought to the last. As he had written to Harrowby in February 1832,

> Why have we been struggling against the Reform Bill in the House of Commons? Not in the hope of resisting its final success in that House, but because we look beyond the Bill. . . . We want to make the 'descensus' as 'difficilis' as we can, to teach young, inexperienced men charged with the trust of government that, though they may be backed by popular clamour, they shall not override

on the first springtide of excitement every barrier and breakwater raised against popular impulses. . . . These are salutary sufferings, that may I trust make people hereafter distinguish between the amendment, and the overturning of their institutions.

It had not been an entirely unstatesmanlike policy. In 1832 it was still not certain that the Reform Act would not produce the destructive effects prophesied by its opponents. And if he was right that there was a large potential conservative feeling in the country, then the future was not without hope. Despite the parliamentary miscalculations which had led Grey into a larger and more desperate course than he had ever anticipated, the Reform Act had satisfied a deep national demand and a new alignment of political forces was now possible. Peel in the end owed more to Grey's courage and imagination than it was possible for him to admit in the autumn of 1832. For Grey's work was ended; Peel's was about to begin.

Chapter 12

The new Conservatism

With the passing of the Reform Act, the unreformed House of Commons came to an end. As soon as the registration of voters prescribed by the act had been completed, parliament was dissolved early in December 1832. The opposition faced the general election with equanimity. They did not expect to win but they thought that the electoral disaster of the previous year would at least be partially retrieved. In the event they suffered a worse smash than in 1831. As reported to Peel early in January the state of the new House of Commons was: Conservatives 150, ministerialists about 320, Radicals and Irish repealers not less than 190. Some estimates put the Conservative total even lower. In any case they were now the third and smallest party in the legislature. The Reform Act seemed more than ever not the end but the beginning of a new era in British politics.

Among the excuses, recriminations and laments which filled Peel's correspondence, were some outright counsels of despair. Lord Mahon suggested that the Conservatives should yield to the Radicals the customary opposition benches on the left of the Speaker and take their place near the gangway as a visible confession that 'we as a party are suspended; or at least that from our weakness we must be umpires rather than parties in the great struggle which the new House is so shortly to witness'. Peel, however, as he shot partridges at Drayton or made his round of great country houses after Christmas, saw no cause for panic. Bad as the situation was, it was not hopeless; and he was clear in his own mind how to meet it. The function of a Conservative Party, however small, must be to resist further radical encroachments on the constitution, to oppose ministers if they yielded to their new allies, to support them if they seemed ready to stand firm. Opposition for its own sake would be worse than useless. Whatever action the Conservatives took must be based on rational, moderate, and intelligible principles. To Goulburn, who advocated a union of all the forces of the right as the only means of creating a strong party, he showed the caution and scepticism that had marked his attitude during the reform crisis; and beneath his temperate language Goulburn sensed a continued unwillingness to enter into an alliance with the ultra-Tories. Peel replied that he did not think discussions on general topics would be profitable; and he was not prepared to make concessions on policy merely to attract followers. As for what the Conservative Party stood for, other than the basic principles of order and authority,

I suppose the 140 members of whom you speak will agree as to the strict appropriation of Church property to purposes *bona fide* connected with the interests of the established religion, and to purposes for which in principle it was originally designed; as to the resistance of all such schemes as excluding the Church from the House of Lords; as to protection to agriculture, the maintenance of public faith to the public creditor, and generally, resistance to the real tyranny which mobs and newspapers, if aided by a popularity-hunting Government, will infallibly establish. I think such a party acting with temperance and firmness and avoiding a Union with Radicals for the mere purpose of annoyance to the Government will soon find in circumstances a bond of Union and will ultimately gain the confidence of the Property and good sense of the Country.

If this rough draft of Conservative strategy was deliberately left vague, it at least allowed him flexibility in tactics and room for writing in the details of policy should he ever come to power.

Parliament assembled at the end of January. In the Commons it was a strange and disorderly assembly. Not much more than half its members had served in the preceding parliament and in the general dislocation of parties the Conservatives found themselves sitting among Radicals and Irish who even invaded the opposition Front Bench. The task of government, difficult enough before, was clearly going to be even more difficult in future. The mention in the king's speech of a measure for repressing Irish disorders provoked an immediate onslaught from O'Connell on what he chose to call 'a bloody, brutal unconstitutional address'; and a series of amendments from Irish and Radicals prolonged the debate for four nights. Though Stanley, the Irish Secretary, retaliated with skill and venom, among the liberals as a whole there was some embarrassment at starting a reform session with a measure which in the past they had been accustomed to identify with their opponents. It was precisely the kind of situation which Peel had anticipated and he exploited it with immense effect. Rising on the third night he spoke for two hours and was cheered repeatedly on both sides of the House. To the new members who had never heard him before it was a signal demonstration of the parliamentary talents to which he owed his commanding position; to the ministers a reassuring and valuable proclamation of support.

What men remembered most about the speech was the attitude he took to the whole question of reform. It was his duty, he said, to support the measure proposed for Ireland, not because he hoped or wished to return to office, not because he felt any greater confidence in the government, but because the national interest required it. The changes made by the Reform Act called for a different approach to public affairs. The old system of party tactics was inappropriate. It was necessary now to look to the maintenance of order, law and property rather than ways of harassing the ministers in office.

He saw principles in operation, the prevalence of which he dreaded as fatal to the well-being of society; and whenever the king's government should evince a disposition to resist those principles, they should have his support.

As for himself, he flatly denied that he had ever been an enemy to gradual and temperate reform.

He was for reforming every institution that really required reform; but he was for doing it gradually, dispassionately, and deliberately, in order that reform might be lasting.

As for the Reform Act, he considered

that question is finally and irrevocably disposed of. He was now determined to look forward to the future alone, and considering the constitution as it existed, to take his stand on main and essential matters.

The meaning of his speech was clear; and the effect immediate. In a confused and indisciplined legislature he held up the standard not of reaction but of sense, firmness and moderation. It was a rallying call to which a surprisingly large number of the House of Commons responded. Without compromising himself with the Whigs, he re-established at a stroke his stature as a national leader. As Greville acutely observed, he had 'contrived to transfer to himself personally much of the weight and authority which he had previously held as the organ and head of a great and powerful party'. If so, a further conclusion was possible. If his party was in fact to become great and powerful again it would only do so by accepting his leadership and his principles. What remained to be seen was how fast and how far they would travel down the road which he opened up for them that evening.

Issues soon emerged on which it was difficult either to collaborate with the government or secure unanimity among the Conservative opposition. The most important of these was the reform of the Anglican Church in Ireland. The repeal of the Test and Corporation Acts in 1828 and Catholic emancipation in 1829 had not so much disarmed the critics of the Establishment as exposed to them its weakness. The third chapter of the revolutionary trilogy, the Reform Act of 1832, strengthened still further the formidable alliance of political radicalism and religious dissent. Though religion was not the touchstone of politics, it came nearer to being so than most other issues; and a growing number of churchmen, both lay and clerical, were already beginning to see the situation in terms of an erastian State set against a spiritual Church. They feared not only a decline in the status but an attack on the wealth and property of the Establishment. Peel was not so apprehensive nor so intransigent as some of his High Church colleagues. He accepted the need for administrative reform in both the English and Irish Establishments and for some conciliatory concessions to both Dissenters and Roman Catholics. He thought the best defence for the Church lay in its own reorganisation and reform; but he was not prepared to see its position weakened and its property impounded by a legislature which had ceased to be an exclusively Protestant, let alone an Anglican assembly.

The Irish Church bill announced by Althorp early in the session neither proclaimed nor rejected the controversial principle of appropriation of ecclesiastical property for secular purposes. Nevertheless the ministerial proposal that any increase in revenue resulting from the projected reorganisation of diocesan property should be liable to parliamentary appropriation came very close to it. It was this, as Peel made clear in an almost personal appeal to Stanley, that was the real stumbling-block for the opposition; all his other criticisms were on matters of detail. The government obtained a majority on the second reading but when the appropriation clause was reached in committee, Stanley announced the cabinet's decision to abandon it. In this the ministers were thinking more of prospective opposition from the peers than of immediate tactics in the Commons. But it was clear that a clause to which even Peel had declared an unalterable objection was unlikely to survive in the headier atmosphere of the House of Lords. The withdrawal of the famous clause 147, however, put Peel in a delicate position. On the one hand he had been labouring to secure the assent of Church leaders, and Church politicians like Goulburn, to some wider reform of Church endowments in Ireland. On the other, he was anxious to conciliate the moderates in the Whig cabinet, especially Stanley, with whom he had been in friendly correspondence over Irish tithes and the Irish Church bill. It was evident that the government was divided on the issue of appropriation but Peel suspected that only a threat of resignation from Stanley had prevented a decision in its favour.

The danger to Peel's central and mediating position lay not in the Commons, where the ministers had comfortable majorities for its amended bill, but in the Lords where despite the dropping of clause 147 there seemed a real risk that the bill would be defeated. Peel had been in touch with Wellington early in July and was satisfied that the duke would not vote against the second reading. But he could not feel equally confident that opposition amendments might not be carried in committee which would wreck the bill and perhaps provoke the resignation of the government. On 20 July he took the unusual step of writing a long letter to the duke pointing out the impossibility of a successful alternative government should the Whigs be driven out on such an issue. The duke replied in a mood of dour agreement and in the event the policy of the two Conservative leaders carried the day against the ultra-Tories and a handful of recalcitrant bishops. Though the government was pressed to the limit of concession in committee, the bill passed the upper House and in August the Commons accepted the revised text. The most dangerous crisis of the session was over and the ministry was still intact.

The remaining business of the session chiefly concerned finance. Not only was this a field in which Peel was an acknowledged expert but it enabled him to resume the congenial role of ally of the government against the currency heresies and irresponsible economies demanded by extremists on both sides of the House. In April he came to Althorp's rescue in fighting off a radical demand for a committee to reconsider currency policy; the same month he helped to secure a reversal of a snap resolution on the malt tax carried against the government by back-bench agriculturalist M.P.s which would have transformed Althorp's modest budgetary surplus of half a million into a deficit of two million. In the long violent debates on currency, taxation and national distress which engaged the attention of parliament and the press in the early summer of 1833 Peel in fact was as much singled out for attack and was as much a defender of financial orthodoxy as any member of the government. He was ready enough to play his part as champion of the ministers; but he was irritated on occasions by their blunders and ineptitude and, Stanley apart, was disposed to think poorly of their talents. His restraint towards them in public was relieved by a certain contempt in private.

> My belief is [he wrote to Croker as early as March] that the Reform Bill has worked for three weeks solely from this, that the Conservatives have been too honest to unite with the Radicals. . . . What are we doing at this moment? We are making the Reform Bill work; we are falsifying our own predictions. . . . It is right we should do this, but I must say it was expecting more than human institutions, intended to govern the unruly passions and corrupt nature of human beings, ought to calculate upon.

His temper was not improved by the fact that the 'unruly passions' were as much in evidence among back-bench Tories, led by such men as Knatchbull and Vyvyan, as among the Radicals.

II

The political difficulties revealed in 1833, with the consequent strains on the ministry and divisions among their opponents, came to a climax the following session. The mild Irish tithe bill introduced by Littleton, the new Chief Secretary, still evaded the crucial issue of appropriation; but the radical language used by Russell in the Commons and the forthright resolution moved by Ward, a Liberal M.P., on the disposal of surplus Church revenues, brought the dissensions in the cabinet to a head. In May Stanley resigned from the government, accompanied by his close friend Sir James Graham, the ex-Tory Duke of Richmond, and the ex-Canningite Lord Ripon. Six weeks later came the final stroke to the tottering reform cabinet. Indecision and indiscretion in the Irish executive over the government's Irish coercion bill led to an open quarrel between Littleton and O'Connell. On 7 July Althorp, who was partially inculpated in the unedifying charges and countercharges hurled across the floor of the House, offered his resignation. But Grey by this time had enough. Sick and angry at the constant wrangling in the cabinet and alarmed at the radical proclivities of some of his colleagues, he sent in his own resignation the following day.

For Peel the sudden end of Lord Grey's ministry was unexpected and, from a tactical point of view, premature. Though he was critical of the government's handling of the Littleton affair, and had taken part in the debate which led to Althorp's resignation, he had not wished to bring about the fall of the cabinet. He knew that there was no possibility of forming a Conservative administration until, both among parliamentary politicians and the electorate, there had been some change of heart in those who in 1831–32 had been supporters of reform. The secession of the Stanleyites was encouraging; but unless the cabinet broke up entirely, there was little hope for the opposition of a successful appeal to the country. The steady drift of Whig policy towards a radical reform of the Church had certainly hardened Peel's attitude; and it had further strengthened his contacts with Stanley. There had been discussions between Peel and Graham on the amended Irish Church bill and Stanley's lieutenant had reported to his chief that Peel had shown himself friendly and cooperative. The shadow of a Conservative alliance was there; but it had as yet little substance, nor was there any real prospect of power.

Nevertheless, Grey's resignation did, however fleetingly, raise the possibility of a different kind of political regrouping. When the king summoned Melbourne on 9 July it was to ask him not simply to carry on the Whig government but to attempt a coalition with Wellington and Peel. Melbourne declined in a reasoned statement based chiefly on his political disagreement with the leaders of the opposition on measures such as Irish tithe and Irish Church reform which Melbourne regarded as 'vital and essential'. Directed by the king to comment on this letter, Peel and Wellington returned separate but concerted replies. They took the line that Melbourne himself had killed any chance of coalition by his statement to the king. Though they disclaimed any desire for office, they had not refused, nor would refuse, to serve the crown if they could do so without restrictions on their freedom of action. If necessary they would have been ready to appeal to the electorate on behalf of a Conservative administration offering, as Peel put it, 'cautious and well-digested reforms' and 'the redress of proved grievances'. Peel even went so far as to send the correspondence to Knatchbull and express a wish to consult him if he should ever be required to form a ministry.

But the curtain dropped almost immediately on this faint vista of the future. After a futile attempt to impose conditions as to men and measures, the king finally gave way, and on 16 July Melbourne took office as prime minister. The Coercion Act, shorn of its more drastic clauses, was renewed; and the Irish tithe bill sent up to the Lords. With the Commons business virtually finished for the session, Peel went off to Drayton at the end of July. The crisis, however, was not quite over. Even before he left London, he had been alarmed at Wellington's apparent desire to resurrect the omitted clauses of the coercion bill. Though in the end the duke allowed it to pass under protest, the Tory peers in August threw out the Irish tithe bill by a large majority, Wellington himself, swayed by the intransigent feeling in his party, both spoke and voted for rejection. This was not victory so much as defiance: Tory opposition as men like Cumberland, Kenyon and Londonderry understood it, rather than the prudent Peelite formula which Wellington had followed in the previous session. For the first time since the Reform Act the hostile majority in the Lords had contemptuously and unconditionally rejected a major government measure.

By any long-term calculation it was a hazardous step. It was one, moreover, of which Peel seemed a curiously distant and powerless spectator. He could not have approved the action of the Lords; yet he did nothing to avert it. He may have said all he had to say to the duke before he left London. He may have been reluctant to strain his credit with the duke on a less vital issue than the Irish Church bill of 1833. He may not even have realised that Wellington's attitude was hardening as the session drew to a close. If the last was true, it argued a dangerous lack of contact between the two Conservative leaders. Though they had been in regular communication over political matters, the relationship between them was still brittle. Wellington's election as Chancellor of Oxford University in January, to which some observers attributed his sudden zeal on behalf of the Church, had certainly deepened Peel's hurt conviction that his loyalty over Catholic emancipation in 1829 had received little recognition from the duke. Though Peel had consistently said that he did not wish to become Chancellor of his old university, he felt, keenly if unreasonably, that he had often been spoken of as a natural successor to old Lord Grenville, that he had close personal and academic ties with Oxford which the duke conspicuously lacked, and that a large party in the university were anxious that he should become a candidate. Yet the very men in Oxford who had secured his defeat in 1829 had now put forward the duke, who was equally responsible with himself for the Emancipation Act; and the duke himself had allowed himself to be nominated without any attempt, direct or indirect, to discover whether Peel might not wish to stand.

Coming so soon after the unhealed breach of 1832, the unmistakable constraint in the relationship between Peel and Wellington in the 1834 session disturbed the friends of both men. Peel made no effort to explain or end the coolness. Wellington, misinterpreting his attitude, thought that Peel disliked him personally. In the end both Arbuthnot and Aberdeen tried to bring about a reconciliation. Their efforts had no immediate success, though they did something to clear the air. Aberdeen admitted to Peel that the duke was largely responsible for the situation which all their friends deplored; but he added frankly that he did not think Peel was entirely blameless. The rift was not perhaps as desperate as the over-protective instincts of men like Arbuthnot sometimes made it appear. Between Peel and Wellington there was great mutual respect. Neither under-valued the political importance of the other; and left to themselves they usually came to similar conclusions. Nevertheless, it was as well for the slow recovery of Conservative strength that the main events of the 1834 session hinged not on the personal relations of the opposition leaders but on the political differences between members of the government.

As it was, the rejection of the Irish tithe bill formed a fitting end to a barren and frustrating session. After the preliminary sparring of the first session of the reformed parliament the lines of battle were now beginning to show more clearly. The Dissenters were angry and resentful at the strength of Anglican opposition to the redress of their public grievances. The Radicals and Irish Nationalists were realising that the House of Lords could prove a formidable barrier even to a reformed House of Commons. The optimistic assumptions which the passage of the Reform Act had trailed in its wake were breaking down on hard political realities; and the temper of reformers were not improved by the painful process of disillusionment. Their opponents were scarcely more satisfied. After the momentary flutter of hope at the time of Grey's retirement, what one observer called the 'high and foolish' Tories were sulky and disappointed. Peel was indifferent to their feelings. He knew what he would do if ever recalled to power; but when that would be seemed as far off as ever.

III

In the autumn of 1834 Peel, Julia and their eldest daughter went off to Italy. Travelling in leisurely fashion they reached Milan at the end of October and after visiting Venice, Bologna and Florence, they arrived in Rome in mid-November. There they planned to spend two weeks in shopping, sight-seeing and entertainment before moving on to Naples for a steamboat which would take them to Genoa or Marseilles on the first stage of their homeward journey. Towards the end of their stay, Peel read in the papers of the death of Althorp's father, Earl Spencer. Though Althorp's elevation to the Lords would clearly mean some reshuffle of the government front bench, he did not otherwise attach much importance to it.

Back at home the event brought to a head the king's mounting

Sir Robert Peel. From H.B.'s Political Sketches No. 290 (December 1833).

Sir Robert Peel aetat. 50. From the painting by John Linnell.

fears about the state of the government and the onward march of reform. What alarmed him most was the attitude of the Melbourne cabinet to Irish Church reform. Melbourne's proposal to replace Althorp by Russell as Leader of the House of Commons seemed to his royal master proof that his ministers were now committed to the extreme policy that had caused the resignation of the Stanleyites in the summer. On 14 November Melbourne returned from an interview with the king at Brighton, carrying with him a sealed packet for delivery at St James's Palace which, with sardonic humour, he realised must contain a summons for the duke of Wellington. For the last time in British history a monarch had dismissed his political servants; and Melbourne's first ministry was over almost before it had got under way.

For Wellington the experience of one disastrous premiership had been enough. When he in turn went to Brighton on 15 November he told the king that his prime minister must be in the House of Commons and that the only possible man was Peel. But for the time being, as an act of practical necessity, he consented to take office as First Lord and Secretary of State with Lyndhurst in charge of the Great Seal. To this William IV cheerfully consented. Only Peel's absence in Italy, he observed with candour if not tact, had prevented him from being summoned in the first place. The same evening the king and the duke composed letters for Peel, and a young officer of the Household named Hudson made ready to start abroad in search of the missing member for Tamworth. While the duke with imperturbable self-confidence moved round Whitehall, directing singlehanded the activities of government departments, the astonished British public settled down to wait for Peel's arrival. When that would be nobody could say; since nobody knew exactly where Peel was. The opening scenes of the new *Hamlet* had to be played without the Prince.

Hudson, pursuing an erratic itinerary as the result of false intelligence, police obstruction, and flooded roads, finally arrived in Rome on 25 November. Running Peel to earth in the Hôtel de l'Europe he was (according to a Foreign Office tradition) unkindly told by the great man that he could have done the journey in one day less. Time in fact must have been Peel's first thought after reading Hudson's budget of letters. It was eleven days since Melbourne had been dismissed; at least as many would be needed for the return journey. It was an inauspicious start for what had all the prospects of being an inauspicious ministry. In his letter William IV had commanded him to come back to England and 'put himself at the head of the administration of the country'. In his reply Peel committed himself to nothing except his immediate return. But as the long miles passed and the wintry landscape of southern Europe slowly receded across his carriage windows, it became increasingly clear to him that on two essential points at least a decision was virtually taken. He would have to take office and there would have to be a dissolution of parliament. By taking office, he would be accepting responsibility for the dismissal of the Whigs; and the justification for that dismissal, on the scanty information conveyed to him, he was inclined to doubt. Yet to refuse office, after a three-week interval during which a provisional government had already been formed, would be to inflict an impossible humiliation on the Crown. Equally clearly, no ministry could hope to maintain itself with only 150 supporters in the House of Commons The only question was one of timing. Pitt in 1784 had braved a hostile House of Commons for three months before making his successful appeal to the country. But 1834 was not 1784. The reformed electorate was more impervious to management, the reformed parliament more partisan in its views, than their eighteenth-century counterparts; and an initial, noisy conflict in the legislature would inflict irreparable harm on the Conservative cause. In any case, a general election could not long be staved off; and to find twenty or thirty M.P.s fit for office who would also be ready to face two elections in quick succession, one on appointment and the second at a dissolution, would be a formidable undertaking.

On one point his mind was made up. His would not be a mere repetition of Wellington's ministry of 1830. Tactics and statesmanship both demanded an infusion of fresh talent and greater liberalism. The reconstruction so mismanaged by the duke four years earlier would have to be carried out by his former lieutenant if the new government was to have any chance of survival. The two men on whom Peel set his hopes were Stanley and Graham. Even this was a predictable reaction to the difficult situation into which he had been unexpectedly thrust. From the time the dismissal of the Whigs had been announced, there had been newspaper speculation on Stanley's future; and the interest was not confined to the press. The combination of office and a parliamentary minority had exercised an agreeably liberalising effect on the minds of many Tories; and Ellenborough was pressing Wellington to make an approach to the Whig seceders even before Peel arrived. In a letter from the duke which Peel received in France on his homeward journey, a draft list of possible ministers had been included which contained the names of Stanley, Graham, Richmond and Ripon. Though Wellington had made no comment on the policy of inviting them to join the new ministry, he had added laconically, 'I think it is expected, and will give satisfaction'.

Late on the evening of 8 December, having stopped only four nights on the road, the Peels arrived at Dover. Leaving his wife and daughter behind him, Peel posted on through the night and by eight o'clock the following morning was at his desk in Whitehall Gardens writing to the king. Within a few hours Wellington arrived and there was another briefer talk with Granville Somerset, the chief of the party's small staff of organisers, before Peel went off at two o'clock for his audience with the king at St James's. At the interview William considerately asked whether he wanted time to reflect before making his decision. But Peel characteristically took the bold course. He told the king that the prospects for the new ministry were doubtful enough but would be made more so if there was any appearance of hesitation. All he asked was permission to invite Stanley and Graham to join the cabinet. Letters to both went off the same day and in the interval of waiting a Council was held at which Peel was formally appointed First Lord of the Treasury. At a dinner at Apsley House, attended by some two dozen leading Conservative peers and commoners, he made his first speech as prime minister. He told them that the issue was not between parties but whether the monarchy and the ancient institutions of the country were to be preserved. For that purpose it was essential that the new government must be formed on as broad a foundation as possible. He had therefore invited Stanley and Graham to join the administration. The news gave general satisfaction to his audience and Peel himself, despite the fatigues of the last fortnight, seemed lively and in good spirits.

Two days later came the first blow. In a long explanatory letter Stanley politely but categorically refused to take office. Though he held out the possibility of independent support, he referred to the disagreement that had existed between them on all matters except the Irish Church and concluded that a coalition would ruin the reputation of one without adding strength to the other. Graham, though equally firm, was more conciliatory and even went to the trouble of making the long journey from Cumberland to assure Peel of his personal regard and of his general wish to support the new government. But the unpalatable fact remained that neither would enter the cabinet. It was more than a disappointment; it was a foretaste of failure. In fact, even before Peel had written, Stanley and his friends had decided against a coalition. They had little personally against Peel; but there was considerable animosity against Wellington and this in the end was perhaps the decisive factor. The duke had been the first to be asked to form a government; he had administered the country for the first three weeks of its existence. 'This circumstance alone', Stanley informed Peel, 'must stamp on the administration about to be formed the impress of his name and principles.' If there had been a chance of securing Stanley at all, it had been destroyed by the accident of Peel's absence in Italy at the start of the crisis.

In the circumstances the cabinet that Peel proceeded to form inevitably bore a strong resemblance to the duke's cabinet of 1830. For himself he took both the Treasury and the Exchequer. Goulburn went to Peel's former post at the Home Office and the duke took over the Foreign Office. Other survivors of his old ministry who reappeared were Aberdeen, Ellenborough, Rosslyn, Herries, Hardinge and Sir George Murray. But there were a few new names. The Earl de Grey, a brother of Lord Ripon, accepted the Admiralty; Alexander Baring, the financier, who had deserted the Whigs during the Reform crisis, became President of the Board of Trade; and Lord Wharncliffe, one of the leading waverers of 1831–32, was pleasantly surprised to be offered the Privy Seal. Lord Haddington, an ex-Canningite, was appointed

Lord-Lieutenant of Ireland; and two former Grenvillites were also included, Wynn as Chancellor of the Duchy of Lancaster, and Fremantle as one of the Secretaries to the Treasury. The chief representatives of that fading political connection, however, were the Duke of Buckingham and his son Lord Chandos. Their refusal to take office except on their own exorbitant terms presented Peel with his most difficult personal and party problem. Their significance lay not in their political talents, which were negligible, but in Buckingham's ducal pretentiousness and Chandos's self-assumed leadership of the agricultural party among the country gentry. Peel did not neglect that interest in composing his ministry. As early as 13 December he had secured the services of Sir Edward Knatchbull as Paymaster-General. But the Buckinghams were made of vainer and more unmanageable material. Peel declined to accede to Buckingham's desire to enter the cabinet or go to Ireland as Lord-Lieutenant; and the duke thought himself too important for a purely ornamental office in the Household which was all he was offered. Chandos, on the other hand, whom Peel was prepared to put in the cabinet, refused to take office without a pledge that the malt tax would be abolished. The failure to secure either caused gloom among the party whips, who feared the mischief they could create in the county elections.

Forced to make his selection of senior ministers from a more limited range than he had hoped, Peel, like Lord Liverpool in 1812, tried to redress the balance by promoting promising juniors. 'All my experience in public life', he had once observed to Wellington, 'is in favour of the employment of what the world would call young men instead of old ones.' The brilliant young Cambridge barrister and journalist W. M. Praed, whom some regarded as the Tory answer to the Whig Macaulay, was made Secretary of the Board of Control. The graceful and aristocratic Sidney Herbert joined him as second secretary. W. E. Gladstone, an Oxford double first and son of the great Liverpool merchant and Canningite supporter, and Lord Lincoln, son of the Duke of Newcastle, were put in the Treasury. All three were friends and fellow-Oxonians who had been new members in the first reformed parliament. Undersecretaryships were also found for two other aristocratic Christ Church men, Lord Mahon at the Foreign Office and Lord Eliot at the Home Office. Inevitably there were grumbles and criticisms; but it is hard to see how Peel could have done much better; and he might have done much worse. Like all prime ministers, he had to balance party claims against administrative performance, seniority against youth, influence and connection against past services and future promise. The critics themselves were singularly reticent in naming anyone of importance likely to accept office to whom offers had not been made. Even so the uncomfortable feeling persisted that the composition of the new ministry would not in itself arouse much national enthusiasm.

Peel himself realised from the start that the success of his minority government would largely depend on his ability to persuade the country in general and the electorate in particular that the new ministers had something to offer. On his arrival in London he had discovered not only that an immediate general election was taken for granted but that candidates were already in the field. He would probably have decided in any case on a dissolution but the choice had been virtually made for him. At the same time he found ample evidence in his correspondence and in the press to confirm what his own judgement might have made him fear: that the arbitrary dismissal of the Whigs and the Duke of Wellington's three weeks' monopoly of power had already alienated many who might otherwise have been favourable. Barnes, the editor of *The Times*, had made it clear that he could only support the new ministry if it was ready to accept measures that had already passed the House of Commons. Several correspondents from different parts of the country emphasised the widespread distrust of Wellington and the need to counteract it by an early statement of government policy. John Walter, proprietor of *The Times* and parliamentary candidate for Berkshire, in a letter to Sir James Scarlett which was sent on to Peel, urged 'some frank explanation, some popular declaration, *previous* to a Dissolution of Parliament'.

Neither Peel nor his colleagues needed much persuading that it would be advisable to make a public pronouncement of their general policy before encountering the hazards of a general election only two years after the Reform Act. It was unusual, virtually unprecedented; but so too were the circumstances. The only question was to hit on the right method. By December Peel had made his decision. Though parliament had not yet been dissolved, by accepting office he had vacated his own seat. There would therefore be no impropriety in issuing an address to his own constituents in which he could outline his views. The document was drafted at once, read to the cabinet after dinner on 17 December, and sent to the waiting presses of *The Times*, *Morning Herald*, and *Morning Post* in the small hours of the morning. On 18 December the *Tamworth Manifesto* appeared before the public. It made, recorded Greville, 'a prodigious sensation, and nobody talks of anything else'. In form an address to Peel's constituents, in substance a statement to the country of the principles of the new administration, the *Tamworth Manifesto* was an electioneering document on a grand and unparalleled scale. Beginning with a brief reference to the circumstances of his taking office, Peel made it clear that he was making through his constituents a general appeal 'to that great and intelligent class of society . . . which is far less interested in the contentions of party, than in the maintenance of order and the cause of good government'. In the seven pages of print which followed he stated his present position and future intentions. He referred to his public record as a reforming minister; he repeated his declaration in parliament that he regarded the Reform Act as 'a final and irrevocable settlement of a great Constitutional question'. If to govern in the spirit of the reform bill meant following every popular whim, promising instant redress for every alleged grievance, he could not do so. But if it meant 'a careful review of institutions, both civil and ecclesiastical' and 'the correction of proved abuses and the redress of real grievances', then 'I can for myself and colleagues undertake to act in such a spirit'.

As a landmark in the history of British political parties the *Tamworth Manifesto* has an assured place. But its posthumous fame should not obscure its contemporary purpose. Peel wrote it at short notice not for posterity but for the public and the electorate of 1834. It was not primarily a statement of the principles of the new Conservatism nor was it a programme of governmental action, though elements of both can be found in it. Above all it was not the announcement of a sudden political conversion. On the reform bill itself Peel was only restating what he had said in the first session of the reformed parliament. On reform in the abstract he was only declaring the beliefs and practices of his whole previous career. Fundamentally the *Tamworth Manifesto* was a considered statement of the attitude of the new government to the main political issues of the day, designed to conciliate neutrals and attract moderates in the forthcoming electoral battle. To Croker, who reviewed the *Manifesto* in the *Quarterly Review*, Peel made the criticism that he tended to ascribe the Tamworth address too much to the necessities imposed by the Reform Act. 'I think', he added practically, 'the necessities rather arose from the abruptness of the change in the Government, and, to say the truth, from the policy of aiding our friends at the election.' What gave the *Manifesto* its importance were the circumstances in which it was issued; what gave it its character was that it was written by Peel. But if the ideas and the language were typically Peelite, the authority behind it was that of a prime minister. It was the combination of the old attitude and the new power which made it the significant document it was.

Much, if not everything, now depended on the results of the general election. In the last week of December it was agreed to dissolve parliament on the 30th and summon the new for 19 February. The government had precisely eight weeks in which to fight an election and prepare their measures. It seemed to Peel that their fate would largely be decided by religious issues. If to many Radicals the action of the Crown had seemed an attempt to rescue the House of Lords by dissolving the Commons, to many Dissenters it seemed an attempt to rescue the Church by evicting the Whigs. No ministry in 1835 could avoid the issue of ecclesiastical reform. Indeed Peel had already committed himself in the *Tamworth Manifesto* to immediate consideration of Church reorganisation and Dissenting grievances. Here, if anywhere, would come the test of the Conservative claim to constitute a genuine reforming party. The new ministry had at least one advantage to set against the continuing hostility of organised Dissent. The Church might yield to the persuasions of its friends what it would refuse to the coercion of its enemies. What the Establishment needed was not merely a stimulus to reform. That had already been provided in the previous few years by Dissenting and Radical attacks, by Anglican consciousness of entrenched abuses, and by the reforming pressure of men like Archbishop Howley of Canterbury and Bishop Blomfield of London. The Whig commission of enquiry into Church revenues had prepared the ground; and the notion of a mixed lay and clerical commission to propose specific measures was already finding advocates. The occasion, as Peel with his instinctive sense of timing realised, was ripe for action. What was required was sympathetic leadership that the Church could trust and follow.

To provide this was the first great act of policy to which Peel turned his attention. Discussions with Church leaders at the end of December gave him the assurance that they would be ready both to initiate internal reforms and support conciliatory legislation for the Dissenters. Under Peel's impetus ministers found themselves individually and collectively joining in the work. The duke and Goulburn were commissioned to use their influence at Oxford and Cambridge; the cabinet took up the problem of Church rates; and committees were appointed to look into the problems of English and Irish tithes, dissenting marriages, and other nonconformist grievances. Early in January Peel had a long conference at Lambeth with the Archbishop and Blomfield at which it was agreed that a royal commission should be set up to reorganise episcopal and diocesan responsibilities and review Church patronage. The commission was issued the following month and its members were set to work immediately. It was the essence of Peel's policy not merely to reconcile the Church to reform but to make the Church the instrument of its own regeneration. The composition of the Commission (two archbishops, three bishops, the Lord Chancellor and six prominent laymen of known Anglican sympathies, headed by the prime minister in person) was a guarantee that the work would be carried on both efficiently and sympathetically; and the responsibility placed on the Commission not only for enquiring into abuses but for proposing remedies ensured that the initiative would remain in its hands. As Peel made clear in correspondence both with the men invited to serve and with distrustful ecclesiastics like the bishops of Durham and Exeter, the whole purpose was to lay 'the safe foundations' of 'progressive reform in the Church'. No reasonable politician doubted that the Church must be reformed. What Peel feared was that resistance by the Church would provoke punitive action by its opponents. Clerical reaction rather than dissenting and radical hostility was the real danger. The Church had to be saved from itself as well as from its enemies.

Every post [he wrote to Goulburn at the end of January] brings me statements which, if they are true, convince me that the deepest responsibility attaches to the Church, or at least to authorities connected with the Church, for the present state of the country in regard to the progress of Dissent.

In the middle of all this cabinet and departmental activity came the general election. Starting in the first week of January it engaged the interest of the public and the calculations of the whips for the greater part of the month. Nearly 400 Conservative candidates eventually took the field. Even so, the party was only contesting about three-fifths of the parliamentary seats and many of these were hopeless from the start. An outright majority was obviously out of the question; but if the party managers' optimistic hope of securing over 300 M.P.s was realised, this might be enough in view of the divided state of the opposition. When the results began to come in even this limited ambition was seen to be beyond their reach. Expected gains were offset by unexpected losses; and at the end of the month the final analysis ran: government 290, radicals 150, Whigs and Stanleyites 218 of whom forty or fifty could be classified as doubtful. It was not victory; it was not exactly defeat. With improvised organisation and hastily recruited candidates the party had won over two-thirds of the seats they contested. In the English counties they had done particularly well, winning twenty-nine seats and losing none. They had nearly achieved their objective of 300 M.P.s; they had almost doubled their numbers; they were the largest single party in the House of Commons. If the opposition remained divided, if the Stanleyites proved friendly, if some moderate Whigs could be won over, if all or some of these things happened, all was not yet lost.

Peel himself, as befitted a leader, set an example of optimism. He was unperturbed by the election results because he had never assumed that the election in itself would give him an absolute majority.

I feel [he wrote to Herries on 11 January] that I can do more than any other man can who means his reforms to work practically, and who respects, and wishes to preserve, the British Constitution. I think this must ultimately prevail, and attract for us more support than we at present calculate upon.

Notwithstanding four weeks of ceaseless activity, in which even Christmas Day afforded no break, he remained noticeably sanguine and energetic. But the opposition, too, had not been idle. Common danger had overcome mutual distrust; and a joint meeting of Whigs, O'Connellites and Radicals at Lichfield House, the day before parliament assembled, formally united the forces of the left for the purpose of evicting the government. The following evening they scored their first success in electing a Whig Speaker in place of Manners Sutton. The voting was close, and it was not primarily a government matter. But the opposition had deliberately chosen the Speakership as a trial of strength, and the defeat was ominous. One battle, however, did not make a campaign. The real test would come over the king's speech in which the ministerial programme was unfolded. Peel had staked his real hopes on attracting independent support by a fair offer of reasonable reform. Much depended on the attitude of the Stanleyites who had cast themselves for the ambitious role of a third party holding and deciding the balance between government and opposition. On 24 February Peel made a vigorous and effective speech, appealing for a fair trial in

> the trust, which I did not seek, but which I could not decline. . . . I make great offers, which should not lightly be rejected. . . . I offer you these specific measures, and I offer also to advance, soberly and cautiously, it is true, in the path of progressive improvement.

Next day Stanley held a meeting at which his followers were joined by a small squad of moderate Whigs. The unfavourable temper of the meeting was reflected in the speech he made the same day. He said he wished to give Peel a fair trial and would not support a hostile amendment to the address; but he added that he could put no trust in the ministry as a whole and regretted in particular that no pledge had been given on municipal reform. It was a grudging and unpleasant speech which annoyed many government, and especially Wellingtonian, supporters. Even worse, though Stanley carried some votes to the side of the ministry, he did not carry enough. On 26 February, after three days of debate, a crowded House yielded a majority of seven for the opposition amendment regretting the dissolution of parliament. For the government it was a crushing blow. It had not been expected and it came after the prime minister had made a personal appeal to the House to suspend judgement on his administration. There was little more he could do now except offer separately what the House had already rejected collectively. At the cabinet next day he was noticeably depressed.

Though the odds had lengthened alarmingly, however, there was no thought of immediate surrender. Peel had said in the debate that an unfavourable decision on the address would not make him resign; and a few tactical successes in March gave a few straws of encouragement to the more optimistic members of the government. But as the session continued the position of the front bench steadily deteriorated. They could not control the ordinary business of the House. On no issue could they be sure of a majority. On many minor matters Peel could not rely either on debating support or even assiduous attendance from his backbenchers. With few sanctions to enforce their authority, the effectiveness of the government whips depended to a great extent on the morale of their troops, and this ebbed perceptibly during March. It was not pleasant always to be beaten. Though in the end a belated effort was made by the rank-and-file to improve their ragged attendance, it came too late. Peel knew in his heart that the government was doomed; the only problem was to find a distinct and satisfactory issue on which to resign. On several occasions he had challenged Russell to move a direct vote of no confidence, only for the challenge to be evaded. Instead, with or without encouragement from their leaders, the opposition resorted to all the obstructive devices which the lax rules of the House allowed. In the absence of effective control the behaviour of the Commons, never noticeably decorous, rapidly degenerated. Shouting, groaning, hooting, stamping of feet and beating of sticks on the ground, became a regular accompaniment to debate; and it was said that there was one set of opposition M.P.s who were making a deliberate attempt to 'bellow Peel down'.

The inevitable end came early in April. The government's Irish tithe bill introduced in March had once more raised the acrimonious question of the Irish Church. Russell, after hesitating in his tactics, finally gave notice of a motion to go into committee to consider the application of the surplus revenues of the Church of Ireland to the 'religious and moral instruction' of all classes of the community. With this explicit renewal of the old appropriation conflict, it was evident that the climax of the session had arrived. Peel had asked for a fair trial; he was given instead a pitched battle, on grounds of his opponents' choosing, on an issue which would unite all the parties to the Lichfield House compact against him. It was true that it would also force Stanley over to the side of the government, but the Stanleyite Third Party was by now a spent force. The only doubt was the size of the adverse majority. For Peel it was not a matter of whether he would be defeated but of when he should resign. On 25 March he circulated a cabinet memorandum arguing strongly in favour of retirement. There was no longer any rational hope of attracting further support, and to remain in office if beaten on Russell's motion would be to throw away a good and intelligible ground for resignation with no certainty of getting a better and every prospect of having to be content with a worse. He did not press for an immediate decision; and some of the peers in the cabinet, insulated from the unpleasant realities of life in the Commons, were still reluctant to quit office. On Friday 3 April, however, after four days of debate, Russell's motion was carried by thirty-three votes. When the cabinet met next day there was general acceptance that resignation was now inevitable. Peel turned down flatly the notion of struggling on in the hope of a successful dissolution and said that the return of a Whig ministry was now a certainty. Though the king had offered a second dissolution if necessary, Peel thought that it could not be justified and would not prove successful. Desperate as the king was at being abandoned to the mercies of the Whigs, all William could suggest was a coalition with such moderate politicians as Grey, Melbourne, and Stanley. But this was too unrealistic to be worth considering. On 8 April, after fresh defeats in the Commons, Peel announced the resignation of the ministry.

In the last few weeks the only question had been not whether, but when, to go out; and in the end the timing of Peel's resignation had been almost faultless. Earlier it would not have been understood by his followers; later it would have incurred justifiable criticism. As it was, the cabinet and the great majority of the party were satisfied that all had been done that was humanly possible. Once the ministry had come to an end, moreover, there was a widespread feeling of respect for its gallant stand in the face of hopeless difficulties. Even Whigs like Mulgrave and Campbell, and Radicals like Hume, joined in what Greville called the general chorus of admiration. From Peel's own followers, headed by Lord Francis Egerton, came a hearty letter of confidence and thanks. Another approving address, containing over a thousand signatures, was presented to Peel by a deputation of metropolitan solicitors. These were only two of countless similar testimonials that came in from all over the country. Despite the unpropitious start, the reputation of the ministry had grown with its defeats and its credit was never higher than when it surrendered power. This paradox was almost entirely the achievement of the prime minister. Not only had he taken on himself the main burden of the parliamentary conflict, but he had done so in a manner which had raised immeasurably the public's estimate of his talents and statesmanship. He had demonstrated a fresh and welcome form of political leadership, dissociated from the anti-reform image of old Toryism and yet different from the radical propensities of the new Whiggery. He had emerged as a national figure and, as the *Annual Register* observed in its review of the year, 'not merely as the first but without a rival'.

It was not only his opponents and the public which had been impressed. Some of his colleagues had been equally surprised. Those who previously had not known him well were struck by his modesty and friendliness. Power seemed to have given him an assurance and ease of a manner which in the past only his intimates had encountered. Young men like Gladstone, older men like Wharncliffe, were all touched by his warmth and kindness. Sir James Graham, the reluctant Stanleyite, was particularly moved by this unexpected side to Peel's nature. He told Greville that the interview he had with Peel immediately after his return from Italy was 'cordial and obliging . . . without any appearance of that coldness and reserve of which he has been so often accused'. Though still loyal to Stanley, Graham was clearly looking forward to an eventual union with Peel and the return of the Conservatives to office 'with as much zeal', noted Greville curiously, '. . . as if he had been a member of the Cabinet'.

A return to power, moreover, was now something more than a distant prospect. The Hundred Days had given fresh heart to the scattered forces of Conservatism in the country at large. It had enabled a 'Conservative Party' in a real sense to come into existence. Previously it had neither numbers nor cohesion; now it had both. If the king had done nothing else, he had made Peel the acknowledged leader of the party; and Peel had made the *Tamworth Manifesto*, as much as anything of that kind could be, the official expression of the party's views. The Conservative forces in the Commons were now almost twice as large as in 1833; they had a majority in the Lords and the open sympathies of the Crown. They constituted an organised opposition in parliament more formidable than anything that had existed since Waterloo. For the first time since the Reform Act they had taken the initiative in the provinces; and the wave of constituency Conservative and Constitutional Associations formed under the stimulus of the general election and the new government provided a basis for further growth. As Bonham, the party's chief electoral expert, wrote to Peel at the end of the year, 'then we had to find candidates, organisers and friends in almost every place. *Now that work is done* and a tenth part of the exertions then applied would at least preserve if not increase our present strength.'

Peel himself was not untouched by the general atmosphere of confidence. In a brief affectionate little speech he made at a dinner to some of his outgoing colleagues in April, he observed that if a Conservative government had not been strong enough to carry on the affairs of the country, at least they were now strong enough to prevent any other government from doing serious mischief. He abstained from further political speculation but it did not require much optimism among those present in the dining-room at Whitehall Gardens that evening to look forward to the time when the party would be in power and Peel in office in circumstances vastly more favourable than those of November 1834.

Chapter 13

Leader of the opposition

The transformation of politics brought about by the events of 1834–35 affected Peel more perhaps than any other single man in public life. The principles he had advocated in the years immediately after the Reform Act had not changed, but they now had to be worked out on the practical level of specific issues and party tactics. Balance had been restored to the parliamentary situation and with the balance, greater tension. The Liberal Party had not exhausted its programme of reform. But it now faced not only an invigorated Tory majority in the House of Lords but a strong compact opposition in the House of Commons. The problems however were not all on one side; Peel too had his difficulties. He was for the first time in his life the acknowledged leader of a powerful party. The question was whether, and on what terms, he could control it. Tamworth conservatism demanded a measured and selective opposition. Mere reaction and obstruction would make nonsense of his recent public utterances and destroy any chance of winning over the moderate opinion for which Stanley and his friends served as a kind of parliamentary barometer. Yet the party unity witnessed during the Hundred Days was too recent to be anything but fragile; and the needs of organised opposition implied novel and unwelcome restraints for his followers. The combination of party discipline and Tamworth conservatism was not a diet to which all his followers would readily take. Nevertheless, it was the only course which would lead them to power and it was one which Peel was determined to pursue. In the process he was to experience more than once the truth of the old saying that most of the problems of a party leader come from his own party.

Between 1835 and 1841 Peel set himself three main tasks: to prevent the Tory majority in the House of Lords from abusing its power; to follow a policy in the House of Commons that would make possible an alliance with Stanley and Graham; and to build up the party's strength and prestige in the country. The most unmanageable task, since it was largely outside his direct control, was presented by the House of Lords. Though his relations with Wellington grew more stable after 1834, the disparity of temperament and experience between the two men was always liable to produce occasional disagreements, misunderstandings and irritations. Lyndhurst, who acted in these years as a kind of self-appointed lieutenant to the duke in the Upper House, was a vain, brilliant, shallow man whose waywardness was only redeemed by his lack of serious political objectives. In any case the Tory peers were men whose rank and wealth often made them indisposed to accept direction from anyone, least of all from the House of Commons

THE LIFE OF PEEL

party and its leader. The party opposition of the Tory majority in the Lords raised, however, the constitutional issue of the function of the Upper House. Irresponsible action by a hereditary majority would certainly intensify the demand for a curtailment of the powers of the Lords and though few politicians would welcome the prospect of another reform bill controversy, Peel for one thought that the only prudent course was for the House of Lords to disarm its critics by statesmanlike behaviour.

The most serious clash, not only between the Tory peers and the government but between the two wings of the Conservative Party, came in 1835 over the English Municipal Corporations bill. Though Peel had his criticisms of the work of the government's royal commission, he accepted that there was an irresistible case for reform and his first step was to obtain Wellington's agreement that it should not be made a party question. The various amendments put forward by the opposition in the House of Commons were duly defeated but Peel had no reason at that stage to feel dissatisfied. The government's bill had been better than had been expected; he had secured the cooperation of the Stanleyites; and the party had shown itself moderate and united. When the bill went to the Lords the situation changed abruptly. There was considerable hostility there to the actual principle of the measure and some peers clearly thought that the government might be driven to resign on the issue. In August, after hearing counsel at the bar in defence of the threatened corporations, the House of Lords under Lyndhurst's flamboyant leadership tore the bill to ribbons. It was not merely an unreasonable and provocative attack on an important government measure; it was a direct challenge to the government itself. Clearly the duty of the Whigs was to stay in office, since no alternative administration was possible. But they were being presented with a gratuitous justification for resignation; and Peel for one was not sure that they would resist the temptation.

He had told Ellenborough at the outset that there was no chance of forming a Conservative ministry and that he could not be party to any hostile amendment in the Lords which he had not supported in the Commons. What angered and disheartened him was that the understanding he thought he had achieved with Wellington and his aristocratic colleagues had collapsed like a house of cards at the first breath of revolt from their followers. At the end of July he warned them that he would not be responsible for the actions of the Lords. As soon as it was evident that Wellington had lost control and that the ultra-Tory peers were running riot, he signalled his displeasure by ostentatiously leaving town. When the mutilated bill returned to the Commons at the end of the month, some Conservatives thought the wisest course would be to leave the government and the Radicals to deal with it. Peel, however, was not prepared to abdicate his authority so easily. On 31 August, fresh from a shooting expedition in Derbyshire, he reappeared in London. The same evening he intervened decisively in the debate.

Though, as was said at the time, he 'threw over the Lords', it was in substance rather than in form. His tone was conciliatory; he welcomed the various concessions made by Russell; and he said it was the duty of both sides to compromise. With both leaders in the Commons bent on settlement, the remaining differences were readily composed.

Everything now depended on the pliability of the Lords, and by September the united front of the Tory peers was beginning to crumble. Even the ultras realised that in the face of Peel's determination there was no hope of forcing a change of government. The more moderate ex-ministerialist group began to exert an increasing influence and at a meeting at Apsley House on 3 September the policy of conciliation was finally accepted. The collision course which the peers had been steering all through August was thus altered at the last minute. But it had been a narrow escape and the crisis left its mark. Though there was discontent among the Conservatives, not least at Peel's behaviour, it was nothing to the dissatisfaction felt by many Radicals who had been outraged by the action of the Lords and resented the concessions made by the government. The theme of House of Lords reform became a passionate topic among politicians of the left and in the autumn O'Connell made an oratorical pilgrimage to Scotland and the north of England to agitate for an elective Upper House. This was precisely the reaction Peel had feared; and despite his success in September 1835, he still feared. There was no certainty that the Tory peers had learned a lasting lesson or that the same situation, with a worse result, might not recur.

The English Municipal Corporations bill had demonstrated in painful fashion the political differences between the two wings of the party. There were other issues which, while not disturbing party unity so profoundly, presented Peel with perhaps more subtle and difficult problems of leadership. The question of the reform of the Irish Church offered few embarrassments as long as the Whigs clung to the principle of appropriation. This, the issue on which Peel had been driven from office in 1835, constituted a clear line of demarcation between the two parties. But the reform of the Irish municipal corporations was a more complicated matter on which Peel made one of his rare tactical errors in these years. It was an error from which it took him some time to recover. In 1836 the government introduced a bill to sweep away the seventy-one old Irish corporations, for the most part small corrupt Protestant oligarchies. They were to be replaced by a system similar to that set up in England, though on a more limited franchise, with popularly elected councils and property qualifications for councillors. The reform in the abstract was unexceptionable. But it raised the dilemma that constantly dogged Conservative policy towards Ireland: how to apply rational reforms to Irish institutions without destroying Protestant Ascendancy. Peel's particular fear was that a remodelled Dublin Corporation in the hands of O'Connell would become an instrument for Irish nationalist agitation and assume something of the character of a permanent Irish assembly sitting in the Irish capital. The problem was to devise an acceptable alternative proposal. Peel and his little committee of Irish experts—Shaw, Fitzgerald, Goulburn, Jackson and others—concluded that the only course satisfactory to Irish Protestants would be to abolish the borough corporations entirely and substitute for them the ordinary machinery of county government with administration and justice in the hands of local magistrates and officials appointed by the Crown.

The plan, backed by the authority of Peel and the House of Commons party, was accepted (though perhaps with no real enthusiasm) by Stanley and Wellington. Peel was always a persuasive advocate for any line of policy he had adopted and his point about O'Connell was a particularly telling one. Both he and Stanley had a personal dislike of the great Irish agitator and it was difficult for either to be completely objective towards him. It was true that O'Connell had hailed the new English corporations as 'schools for teaching the science of agitation'; and what was rhetoric in England might become reality in Ireland. But to found a policy on O'Connell's oratorical excesses was itself to give way to exaggeration. Whatever the political justification, to deny Ireland the reformed municipal institutions granted to England was a national insult with which the Conservative opposition as a whole was never happy and Peel in the long run found it impossible to persist. The only immediate advantage was that it provided a policy which kept himself, Stanley and the duke in agreement and made slightly more respectable the slaughter of the government's bill in the Upper House. In 1837, however, after a similar bill had been introduced and similarly opposed, Stanley suggested the more flexible course of postponing consideration of the Irish Municipal bill until more satisfactory terms had been secured for the other ministerial Irish measures relating to Poor Law and tithe. This at least held out the prospect of a packet of compromises which might include the withdrawal of the appropriation clause from the tithe bill. Peel was ready enough to modify his tactics. His House of Commons party had never shown much stomach for a fight on the corporations issue; and Stanley and Graham were reluctant to hold up Irish municipal reform for yet another year. None of them wished to provoke a constitutional collision between Lords and Commons or drive the cabinet into resignation. The real problem lay with Wellington, who disliked political manoeuvring and had his own followers to consider. In the end Peel was able to guide his colleagues to agreement on the change of tactics. With the belated substitution by the Whigs of a tax on ecclesiastical revenue for the controversial appropriation clause of the tithe bill, the way was clear for compromise on all three of the government's Irish measures. Only delays in the legislative timetable and the death of William IV in June 1837 postponed the decision to yet another session.

What the character of the new parliamentary era would be, with another sovereign and a new parliament, could only be a matter for speculation. But in retrospect the session of 1837, barren and disappointing for the Whigs, had brought Peel marginal and hard-fought gains. From the start he had acted as mediator and arbiter, especially in the matter of the Irish corporations. He had put Wellington's views to Stanley and Graham, Stanley's views to Wellington and Lyndhurst, the commoners' views to the peers and the peers' views to the commoners. His chief concern had been to prevent separate action by Stanley in the Lower House and by Wellington the Upper. In this he had succeeded; and in so doing had further eroded the position of the Whigs. But though unity had been preserved, it had only been by constant effort. Between Stanley and Wellington there was still the sediment of old hostilities, and the two sections of the party did not always find it easy to run in double harness. 'Few people', Peel wrote reflectively in July in a memorandum which he placed with his Irish municipal papers.

> can judge of the difficulty there has frequently been of maintaining harmony between the various branches of the Conservative party— the great majority in the House of Lords and the minority in the House of Commons consisting of very different elements that had been in open conflict within a recent period.

II

Whatever the problems of its leaders, the party as a whole was immeasurably stronger at the end of William IV's reign than it had been even two years earlier. By 1837 the last delicate stage in Peel's long courtship of the Stanley group had been reached; and that session had witnessed a silent transformation in their relationship with the Conservative party. From being political allies they had become political associates, and personal consultation had increasingly replaced formal correspondence. The English Municipal Corporations bill had marked one stage; the Irish Corporations bill another. In the summer of 1835 the hostile attitude of Whig backbenchers had forced the Stanleyites to abandon their old seats on the ministerialist side of the House and move across to the benches behind Peel. Two years later that symbolic shift of allegiance had become a reality. In April 1837, for example, Stanley and Graham were present with Peel at a meeting of Conservative peers at Lyndhurst's house to discuss the Irish bill. They attended a similar meeting at Peel's house a few days later and again at Aberdeen's house in May. In June they had been members of an opposition committee to prepare amendments to the bill in the House of Lords. The Derby Dilly had found stabling at last; and though they numbered now little more than the 'six insides' of O'Connell's famous jibe, they brought prestige, debating skill, and an element of liberalism to the parliamentary forces at Peel's disposal.

The party was also better organised. For all Peel's distaste for the petty arts of politics, the management of the Conservative party under his leadership achieved a degree of professional competence that it had never possessed before or was to possess again until after the second Reform Act. The Chief Whips he appointed, Sir George Clerk in 1835 and Sir Thomas Fremantle in 1837, were a marked improvement on Holmes, Ross, and Planta who had served in the pre-reform era. Lord Granville Somerset, the brusque but efficient aristocrat who had served his apprenticeship under Lord Liverpool, acted as unofficial chief of staff. In the indefatigable F. R. Bonham, an Oxonian and former M.P., with his voluminous correspondence and strapped book full of constituency secrets, Peel had an electoral expert of equal competence and higher social standing than Parkes and Coppock, the two radical solicitors who carried out similar functions for the Liberal Party. It was at Bonham's suggestion in 1835 that a small permanent committee under Granville Somerset's chairmanship was set up to supervise elections, provide money and candidates, and collect information on the state of registration in the constituencies. It was Bonham too, a personal friend and frequent visitor to Drayton, who acted as Peel's eyes and ears in the party. There was scarcely a ripple of opinion among the Conservatives which was not reported to Peel by his faithful watchdog in the Carlton. Whatever other difficulties Peel faced in opposition, he lacked neither detailed information on the mood of his followers nor expert advice on the outcome of any prospective general election.

He himself showed in these years a growing confidence and authority as leader. Strong-willed by nature, intellectually scornful of the backwoodsmen of the party, he had no intention of letting the tail wag the head. But a quarter of a century in politics had schooled him to patience and conciliation. From 1835 onwards he was evolving his own technique of party management and consultation. In December or January, before the session began, came the annual gathering of the inner ring of his colleagues at Drayton. During the session there were periodic discussions with the leading debaters and experts on particular issues, reinforced by occasional conferences with Wellington and the more influential peers. Sometimes, but less often since Peel had no great liking for them, there was a full meeting of the House of Commons parliamentary party to explain policy. These were flanked on a more social plane by Peel's regular political dinners at Whitehall Gardens and a personal appearance from time to time at the Carlton. For a man denied by nature the indolent charm of Melbourne or the cheerful insouciance of Palmerston, these latter activities were more perhaps a duty than a pleasure. Nevertheless the common charge against Peel of coldness and uncommunicativeness towards his followers is largely coloured by the subsequent events of the 1840s. As leader of the opposition in the late 1830s he showed a remarkable degree of tact and patience in keeping his party together without compromising his essential objectives; and his success was seen in the relative absence of any serious difficulty with the House of Commons party during these years. Only after 1841, when office robbed him of leisure and the demands of national policy conflicted with the interests of his followers, did his control begin to weaken.

Peel's work in opposition was not confined to the narrow arena of parliamentary tactics or electoral preparations. Indeed, these efforts might well have failed to achieve their goal had it not been for the wider propagation of Conservative views which he carried out in these years. It was a task for which there were few opportunities and little precedent. Outside parliament and his own constituency a politician, particularly a former minister of the Crown, was inhibited by convention from political speech-making on all but the rarest of occasions. The demagogic methods of O'Connell or Hunt were not those that could be followed with propriety by a Privy Councillor. Nevertheless, from the time of the Reform Act, Peel had realised that the only hope for the Conservatives lay in winning back part at least of the moderate middle-class opinion which had supported Lord Grey in 1831–32. In the *Tamworth Manifesto* he had made an appeal to the politically uncommitted classes interested in the defence of property, order and good government. In May 1835, at a dinner given in his honour by the merchants and bankers of the City, he renewed the message in more explicit terms. The nature of the government, he reminded his audience, was now decided by the composition of the House of Commons. To gain control of that assembly by open and constitutional means was the prime task of Conservatism. Between them and the reformed electorate there were, or should be, no barriers.

> We deny that we are separated by any line of interest, or any other line of demarcation, from the middling classes. . . . What was the grand charge against myself—that the King had sent for the son of a cotton-spinner to Rome, in order to make him Prime Minister of England. Did I feel that by any means a reflection on me? . . . No; but does it not make me, and ought it not to make you, gentlemen, do all you can to reserve to other sons of other cotton-spinners the same opportunities, by the same system of laws under which this country has so long flourished, of arriving by the same honourable means at the like destination?

After rehearsing once more the main points of the *Tamworth Manifesto*, he argued that the maintenance of the existing mixed and balanced constitution, above all a refusal to allow any further slide towards a democratic republic, was in the true interest of the middle classes of the electorate. Public order and national prosperity depended on it. 'That is what I apprehend by the Conservative principle and such is the ground on which we make our appeal to the country at large.' Reported prominently in *The Times* next day the speech made a sensation more perhaps from the vigour of its language than from the novelty of the argument. The party, as Greville reported, praised it to the skies and distributed copies all over the country.

It was the most significant public pronouncement outside the walls of Westminster that Peel had ever made; and in less than two years he was given another opportunity to address himself to a large and representative middle-class audience. In November 1836 he was elected Rector of Glasgow University. To fill an office held by Mackintosh, Brougham and Stanley was an honour; to have won it against a Whig candidate, the future Lord Chancellor Sir John Campbell, was a triumph. Though acceptance meant a journey of four hundred miles in the depth of winter and on the eve of a parliamentary session, Peel did not hesitate. His main speech, however, was not that delivered on 11 January to his student constituents in the university but one given two days later at a political banquet in celebration of his visit. Public speeches by ex-prime ministers were even more of a novelty in Scotland than in England and a huge temporary hall of timber and tarpaulin had to be constructed to accommodate the 3,400 guests who subscribed twenty-five shillings a head to hear him. After the dinner Peel spoke for nearly two hours to his vast and applauding audience. Though much of his speech was devoted to the burning contemporary topics of the House of Lords and Church Establishments (with an appropriate emphasis on the Church of Scotland), what gave it a special flavour was the direct appeal he made to his hearers. He invited all those who had supported the Reform Act to join him in protecting the constitution that had resulted from that epoch-making statute. 'I see the necessity', he told them, 'of widening the foundations on which the defence of the British Constitution and religious establishments must rest. . . . With me you ought now to combine for the defence of the existing institutions of the country.' He shared their wish to end corruption and abuse. He did not want the great engine of government to stand still. He wanted to see it functioning properly, 'animating industry, encouraging production, rewarding toil, correcting what is irregular, purifying what is stagnant or corrupt'. But it could only operate well if its foundations were secure and its operations free from perpetual meddling and disturbance.

A year and a half later came the turn of his own party. In May 1838, over three hundred friends and supporters under the chairmanship of Lord Chandos, nearly all members of the House of Commons, organised a banquet in his honour at the Merchant Taylors' Hall in London. With Stanley and Graham sitting beside him, Peel took this unprecedented opportunity of expounding to his followers his conception of the nature and policy of Conservatism. His object, he told them, for some years past had been to diminish the risk of a collision between the two Houses of Parliament and check the radical pressure for precipitate alterations in the laws and constitution of the country. Though they were now a great and powerful party, they were still a Conservative party. Their function was not to resist but to preserve. On

many occasions they had supported the government against its own
supporters; they had rejected the temptation to ally for the sake of
tactical advantage with those with whom they had nothing fundamentally in common. By doing their duty even in support of the government they had established new claims on the confidence of the electorate
for becoming the government themselves. It was the Tamworth message
over again: defence of the settled institutions of the state; progressive
reform rather than radical innovation; and the broadening of the
party's electoral basis. Even in his patronage as prime minister during
his short 1834–35 ministry he had not been unmindful of this last consideration. In recommending a discreet bestowal of pensions to scientific figures he pointed out to the king the political advantages of
'conciliating the confidence and goodwill of that most powerful class
. . . connected with the literature and science of the Country, and of
encouraging the application of great talents and great acquirements to
the support of the ancient institutions of the Country'.

III

With the Whigs encouraged by the accession of a young and partial
sovereign and the Conservatives seeking to enlarge the advantages
gratuitously presented to them by William IV two years earlier, the
general election of 1837 was the hardest fought and in some respects the
most critical contest between the first and second Reform Acts. But
even with the influence of office behind them the Whigs were still unable
to halt the Conservative advance. With twenty-three English county
seats falling to their opponents, their domination in England and
Scotland finally disappeared and only Ireland and O'Connell stood
between them and a Conservative government. By the time all the
election returns had come in it was clear that their majority in the
previous session of under sixty had been reduced to one of just over
thirty. For their opponents it now seemed only a matter of time and one
more trial of strength before they were evicted.

In November a cheerful mass of Conservative M.P.s gathered in
London for the opening of the new parliament. At a meeting of some
three hundred of them at Peel's house, Stanley for the first time was
present, thus tacitly acknowledging his junction with the Conservatives. As though recognising the changed parliamentary situation, the
queen's speech introduced no fresh controversial proposals and made
only mild references to the unfinished business of the previous session:
Irish municipal reform, Irish tithe and Irish poor law. Russell as leader
of the House signalled the cabinet's retreat with a speech repudiating
any further electoral reform which earned for him from the disappointed Radicals the nickname of Finality Jack.

With a powerful opposition eager for attack and a section of their
own supporters restless and frustrated, the prospects for Melbourne's

government seemed more precarious than ever. Peel's chief problem was how to keep his troops under control without damping their ardour. It was too early yet to think of evicting the Whigs; and Wellington in particular was unwilling to lend himself to any attempt to force a Conservative ministry on the new queen. The Canadian crisis that blew up in the winter of 1837–38 exposed all these complexities in the parliamentary situation. The Whigs were torn between their instinct to make liberal concessions and their responsibility as the imperial executive; the Conservatives between their traditional support for executive authority and the temptation to make the most of their opponents' difficulties. Only the Radicals, with their scarcely veiled sympathy for the Canadian rebels in their attack on oligarchy, privilege and Church establishments, could afford the luxury of a doctrinaire attitude. Peel, Wellington and Stanley were agreed that though the government's policy was open to large criticisms in detail, it must be supported in the practical proposals to end the Canadian revolt. In this they were aided by the cabinet's prudent readiness to accept many of Peel's suggestions. When in March Molesworth launched a radical attack on Glenelg, the colonial secretary, skilful tactics on Peel's part enabled the official opposition to express their criticisms of government policy while rendering it impossible for the Radicals to make a temporary and dangerous coalition in the voting lobby which might have brought down the administration.

From the position of controlled power in which he had been left by the Canadian crisis, Peel was now able to negotiate a settlement of the interminable controversies over the government's Irish reforms. In a guarded exchange between the two leaders in March 1838 Russell signified his readiness to abandon the contest over appropriation and Peel responded by expressing a wish for a settlement of the tithe and corporation issues. Before the session was over the Irish tithe and poor law bills had gone into the statute book; and though dissatisfaction among his own followers prevented Russell from accepting a compromise £10 rating franchise for Irish municipal electors, the gap between the two sides had narrowed sufficiently to bring the end of the dispute in sight. For Peel, who with difficulty had brought his party to accept the compromise, the result was not unduly displeasing. He had extricated himself from the untenable policy of abolishing the Irish corporations; and the 'Fabian policy' as Graham called it, of wearing down the government and extracting valuable concessions had shown a handsome profit. A future Conservative ministry would at least not be faced with a daunting list of unsolved Irish issues on which they would be fettered by their attitudes in opposition.

Though there was some grumbling and dissatisfaction among the Conservatives at the cautious policy of their leaders, in fact the 1838 session had virtually brought to an end the reforming phase of the post-1832 Whig governments. On many major matters they had been forced to accept the limitations prescribed by the opposition; they would give no clear lead on such issues as the ballot or the Corn Laws; and their Radical allies were increasingly disillusioned and disheartened. These were not their only troubles. O'Connell was beginning a fresh agitation in Ireland; the resignation of Lord Durham was embarrassing their Canadian settlement; and in April 1839 a new colonial crisis arrived in the shape of a constitutional conflict with the Assembly in Jamaica. Meanwhile at home, after a decade dominated by constitutional and religious problems, the economic depression was thrusting social and economic questions once more into the foreground. Two extra-parliamentary movements started in 1838, Chartism and the Manchester Anti-Corn Law Association, were early signals of the change in national mood. It was a change which Melbourne's cabinet, politically and temperamentally, was ill-equipped to meet.

For Wellington the mounting difficulties of the government at home and abroad seemed an additional argument for not bringing pressure to bear on them. He went so far as to opine to Arbuthnot that the Conservatives should not take office even if they had a majority. While sharing many of the duke's misgivings, Peel was not prepared to adopt quite such a despairing attitude. An opposition party, he argued, could not be held together unless it opposed; and only the strength of the opposition had prevented the cabinet from carrying out a more radical policy. Though not eager for office in existing circumstances, he would not evade it if the need arose; nor on the other hand would he provoke the Whigs into resignation or seek any tactical success with the aid of Radical malcontents. He would, in other words, continue cautiously along the same road he had been following since 1833. Indeed, if Tamworth Conservatism was to mean anything, he had no other choice. At the start of the 1839 session a kind of deadpoint in the balance of political power seemed to have been reached. If it was a situation which fretted the more impetuous Conservatives, it was even less to the liking of some Radicals. Leader warned the government in the spring that on a general motion of confidence some ten or twelve Radicals would vote against them. The position of the ministry, observed the indignant member for Westminster, was that Mr O'Connell governed Ireland, and Sir Robert Peel governed England. The leader of the Conservatives was satisfied with power without place or patronage; the Whigs with place and patronage without power.

It was this fundamental insecurity that explained, if it did not justify, the abrupt resignation of the cabinet in May 1839 over their bill to suspend the Jamaican Assembly. While Peel had been critical of the government's tactless handling of the West Indian planters, the decisive action was taken by a group of left-wing Liberals. The ministers were not beaten, but their majority sank to five; and nine of their usual supporters voted against them. In the context of all that had passed in the earlier part of the session it was enough. On 7 May Melbourne resigned and advised the queen to send for Wellington. The situation which had been talked about so long had suddenly arrived.

On Wednesday 8 May a curt note from Victoria desired Peel's immediate attendance at the Palace. He was under no illusion as to what awaited him. The queen was sending for him because she had no choice; and if he was not already aware of his deficiencies in dealing with strange females, he had just been reminded of it by a note from his old friend Lady de Grey who warned him with more truth than tact that it would be difficult for a man of his reserved and cautious temperament to overcome the queen's partiality for Melbourne. Waiting for him in the Palace was a short, sulky young woman of twenty in a state of suppressed anger, misery and nervousness. The opening exchanges were stiff but civil. Victoria made it clear that she would not agree to a dissolution of parliament, that she wished Wellington to be a member of the new administration, and that she intended to continue her friendship with her late prime minister. Peel assented to all this but emphasised the difficulties of his parliamentary position and said he would like the queen to demonstrate some confidence in her new ministers and that the Household would be a sign of this. Discussing the situation with his colleagues that evening the question of court appointments came up. It seemed a minor if inescapable problem. As a result of Melbourne's careless partisanship an unusually large number of the women holding Household posts were wives or relatives of the outgoing Whig ministers; and under the rule of the dominant Paget clan the whole tone of court life was notoriously lax. It was assumed that those ladies with close Whig connections would resign immediately and Peel talked briefly with Lord Ashley on suitable persons to form the entourage of a young unmarried queen.

These were rational assumptions. What the Conservative politicians failed to realise was that the emotional relationship between Victoria and Melbourne made both of them less than rational in this moment of separation. Encouraged by Melbourne, to whom she sent an immediate report of the interview, Victoria the following day cut Peel short as soon as he moved to the question of Household appointments and peremptorily told him that she wished to retain all her ladies. He tried to reason with her; but the determined and excited young Victoria was beyond the reach of reason. The duke of Wellington was brought in to add his persuasion but with equal lack of success. When the stillborn cabinet discussed the matter there was general agreement that their precarious position in parliament made some public mark of confidence indispensable. Meanwhile, on the strength of Victoria's account of the negotiations with Peel, the outgoing Whigs advised her to reject his proposals. Not until the day after, when he read Peel's formal letter to Victoria recapitulating all that happened, did Melbourne realise that Peel had only asked that some, not all the ladies of the Bedchamber should be changed. But some or all, said the happy exhilarated young queen, was the same.

When the news spread that the Whigs were in again, there was the usual spate of rumour. Disappointed Tories spoke of planned intrigue;

Whigs of Peel's dictatorial and unreasonable behaviour. The guarded explanations given by the party leaders in both Houses did little to remove the obscurity. In fact Wellington told Greville that he had never seen Peel so gentle and conciliatory and that there was nothing at which Victoria could have taken offence. The difficulty had been in Victoria herself. It was evident that she had made up her mind to yield as little as possible to Melbourne's successor. Her hostility was because she was losing her minister, not her ladies. As she said to Russell afterwards, 'I have stood by you, you must now stand by me'. It would have needed unusual charm and flattery to have coaxed her out of her rebellious mood. All that Peel could offer was patient reasoned argument by a large, shy, self-conscious man. Victoria recorded afterwards that she found him cold and odd, and that she could not make out what he meant; but she was scarcely an impartial witness. Though there was clearly a temperamental antipathy, this was not the most important consideration. The old duke, more versed in the ways of women, she liked better; but his arguments still made no impression. For Victoria, however, there were human excuses. There were none for the Whigs, who had put both themselves and their youthful sovereign in an unfortunate and unconstitutional position. The core of the trouble was Melbourne's contradictory role as prime minister and private secretary to the crown. He was the only person to whom the young and unhappy Victoria could turn for guidance; and this in turn created the anomalous situation in which the queen took advice from one cabinet on how to deal with another. It was true that the Whigs had been misled by Victoria about the extent of Peel's request; but they had taken remarkably little trouble to find out. Melbourne had every disposition to be fair to his successor but he had let himself be carried along by Victoria's adolescent ardour and his own elderly affection.

Failure to win office under the cramping conditions of 1839 was no great loss to the Conservatives. But Peel had gone to the Palace ready to show respect and sympathy and he would have been less than human not to feel that part of the hostility he had encountered was personal to himself. What rankled most was the charge that he had behaved in a mannerless and overbearing manner to the young girl who was his sovereign. Nevertheless he refused to retreat an inch from the constitutional position he had taken up. In reply to a public address from Shrewsbury in June he said firmly that the sex of the persons made no difference to the general principles governing court appointments, however much the exercise of ministerial power might be restrained by personal consideration for the monarch; and he added pointedly that the necessity for changes was not of his making but of the ministers who in previous years had given such a political character to the Royal Household.

Meanwhile, with a powerful opposition temporarily disabled from office and a weak ministry temporarily disabled from resignation, parliamentary politics in the remainder of the session took on an even more desultory appearance. The cabinet seemed floundering in a sea of executive problems. They could do little without the tacit connivance of the Conservative leaders; and in the general paralysis of liberal policy the enthusiasm drained from their supporters both in the Commons and in the country at large. Their educational scheme brought forward in June foundered on massive Anglican opposition out of doors; their legislation for Canada and Jamaica had to be trimmed to meet the objections brought forward by Peel in the Commons. After the session had ended the still smouldering resentment of lesser Tory politicians against the queen continued to break out on various public occasions during the autumn. Even the news that the queen was to marry the young and virtually unknown Prince Albert of Saxe-Coburg-Gotha failed to soothe party hostility. The most that could be said for the marriage from the Conservative point of view was that it might weaken Victoria's dependence on the Whigs. As Graham resignedly expressed it to Peel in November: 'No change can well be for the worse; and in such circumstances almost any change becomes desirable.'

Chapter 14

Squire of Drayton

Although the Peel family never again exhibited the vast concentration of wealth present between 1815 and 1830, Peel himself had been left a rich man. His father's real and personal estate at the time of his death amounted to nearly £1½ million. Though a third of this was distributed among his five younger sons and two daughters, the main Tamworth estate, probably worth nearly £500,000, and a substantial amount in stocks and annuities was inherited by his eldest son. With an annual rent-roll of some £25,000 Peel after 1830 was in possession of a gross income from all sources of over £40,000 per annum. In the previous decade the sums settled on him by his father, together with his official salary as Secretary of State and some small personal property, had brought him in about £20,000 a year. But his marriage, his new house in Whitehall Gardens, his purchases of pictures, had involved him in heavy expenditure and he was overspending his income up to the time of his father's death. The inheritance which came to him in 1830, therefore, was peculiarly welcome. It lifted him out of his indebtedness, absorbed the loss of his official salary, and provided him with a comfortable surplus on which to live.

As squire of Drayton and leader of a party, he inevitably found his expenses rising with his new status. Accustomed since boyhood to a luxurious standard of existence, Peel liked to live well and generously. He enjoyed good food, fashionable clothes, expensive furnishings. His town house saw a constant succession of dinner-parties during the session and Drayton was rarely without guests during the autumn and early winter. His entertaining was famous for its quality and style. At Whitehall Gardens the guests usually found themselves eating off plate in company with about twenty or thirty others attended by a platoon of servants in their orange and purple livery. The meal itself equalled the setting. Even the cynical and irreverent Disraeli was impressed when he dined at Peel's house in February 1839. He arrived late to find 'some twenty-five gentlemen grubbing in solemn silence'. But, he told his sister appreciatively, 'the dinner was curiously sumptuous— "every delicacy of the season", and the second course of dried olives, caviare, woodcock-pie, *foie gras*, and every combination of cured herring, etc. was really remarkable'.

If Peel entertained handsomely, he also gave generously. Most M.P.s were expected to subscribe to local and charitable appeals; and as a wealthy man with property in three counties, Peel was more than ordinarily exposed to demands on his purse. Where his personal

inclinations were revealed was perhaps in the frequency of his do-
nations for religious and educational purposes. In one year for example
(1839) a surviving memorandum book shows that among other items
he gave £10 to Drayton Sunday School, £500 to the Lichfield Diocesan
Church Building Society, £50 and an annual subscription of five
guineas to the Lichfield Diocesan Education Society, as well as £500
to Tamworth Corporation for widening the Lady Bridge. Without
being spendthrift, Peel clearly thought that wealth was to be used
rather than hoarded. During his decade in opposition from 1831 to
1841 there was no sign that he was saving money. Though his buying of
paintings had fallen off, he was steadily enlarging his landed property.
In 1837 he told his electors at Tamworth that 'all my present pecuniary
and personal interests are centred in the prosperity of agriculture'.
Five years later he extended those interests still further by paying
nearly £5,000 for the manor of Hampton-in-Arden in Warwickshire,
designed perhaps for his seond son Frederick to whom he bequeathed
it in a will drawn up the same year.

After that his activities slackened. He told his brother William in
1845 that he had already bought more land than he proposed to leave
to his eldest son and was not anxious to increase his estate except in
special circumstances. In later years his investments, probably with a
view to settlements on his other children, were mainly in securities. At
the end of his life his private fortune, apart from the entailed estate and
two large trust investments, totalled about £120,000, more than half
of it in land. This was in addition to the house in Whitehall Gardens,
his paintings, library, furniture and farm stock. He had spent or given
away more than he had received and, though a wealthy man, was less
wealthy in 1850 than he had been in 1830. On the other hand he had
become a more considerable landowner than his father and the
decline in his funded property was at least partly accounted for by his
real estate purchases. Though his political enemies alleged that he had
increasingly disengaged himself from the landed interest, he had in
fact committed himself more deeply to it. 'So far from my brother
having increased . . .' wrote Colonel Jonathan Peel in October 1850,
'I should think he had decreased his personal property by at least the
value of the Land he purchased.'

One expensive personal luxury he did allow himself: the building
of new Drayton Manor. Certainly his father's old house was too small
and plain to warrant retention or justify extension. Yet the zeal and
money Peel devoted to his new house derived as much from his interest
as patron of the arts as from his social needs as landowner and politician. The combination of Peel wealth and taste, Robert Smirke, the
fashionable architect of the Tory aristocracy, and William Gilpin, the
great landscape gardener, promised a spectacular achievement. Plans
for the new house were drawn up as early as the autumn of 1830. By
1832 the gardens had been laid out and the body of the house was
being roofed. But it was not until the end of 1835 that Peel was able to

entertain in it for the first time and not until 1836 that the great work finally came to completion.

Peel Fold at Oswaldtwistle, the old home of the Peel family, was a humble yeoman's farmhouse; old Drayton Hall, built by his father, a plain unimaginative country mansion; new Drayton Hall a great Victorian pile. Peel set out to construct a house which should combine the elegance of an Elizabethan or Jacobean manor with the comfort and opulence of contemporary taste. With no restrictions of space and almost none of time and money, the result was by the standards of the twentieth century a florid and ambitious failure. Built in the reign of William IV, it was one of the first great examples of the disintegration of style commonly associated with the reign of his successor. Cupolas, balustrades, towers, gables, mullioned windows, an Italian campanile, marble and mahogany, stained glass and parquet floors, failed to conceal the essential ponderousness of the building while successfully obliterating all sense of architectural tradition. It was the fault not of a single patron or architect but of the age. Drayton Hall was conspicuous only because it was an early example of Victorian eclecticism on a grand scale; it was to be followed by countless others in the course of the century. What struck the first visitors to the house, however, was its opulence and comfort. 'A very handsome house with every conveniency and even magnificence', reported Lord Talbot, Peel's former Lord-Lieutenant. Haydon, the painter who stayed at Drayton in 1838, wrote in his diary that 'the House is splendidly comfortable'. And Victoria, after her visit with Albert in 1843, said to Aberdeen, 'Well, what you told me is quite true. Drayton is certainly the most comfortable House I ever saw.' In a society accustomed even among the rich to draughts, discomforts, smells and general inconvenience in all its old houses, the provision of efficient plumbing, mechanical heating, and furnishings designed for physical ease, was appreciated more highly than by a posterity able to take such amenities for granted.

Whatever its qualities, it was Peel's favourite house for the rest of his life. With its dogs and horses, home farm, estate office, dairy and stables, Drayton Manor was essentially a country mansion, the heart of a substantial landed estate; and Peel and his wife had simple tastes which they could enjoy to their heart's content in their Staffordshire home. Peel could feed partridges from the French windows of the breakfast-room and Julia drive her pony carriage round the park. When her husband was detained in London during the spring and early summer, she would send him violets, strawberries and new potatoes to bring a breath of country air to Whitehall Gardens. From his great library overlooking the busy Thames Peel could reply, as he did in September 1843, 'My heart is far away, basking with you in the bright sun on the terrace or dawdling about on your walk'. Of all the houses in which they lived together, it was the one that Peel and his wife loved most. Outside politics, paintings and books, Peel in fact was by inclination more of a countryman than a towndweller. Social visits, formal dinners, public occasions he learnt to tolerate but rarely to enjoy. For club life he had little time and less interest despite his dutiful appearances from time to time in the Carlton. When his eldest daughter, in her mother's absence, had to be chaperoned in London, Peel undertook the duty in the spirit of a necessary but penitential exercise. 'Julia has had very nice partners at her two balls,' he wrote to his wife in July 1839, 'and offers for every dance if I could have stayed, but I do get so tremendously bored after a certain time.'

Life in Staffordshire, on the other hand, was a pleasure beyond mere relaxation from political affairs. He told his neighbours on his father's death how much he looked forward to settling down as a country gentleman; and despite the demands and restraints of his public career, he took an unobtrusive part in the life of the county. Local gentry and their ladies were constantly invited to his house; he attended the Lichfield Races and acted on one occasion as a steward of the course; he applied his mind to the problems of turnpike trustees and the introduction of the new poor law; he became president of the farmers' club started at Tamworth in 1843; and was vice-president of the Lichfield Agricultural Show the same year. With the borough of Tamworth he had, through his family and property, an interest that went beyond the mere constituency connection. He was trustee of the Free School which his father had founded in 1820 and built a new edifice for it which he opened in person in 1838. When this in turn proved inadequate, he had a larger school building constructed in 1850. He founded the first public library and reading-room in Tamworth and delivered the inaugural address in 1841. In succession to his father he became High Steward of the borough and was the last person to hold that traditional office, which became extinct with the Municipal Corporations Act of 1835. Though perhaps to the ordinary townsfolk of Tamworth he remained an aloof and awe-inspiring figure and his measured periods were more suited to the House of Commons than to the tavern dinner or marketplace hustings, they were proud of his national reputation. For Peel in turn his connection with the borough, like his experiences as landlord and Staffordshire magnate, was not without value for his work at Westminster. As squire of Drayton and M.P. for Tamworth he had his own roots in English provincial life.

II

By the autumn of 1837 Peel was into his fiftieth year. Sedentary employment and good living had left their mark and the long determined face painted by Lawrence in 1825 had grown broader and more fleshy. His hair, though duller, was still luxuriant. As he grew older he tended to wear it in long waves on each side of his head, a style which increased the florid appearance of his face when seen from the front. Only the profile showed the curving line of the nose and the firm chin.

His general health remained excellent. He still suffered from an occasional suffusion of the eyes; and an experiment with a new type of cartridge in the 1820s had damaged his left ear and left a continual buzzing which grew worse when he was tired and overworked. Otherwise his constitution was unimpaired and despite his height and increasing weight his legs could still carry him through a day's shooting over the roughest moorland. His first serious indisposition, an attack of sciatica, came in 1837 towards the end of the parliamentary session. He was confined to his room for several days and though he attended the debate on the address to the new queen, he had to use a crutch. News of his illness was reported in the press and sympathetic members of the public wrote to him with remedies. To Aberdeen, who had forwarded to him one lady's prescription for a cure—a holiday in the south of France—he replied amusedly that 'my gratitude to those who are good enough to suggest remedies varies (not very rationally perhaps) with the Pleasantness of the Prescription'. Even when he went down to Drayton the pain and lameness continued. But he soon tired of the role of invalid and went off to shoot with the Duke of Rutland at Longshawe.

> Having tried what *materia medica* and what Repose would do for Sciatica [he reported to Aberdeen] and without complete success, I bethought me of a novel remedy—Grouse shooting upon Ground which for Rocks, pitfalls, Bogholes and quagmires Scotland has no parallel. I went on persevering (in Torture after a tumble) until I was well, at least able to walk 7 or 8 hours a day without pain for the first 4 or 5 and free from it the next morning. Pray note the prescription, should you ever be troubled with a similar disorder.

Even this heroic treatment was not completely efficacious. When Graham came to Drayton at the end of September, Peel was still lame; though this did not stop him from going out shooting with his guest three days running.

While Peel was beginning to experience these first signs that even his superb constitution was not invulnerable, his wife's health perceptibly improved during the 1830s. With her last confinement in 1832 and her husband free for almost a decade from ministerial ties, it was perhaps the happiest period of her life. Always a temperamental woman, Julia Peel became more nervous and emotional with middle-age. Her passionate absorption in her husband, after the early jealousies, had settled into a close and affectionate companionship. Her dependence on him increased with the passage of years. When they were apart they corresponded constantly; and Julia was never tired of telling her sons about their father's doings and urging them to read his speeches. Apart from her husband her only interest was in her home and children. As Peel rose in the public eye, she seemed to withdraw from it. She never became a great hostess; her intimates were few; her social life no more than dutiful. In her husband's essentially masculine world, she was content to remain on the fringe. Only old friends like Goulburn, Croker, Hardinge and Bonham came to know her well. She often did not accompany Peel on visits when her presence would have been natural. London she never seemed to care for. She escaped to Drayton as early in the summer as possible, even at the cost of separation from the husband of whom she saw so little during the parliamentary session. Her attitude to grand festivities was not unlike that of Peel. 'I was civil to all,' she wrote to him unenthusiastically after a Tamworth ball in 1843, 'and spoke to all I knew.' Like him, she was happiest at Drayton among her children and flowers—'the place of all I love best'.

With seven children, five of them boys, the years after 1832 saw a procession of comings and goings at the start and end of term. Robert, the eldest, went to Harrow in 1835, followed by Frederick in 1836 and William in 1837. The two youngest broke with tradition by going to Eton. Peel had not been satisfied with Frederick's experience at Harrow and the change was perhaps a silent criticism of his old school. He made a similar decision in the matter of universities. Robert went as a matter of course to his father's old college. But Christ Church in 1841 was no longer the place it had been under Jackson, Gaisford and Lloyd; and the next boy Frederick went instead to Trinity College, Cambridge. 'With every prepossession in favour of Christ Church,' wrote his father to Gladstone in 1845, 'I sent my second son to Cambridge, after recent experience of the want of discipline and neglect of the opportunities of application and of academic distinction, prevailing at that College.' Robert, who sauntered away his Oxford days with a servant and an allowance of £500 a year, was a disappointment for his parents. But the fault was not entirely in his college. Small, dark, almost foreign-looking, Peel's eldest son was a freakish contrast to the three generations of Robert Peels who had preceded him. His good looks, vivacity, and quick intelligence were unaccompanied by the traditional Peel qualities of soberness, integrity and purpose. He came down from Oxford without a degree and when he chose the typically dilettante profession of diplomacy, he was already a source of anxiety.

It was fortunate for his parents, as they watched his capricious nature unfold, that the other sons in their different ways showed more reassuring qualities. The ablest intellectually, and in character the most solid and dependable, was Frederick. At Harrow he became head of his house, won the essay prize which his father had founded, and ended his school career by obtaining the Lyon scholarship in 1841. Peel's unacknowledged favourite among his sons, however, was the active and spirited William who joined the navy as a midshipman in 1838 at the age of thirteen. Two years later, on board the *Princess Charlotte*, he saw action off the coast of Syria and sent home accounts of the operation showing such sense and maturity that his proud father could not refrain from passing them round among his friends, including

Sir Robert Peel. From an undated painting by H. W. Pickersgill R.A.

The rise of a family: Peel Fold, Oswaldtwistle (the old home of the Peels), Old Drayton Hall, built by the first Sir Robert Peel; Drayton Manor built by Sir Robert Peel 1831–35.

that supreme authority on all service matters, the Duke of Wellington. The duke returned them with laconic advice to encourage William to write down his observations on any action in which he took part, revising the account afterwards and leaving on the paper both errors and corrections. 'This habit will accustom him to an accurate observation and report of facts; which are most important, destined as he most likely is to direct and carry on great operations.' This comment by the greatest captain of the age moved Peel as no praise of himself could have done.

William's early departure made the first gap in the row of growing children. The next came in 1841 when the Peels' handsome elder daughter married Lord Villiers, son and heir of the Earl of Jersey. For a great-granddaughter of old Parsley Peel of Fish Lane to become a future countess, and for the yeoman stock of the Peels to ally with a family which had supplied a minister to one Stuart monarch and a mistress to another, was not without a certain piquancy. Until Villiers's parents showed their own inclinations, Peel's pride held him back from any approach. 'I think our object should be', he wrote to his wife in July 1839, 'to keep on good terms just as usual but to show, very decisively if it be necessary, that we think of no closer connection.' Fortunately there were no political hindrances to vex the course of young love. Jersey had held an appointment in Peel's 1834 ministry and Villiers himself, as Conservative M.P. for Weymouth, was one of Peel's parliamentary followers. The marriage, in July 1841, was one of the social events of the season; and the following year at Grosvenor Place a third Julia was born to the young couple. Peel and his wife were now grandparents.

III

The Peels had brought their children up in a close family relationship governed by firmness and affection. Whether recommending useful classical authors for Frederick to study, seeing that the homesick John was comforted in his first weeks at Eton, or urging William at sea to read Southey's *Life of Nelson*, Peel was always prompt to guide and assist his sons' development. When there was trouble at Harrow he sent a stern warning to Frederick telling him that he must resist the temptation to follow weakly the example of his companions.

> Do not listen to the silly advice that only turns industry and honourable exertion into ridicule. . . . Write to us immediately and comfort us. Tell us that you are fulfilling the promise you made to us, and that you are resolved not to swerve from the path which will lead you to honour.

This close parental supervision continued even after school was behind them. 'My dearest Frederick,' his father wrote in December 1841, 'however occupied I am, you are never out of my thoughts. Let me know how you are going on at Trinity College, who are your friends and what you are reading.' It was an age when moral exhortation and parental vigilance was a matter of course not only among the respectable middle classes but increasingly among the aristocracy of English society. What would otherwise have been commonplace was given a personal character by the affection Peel had for his children and the religious conviction which underlay his code of behaviour.

Peel's Christianity was undemonstrative. He paraded his religion as little as his emotions; but it would be absurd to doubt the genuineness of either. In the country he regularly attended church either at Drayton across the park from the manor-house or at nearby Tamworth where he frequently walked to Sunday service and back to spare the servants and horses. In town he was an inconspicuous visitor at various London churches. Greville noticed him in the somewhat incongruous company of Lord Brougham at the Temple Church in May 1843. The same year he attended Whitehall Chapel on Good Friday and took Holy Communion there with his daughter on Easter Sunday. At Drayton he made it a rule to read prayers to the whole household, including family, guests, and servants; and though few knew of this, he practised his own private devotions. He rarely made references to such matters even in letters to his wife. Yet it was conviction rather than convention that made him end his rectorial speech at Glasgow with a plea to look to religion for support in tribulation, admonition in prosperity, and comfort in time of death.

His own beliefs were essentially moderate. He thought it proper for the State to support the Church but he had little love for dogmatic exclusiveness or priestly monopoly. He could not bear the clerical authoritarianism of the Roman Church. He disliked the doctrinal extremism of the Anglican Tractarians. Though he was a loyal churchman all his life, his Anglicanism was not in the Laudian High Church tradition of his old tutor, Bishop Lloyd, who had cause before his death to lament the low Protestant views of his most famous pupil. To Peel the Church of England was the seemly embodiment of the purified religion adopted by the English people at the time of the Reformation. His definition of the Establishment was entirely secular. '*That* is the Established Church of England to which the King must conform—whose chief ministers have a right to seats in the House of Lords—which has an unalienable claim to ecclesiastical property', he wrote to Lloyd in 1828. A supporter of Protestantism from conviction of its rightness, a supporter of the Establishment from conviction of its utility, he was prepared to defend the Church of Ireland as the missionary church of the minority and the Church of England as the institutional church of the majority.

Tolerant and undogmatic as he was, moreover, there were limits to his tolerance. When Robert Taylor, the anticlerical agitator, was imprisoned for blasphemy during his Home Secretaryship in 1828, Joseph Hume wrote admonishingly to him asking him to peruse a sermon by Tillotson on persecution. Peel, who knew his English theological writers as least as well as Hume, retorted by recommending two other sermons by Tillotson, one on the dangerous folly of scoffing at religion, the other on the rights of the civil magistrate 'to establish the true worship of God in such a manner as he thinks best, to permit none to affront it, or to seduce from it those that are under his care'. Fourteen years later Peel was writing to another Home Secretary about 'the exhibition of revolting infidel publications and placards' in Holywell Street off the Strand. He added, 'you may safely go to the extreme range of the law in suppressing these nuisances and it would be as well, I think, to direct the special attention of the Police Commissioners to the subject and desire them to *harass* the offenders'.

For Peel religion was something inward and personal. He disliked undue manifestations of piety in those not required by their calling to bear witness to their faith. When bigots began to wrangle, it was his experience that Christian charity and humility flew out of the window. He did not relish religious exhibitionism, sectarian monomania, or collective sanctimoniousness, though he lived in an age when all three were conspicuous features of society. If it was the duty of the magistrate to defend religion, it was not for secular government to appeal to the Deity as a political ally. When Lord Kenyon in 1845 suggested a public acknowledgement of dependence on God's mercy at the time of the Irish famine, Peel dryly commented that it might seem somewhat inconsistent at the same time to leave in operation human restrictions on the import of food. He made an even more cutting criticism of the pious Sir Robert Inglis's suggestion that the parliamentary vote of thanks for the victories in India in 1846 should include a reference to Divine Providence.

> Considering the sanguinary nature of great battles [he wrote], and that (however just the cause) many thousands forfeit their lives through no fault of their own, too direct a reference to the special intervention of Almighty God is not very seemly.

As it was he had already had to tone down the religious fervour of the draft resolutions of the House.

> They almost made it appear [he told the Queen ironically] as they were originally drawn, that the fire of artillery on the confused mass of Sikhs, after they had been driven into the Sutlej, had been directed by Divine Providence, and was an agreeable sight to a merciful Creator.

His own religion was a simple, rational, pious Protestantism. The enthusiasm of the 'Saints', the high sacerdotal principles of Gladstone, were as foreign to him as the intellectual pessimism of Melbourne or the tortured self-examination of Lord Ashley. When a copy of Gladstone's book, *The State in its Relations with the Church*, arrived at Drayton in 1838, Peel glanced through it and then laid it aside with the dry remark that 'that young man will ruin a fine career if he writes such books as these'. For himself he felt that his duty was with the affairs of this world and that Christianity was something to be expressed in practical conduct rather than in external observances or metaphysical specu- lation. Because religion meant to him in effect duty and conduct, he also had faith in the progress of society and in the spread of education and science. With so little dogmatic content to his own mind, he apprehended no danger to religion from the growth of secular knowl- edge. Indeed he welcomed it as a means of curing some of the evils and bridging some of the divisions of his troubled society. In his speech at the opening of the Tamworth Reading Room in 1841 he expressed the belief that there was nothing in knowledge which should harm religious faith. Only the unwise and foolish formed unworthy conclusions about Divine Nature and the Divine Universe; and he affirmed his con- viction of the harmony of the Christian dispensation with all that reason assisted by revelation told them of the course and constitution of nature. In religion as in politics, Peel was robust, optimistic, unmeta- physical and practical.

Yet there was one matter in which he refused to allow either the precepts of religion or consideration for his wife and family to guide his conduct. Though he had schooled his nature to patience and for- bearance in ordinary personal and political dealings, what he could never tolerate was any reflection on his courage or integrity. On several occasions his keen and sometimes unreasonable resentment led him to the time-honoured demand for apology or satisfaction. The nature of duelling makes it the remedy of the injured party and Peel never received a challenge in his life. In public life he was scrupulously courteous to his opponents. Few politicians so carefully avoided giving offence. Few, however, reacted so sharply to insult. The duelling code was still an accepted social convention. In the House of Commons there were plenty of men who had been involved, or had narrowly escaped being involved, in affairs of honour; and the last actual encounter in England took place after Peel's death. When he started his public life duelling was an inescapable contingency of social life for all who called themselves gentlemen. Peel's plebeian origin would have come in for the inevitable sneer had he seemed to shirk this final test of breeding and courage. Nevertheless, there was at bottom something excessive about Peel's sensitivity on points of honour. It would be superficial to ascribe it simply to the social uncertainties of a parvenu, concerned to prove himself a gentleman precisely because others did not take it for granted. Other politicians of no better social origin did not show the same sensitivity. It might be more convincingly explained, along with such other traits as his shyness, his reserve with strangers, and unusually affectionate manner with intimates, as the marks of a childhood that had known too much discipline and too little love. What is beyond argument is that underneath the intellectual caution and professional restraint of Peel's character was an emotional, impulsive and self-conscious nature. Anything which touched his proud and prickly temperament on the raw evoked a response which was too strong for reason or reflection.

The most serious incident of this kind occurred in 1837. In the general election of that year a new Conservative candidate, Captain A'Court, secured the second seat at Tamworth previously held by William Peel. Though Peel denied that he had used his influence, directly or indirectly, to decide the fate of his brother's seat, this was angrily contradicted on the hustings by the defeated Whig candidate, Captain John Townshend. Even more provocatively he was reported in the press on two subsequent occasions as having publicly charged Peel with a deliberate violation of truth and honour in the matter. On 22 August, when the first of these reports came to his notice, Peel composed a stiff letter and placed it in the hands of his old military friend Sir Henry Hardinge for delivery to Townshend. After consulting Wellington, Hardinge prudently kept back the letter and wrote himself to Townshend who meanwhile had gone off to Ireland. The delay, coupled with the speculation caused by Townshend's public insults, made it difficult to preserve secrecy, and for a while Bonham was brought in to act as intermediary. When eventually located Townshend showed no disposition to retract and for a time it looked at if a meeting was unavoidable. On 5 September Peel asked Bonham so smuggle his case of pistols from the library at Whitehall Gardens and Hardinge made arrangements to join his principal under the cover of a shooting party of the more conventional kind. In the end, however, the seconds settled the affair. Townshend withdrew the offensive words, admitting that they were based on an erroneous impression. The old duke pronounced the apology 'satisfactory and complete' and the retraction appeared in the press. Peel himself had remained throughout outwardly calm and cheerful. His only burst of indignation came when Townshend was appointed to the command of a ship soon after the offending speech. What would have been thought, he asked irately, if he had done the same for an obscure post-captain who had tried to insult Melbourne or Russell.

One pleasure he could feel in this period of anxiety: the support and loyalty of his friends.

> Never mention any personal inconvenience [Hardinge wrote on 29 August]. The occasion is to be lamented but any honest man owes you such a debt of gratitude, that exclusive of my personal attachment, I shall ever be anxious to prove how sincerely and devotedly I am yours.

It was characteristic that the reserve shown by Peel in public was offset by the affection he inspired among the small circle of his friends. If they were few, they were staunch and as he grew older he never lost the capacity for making new ones. One of these latter was Sir James Graham. Defeat in the same general election that produced the Townshend affair brought him to the point at which his personal as well as his political allegiance was finally transferred from Stanley to Peel. Receiving a friendly message of condolence from Drayton on his electoral failure, he replied with obvious emotion:

> In my retirement I shall constantly remember the generous kindness which you have shown to me on every occasion, and, if you will allow me the expression, I trust we shall always continue friends. I do not believe there now exists between us one shade of difference on public matters.

With that letter a decisive point in Graham's career was reached. It was symbolised by his acceptance at last of an invitation to stay at Drayton the following month. It was the end of the Derby Dilly and the beginning of one of the closest friendships in the lives of both men.

Chapter 15

The year of victory

By the start of Victoria's reign most observers recognised that Conservatism as a political force was something other and larger than landed Toryism. The latter supplied the nucleus of strength; but Conservatism provided the element of growth. In parliamentary terms Peelite Conservatives still formed a minority of the party, but they comprised nearly all the leading men and they represented an element in the electorate which was decisive for the passage from opposition to office. If the opposition was to succeed, it had to become a national party; and a national party, even with the limited post-1832 electorate, had to be a composite party. The Whigs had been grappling, uncertainly and sometimes half-heartedly, with that necessity. But by 1840 they were being outgunned and outmanoeuvred by the leader of the opposition in the battle for the confidence of central moderate opinion. For the task of harmonising upper- and middle-class interests all Peel's previous career seemed to have prepared him. His aristocratic training and sympathies, his middle-class origin and affinities, his administrative outlook, his non-partisan intellect, his passion for efficiency, his immense parliamentary experience, all these qualities which had been in conflict in 1831–32 had by 1840 fallen into a unified pattern. If there were discords and complexities in his own position and in the nature of the party he led, these were inseparable from the forces that had brought him and his followers to the brink of power. A more homogeneous party under a less sophisticated leader would have experienced less strain. It would have suffered from only one disadvantage: that of never coming into office.

Office, however, was something for which Peel's party seemed to hanker more than Peel himself. By the end of 1839 it seemed only a handsbreath away. The fiasco of the Bedchamber had merely piled frustration on top of impatience. Peel was as aware as anyone that the point had been reached when he might soon have to face the practical consequence of power which was office; and office meant not only loaves and fishes for his followers but responsibility for all the problems with which the Whigs had been struggling and others which time would certainly uncover. To Goulburn, who in November was suggesting a motion of censure on the government's budgetary deficits, he rejoined that they ought rather to be thinking about how to remedy them. 'In other words, more startling to a House of Commons,' he added dryly, 'what new taxes could be imposed?' Nevertheless it was clear that party morale would suffer if the Fabian waiting policy were pursued much longer, and in December it was decided to go over to

the attack at the start of the following session. Though Wellington and
Stanley had misgivings, Graham and Goulburn thought that the feeling
in the party left them with no choice and they agreed with Peel that
in those circumstances a direct vote of no confidence was the best
mode of procedure. The party managers, Fremantle and Bonham,
believed that the vote might succeed and that the party would certainly
secure a majority at a general election.

The motion, on 28 January 1840, was entrusted to a solid country
squire, Sir John Yarde Buller of Devonshire. It led to four nights of
wideranging debate in which all the leading speakers on both sides
took part. Macaulay, one of the three new Liberal ministers brought
into the cabinet the previous session, threw out the taunt to Peel that
if he came to power he would lose the confidence of his party without
gaining that of Ireland. When, on the final evening, Peel came to make
his own contribution, he retorted that he would never purchase
support at the price of concealing his own opinions nor would he be the
instrument for giving effect to opinions in which he did not concur.
He would maintain the new and unpopular Poor Law; he would
preserve the independent educational system of the Dissenters; he
would observe the principle of civil equality in Ireland provided this
did not imply encouragement to agitation or injury to the Established
Church. It was unlikely that his speech made any converts but he had
done two things of significance. He had indicated, as far as circumstances and his own caution allowed, the nature of his future administration; and he had given notice to his own followers that if he was to
govern, it would be on his terms and only his.

Yet after all the careful calculations on the eve of session, the
attack failed. When the division took place the opposition saw their
motion defeated by 308 votes to 287, a large and unexpected majority
of 21 for the government. Two factors had shattered the optimistic
forecasts of the whips. Of the independent Radicals, ten voted with the
government; five were absent; only one voted in the minority. In the
second place, the Whigs had been strengthened by the return of six
members in by-elections since the session had started; and they had
only eight absentees as against nine Conservatives. The direct threat
to the ministry had rallied the Liberal party; and the opposition not
only failed to pick up floating votes but had shown less zeal in attendance than their opponents. It was a humilating failure and Peel felt,
not altogether justly, that he had been misled by the whips and hurried
into a false position. The result safeguarded the cabinet for the rest of
the session and aggravated the endemic divisions within the Conservative Party. The remainder of 1840 was marked by a kind of
brooding restraint on the part of the opposition which was a sign of
tension within.

One particular cause of anxiety was a renewed coolness between
Peel and Wellington. Though the duke in the end showed admirable
party discipline in accepting the government's Irish Corporations and

Canada bills when they came up from the Commons, there had been considerable doubt beforehand about his intentions. Over the Hansard case, in which Peel had offended many of the party by his obstinate defence of House of Commons privileges, it was notorious that there was a complete divergence of views between the two Conservative leaders and after Easter the marked absence of any communication between them threatened an open breach. There was in fact not only real disagreement but unnecessary pride on both sides. The duke, looking morbidly into the future, did not like to give the seal of his approval to anything which he thought might damage the stability of British rule. Peel, also looking to the future, did not wish to handicap a prospective Conservative government with a load of unsolved problems. Given differences of opinion, differences of temperament made personal explanations peculiarly difficult. The enormous respect which Peel felt for Wellington as a great national figure made him dislike entering into any argument with him on policy. This *mauvaise honte*, as Hardinge once described it, which afflicted all his relations with the duke, made him refuse all the entreaties of Arbuthnot, Graham and Aberdeen to talk privately with him about the Canada bill. Wellington, on the other hand, conscious of his age and deafness, disliked and avoided formal party meetings. Though in his more pessimistic moods he fancied Peel deliberately concealed his opinions, he himself somewhat illogically preferred not to state his own views unless he were asked. At the beginning of September the separation seemed so wide that Arbuthnot wrote that he despaired of ever seeing Peel and Wellington act cordially together.

The situation gradually righted itself. In October Arbuthnot went to Drayton and reported back that Peel's views on public affairs were exactly the same as the duke's. This drew from Wellington his invariable comment that though he and Peel were kept apart by their different occupations and distant residences, he found that without consultation they generally came to the same conclusions. Peel for his part told Arbuthnot that nothing gave him more pleasure than unreserved communication with the duke and no occasional difference of opinion on isolated topics could diminish their mutual respect or decrease their cooperation. The old duke was pleased and Peel went out of his way to demonstrate his friendliness by sending him his son William's letters about the operations off the Syrian coast. By the time the first frosts were on the stubble and politicians' thoughts were turning with perennial zest towards the new session, the rift was healed. It had not been as great as some of their over-protective friends had feared; and, what was more remarkable, it had been kept from the public. What might have caused an upheaval in the party six years earlier, could now be absorbed with little shock. If the 1840 session had been disappointing, it had not been disastrous.

II

The memorable year 1841 began quietly. The great controversies seemed laid to rest; Whig policy seemed exhausted. The government presented the spectacle of an engine continuing to glide forward under its own momentum though the power had been shut off. It was the end of the reform bill decade and of all the hopes and fears inspired by that epoch-making measure.

Nevertheless, if office did not give the Whigs power, it left them with the initiative; and there were rumours in April that they were planning a bold stroke in the field of finance. Bonham urged Peel to strike at the government before they could bring in their budget, 'which will, I fancy, be attractive but revolutionary, in proportion to the desperate position in which they are now placed'. They were certainly in need of something new in the way of budgetary devices. Since 1831 they had followed a hand-to-mouth financial policy, responding to the radical pressure for 'cheap government' by reducing direct taxation, without finding a reliable substitute. After 1837, with an industrial slump and increased expenditure on colonies and the armed services, their fiscal nakedness was plain. They had no surplus in 1837, a deficit in 1838 and in 1839. Increases in assessed taxes and tariffs in 1840 failed to extricate them from their annual insolvency. Some other device was needed. It was found in the recent report of Hume's radical free trade committee on import duties which argued that a lowering of duties on imported consumer goods would lead to a higher revenue because of increased consumption.

The resultant Whig budget of 1841, sharply reducing duties on timber, sugar and corn, transformed a fiscal expedient into a political demonstration. It was an anti-monopoly rather than a free trade budget and financially it was a gamble since it depended on the untested prognostications of a doctrinaire committee. But in the atmosphere of 1841, with Chartist agitation, the Anti-Corn Law League, industrial depression and social disorder, it inevitably took on a political colouring. If to Whig members of the cabinet it was a painless way of curing a deficit, to their Liberal and Radical supporters it could be made to signify free trade versus protection, freedom versus monopoly, a large loaf versus a small. It was turning away from the exhausted controversies of the past to erect a new banner under which the party could fight. Yet despite the apparent hustings appeal of the new policy, it failed to arouse much national enthusiasm or conviction. The Whigs had left their initiative too late; their policy smacked of desperation.

Nevertheless, it presented the opposition with considerable problems. If free, or greater freedom of, trade was the national trend, protection was still the national system. No great party could have a simple approach to the question. For the Conservatives who could look back to such liberal economists as Pitt, Liverpool and Huskisson, it would have been suicidal to allow a protectionist or monopolist label to be affixed to them by their opponents. The truth was that the Whigs had suddenly decided to make an issue of a question which so far had not been a party matter at all. Even corn had been left an open question, despite the importance now attached by Russell to the merits of a fixed duty over the sliding scale. Peel approached, therefore, the task of countering the government's new policy with considerable doubt and caution. After canvassing various alternatives with his colleagues and leading House of Commons men, he eventually came down in favour of an attack on the revised sugar duties. It was a tactic that had the merit of simplicity; it would undoubtedly get the support of some Liberals; and it would not tie Peel's hands on larger issues since the recent emancipation of the West Indian slaves made British colonial sugar temporarily a special case. There was every prospect of beating the government; and though this would not necessarily force the cabinet to resign, it would pave the way for a direct challenge on the grounds that the administration had lost the confidence of the House.

In the protracted debate which followed the opposition motion on 7 May, the government spokesmen endeavoured to widen the issue to the general principle of free trade; and Peel was challenged to say how he himself would deal with the financial deficit. But he was too old a parliamentary hand to be caught by this. It was hardly for the Whigs, he observed, after their 1840 budget, to declare a proprietorial interest in free trade principles and threaten, if driven from office, to pack them up and carry them away. The deficit was the responsibility of the party which had held power for the previous decade. 'Can there be a more lamentable picture than that of a Chancellor of the Exchequer, seated on an empty chest, by the pool of bottomless deficiency, fishing for a budget?' Then he added, to the laughter of his supporters in which he joined himself, 'I won't bite; the Rt. Hon. gentleman shall return home with his pannier as empty as his chest.' He spoke with the confidence of success and the division at the end of the debate bore out his confidence. The Conservative motion was carried by 317 votes to 281. Fifteen Liberals voted against the government and eighteen more were absent. It was an emphatic victory and even if it owed everything to Liberal defections, Peel had emerged from the debate without compromising his carefully uncommitted position.

What nobody knew listening to him on the night of 18 May, was that he had just been given private and additional grounds for confidence. Nine days earlier, in anticipation of the government's resignation, George Anson, Prince Albert's private secretary, had come to him on behalf of his master, though with Melbourne's knowledge, to negotiate an amicable agreement about the Ladies of the Bedchamber. The prince's suggestion was that if Peel did not insist on any formal procedure, it would be possible to arrange for the resignation of the three principal Whig ladies, or indeed any others to whose continuance at court Peel might object. Peel agreed at once that there was no need to raise any constitutional issue and after more visits by Anson it was finally settled that the prime minister would notify the new ladies of the queen's intention to appoint, and the queen would announce to them personally their actual appointment. Anson, whom Peel found a sensible and sympathetic intermediary, assured him of Albert's support; and Peel did all he could to soothe the queen's still ruffled feelings. It was essential, he said at one point with an awkwardness that betrayed how much the ill-founded charges of 1839 had wounded him, that the queen should understand he had the feelings of a gentleman and when his duty did not forbid, he could not act against her wishes. In the end it was all premature. Immediately after the defeat on the sugar resolution the cabinet, against the inclinations of their chief, reversed their previous decision and agreed to dissolve parliament rather than resign. But Peel had every cause for satisfaction. A great obstacle had been removed from his path and he had received the first sign that in the young Prince Albert he possessed a friend at court.

Whatever happened next, a general election was inevitable. The great debate of May–June 1841 on a direct opposition motion of no confidence was to that extent a sham battle. But since Peel had been challenged by more than one speaker to state his policy on the Corn Laws in more detail, he repeated at length in his closing speech the fundamentals of his position: his concern to maintain an adequate protection, his conviction of the interdependence of manufacturing and agricultural prosperity, and his refusal to bind himself to the details of the existing law. As the debate approached its conclusion it was clear that the rebels of May were rallying to the government once more. No one could predict with certainty the outcome and when at 3 a.m. on the morning of 5 June the House finally divided, it was in an atmosphere of unbearable excitement. When the tellers forced their way through the crowd on the floor of the House and the black hair and luxuriant whiskers of Fremantle were seen to be on the right, a great roar went up. The Conservatives shouted and stamped and clapped; and when the result was read out—for the resolution 312, against 311—they shouted and stamped again. Every single member of the opposition had either voted or paired, and eight absent ministerialists had decided the issue. The following Monday Russell announced the government's intention to dissolve.

The general election which followed vindicated the Conservative party experts. Like all early Victorian elections, it exhibited a medley of local cross-currents, special influences and unexpected results, overlaid by violence, corruption and compromise. But beneath the confusion the general drift of opinion could be dimly discerned: disillusionment with the last procrastinating and inept years of Whig rule and a readiness to confide in the opposition, above all in the dominating figure of their leader. 'The elections are wonderful,' wrote

Croker on 20 July, 'and the curiosity is that all turns on the name of of Sir Robert Peel.' This was exaggeration; but it was probably true that without Peel the great Conservative victory of 1841 could not have been won. In the English counties their predictable progress continued with a net gain of twenty-two. But they also made ground in the English boroughs and even Ireland added to the tale of success with a net gain of eight seats, including one captured from O'Connell in Dublin. The Conservatives were still principally the party of England and especially of the English counties. Nevertheless, over the United Kingdom as a whole, without the forty-four Conservative M.P.s returned for the larger boroughs of over 1,000 electors there could have been no victory. The result was a Conservative majority of about seventy-six, or as Fremantle preferred to express it, a round figure of eighty. This was enough, as Ripon cannily observed to Graham, for a working majority but not so large as to encourage the extremists of the party to try any undue pressure on Peel. It was in its way the first modern general election that the country had experienced. For the first time in British history a party in office enjoying a majority in the Commons had been defeated at the polling booths by an opposition previously in a minority. The powerful party organisations built up since 1834 and the appeal of a great national leader had imposed on the defective and old-fashioned electoral structure left by the Reform Act of 1832 something which Britain was not to see again until after the Reform Act of 1867.

By constitutional convention the Whigs remained in office to meet the new parliament; but certainty of the outcome robbed the second no confidence debate in August of any flavour or excitement. Speaking on the final night Peel exhibited the calmness and objectivity that befitted a man on the brink of office. On matters of immediate policy he refused to commit himself to more than he had said in the previous parliament. On social distress he reaffirmed in more striking language that

> if I could be induced to believe that an alteration in the Corn Laws would be an effective remedy for those distresses . . . I would earnestly advise a relaxation, an alteration, nay, if necessary, a repeal of the Corn Laws.

But what remained longest in people's memories was the warning he threw out to his own party. He had been told, he said, that in exercising power he would have to be the instrument of opinions and feelings he himself repudiated. He was little disposed, he observed contemptuously, to add this degrading condition to the other sacrifices which office entailed.

> If I exercise power, it shall be upon my conception—perhaps imperfect, perhaps mistaken—but my sincere conception of

public duty. That power I will not hold, unless I can hold it consistently with the maintenance of my own opinions; and that power I will relinquish the moment I am satisfied I am not supported in the maintenance of them by the confidence of this House and of the people of this country.

III

On 30 August, the day when the resignation of the Whig government was announced in parliament, Peel drove to Windsor in response to a frigid summons from Victoria. It was the end of a decade of opposition, the start of a new period in his life, and perhaps in that of the country as well. He was inured to office and he knew what it was like to be prime minister. But power of the kind which was about to be placed in his hands was something he had never had before. At the age of fifty-three, with wider experience of public affairs than any other man in politics, he was as much his own master as a parliamentary statesman can ever be. He was as uncommitted as any man in his position could hope for; to a degree in fact which had evoked the exasperated comments of his opponents. But the limitations were there; and no one knew better than Peel how commonly the world overestimates the freedom of action of the person at the head of a nation's affairs. The principles that had served him in opposition would hardly furnish more than the bare bones of policy in office; but with the right men in power, he believed the details of policy would come right too. After ten years in which his administrative talents had lain fallow, he could set to work once more. In the prime of life, with his experience still matched by his stamina, he could face with confidence and self-reliance the greatest challenge of his career. It was a cautious, experienced but masterful man who was ushered into the queen's presence that afternoon.

In the event his relations with Victoria turned out to be among the least of his problems. With the discreet assistance of Albert and Anson, the long list of Household appointments was filled up during the early weeks of September to the general satisfaction of both sides. Wherever he could Peel went further than might have been expected to defer to the queen's wishes. She admitted herself that Peel had behaved very handsomely to her; and when old Lord Melbourne heard the details from Anson, he grumbled like any traditional Whig that 'Sir Robert had allowed the Queen *far too wide a discretion* in the formation of the Household'. As for Peel he let it be known that the queen had behaved most kindly and generously; and he confided to Ellenborough that 'Prince Albert is altogether with us'. For these large political advantages a handful of court appointments was a small price to pay.

The main structure of his administration was rapidly erected. As far back as June he had been thinking about the problem and after detailed consultations with Fremantle and Bonham in August he was able to go to work immediately after receiving his commission from the queen. In general three considerations governed his choice. He felt he owed a debt to those who had supported him in the forlorn venture of 1834; key posts had to be found for Stanley and Graham, the great converts of the post-1835 years; and for the sake of party unity he had to make some gesture to the agriculturalists. Keeping his cabinet at its former figure of fourteen, he was able to bring in Stanley as Colonial Secretary, one of the most difficult posts of recent years: Graham as Home Secretary; and Ripon as President of the Board of Trade. The Duke of Wellington, because of his age and infirmities, was relieved of departmental responsibilities and Aberdeen took over the Foreign Office. The Chancellorship of the Exchequer, which Peel had held in 1834–35, was given to Goulburn. Others like Lyndhurst as Lord Chancellor, Ellenborough at the Board of Control, and Knatch-bull as Paymaster-General, returned to their old posts. The one cabinet vacancy left was offered as a calculated measure of expediency to the former Lord Chandos, now Duke of Buckingham. He was a man without talents or even businesslike habits; but he had electoral influence; he was the darling of the Buckinghamshire farmers; and in the decade since the Reform Act he had made himself the titular leader of the Tory agriculturalists. With both Buckingham and Knatchbull in the cabinet that interest had been given a gratifying representation and at the same time a potential source of dissidence was substantially weakened. Two passengers in a crew of fourteen was not in political terms an excessive supercargo; and for the rest it was a workmanlike combination of experience and prestige.

The task of filling the junior appointments went forward with almost equal promptitude. Gladstone, despite his misgivings over such a mundane post, accepted the vice-presidency of the Board of Trade. Of the remaining young men of the 1834 vintage, older now by seven years, Lincoln became Commissioner for Woods and Forests, Herbert Secretary to the Admiralty, and Eliot Chief Secretary for Ireland. The party managers too came in for their share of rewards. Clerk was appointed financial and Fremantle patronage secretary to the Treasury. Granville Somerset took the Duchy of Lancaster, though it came without the cabinet seat he had hoped for; and the indispensable Bonham, though not in parliament, returned to his old niche as Storekeeper to the Ordnance. There were inevitable disappointments. Herries, who would otherwise have been in the cabinet, had lost his seat at Ipswich at the general election and refused a subsequent offer by Peel of a safe seat at Ripon because it came unaccompanied by the promise of a ministerial appointment. In the end, though one of the acknowledged financial experts of the party, he remained out of parliament until 1847. An even more prickly and tortured man was Lord Ashley. When offered a court appointment he took the line that he was so committed on the factory question that he could not hold office unless the government fully accepted his policy on that issue. Peel used all his patience and persuasiveness to get him to change his mind; but Ashley was in too irrational and emotional a mood to be swayed by ordinary argument. Though he had probably made up his mind not to take office in any case, he was privately mortified at not being offered a political appointment. A third difficulty was India, where there seemed insuperable objections to any candidate that was put forward. Finally, in October, Peel cut through the dilemma by asking Ellenborough to go out himself as Governor-General, leaving his place at the Board of Control to be filled by Fitzgerald.

In the meantime, by dint of working sixteen to eighteen hours a day, Peel completed the rest of his arrangements. As late as October he was still spending a couple of hours daily answering applications from those who, as he expressed it dryly to Arbuthnot, 'either have no profession, or seek civil office instead of professional employment'. The pressure was equally great from those who merely sought social advancement. Austere by nature in his attitude to patronage, Peel could not persuade himself that the recent history of the House of Lords warranted an immediate reinforcement of new Tory peers. This did not save him from a heavy correspondence with Wellington on honours, promotions, lord-lieutenants and bishoprics. With the approaching confinement of the queen, there was another surge of aspirants who optimistically assumed that the birth of a future Prince of Wales would be celebrated by a large creation of peers and baronets. It was an expectation the prime minister had no intention of satisfying. 'The distinction of being without an honour is becoming a rare and valuable one,' he wrote with mild irony to Graham in late October, 'and should not become extinct.'

IV

During the last few months of 1841, while cabinet ministers and their juniors were accustoming themselves to the routine of office, the rather brittle relations between the prime minister and the queen settled down on a more durable basis. It needed some time for Peel's self-consciousness to wear off and his constant, unnecessary reiteration that his one desire was to consult the queen's happiness clearly sprang from a painful sense that there were still memories and prejudices to overcome. The queen complained that he was so shy that it made her shy too. At the second council on 17 September, though Victoria seemed more at ease with her new ministers, Greville mordantly observed that when she talked to Peel, he could not help putting himself 'into his accustomed attitude of a dancing master giving a lesson'. But these early embarrassments were soon left behind. In the growing correspondence between them on parliamentary affairs, foreign policy and patronage,

Peel was punctiliously polite, even though he gave nothing away on points of substance. Relations were softened in small ways. The queen offered a post of groom-in-waiting for one of Peel's younger sons; and Peel, while declining that honour on the score of youth, successfully proposed that Prince Albert should be head of a Royal Commission on Fine Arts which he wished to set up. Closer contact with Albert had already produced a markedly friendly relationship. The German prince, young enough to be Peel's son, with few friends and prepared by Anson to meet the prime minister on terms of trust, was a willing disciple for the great English statesman, and the warmth of the prince's regard insensibly infected the queen. By the start of the new year relations had become close enough for Peel to be given an impromptu invitation to join Albert in one of his few relaxations, an hour or two shooting in the morning before Victoria claimed his attention. With a borrowed gun and dressed in his usual town clothes—thin shoes, pepper and salt trousers, and a blue frockcoat—the prime minister took part in a ninety-minute foray against the pheasants, hares and rabbits of Windsor Great Park.

The only remaining complication was Victoria's notorious intimacy with Melbourne. Though Peel made it clear that he had no jealousy of his predecessor's continued friendship with the queen, he might well have suspected that Victoria's emphatic views on men and affairs owed something to the other man's prompting. For the time being he kept his thoughts to himself. But when Baron Stockmar, who was making energetic attempts to detach Melbourne from the queen, came to see Peel in November, the prime minister took advantage of the opportunity to express his feelings to the prince's old tutor and family friend. He told Stockmar that he was ready to ignore any reports that came to him of Victoria's private life and opinions. But, he repeated with emphasis, the moment he knew that the queen was taking advice on public matters from another man, he would resign office. The warning, relayed by Stockmar to Melbourne, had its effect. Though Melbourne's letters to the queen did not stop immediately, they came less often and their contents were increasingly less political.

There were other influences at work to weaken the relationship. A second child, growing domesticity, her deepening emotional dependence on Albert and his increasing participation in the business of the monarchy: all these new elements were gradually weaning Victoria from the first adolescent stage of her reign. Anson noted at Christmas that she was becoming less interested in politics and less prejudiced against her ministers, even if she would not have been prepared to admit any change in her attitude. The problems of the new Conservative ministry were unlikely now to arise at Windsor or Buckingham Palace.

Chapter 16

The condition of England

Few governments in the nineteenth century took office in circumstances as discouraging as those of 1841. Abroad there was war with China and Afghanistan; a continuing dispute with the U.S.A. over the Canadian frontier aggravated by local acts of violence on both sides; and strained relations with France over Syria. At home there was an accumulated government deficit of £7½ million; trade was depressed; industry stagnant. The textile areas were suffering from severe distress. In towns like Bolton and Paisley thousands lived on private charity and public subscriptions. There had been a run of bad harvests and the cost of living was abnormally high. A population increasing remorselessly by 15 per cent each decade seemed to be outrunning its ability to feed, clothe and house itself. Industrialisation, which to some appeared the promise of a golden age, to others seemed a cancer at the heart of society.

In the few short years of Victoria's reign the old conflicts of the reform era had been pushed into the background by what Thomas Carlyle in his pamphlet on *Chartism* the previous year had called *The Condition of England Question*. The problem was manifest; the remedies offered varied and dubious. There was Ashley's Ten Hours factory campaign; the anti-Poor Law protest; the Complete Suffrage agitation. There was the passionate working-class movement known as Chartism which concealed a diversity of aims and methods beneath the simple banner of democratic parliamentary reform. There was the smaller, wealthier and better organised Anti-Corn Law League, more astute and singleminded but as violent and emotional in its denunciations of landlords and aristocrats as the Chartists in their attacks on mill-owners and capitalists. The agriculturalists themselves, in the Duke of Buckingham's Protection Society, were making their first show of organised resistance to the free-traders and Manchester men. Like Kilkenny cats the classes of British society seemed bent on devouring each other; and if Peel needed any reminder of the intensity of feelings in the divided nation over which he presided, he promptly received it from the various delegations which came up to see him in the course of the autumn.

The immediate problem facing the ministers was financial. What parliamentary reform had been to Grey's ministry in 1831, finance was to Peel's ministry in 1841. Whatever else they accomplished, if they failed in this, they would fail absolutely. Money, the sinews of war, was the backbone of any policy which sought to bring peace to their distracted society. Abstractly the problem presented no great difficulty.

Most financial experts would have agreed that an income tax alone offered a reasonable prospect of raising the additional revenue needed in a form that was effective in operation, predictable in its yield, and equitable in its burden. The question was not what tax, but what government would be courageous enough to revive a tax psychologically identified with the dictatorial powers of a state at war and unique in its inquisitorial basis of assessment. Ever since the House of Commons had forced Liverpool's ministry to abandon it in 1816, it had lain unused in the armoury of theoretical policies, unused, repugnant, but not forgotten.

It is probable that Peel had made up his mind from the start to reintroduce the income tax. But he knew it would take much persuasion before all the members of his cabinet could bring themselves to accept it. The general election was barely over before he broached the subject to Goulburn, his prospective Chancellor of the Exchequer. In his judicious civil service fashion, Goulburn drew up a balance sheet of its advantages and disadvantages.

> In point of reason and sound policy [answered Peel on 28 July] the former in my opinion predominate. We well know however that that consideration constitutes no conclusive argument for the adoption of a financial measure. We will of course say nothing whatever on the subject, though as my belief is, that 'to this complexion we must come at last', we may as well be turning the subject in our minds.

His caution was justified. When Graham and Stanley were brought into the discussion they both recoiled in typically Whig fashion from such a revolutionary measure. Stanley expressed a hope that it would only be resorted to 'upon the most evident necessity' and privately told Graham that he thought any discussion of it at that moment was premature.

Once the administration had been formed in September, Peel returned to the subject in a more formal way. An unexpected ally was found in the duke; and Ripon, who like Peel had been bred up in the Liverpool–Huskisson school of economists, hailed Peel's suggestion as a 'bold and most judicious plan of finance'. Even their former colleague Lord Ashburton, a banker and orthodox financier, agreed that it offered the best way out of their financial difficulties, provided it was a temporary expedient. 'It would be next to insupportable', he added with feeling, 'to live in a country where such a tax were permanent.' Herries, out of office, also gave it authoritative support though Gladstone, Ripon's junior at the Board of Trade, argued strongly against an income tax and in favour of a house tax. Peel circulated his paper and returned a detailed and courteous answer; but his private opinion was that a house tax would be even more odious than an income tax. In the following weeks his senior colleagues gradually came round to an acceptance of the prime minister's proposal as the basis of their budgetary policy; and towards the end of January the final plan was drawn up. In its final form it showed several important differences from the wartime tax of Pitt and Addington. The income exemption limit was fixed at £150 instead of the previous £60; and the profits of farming were assessed at half instead of three-quarters of the rental. These concessions materially modified Goulburn's summer calculations of a yield of £5 million from a rate of sixpence in the pound. To obtain an effective revenue it was found necessary to raise the rate to sevenpence, and even so other minor taxes had to be devised to bridge the remaining gap.

From the start there had been general agreement that if the massive and unpopular engine of the income tax were to be revived, it would have to be used not merely to end the deficit but to create a surplus; and that this surplus would, both from a political and fiscal point of view, be best employed in reducing duties on consumer goods. The income tax was not introduced to make possible a reform of the tariff; but its introduction made tariff reform both possible and expedient. To Ashburton in October Peel had argued that capitalists would be serving their own interests by submitting to an income tax for a number of years to enable the government 'to make without risk a decisive experiment in the reduction of duty on some of the great articles of consumption'. He went on,

> I would combine with this measure a review of the existing Corn Law . . . relaxing the amount of protection where it might safely be relaxed; and attempting to reconcile all just protection for agriculture with greater steadiness in trade.

Tariff reform and a new corn law were therefore the two flanks of the income tax, disarming opposition to the central measure by their promise of greater social justice and sounder commercial policy. Hume's Import Duties Committee, the Whig budgetary proposals, and newspaper discussions in 1840 and 1841, had familiarised the public with the notion that a reduction of duties might actually strengthen the tariff system as an instrument of revenue as well as bringing relief to commerce and industry. But the Conservative ministers in 1841 did not have the same confidence as the Whigs in the doctrinaire views of radical economists. Their proposals were designed as conscious experiment rather than as dogmatic policy. Their object was to relieve consumers and manufacturers rather than stimulate the revenue; and the expected financial loss was covered by the introduction of the income tax. It was this which made the difference between Whig policy in 1841 and Conservative policy in 1842.

Once the principle of the income tax was accepted, Goulburn's initial suggestions in July were widened in discussions between Peel and Ripon to cover a large number (running to over six hundred items) of raw materials and consumer goods. In all Ripon budgeted for a loss of over £2 million; though even after meeting the current deficit the income tax would still leave them with a surplus of nearly £500,000. Major changes in the sugar duties were reluctantly set aside since they were dependent on negotiating a new commercial treaty with Brazil. If the 1842 financial experiment proved successful, however, it was hoped that further relief to consumers could be made in future years. No tariff reconstruction, however, could avoid the question of the corn laws. The agitation of the League and Russell's proposal for a fixed duty in 1841 had made it a burning contemporary issue; and many politicians were prepared to admit that the existing law was either objectionable in principle or defective in practice. Peel had studiously refrained from committing himself to a defence of the 1828 act as distinct from protection in the abstract and it was generally accepted that the new government would revise the law. To have left it alone would have been taken as mere truckling to the agriculturalist wing of the party.

In October Ripon prepared a new scale of corn duties considerably lower than under the existing act. Even so, it did not go far enough for Peel; and he urged Ripon to consider the possibility of lowering tariffs on other articles of food. 'We must substitute protection for prohibition and must set about considering what will constitute fair protection. Live animals, or fresh meat, can surely require no great amount.' He was clearly sceptical of some of the Board of Trade's basic assumptions; and under his brisk direction more wideranging and systematic attempts were made during November to acquire reliable information on such technical matters as corn exports from northern Europe, the effect of British food tariffs on foreign trade, the possibility of reciprocity treaties with such wheat-exporting countries as Russia, the operation of the 1828 act at home, and the views of practical agriculturalists and county M.P.s Further research brought Ripon round to Peel's view of the inability of the foreign grower to put large quantities of cheap corn on the British market, and growing bolder as he went along he reduced his original scale by half. Gladstone, educating himself even more rapidly, put forward a scale aiming at providing no real inducement to imports of foreign wheat under 54s a quarter and no real protection to the domestic grower above 61s. This was going faster and further than Peel thought the agriculturalists would tolerate. It would not do, he told his zealous young subordinate, to propose to them a mere 6s duty when the market price in Britain was 61s.

By December Peel felt that the ground had been sufficiently prepared for a discussion in the cabinet. His first official memorandum was merely designed to obtain consent for the principle of revising the 1828 act. The next and more difficult step was to obtain agreement on the details of a new measure. On 22 January he read a second memorandum to his colleagues. Three considerations shaped his proposals: the high level of British farming rents as an element in production costs, the need to encourage domestic agriculture and particularly wheat-growing, and the importance of eliminating fluctuating supply, speculation and fraud. Taking 56s a quarter as a fair remunerating price for the British farmer and 45s as the minimum price at which European wheat could be placed in any quantity on the British market, he concluded that in the previous decade a duty of 12s would have been enough even in cheapest years to provide ample protection for the domestic producer. What he actually proposed was a graduated scale of protection providing a duty of 20s when the price was 50s, 16s when the price was 56s, dropping to a minimum of 1s at 73s. At certain key points the rate of descent was slowed down to discourage hoarding and speculation.

In effect therefore his detailed recommendation was less drastic than his general argument. In leaning to a Conservative rather than a Liberal policy, however, his tactics were dictated by an unwillingness to startle those of his colleagues who had not shared in the preliminary discussions and an appreciation of the alarm that would be caused among the more timid agriculturalists by any appreciable lowering of the tariff. What is beyond doubt is that the bill was drawn to Peel's design and that he was determined to dispose of it at the earliest possible moment. If the party had to swallow unpalatable medicine, it would be best to administer it at the very start of the session. Though it fell short of what the more ardent free-traders in the government would have liked, it corresponded closely with the views of the more moderate and intelligent agriculturalists. Immoderate ones he could not hope to satisfy; but he did not want to add unnecessarily to their number. As it was the Duke of Buckingham strongly opposed the plan and since he was alone in his opposition it was expected that he would resign. The rest of the cabinet gave a hearty approval and favoured immediate action.

To have brought his colleagues to agreement on what was politically the most difficult of their decisions was a decided success for the prime minister. It was due to two things; to the careful preparation that had gone on since October, and Peel's refusal to drive the cabinet into a quick or drastic solution. The final plan fell short of his private economic convictions but his abstract views were tempered by his judgement of what was feasible. His recommendations to the cabinet were thus able to appear less extreme than those of the Board of Trade. To the mutinous Gladstone, who momentarily talked of resignation, he pointed out that most of their colleagues had their doubts on some point or other; but 'they look to that point, which must always be looked at by the members of a government, the prospect of carrying the measure they propose'. Had he been able to consider only abstract arguments, he confided to him later, he would have proposed a lower rate of protection; but 'it would have done no good to drive Knatchbull out of the cabinet after the Duke of Buckingham, nor could I hope to pass a measure with greater reductions through the House of Lords'.

II

Parliament opened on 3 February and six days later Peel rose in a crowded House to announce the details of his promised corn bill. It was a dry, balanced speech, weighted with a mass of statistical information, and of necessity somewhat defensive in character. To agriculturalists he stressed the justice of some reduction and the benefits to be expected from greater price stability. To free-traders he argued that agriculture was a national interest which deserved favourable treatment because of the special burdens laid on it and pointed out that under the new scale the duty between 59*s* and 60*s*, for example, would be cut by half. A middle of the road policy sometimes commands intellectual respect; it rarely excites enthusiasm. Nevertheless it was something in which moderate men could concur and, given his premisses, the technical solution Peel offered seemed workmanlike and adequate. Its greatest defect was that it provided no final, absolute solution. Its greatest merit was that it offered an immediate practical one. Public opinion was so fragmented that no proposal would have commanded wide support and Peel's plan was acceptable as the mean average of conflicting views and interests. Subsequent debate in the House confirmed this. Alternative proposals from Russell for a fixed duty, from free-traders for total repeal, and from protectionists for a higher duty, were all decisively defeated. A meeting of the party before the main debate made it plain that though many Conservatives would have preferred a higher degree of protection, they were ready as a body to support the government's measure. The excitement was outside the House, in the violent proceedings of the Anti-Corn Law League in London, and in the industrial areas of the north and midlands, where Leaguers, Chartists and Complete Suffragists met in innumerable angry meetings, and effigies of the prime minister were publicly burnt. But in March the second reading of the bill was carried by over a hundred votes and before the spring was out the new corn bill was safely through to the statute book.

Meanwhile the second instalment of the budget had been unfolded. On 11 March Peel informed the House of the government's financial proposals. If corn had been the great social issue, this was the great technical issue. The secrecy surrounding the cabinet's decision had been complete and up to the last the Whigs did not believe that Peel would dare in time of peace to reintroduce the income tax. His speech, lasting over three and a half hours, was a model of lucidity which had all the greater effect because of the shock of the principal proposal. 'The success was complete,' wrote Greville, 'he took the House by storm.' The bombshell came at the end of the first hour and there was a moment of stunned silence before members recovered their senses and interruptions broke out. When order was restored Peel continued with the rest of his statement. With a total of £4.3 million to be expected from the income tax and various subsidiary sources, he estimated the net surplus at £1.8 million. This was to be applied to a vast remodelling and rationalising of the tariff system, on the general principle of removing all prohibitory duties, reducing all duties on imported raw materials to 5 per cent or less, and those on foreign manufactured goods to 20 per cent or less. Of the 1,200 dutiable articles in the cumbrous book of rates, 750 would have their duties reduced. As a result of these major, and a few minor changes, the government would be left with a surplus of half a million. His elaborate but skilful analysis over, he pitched his argument to a more rhetorical note and adjured his audience to rise to the needs and perils of the time as their fathers had done to the challenge of the revolutionary France. 'If you do permit this evil to continue,' he finished grandly, 'you must expect the severe but just judgement of a reflecting and retrospective posterity.'

His speech was delivered on a Friday evening and over the weekend two things became clear. He had thrown the opposition into confusion and put himself into a position which in a sense transcended party. The fundamental proposition he had laid down was that the rich should take on their shoulders the cost of rescuing the country from its financial ills. This was not class but national policy. Over corn the ministers had been criticised for timidity and social bias; over the income tax they startled parliament and the country by the boldness of their proposals. They had demonstrated their ability to solve a problem on which their opponents had signally failed; and the country could feel that it was being governed by men who knew what they wanted and how to do it. Some of his parliamentary opponents were as sensible of this as his friends. One Whig M.P. came into the Travellers' Club on the Friday night to give an account of the speech. 'One felt,' he said honestly, 'all the time he was speaking, "Thank God, Peel is Minister".' This did not mean that there was no opposition; but over the income tax the Whigs found no great national support and over tariff reform they were confined by their own record to piecemeal criticism. Peel's own impression was that in the country at large there was less feeling against the income tax than in parliament and a wider endorsement than might have been expected for his dictum that 'it is for the interest of property that property should bear the burden'. The most awkward moment came in May when eighty-five Conservative agriculturalists voted against the government in favour of an amendment to restrict the import of live cattle. But with the help of 172 Liberals the ministers were able to ride comfortably over this minor agricultural revolt and by June the whole of their fiscal and financial programme had gone through intact.

Despite the growing discontent of the Tory agriculturalists and their constituents, Peel steadily refused either to make concessions during the passage of the bills or to utter soothing words afterwards. To Croker, who was collecting material for the defence of the government which appeared in the September *Quarterly*, he wrote sharply that the difficulty would be to prove that they had gone far enough. Something had to be done to revive industry and commerce; something had to be done for the starving thousands in towns like Paisley. What he had done was not in response to agitation. 'There is nothing I have proposed which is not in conformity with my own convictions. I should rather say, I have not gone, in any one case, beyond my own convictions *on the side of relaxation*.' Unless there was some improvement soon, he added sombrely, they would be on the brink of a social crisis.

What coloured Peel's mind increasingly in the summer of 1842 was the condition of Britain. Starting with an enquiry into the best means of balancing the budget, he ended with the broad concept of attacking poverty and restoring social stability. The only way open to the government to do this was by reducing unemployment and lowering the cost of living, or in the more abstruse language of the textbooks, to reprime the economy by stimulating consumption. However much dictated by the limitations of early nineteenth-century government, it was a curiously modern formula; and he had arrived at it by a process of practical commonsense rather than through any doctrine. In the end his preoccupation was with the means whereby government could meet the dangers of a spawning, impoverished and disorderly industrial society. The harrowing experience of governing England in 1842, the worst year perhaps which the British people endured in the whole of the nineteenth century, acted as a forcing-ground in which his ideas developed almost from month to month. Revolutionary as the great budget of 1842 was, by the end of that terrible year of starvation and violence Peel was convinced he had done too little rather than too much. The 'condition of England question' was a more savagely educative process than any textbook.

III

As far back as the autumn of 1841 it had been obvious that the combination of Chartist agitation, Anti-Corn Law League propaganda, and widespread unemployment threatened a winter of unrest. Though Ashley, angry at the government's refusal to accept his Ten Hours factory bill, had prophesied that the workers would ally with the League, it was to Chartism rather than the Manchester mill-owners that the industrial proletariat turned in the months when Peel was working his corn, tax and tariff proposals through parliament. Though Cobden, at League meetings in the spring, had used violent language about the need for physical force to overawe ministers and did what he could to vilify and discredit aristocratic government, he failed to attract much support. Even in Manchester the *Guardian* praised the income tax and with the passing of the new corn bill called for a halt in the activities of the League.

The Commons, as a debate in July had demonstrated, was genuinely concerned at the social consequences of the economic depression. Nevertheless nothing that parliament had done so far had any effect on distress in the country. The government did not need debates to remind them of the grim state of some of the industrial areas. From the time they took office petitions, deputations, and the correspondence of the Home Department had kept them in daily awareness that the country was passing through its worst period in living memory. A memorial from Paisley in February, for example, had drawn a grisly picture of long-standing and increasing destitution. In that one town some 17,000 persons were enduring slow starvation, and the local relief committee with failing funds was having to reduce the already inadequate assist-ance. In Leeds some 16,000 persons out of a population of 80,000 were in receipt of assistance from the workhouse board. These were only single items in a general catalogue of misery which included areas as different and far apart as Manchester, Marylebone, Clydeside and the Potteries. Almost everywhere the story was the same. Poor relief and local charity were both breaking down under the prolonged and unpre-cedented strain. Though the government took energetic steps to promote a national relief fund campaign, this could only be a palliative; and though the weather was good and the harvest promised well, ripening corn in the fields was no remedy for starvation in the streets.

Meanwhile the frustration of Chartists and Leaguers was driving them into desperate courses. In the spring of 1842, for the first time since the Reform Act crisis, there seemed a possibility of an alliance between lower and middle-class agitators for an attack on aristocratic government. Many League members who were mayors of boroughs or local magistrates in the distressed areas openly declared that they would not try to preserve law and order unless the ministers made concessions to public demands. The League leaders were talking in private of a campaign to withhold taxes, and more sinister still, of closing down factories to produce unemployment on such a scale that the government would be forced into submission. Though their correspondence on this subversive topic remained unknown to the authorities, there was enough wild talk from lesser men in the move-ment to make the Home Office aware of this new and dangerous threat. Meanwhile their propaganda charged the government with direct responsibility for the sufferings of the people. In May 1841 the *Anti-Bread Tax Circular*, the official organ of the League, had argued that those who upheld the Corn Laws were 'virtually the murderers of their fellow-creatures'. Equally violent language was a feature of the angry recriminations which filled the summer of 1842. At a free-trade meeting in London in July one speaker mentioned a conveniently unnamed acquaintance who had expressed a readiness to assassinate Peel; and, while not himself approving of such extreme measures, he added that few tears would be shed on the day of Peel's funeral.

In August all the sweltering discontents of that hot summer came to a head. In many industrial areas crowds of unemployed men went round the countryside ostensibly begging for assistance but overawing the local inhabitants by their appearance and numbers. Where men were not unemployed they were often on short time or reduced wages.

THE CONDITION OF ENGLAND

In July an attempted reduction of wages at a colliery near Longton in Staffordshire precipitated a general turnout in the Potteries. The strikers went round the pits extinguishing the steam-engines and pulling out the boiler plugs so that they could no longer be used. Thousands moved into Shropshire and Cheshire with the intention of enlarging the area of the stoppage. Simultaneously cotton-mill owners in north-east Cheshire began a series of wage reductions and at meetings to consider strike action the men were harangued by local Chartists. At the beginning of August the two streams of industrial unrest merged into one violent movement to withhold all labour until the Charter was the law of the land. Colliers and mill-hands, armed with bludgeons, pitch-forks, flails and pikes, went round in vast crowds, closing down pits and mills, breaking into buildings, and requisitioning food and money. Houses of magistrates and clergy, public buildings, police stations, and workhouses were looted and set on fire. Two policemen were killed in Manchester and an attack made on the railway. The original distur-bances were in Staffordshire, Cheshire, and Lancashire; but the example of disorder was soon followed in Yorkshire, on Tyneside, and in Wales and parts of Scotland. By this time the Chartist leaders were being carried along, exhilarated or frightened according to tempera-ment, by the violence raging all round them. The Chartist Convention Council meeting in Manchester showed the familiar divisions of policies and personalities, but before it broke up a fierce manifesto was issued to the working classes appealing to the God of Battles and urging a universal strike.

The authorities in London had already begun their counter-measures. On 13 August alarming reports from Manchester were confirmed by the arrival of several magistrates. The 16th was the anni-versary of Peterloo and it was feared that there might be an outbreak of demonstrations on that red-letter day in the working-class calendar. Peel promptly summoned the cabinet and it was agreed to despatch a battalion of the Guards north by rail that evening. The same day a hastily convened Privy Council at Windsor issued a royal proclamation warning all subjects against attending tumultuous meetings or com-mitting breaches of the peace. Under this energetic leadership the local authorities, many of whom seemed paralysed during the first week of violence, began to recover their nerve. Gradually the overstrained military forces in the industrial districts reasserted their control. In several places they had to open fire and there were a number of casual-ties, including some killed at Preston and Burslem, before order was finally restored. The speed with which troop reinforcements had come up by rail from London and the south had a disconcerting effect on the rioters and by the end of the month the worst was over.

The work of coordinating the efforts of magistrates, police and mili-tary, arresting ringleaders and preventing further outbreaks, was the responsibility of Graham's department. But throughout the crisis the prime minister remained in close touch with the Home Office. One

221

personal anxiety was the presence of his wife and children at Drayton in the very heart of the disturbed areas. In the middle of August he snatched a couple of days to see to their safety, only to hear at Drayton a report that the queen had been assassinated. On the 17th he was back in London and next day went through all the provincial correspondence with Graham at the Home Office. London itself was threatened by disturbances, though the existence of the Metropolitan Police made it unlikely that the violence of the north would be repeated in the capital. A meeting at Lincoln's Inn Fields on 18 August was promptly countered by Graham with an order to disperse the crowd and arrest the ringleaders. Chartist meetings at Kennington Common and Paddington were met with a similar display of executive authority, backed by a strategic disposition of men and guns. Friday, 19 August, was a particularly arduous day. Peel and Graham, dining late at Whitehall Gardens on Thursday evening, had their meal interrupted by a report from Mayne, the Police Commissioner, of a great gathering at Lincoln's Inn Fields. They at once adjourned to the Home Office and Peel was there until the small hours of the morning supervising police and troop dispositions. Next day he was back again conferring with provincial magistrates, the City authorities, and the Attorney-General. That morning a report had come in of renewed disturbances in the Potteries and a threatened attack on Drayton Manor. In the midst of all the hubbub Peel scribbled a letter to Julia, telling her to come up to London at once if there was any danger. A brief note arrived from her that evening telling him that all was well and that he was not to come down himself. An alarm there had been and preparations had been made by Julia and her steward to resist an attack. The indefatigable Bonham at the Board of Ordnance had sent down carbines and ammunition and the little garrison at Drayton, wrote Julia the following Sunday,

> should have been equal to an attack from two or three hundred till assistance had come. But then we expected three or four thousand. I am confident, however, that no men actually attacking doors and windows here would have left this place alive. . . . I have felt *furious* with the vile mob who contemplated an attack.

Like her husband, Julia Peel's spirit always rose in an emergency; all her anxiety was for her husband.

Peel himself was clearly in need of rest after the strain of the parliamentary session; but there was little respite for him that year. At the end of August came the royal visit to Scotland on which his presence was required. With distress as severe as in England and disorder almost as widespread, it was hardly an auspicious time to visit the northern kingdom. But the visit had been long planned and postponement would be psychologically damaging. In the event everything passed off well except for the weather. But anxiety for the queen's safety, constant official functions, and the never-ending flow of red-boxes from London made it hardly a holiday for the prime minister. 'I have no great anxiety for the repetition of a similar visit,' he wrote dryly to Graham. But at least he was reassured that loyalty to the monarch was a deepseated feeling among the mass of the people. He himself had not been without some marks of popular favour. After going through Stirling and Linlithgow his hands were bruised and swollen with the constant handshaking with the crowd who pressed round his carriage. It was an experience he endured with some distaste. 'It is better, however,' he wrote to his wife, 'than having stones thrown.'

IV

By 22 September Peel was back at Whitehall to deal with the aftermath of the August disorders. Special Commissions had been appointed to deal with the rioters captured in Staffordshire, Cheshire and Lancashire; and a number of leading Chartists had been subsequently arrested. Against the latter the law officers advised simple charges of conspiracy, since treason would be difficult to prove. A state trial of the Chartists was avoided and they were left to make their appearance in court along with the ordinary rioters. In the event they escaped with lighter sentences than their convicted fellow-prisoners. In general the evidence collected by the Home Office pointed to economic rather than political causes for the disturbances. On this score the sympathies of the government were entirely with the workmen. At the start of the troubles Graham had reported to Peel that the masters were more to blame than the men; and he instructed the commanding officer of the Northern and Midland District not only to avoid any appearance of conniving with employers to make the men return to work but to urge the manufacturers, wherever it seemed that their employees had reason for complaint, to meet their grievances. Peel completely endorsed this distinction between the preservation of order and the protection of the masters against what he called 'just and peaceable demands for a rise of wages'. Up in Scotland the problem of employers and workers had continued to exercise his mind.

> I wish [he wrote to Graham on 2 September] that we could with perfect safety and without adding to the excitement which prevails, appoint a Commission for the purpose of ascertaining the real truth as to the state of the relations between the employers and employed in the Collieries. I think it would be found that there are practical grievances—possibly not to be redressed by law—of which the employed have just reason to complain. What law cannot effect, exposure might. I strongly suspect the profits in many of those collieries would enable the receivers of them to deal with much more liberality towards their workmen than they do.

Graham acted immediately. A week later he sent Peel a confidential memorandum on the grievances of the colliers and promised a commission of enquiry as soon as the men returned to work.

From the government's point of view the most disturbing aspect of the August rioting was the equivocal behaviour of some of the magistrates and the fomenting of disorder by the Anti-Corn Law League. A whole file of complaints against local J.P.s had been amassed by the Home Office and in September Graham instituted a formal enquiry into the allegations. But while there were ample grounds for suspicion, it was not easy to obtain proof of criminal negligence as distinct from timidity or supineness. Though Graham hankered for a few summary dismissals, Peel finally ruled that no magistrate should be removed except on firm evidence and after he had been given an opportunity to defend himself. A professional standard of efficiency could not reasonably be expected from an amateur unpaid magistracy. Whatever their shortcomings, they constituted the government's first line of defence for the preservation of order and property. In any case the defects of the local authorities exposed by the riots were only partial. In many of the worst affected towns the magistrates, even when politically opposed to the government, had shown both courage and initiative.

What exercised Peel more than the magistracy was the role of the Anti-Corn Law League in the riots. There was a widespread impression that the League members, by reducing wages and closing mills, had deliberately invoked disorder to bring pressure on the government. In Chartist mythology the Plug Plot, as the riots were known in Lancashire, was long attributed to a conspiracy of League mill-owners. It was a belief shared at the time by many Conservatives. Even if the League as an organisation could be acquitted of guilt, it could not be absolved from blame. Not only economic distress but political agitation also had been prevalent all over the midland and northern industrial areas; and the orators of the League had been as influential as the Chartists in producing a sense of unendurable evils wantonly inflicted. 'Their paid lecturers', reported the police commissioner in Manchester at the height of the disturbances, 'worked the people up to a frenzy.' Peel had no doubt in his mind that it was an aspect of the riots that needed investigation and even before he left for Scotland he instructed Graham to institute an enquiry.

> If we can bring no legal offence home to the League, it would have an excellent effect, having collected our evidence and arranged our proofs, to arraign the League in a careful publication, so careful as to admit of no reply, at the bar of public opinion. . . . I cannot tell you how strongly I feel the advantages of a *thorough* exposure, *founded on proof*, of the Anti-Corn Law League.

The materials for investigation were certainly present. It was not until

November that Graham's bulky dossier was in a state to be printed and privately circulated.

All it could demonstrate, however, was the League's responsibility for bringing about a dangerous situation, not their actual complicity in the riots themselves. Direct governmental publication was therefore inadvisable. Instead the document was handed to Croker to form the basis of the article on 'Anti-Corn Law agitation' which appeared, after careful instructions and revision by the prime minister, in the December issue of the *Quarterly*. In ensuring the denunciation of the League as a dangerous, immoral and quasi-unconstitutional organisation, the government went as far as it could in striking back. But their suspicions had gone beyond the facts. There had been no plot and some Tory mill-owners had behaved as badly as members of the League. But League propaganda had certainly contributed to disorder and League members had talked both publicly and privately of creating exactly the kind of situation that occurred in August. The League leaders in fact had stopped short on the brink of illegality and their loud and disingenuous protestations of innocence concealed a lively fear that they had put themselves in danger of prosecution. It was many months before the nervousness and strained tempers on both sides died down.

The riots and the judicial action which followed crippled Chartism and frightened the League. But they did nothing to remove the economic causes of the disturbances. Distress, unemployment, and low wages continued. From Paisley, a town which haunted Peel all through 1842, came another memorial in December, reporting that their relief funds, despite a large grant from the national Relief Committee, were almost exhausted and that there were 10,000 persons in the town for whom the choice would soon be between starvation and crime. The only consolation for the government was that nature, if not man, had been kind to them that summer. It had been one of the warmest seasons in living memory and each time Peel travelled on the new railroad that now linked London with Birmingham, he gratefully noted the signs of a bountiful harvest. When the agriculturalists of his party, still brooding over the legislation of the session, began to complain of falling wheat prices, he reacted sharply. 'My firm belief is', he wrote to Arbuthnot, 'that you could not have during the coming winter the high prices of the last four years and security for property.' At the heart of his policy now was the conviction that the only way to overcome both the human misery and the social threat was to increase the purchasing power of the masses. Poor relief, emigration, charity, were only palliatives. Steady employment and cheap food were the only permanent remedies. As he told Croker in August, 'we must make this country a cheap country for living, and thus induce parties to remain and settle here, enable them to consume more by having more to spend'.

All the experience that had come to him in 1842 convinced Peel that he must press on with a further reduction of the tariff. Butter and cheese must follow meat and cereals; even the complicated problem of sugar must be looked at again. But it was left for Graham, the man who had come to share Peel's inner thoughts and feelings, to make the most startling observation of that year of distress and disorder. The occasion was the minor question of colonial preference for which Stanley had promised the Canadians he would introduce legislation the following session. 'It is a question of time,' wrote Graham to the prime minister in December. 'The next change in the Corn Law must be to an open trade. . . . But the next change must be the last; it is not prudent to hurry it.'

"A Pit-iable Situation" – Constable Peel moved the Whigs on (June 1841). In the
no-confidence debate of May–June 1841 Peel pokes fun at the Whigs for using the
precedent of Pitt in 1784 as a justification for remaining in office when unable to carry
their measures. "It is only under the refuge of the mantle of Mr. Pitt that they can seek
safety". The three Whigs are (left to right) Hobhouse, Morpeth and Russell.

"A pleasant situation!" – facing two dangerous animals (November 1842). Peel between the snapping crocodile of the anti-Corn

Chapter 17

Midpassage

The end of 1842 came with no sign that the new year would be any better than the old. The prime minister still stood, as HB the great political cartoonist of the day portrayed him in November, between the snapping crocodile of the League and the couched lion of the agricultural interest, brandishing his Corn Law in one hand and his tariff in the other. The industrial depression continued with its gaunt companions, unemployment and starvation. The success of Peel's tariff experiment hung in the balance and even the revenue had not recovered. Though the reduction in import duties took effect at once, the machinery of the income tax could not be set up in time to collect the full year's assessment. Like its Whig predecessors Peel's government was heading for yet another deficit. When the cabinet started its presessional discussions in October, it was painfully clear that there could be no more tariff innovations while the 1842 budget itself was still on trial.

The sombreness of the political outlook was intensified by a personal tragedy in Peel's own household. On 20 January 1843 at the Charing Cross end of Whitehall his private secretary Edward Drummond was shot in the back by a man called Daniel MacNaghten and died a few days later. It was soon discovered that his assailant had mistaken him for the prime minister. MacNaghten was a Glasgow mechanic of illegitimate birth suffering from persecution mania. He had bought his pistols in Scotland at the time of the queen's visit and it is possible that he had seen Drummond occupying Peel's carriage in the royal processions. Peel frequently travelled with the queen or Aberdeen, leaving his secretary to occupy the conspicuous Peel equipage with its coat of arms and liveried servant. Drummond himself had joked about the mistake which many people must have made of thinking that he was the great man in person. In any case MacNaghten, who had been haunting Whitehall for some days, must frequently have seen Drummond moving between the Treasury and Peel's private house. Only this mistake of identity in the crazy mind of a morose and unsociable Scot had prevented, thirty-one years after Perceval's death, the assassination of another British prime minister.

Though it was obvious that MacNaghten was mentally unbalanced, and the police could find no evidence of political motives, there had been too much talk of assassination in the previous year for his act to be entirely dissociated from the continued agitation in the country. Indeed, Drummond's death was followed by a number of threatening letters to the prime minister. All this gave a sharp edge to a passage between Peel and Cobden only three weeks after Drummond's funeral. In a debate on the economic distress Cobden savagely charged the prime minister with individual responsibility for the dangerous state of the country. Speaking with great intensity in a House already keyed up by Cobden's passionate attack Peel retorted sharply to what he called his opponent's menaces. For some minutes there was an excited scene in the House during which neither Peel nor Cobden could make himself heard. Eventually, and with ill grace, Cobden disclaimed the charge of personal as distinct from official responsibility and Peel coldly accepted the semi-apology. There is little doubt that Cobden had made up his mind before the debate to concentrate his attack on Peel personally. 'If I had only Bright with me, we could worry him out of office before the close of the session,' he wrote to his brother. Though he bitterly resented the accusation that his speech was a direct incentive to violence against Peel, he was too much in the habit during these years of letting his vocabulary outrun his judgement. As far as Peel was concerned, the episode was soon dismissed from his mind. It was another three years before he realised how much it had continued to rankle with Cobden.

The session which began so unpleasantly continued with little comfort to the ministers. In the queen's speech they had avoided controversies and made no mention of major legislation. The parliamentary gap thus created was promptly filled by the opposition. Motions of all kinds were brought forward which, if useless for practical purposes, enabled them to monopolise parliamentary time and score debating points against the government. If these tactics were less effective than they might have been, it was only because the opposition themselves were deeply divided on the right solutions for the problems they insisted on discussing. Though Gladstone at one point alarmed the agriculturalists of his party by a too doctrinaire defence of free trade, it was evident that the Commons as a whole had no great liking either for a general enquiry into the Corn Laws or for Russell's tentative argument in favour of a fixed duty. The only government proposal which threatened to stir up feeling on this sensitive topic was Stanley's bill to admit Canadian corn at a nominal duty. It was presented as a measure of imperial reciprocity rather than of free trade and at a general meeting of the party beforehand Peel and Stanley carefully explained both the reasons for the bill and the consequences of rejecting it. Their speeches were well received and since the Whigs themselves were divided on the issue, the measure went through with little difficulty.

At the beginning of May Goulburn introduced the budget in a speech which was largely a tale of deceived expectations and unexpected losses. With the returns from customs and excise lower than was forecast and the new taxes, particularly the income tax, failing to produce their estimated yield within the financial year, there was a net deficit of over £2 million in place of the expected surplus of £500,000. Nevertheless, neither Peel nor Goulburn were disposed to stand in a white sheet. The revenue had clearly reflected the abnormal depression of 1842 and there were already signs of recovery. Even in Paisley, that grim barometer of the country's health, there was rising employment and falling demand for relief. It seemed unnecessary therefore to make specific arrangements to meet what could clearly be regarded as a temporary deficit. In his own contribution to the debate Peel pointed out that if they had been able to collect the whole of the income tax due, the deficit would have been only slight; and he reaffirmed his faith in the government's policy and their determination to press on with tariff reductions as soon as the state of the revenue permitted. If there was one lesson which stood out, it was that the income tax had stood between the country and financial disaster. 'Where', he asked the Commons, 'should we have been now if the income tax had not been imposed?'

On this major proposition the House of Commons was inclined to agree with the prime minister, and reproaches for his mishandling of the financial situation were among the least of the burdens he had to bear during the 1843 session. With the growing feeling that the country had at last turned the corner of the great depression, it was not easy for fairminded men to escape the conviction that the government's policy was fundamentally sound. Peel's reputation as a financier was in no way impaired by the uncertainties surrounding the first year's working of the new budget, even though it was obvious that it would need two years and not one before its benefits were realised.

In the more passionate and controversial field of religion the government had a less easy passage. Despite Peel's temporising policy during 1842 the longstanding dispute in Scotland over ecclesiastical patronage ended with the Disruption of May 1843 when over four hundred ministers seceded from the established Kirk. In June Graham's factory regulations bill had to be withdrawn because of fierce Dissenting opposition to the educational clauses, which seemed to put the new schools for factory children under the practical control of the Anglican Church. In August O'Connell's campaign for the Repeal of the Union, supported by many bishops and clergy of the Roman Church, reached its climax with the legendary 'meeting of the million' at Tara. It was clear that even the great industrial depression had not weakened the power of religion to stir up historic discords in British society.

The spectacle of embattled clergy in all three kingdoms strengthened Peel's conviction that a Conservative government could not afford to show undue partiality to the Church of England, least of all where the tax-payers' money was concerned. Ever since the ministry had started it had been under pressure from its supporters to assist the Establishment's extension programme; and the industrial disturbances of 1842 had reinforced the case for building new churches and schools in the manufacturing areas. The difficulty was finance. Peel felt as strongly as anyone that there was a need for the Church to apply its own pastoral remedies for the social evils of the time. But the extreme Anglican argument of state Church, therefore state support, merely irritated him. Inglis's proposal for a parliamentary grant of two or three million pounds merely exposed his political naïvety; and even Goulburn's suggestion for a more modest subsidy found no favour with the prime minister.

> It is very well for clergymen and for Sir Robert Inglis [he wrote to Graham in December 1842] to argue that it is the duty of the State to provide religious edifices wherever they are wanted, and that Dissenters are bound to build and repair and endow their own churches, and those of the Establishment also—and this by new Taxation whenever requisite—but you and I know that the Church and religion would suffer, and peace and charity would be sacrificed.

The solution, Peel thought, lay not in an appeal for public money, which would simply lead to an acrimonious debate, but in better use of the Church's own property and more generous private assistance from the laity.

In January 1843 Peel and Goulburn met the Archbishop of Canterbury and the Bishop of London and impressed on them the need for a special effort at Church extension in the industrial areas; and in the course of the session an unobtrusive piece of legislation was put through to facilitate the Church's voluntary efforts. This was the Populous Parishes Act, which empowered the Ecclesiastical Commissioners to create new parishes with stipends and for this purpose to anticipate their revenue by loans from the Queen Anne's Bounty. In introducing the bill the prime minister appealed to the wealthy to assist in the endowment of those new parishes. He turned precept into practice by privately subscribing £4,000 for the Commissioners to use in London, and the industrial districts of Staffordshire, Warwickshire, and Lancashire: all the localities in fact in which he held property. Equally characteristically he forbade any publicity for this handsome donation. This was not the only contribution he made to the voluntary efforts of the Church. When, after the failure of Graham's bill, the Anglican National Society started a special fund for establishing schools in industrial areas, he headed the list of original donors with a subscription of £1,000. His only concern was that there should be no quarrelling over the purpose of the fund. If agreement could be reached, he told Graham, 'I mean to subscribe liberally less as a minister than from connection with the manufacturing districts'.

The long, harassing and largely unproductive session of 1843 ended in August and with it the ministry had virtually completed two years of office. There had been few changes in its composition. Peel tended to keep his colleagues as long as possible in the office to which he had appointed them; and the one minor reshuffle of 1843 was forced on him. Fitzgerald died in May and Ripon asked to succeed him. His chief's ill-health had for some time put Gladstone in virtual charge of the Board of Trade and Peel without delay promoted him to the presidency and a seat in the cabinet. Gladstone's post was filled by Dalhousie, a young Scottish peer favoured by Wellington whose promotion had the additional advantage of not causing a by-election. For a government in mid-passage trials of electoral strength were best avoided.

There was little doubt in fact that support for the ministry had waned since 1841. There was a mood of anticlimax, of expectations aroused and unrealised, of personal disappointment and disillusionment. Partly this was due to the fact that the great problems confronting the ministry had still not been solved; partly to the middle course which Peel had followed on many questions; partly to his inability to compensate for the inevitable rubs of political life with the small change of flattery and attention. Within the party the suspicions of the agriculturalists were still fermenting and later in the session a more exotic note was given to the party's discontents. In August Greville contrasted the civility of Peel's regular adversaries in the Irish debates with the bitterness and insolence of his *soi-disant* supporters. 'Disraeli and Smythe, who are the principal characters, together with John Manners, of the little squad called "Young England", were abusive and impertinent.' But though they were a minor source of worry to the whips, the Young Englanders were only a symptom of the general period of depression through which the ministry was passing. In November the queen surprised Aberdeen by asking whether the government was stronger or weaker. The Foreign Secretary replied diplomatically that it was certainly less popular but this had little to do with strength or weakness. Greville had reached the same conclusion in August. Even if the ministry had lost credit, he thought, no other party or set of men had enhanced their position and there was in fact no rival to Peel.

Certainly there was no desire at Windsor for a change of administration. All that had happened since 1841 had merely strengthened the prime minister's standing at Court. Even the personal relationship between Peel and Victoria was growing warmer. On his visits to Windsor Peel was relaxed enough to drop into his mild joking vein at mealtimes and he was evolving his own way of dealing with the royal couple. When misgivings were expressed in cabinet over their projected visit to Ostend to see King Leopold, Peel assured his colleagues that

> they will be as reasonable as possible—but it does not do to thwart them. I know how to manage them—the way is to receive the proposals without objection and show a willingness to meet their desires—then as difficulties appear, they will grow cool.

The final mark of favour came in November when to the chagrin of some of the Whigs, Victoria and Albert stayed with the prime minister at Drayton. To add to his satisfaction a visit by the prince to nearby Birmingham, where he toured factories and was entertained by a Chartist mayor, passed off, as Peel reported to Stanley, with an enthusiasm 'very striking amid all the discontent, disunion and disloyalty'.

In his own more feudal neighbourhood Peel commemorated the royal visit by giving a shilling to each of the schoolchildren of Tamworth and Drayton who lined the royal route and a hundred guineas to be applied to 'some sort of carousing' for the poorer inhabitants of the borough, including the inmates of the workhouse.

It was a satisfactory end to a not very satisfactory year. To Ellenborough in distant India he described the same month the state of the country.

> The balance of good predominates. We have friendly feelings established with France and the United States. Apparent harmony and prosperity in Canada—a moderate price of provisions. The Income Tax producing more than we calculated and causing little grievance and even little complaint—a surplus of revenue instead of a great deficit. The cotton manufacture flourishing—trade generally reviving. On the other hand . . . we have that great standing evil which counterbalances all good, the State of Ireland.

That was the rub. For all the signs of recovery in England, the problems of the sister-island seemed as intractable as ever.

II

When Peel came to power in 1841 English affairs inevitably took precedence in his mind. The decade that had just ended had seen a substantial number of Irish reforms and of the remaining problems there was nothing that called urgently for legislation. Though O'Connell had started his campaign for the Repeal of the Union, that issue in itself isolated him from the Whigs; and for the first two years of its existence the Repeal Association made little headway. As long as Ireland was moderately peaceful, Peel was content to leave it so. He told the Lord-Lieutenant that the Association's proceedings suggested a desire for martyrdom which the Irish government should carefully abstain from gratifying. To Graham he observed that 'when a country is tolerably quiet, it is better for a Government to be *hard of hearing* in respect to seditious language than to be very agile in prosecuting'.

In the first eighteen months of the new administration Peel was mainly concerned to remove the friction which soon developed between Earl de Grey, the jaunty ultra-Protestant Lord-Lieutenant, and his liberal-minded but rather prickly Chief Secretary, Lord Eliot. While conscious of Eliot's occasional tactlessness and forced by political expediency to make greater allowances for Irish Conservative opinion than his impetuous younger colleague, Peel was generally on the side of the Secretary in his struggles with unsympathetic officials in Dublin Castle. Both he and Graham were increasingly dissatisfied with de Grey's persistent refusal to carry out the government's stated policy of admitting Roman Catholics to a reasonable share of patronage. On this question Catholic emancipation had worked a great change in Peel's mind compared with his youthful attitudes when he first went to Ireland in 1812. To govern on the old Ascendancy principle that there were only two classes of people in Ireland, friends and enemies, would now in his view be fatal. Even the specious argument that, when Protestant candidates were better qualified than Catholics, they should be appointed, was not one which should be adopted too literally. 'We must *look out* for respectable Roman Catholics for office.' To that extent political expediency had to take precedence over alleged administrative efficiency.

Even before he took office in fact a new approach to Ireland had begun to take shape in his mind. In private conversation at Drayton five years earlier he had observed that the fundamental weakness in Ireland was the inability to secure the ordinary administration of justice, since its basic institution, the jury, rested on a presumption of identity between the jurymen and the state which simply did not exist. Two years later, in December 1837, he let fall the significant remark that what the English had conspicuously failed to do in either Ireland or Canada was to establish a working relationship with the Catholic Church. Diagnosis was a logical preliminary to prescription. Pessimistic as these observations were, they contained the germ of Peel's later Irish policy. Though his larger schemes had to wait their opportunity, he thought that a judicious use of government patronage might at least be made a starting-point for winning the confidence of the Irish Catholics. Long years of religious, social and political privilege had given the Irish Protestants a marked advantage in the acquirement of official posts. If that historic monopoly was continued by deliberate governmental action, he wrote in an impressive memorandum to de Grey in August 1843, it would make the more active and ambitious Roman Catholics use the political opportunities open to them since 1829 to work systematically against the whole system of government. 'Every avenue to popular favour is opened, and if every avenue to Royal favour is closed, we have done nothing by the removal of disabilities but organise a band of mischievous demagogues.'

By that date everything was overshadowed by the activities of O'Connell's Repeal Association which in the first six months of 1843 had come suddenly and explosively to life. Monster meetings were held all over Catholic Ireland. The flow of subscriptions rose sharply. Clergy and educated laity as well as peasants began to enrol. A number of Catholic bishops became members, including the redoubtable MacHale of Tuam who like some medieval prince-bishop joined at the head of a hundred of his diocesan priests. The radicals of the Young Ireland group threw their weight into the campaign. Financial support and the cheaper currency of anti-English abuse came from Canada and America; and offers of aid in the forthcoming struggle were made in the bellicose French press. Flushed with success O'Connell increased the pressure. He proclaimed as his objectives a membership of three million, repeal wardens in every parish, and a national convention to prepare for a repeal of the Union. The year 1843, he announced, was to be the Year of Repeal.

The Lord-Lieutenant, who had previously underrated the danger, reacted violently when he realised the extent of the crisis. To ministers in London the situation appeared more complex than it did to de Grey. The other Irish officials were not unanimous; Eliot would clearly not relish piloting a coercive measure through the Commons; and with the Anti-Corn League imitating O'Connell's tactics and language in England, it would be invidious to single out one organisation for attack and folly to attack both. Peel made a stiff parliamentary statement on 9 May, saying that the government would do all in their power to maintain the Union and that though he deprecated war, and above all civil war, there was no alternative which he did not think preferable to the disruption of the empire. For the time being however the cabinet were not prepared to go much further. The Irish arms bill introduced by Eliot a few weeks later provided a clear warning of the difficulties that any coercive policy would encounter. In itself it was a normal security measure of the kind passed by the Whigs in 1838, dealing with the registration of firearms, sale of gunpowder, and possession of lethal weapons such as pikes and daggers. But it was fiercely opposed by the English and Irish radicals, and severely criticised by the Whigs as a confession of bankruptcy in the government's Irish policy. The obstruction to the bill and the fresh Irish debates it provoked, threatened in fact to wreck the government's whole timetable. They had to jettison several minor bills and it was only by organising a body of supporters ready to sit up all night if necessary to counter the filibustering tactics of the opposition that they were able to force the arms bill through before the end of the session.

Between the pressure of the opposition and the pressure of Conservative feeling out of doors, the ministers were for a time pinned in an uncomfortably tight corner. Though the Lord-Lieutenant demanded further coercive legislation to deal with Irish agitation, the cabinet in the end decided that a mild measure would be useless and a harsh measure impolitic. It would simply be a stimulus to agitation; and the agitation would not be confined to Ireland. Peel wrote to de Grey in June:

> I firmly believe, in the present state of things, from the party opposed to us, there would be banded against the measure, that is against a measure of simple unqualified coercion, the Whig party, the Radical party, the Chartist party, the Anti-Corn Law League party—all those parties, by whatever name they are called, who are in favour of democracy or of mischief and confusion.

A policy of forbearance by the government and the chance of some blunder by O'Connell seemed the only hope of weathering the crisis. It was a policy of sense; but it was not heroic and it brought on the government the bitter complaints of the Irish Protestants.

By the autumn there were some signs that the tide was beginning to turn. The very success of O'Connell's campaign had excited Irish expectations to the point where it would be dangerous for him to go further and humiliating to retreat. Meanwhile materials for legal action against the great agitator were beginning to accumulate. He had criticised the queen's speech at the end of session in a manifesto which implied that there was no redress for Irish grievances by constitutional means and the announcement of a final monster meeting at Clontarf in October was couched in more martial language than usual. The issue was decided by the appearance of placards summoning the attendance of 'Repeal Cavalry' at the meeting. The law officers ruled that there was sufficient evidence to sustain a charge of treasonable conspiracy and that the Clontarf meeting was illegal. Now that the opportunity had presented itself Peel and Graham were determined to see the matter through; and the duke, who to the alarm of his civilian colleagues had been aching to go to Ireland to take charge of the situation, was enchanted at the prospect of action at last. On 7 October appeared the Lord-Lieutenant's proclamation banning the Clontarf meeting. A week later O'Connell and half a dozen leading repealers were arrested.

For O'Connell, who had promptly obeyed the proclamation and in the interval before his trial instructed his followers to act 'patiently, quietly, legally', it was to prove the virtual end of his long tempestuous career. But this was obvious only in retrospect. At the time there was no disposition on the part of ministers to underestimate the wiliness of their adversary. O'Connell in an Irish law court was like an old fox in his home covert. For that reason his continued retraction of some of his former language, including a statement of his willingness to accept a form of federation instead of repeal, aroused the curiosity of the prime minister. 'What has chiefly surprised me in the recent events in Dublin', he wrote to Stanley in October, 'is that O'Connell does not see the impolicy of the submissive tone which he now takes. What must his former partisans think of him?' It was a long time before Peel and Graham realised that in bringing O'Connell to trial they had not only halted the Repeal movement but broken the morale of the old Irish leader.

III

To the prime minister the check administered to the repeal movement in the autumn of 1843 was the beginning rather than the end of his Irish policy. If O'Connell had done nothing else, he had reinserted the Irish problem into the centre of British politics. What Chartism had done for the condition of England, the repeal movement had done for the condition of Ireland. With his economic schemes launched and the crisis of 1842 behind him, Peel now had both opportunity and incentive to begin a constructive approach to the Irish problem. In a letter to Graham shortly after O'Connell's arrest he laid down the axiom that 'mere force, however necessary the application of it, will do nothing as a permanent remedy for the social evils of that country'. It was to the long-term remedies that he now turned his attention.

One step had already been taken. In the parliamentary debates of the previous session the uneasy relations of landlord and tenant in Ireland had figured prominently in the speeches of both government and opposition. Peel himself had hinted at legislative protection for tenants wantonly evicted without compensation and promised to take the whole question of land occupation in Ireland into consideration. The upshot was the appointment of a small Commission under Lord Devon, a sensible, liberal-minded landowner with some legal knowledge who owned property in both England and Ireland. The other members were impartially selected from both the main political parties, and included one Catholic. By the start of 1844 the Devon Commission was already at work. In a society dominated by landowners and in an age which attached considerable sanctity to the rights of private property, Devon and his colleagues were clearly treading on dangerous ground. But Peel was prepared to venture even further into the Serbonian bog of Irish affairs which had engulfed so many English governments. Dealing with a nation three-parts Catholic, it seemed logical to come to terms with the Roman Church; and it made sense tactically to isolate O'Connell and the Repealers by driving a wedge between them and the Catholic hierarchy. British diplomatic influence with the Papacy, though not neglected, was too indirect and slow to be more than a marginal element in Peel's plans. An increase in the parliamentary grant for the Catholic Irish seminary at Maynooth, for which Eliot had long been pressing, seemed a more immediate and practical step towards improved relations with the Irish Church. In the long run, and more speculatively, it might even be found expedient to pay the salaries of the Irish parochial priests if that would free them from dependence on their parishioners.

There were few illusions in the minds of Peel and those of his colleagues whom he consulted in the autumn of 1843 about the political difficulties such an approach would encounter on all sides. There was no certainty that the Catholic hierarchy would cooperate; every likelihood that Protestant opinion in England would be hostile. Since Catholic emancipation in 1829 anti-Catholic feeling in Britain had strengthened rather than diminished, partly because of the continuation of Irish Catholic agitation, partly because of the progress of the apparently Roman-inspired Tractarian movement in the Church of England. As Stanley cautiously observed when supporting an enquiry into the state of Maynooth, it would at least 'render familiar ideas which at present would not even be permitted to be discussed'. When the regular cabinet meetings started again in November, members realised that the informal discussions which Peel had been having with his immediate Irish advisers would soon be issuing in more formal proposals. Peel did not attempt to hurry his colleagues. There was enough business before them to last until after Christmas; and when the queen's speech was drafted for the opening of parliament in February the only references to Ireland were the Devon Commission and a reform of the county franchise. Opposition motions in both Houses, however, were a clear signal that the Whigs were planning a grand assault on the ministers' Irish policy, the weakest flank in Whig traditional thinking of any Conservative administration. It was equally obvious that if the cabinet was to present a firm front to the attack, more discussion and agreement on future Irish legislation were needed than had taken place so far.

In the circumstances the great parliamentary debate launched by Russell on 13 February was, on the government's side, little more than a holding operation. The important discussions took place in cabinet on the three great Irish memoranda placed before them by the prime minister the same month. In the first, circulated a couple of days before the parliamentary debate, he asked his colleagues to consider constructive ways of conciliating Irish Catholics, in particular a more generous endowment of Maynooth, and strengthening the financial independence of the Irish parochial clergy. On the latter he proposed, not direct payment by the state, but the milder palliative of a law to facilitate private endowments. While admitting the difficulties he stressed the advantages, 'now that we have resisted agitation and steadily enforced the law', of detaching from the ranks of the agitators those not yet committed to violent attitudes and still prepared to uphold the Union. This document had a mixed reception in the cabinet. Though a majority favoured an increased grant to Maynooth, there was enough opposition, particularly from Gladstone, to put out of the question for the moment any parliamentary announcement.

Before the end of the long, and from Peel's point of view unsatisfactory, debate in the Commons, he sent round another document. Its tone was sombre. 'I view', wrote the prime minister, 'our future position in respect to Ireland and the administration of affairs in Ireland with great anxiety.' Once more he impressed on the cabinet the need to make reforms while it was safe to do so. He reiterated that law and order in Ireland depended on the cooperation of respectable and influential Catholics; and he laid down the naked principle that every concession must be made, short of abandoning the Church of Ireland and the Union, if those two basic features of Anglo-Irish relations were to be preserved. As a sample he mentioned a few possible topics for discussion: further reform of the Church of Ireland, university institutions for Catholics, and widening the municipal franchise. This was radical reform with a vengeance and a somewhat shaken cabinet recoiled instinctively from any immediate decisions. Nevertheless at the end of the month Peel pressed home his arguments in a third memorandum.

He listed the principles on which they were already agreed and asked what could be done immediately to put them into practice. The areas he suggested were municipal and parliamentary franchise, higher education and Roman Catholic endowments. He devoted much space to the question of a reform of Maynooth and on this his language was particularly strong.

> The Lord-Lieutenant tells us that the real enemies of the Government and the really powerful incendiaries are the young priests. . . . The College of Maynooth as at present governed and scantily provided for, is a public nuisance. . . . The wit of man could not devise a more effectual method for converting them into sour, malignant demagogues.

This broadside delivered, he returned to his theme of the endemic danger of the Irish situation and the need to snatch the fleeting opportunity that presented itself to bestow reforms on Ireland then rather than have them extorted later.

In this trilogy of Irish papers in February 1844 Peel had in fact exposed both the essence and the detail of his whole future policy. Though the form and timing had been dictated by the parliamentary situation, the argument was an exercise in rigorous logic. As long as Ireland remained disaffected, the United Kingdom was embarrassed in its diplomacy and vulnerable in war. Ireland would remain a source of danger until it was efficiently governed. It could not be efficiently governed as long as Irish courts and Irish juries were useless to provide the foundation of law and order. They would continue to be useless until the Catholic middle classes identified themselves with the state. They would not do so until they and their Church were given political and cultural as well as legal equality. That equality would only come if professionally, educationally and socially they were given the same opportunities as Protestants. To achieve this after centuries of inferiority parliament and the taxpayer must come to the assistance of Roman Catholics both lay and clerical. To his colleagues in the cabinet this devastating dialectic was almost unanswerable. Even Buccleuch, who started out with a strong Protestant bias, confessed himself completely converted. Only Gladstone, on grounds of past pledges and present principles, remained unhappy and unconvinced; and even he, under the private persuasions of the prime minister, was prepared for the moment to let matters take their course. The difficulty before the cabinet in the spring of 1844 was not their objectives but how to arrive at them.

Chapter 18

Difficulties and dissensions

The year 1844 which saw the beginning of Peel's new deal for Ireland was one of mixed fortunes for the government. At the start of the session the cabinet was in a mood of cautious optimism. Trade and industry had continued to improve; the financial situation had righted itself at last; parliamentary opposition was fragmented; Chartism had declined. The Corn Law of 1842 had shown itself the best technical instrument so far devised for reconciling the demands of consumer and producer. Since September the price of wheat had averaged between 50s and 52s a quarter, a lower level than had been recorded in all but seven of the previous fifty years. The instinct of the ministers was to leave well alone. When Wharncliffe suggested that, if they were asked about the Corn Law, they should speak up stoutly on its behalf, Peel replied that it would be impossible to commit themselves on that, as on any other question, irrespective of circumstances. The law had fulfilled expectations and they had no intention of changing it. The choice, he added significantly, was between the 1842 act and total repeal; at least there was no other step they could take. When Wharncliffe insisted that the important thing was to express their conviction of the continued need for protection, Peel avoided any direct answer. Nevertheless, in the debate on the address he did something to reassure the agriculturalists by saying that the government did not contemplate and had never contemplated, any change. This, if not the positive affirmation of faith for which Wharncliffe had asked, was at least a subscription to orthodoxy; and it did much to put the corn issue at rest during the 1844 session.

What Peel described as 'the most important Bill of the Session' resulted in the Bank Charter Act. With a statutory opportunity presenting itself that year to revise the Bank of England's charter, Peel used the occasion for adding a second fundamental piece of legislation to his currency act of 1819. That act had put the country back on the gold standard, but it did not in itself ensure that there would always be enough bullion to cover the note issue. There was no legal restriction on the issue of paper currency and the position was complicated by the existence of over four hundred private banks entitled to issue their own notes. Four great financial crises since 1819, all followed by widespread bankruptcies among the country banks, had underlined the dangers of an unrestricted credit system. From the start therefore the question of rewriting the Bank's charter revolved round the currency question. In approaching the issue Peel could draw on his experience of no less than four official currency investigations between 1819 and 1841.

Sympathetic as he was to the orthodox banking school of thought which favoured a fixed ratio of issue between notes and bullion, a single national bank of issue, and an end to the circulation of private banknotes, he also had to bear in mind political considerations. To entrust a monopoly of note issue to a government department controlled by politicians seemed financially dangerous; to give it to the Bank of England was still politically inexpedient. There were many country banks and they had many friends and clients in the House of Commons. In those circumstances the prime minister characteristically looked for a middle way between existing practice and ultimate objective.

The government solution, put forward by Peel in the House of Commons on 6 May, was that the Bank of England should be divided into separate departments of banking and issue; that the volume of notes issued should be related to specific amounts of bullion and securities; and that the fiduciary issue should be limited to £14 million. Private banks of issue were to be restricted; no new ones were to be created; and when a private bank terminated its issue rights, they should be taken over to a limited extent by the Bank of England. Some bankers thought that the credit restrictions imposed by the bill were too rigid and that any future financial crisis would be intensified by the inability of the Bank to use its discretion, as in the past, in issuing and lending in time of bullion shortage. To Peel, however, the essence of the bill was that it should restore confidence in the currency by the guarantee of convertibility to gold at all times. It was better, he thought, to leave emergency legislation to the actual emergency rather than write it into the permanent act. Like many other financial experts at the time, he probably oversimplified the relations between note issue and financial stability. But the danger at the time was from an unregulated rather than from an over-regulated system. For all its rigidity the act of 1844 served as the basis of the country's currency policy for the next eighty years. Only three times in that period did it prove necessary to take emergency powers to extend the fiduciary issue; only once was the statutory limit of £14 million actually exceeded. For the House of Commons and the public at large Peel's arguments were as convincing as his explanations were lucid. The stately progress of the measure through parliament was a tribute to the confidence felt in the prime minister's judgement on a highly technical subject.

It was a different story with two other important pieces of legislation brought forward by the government that session. In March the ministers were beaten in committee by 170 votes to 179 on Ashley's amendment to Graham's factory bill reducing the maximum hours for women and young persons from twelve hours to ten. It was not a party issue. Among those who voted for Graham's bill were Liberals, Radicals and leading Whig economists; among those who voted with Ashley were many influential backbench Conservatives. In maintaining

the twelve hours maximum the government was only continuing the
precedent set by the Whigs in the 1830s and it was common, if mistaken,
ground that a reduction of hours in the textile industry would lead to a
loss of production, of profits and ultimately therefore of wages. Peel
and Graham had been advised by their most experienced factory
inspectors that the reduction of the working day from twelve to ten
hours would produce a 25 per cent reduction in wages. Even Buller, a
supporter of Ashley, accepted that there would be a fall of 9 per cent.
The issue was therefore not a simple one between humanitarians and
economists, or between *laisser-faire* and state intervention. The ad-
missibility of government interference was acknowledged by all but a
few diehard Radicals. The real question was what kind of intervention
was justified in this case and what the consequences would be. That
many of the assumptions in the debate proved in the end wrong or
exaggerated did not make the contemporary dilemma less genuine or
painful.

Peel in particular bitterly resented the imputation that the
advocates of the ten hours clause had a monopoly of Christian kindness.
The national importance of the textile industry, which accounted for
about 80 per cent of British exports, ensured that any damage inflicted
on it would be felt throughout the entire economy. What he feared was
that the proposed reduction, amounting to a loss of some seven weeks
in the working year, by crippling British textiles in the foreign market
would soon force a reduction of wages at home; and that this in turn
would lead either to decreased home consumption or prolonged
industrial strife. Stagnation in commerce meant hardship for the poor;
and prolonged industrial depression was something he never wished to
witness again. 'I shall never forget as long as I live,' he told the House
of Commons, 'the situation in Paisley in 1841 and 1842.'

There were other considerations of a more political nature.
Conditions as bad as or worse than those in the textile manufacture
could be found in many other branches of industry. Why, he argued,
should parliament single out somewhat invidiously a few particular
kinds of labour 'which are at your mercy, because they are congregated
in large factories and brought under your eye'. Though many of
Ashley's supporters among the younger Conservatives were inspired
by humanitarian motives, much of the readiness of the country gentry
to vote with them clearly derived from their resentment against the
mill-owners of the League. To indulge in such resentments, Peel and
Graham believed, was the surest way to exacerbate class hostility and
drive the League to greater activity. 'A great body of the agricultural
members', Peel wrote to the queen, 'voted against the government
partly out of hostility to the Anti-Corn Law League, partly from the
influence of humane feelings, not foreseeing the certain consequences
as to the Corn Laws of new restrictions upon labour.'

Though defeated in committee Peel and Graham stuck grimly to
their guns. On 22 March, however, the House plunged itself into

inextricable confusion by voting against both Ashley's ten hour amendment and the government twelve hour clause. After Easter a new bill was introduced and the tussle renewed with tempers which had hardly cooled in the interval. In cabinet Peel, Graham and Stanley stubbornly opposed any compromise. Apart from all other considerations they resented the fact that the party had allowed a motley majority with wildly assorted motives to override the deliberate policy decisions of the government. When in May Ashley once more brought forward his amendment, Peel made it clear that the government would resign if defeated again. Faced by this ultimate sanction and exhorted by the whips, the party mustered in strength and Ashley's amendment was heavily defeated. The hard line had proved successful and the bill quietly passed into law in June.

Yet within a month the cabinet was facing an exactly similar crisis. This time it was over the old matter of the sugar duties. Since the great controversy of 1841 the government had shown a prudent inactivity on the issue; but by 1844 they could avoid legislation no longer. Their earlier reluctance was understandable. The whole question was an explosive compound of commercial, financial, political, humanitarian and religious elements. The virtual monopoly of supplying sugar to the United Kingdom enjoyed by the West Indian plantations, with their shrinking production and rising prices, was not one which the public would tolerate much longer. To reduce the duty on West Indian sugar would simply enrich the grower without bringing corresponding benefit to the consumer. It would also adversely affect the revenue since sugar was by far the most valuable single item of dutiable imports, accounting for a third of the total return from the customs. The alternative was to find other sources of supply to compete with the West Indies and keep down prices. Slave-grown sugar was politically and morally inadmissible; the Conservatives themselves had used the anti-slavery argument in 1841. The expiry of the Brazilian treaty in 1844, however, made it possible to admit 'free' sugar from the East Indies on favourable terms, though the amount available from that source was still limited. It seemed essential therefore to encourage the East Indian planters to increase their production by giving them a practical pledge of the government's intention. The cabinet plan was in two stages: the first to take effect in 1844, the second in 1845. For 1844 it was proposed to reduce the duties on foreign sugar while still leaving a preferential, though much reduced, margin of 10s for imperial sugar. It was hoped to make a permanent arrangement in 1845 when it was known whether the income tax would be renewed and to what extent therefore further tariff reductions could be made.

The ministerial proposal ran into crossfire from free traders who wished to reduce the duty on all foreign sugar, free or unfree, and from protectionists who objected to the decrease in imperial preference. In June an artful motion by P. Miles, the Conservative M.P. for Bristol and a leading West Indian spokesman, decreasing the duty but enlarging the margin of colonial preference, brought together both sets of critics and was carried against the government by twenty votes. Peel had already been aware of the danger of an alliance between the opposition and a section of his own supporters. Taught by his factory bill experience he summoned a party meeting gathering on the day before Miles's motion but said grimly afterwards that it was 'the most unsatisfactory meeting he had ever known'. The split in the party was therefore not unexpected; but its extent was shattering. When the cabinet discussed the situation next day Peel was in a mood of profound pessimism. He said he could see no way they could extricate themselves from their predicament and seemed fatalistically inclined towards resignation.

Though Stanley and Graham seemed to agree with him, the rest of the cabinet were against any desperate course taken in the heat of the moment, on an issue which would not be understood in the country. In the next few days, though still feeling hard, Peel became slightly less intransigent. Nevertheless he told the cabinet he could neither accept Miles's motion nor fall back on a tame continuation of the old duties; and both he and Stanley talked of the inability of discredited ministers to serve their country. Despite Graham's gloomy observation that the mass of the party was not only unruly but positively hostile, there was considerable evidence that most of their supporters were anxious to avoid the resignation of a Conservative administration, even if they were not willing to rescind their vote. In fact a meeting of some two hundred Conservative M.P.s under the chairmanship of Sir John Yarde Buller passed (with five or six dissentients, including Disraeli) a warm motion of confidence in the government.

In the end a motion was concocted, restoring the preferential margin of 10s while leaving those who had supported Miles's motion technically free to vote for the new resolution. The ground for manoeuvre had been minimal; and the device was paper-thin. Not surprisingly the opposition took the view that what the House was being asked to do was to rescind its previous vote; and not only the opposition. Disraeli made a clever, mocking speech, which attracted considerable applause, attacking the prime minister for 'menacing his friends, and cringing to his opponents'. But the atmosphere, bad enough, had been made worse by Peel who showed undisguised resentment at the means whereby Miles had carried his motion. He talked of a combination between the opposition and some of the government's usual supporters; said that acquiescence would only encourage similar combinations in future; and concluded grimly that the government would continue to do what they thought right, even if they did not get the support they deserved. His manner was sharp and offensive, and he spoke as if he was completely detached from the men on the benches behind him. Gladstone at his side felt at the close that he had been listening to the government's death warrant. Peel himself thought that it was the end; perhaps it was this conviction that made his speech so hard and unforgiving. In a brief note to the queen, scribbled after he had sat down, he warned her that the House was likely to reject his motion by a considerable majority and this second rejection would probably bring about the fall of the ministry.

If anyone saved the day, it was Stanley who made a soothing appeal to the government's old supporters for fair and generous treatment. When the division was taken it showed a majority for the motion by 255 votes to 233. What those figures could not reveal, however, were the feelings of those who made that majority possible. Talking afterwards with various Conservative M.P.s, Gladstone was convinced that a deep wound had been inflicted on the party's morale. 'A great man', he recorded sorrowfully, 'had committed a great error.' Peel himself, once his victory had been won, realised how far he had put himself in the wrong. A few days later he took the opportunity to acknowledge the 'generous support' his party followers had frequently given him and to disclaim any such 'arrogant a sentiment' as that the party should always vote for every detail of every measure introduced by the government. What could not be patched up so easily was the shattered confidence on both sides. That there had been much misunderstanding was clear enough. To Peel the revised tariff was a cardinal aspect of the government's long-term economic policy; its defeat a wanton dereliction of duty on the part of his followers. To the rank and file of the party the sugar duties seemed a minor issue and the rumours of resignation that had swept over London a matter for surprise. Lord Sandon, who wrote to Peel remonstrating against resignation, argued that defeat on Miles's motion was only a matter of detail which did not affect the government's general stability. His attitude was simple, probably not unrepresentative, and certainly revealing. Plainly the party did not realise how seriously the cabinet would view the matter; nor did the cabinet, or some of them, realise how unimportant the matter seemed to the party.

Beneath the misunderstanding, however, was a larger issue. Party leaders when ministers of the crown claimed the right to propose measures they thought in the national interest even if they conflicted with the views of their followers. Individual M.P.s tended to interpret party allegiance as only committing them to support on matters of general principle. As Sandon wrote in his letter of 15 June, 'you cannot expect . . . the whole of your supporters should sacrifice everything to this general but honest allegiance'. In the new party machines built up so rapidly after the Reform Act this looseness provided perhaps a necessary margin of tolerance. A more rigid party structure would probably have snapped under the strain. But for a masterful prime minister and a government working under pressure in an antiquated parliamentary framework, the weakness of the system was hard to bear.

Declarations of general confidence, [Peel replied laconically to Sandon], will not, I fear, compensate for that loss of authority and efficiency which is sustained by a Government not enabled to carry into effect the practical measures of legislation which it feels it to be its duty to submit to Parliament.

A great deal in those circumstances depended on management; and in June 1844 neither the prime minister nor his recalcitrant followers were in a very manageable mood. It seemed to Gladstone that Peel and those of his colleagues who shared his attitude were influenced not only by the principles at stake but by their weariness with the un-ending drudgery of office and a resentful feeling that the party only exerted itself to criticise its leaders. There was a similar disillusionment in the party among those, protectionist by interest or conviction, who saw the government following a general policy of free trade, who heard Peel and Gladstone talk the language of radical economists, and who hungered in vain for some words of sympathy from their leader for the threatened cause of agriculture. Opinion on the propriety or justi-fication of Peel's action might differ. What was undeniable was that he handled the whole episode as badly as any in his long parliamentary career. Though the strained feelings died down in time, the relationship between Peel and his party could never be the same again.

II

In the field of Irish affairs 1844 brought equally mixed results for the government though on balance the credits outweighed the debits. O'Connell's conviction in the spring had been quashed on appeal to the Lords in September. Eliot's county franchise bill ran into ob-struction and was finally abandoned. On the other hand the Charitable Trusts bill, designed to encourage the private endowment of Catholic clergy, passed with only minor opposition. The success of the measure depended on the cooperation of the Roman hierarchy in Ireland and a strong counter-campaign to prevent this was waged by O'Connell and Bishop MacHale. By November, however, three Irish Catholic bishops headed by their primate had agreed to serve and the battle of the Board was won. There had also been a change for the better in the Irish executive. In the summer de Grey had been replaced by the more liberal Lord Heytesbury, a career diplomat with an admirably cool, objective mind. It was fortunate for the government that it was he and not de Grey who had to handle the delicate negotiations with the Irish bishops in the months following his arrival.

During the late autumn Graham and the new Lord-Lieutenant worked out the details of the various Irish educational schemes, and in November the cabinet began its discussions of the proposed measures. It was agreed with little dissent to set up provincial colleges at such places as Cork and Belfast and group them into a new university with powers to grant degrees in arts and law. The assumption was that the

Belfast college would be primarily for Presbyterians and the others for Catholics. The cabinet then gingerly turned to the question of Maynooth. Here too there was general acceptance that something must be done. The only discordant note was struck by Gladstone who made it clear that he could not support the scheme as a member of the government though he added somewhat mystifyingly that he would not necessarily oppose it as a private member. Even now Peel tried to avoid an open breach; and at the final cabinet in December he recommended that Graham should leave the details of the Maynooth bill until the new colleges were disposed of. On that temporising note the round of autumn cabinets came to an end.

From Hawarden in January 1845 Gladstone wrote a long and involved letter to the prime minister. 'I really have great difficulty sometimes in exactly comprehending what Gladstone means,' Peel commented dryly to Graham, '. . . I take it for granted, however, that the letter means to announce his continued intention to retire, and I deeply regret it.' Meeting Gladstone in town a week later he treated him with his usual kindness, asked him to stay in office until the last possible moment, and talked of the real danger that the government might be shipwrecked on the issue. During December and January in fact it had become increasingly clear that the Maynooth proposals, combining as they did the obnoxious principles of state support and encouragement to Romanism, would encounter a storm of disapproval among moderate Anglicans, Scottish Presbyterians and English Dissenters. Goulburn, who had been hearing opinion in Cambridge on the subject, wrote a long letter to Peel which concluded pessimistically that 'I should not be surprised if the flame of real religious apprehension of the consequences of the measure was to burn as fiercely as ever'.

Gladstone's resignation made little impact when parliament reassembled in February. The attention of the House was concentrated not on Maynooth but on the financial and commercial matters which occupied the first eight weeks of the session. In bringing forward the budget only ten days after they had assembled Peel justified the early date by the approaching expiry of the income tax. But it is not improbable that he wished to launch a budget which proposed not only a continuation of the income tax but a final settlement of the sugar question, before the House got entangled in the acrimonies of Irish legislation. What he had to offer however was a series of exceptionally well-matured measures which had been engaging the attention of himself and the Chancellor of the Exchequer for the previous twelve months.

In a long-range forecast in the spring of 1844 Goulburn had been in the happy position of being able to assume a substantial surplus for 1845. After that everything depended on the renewal of the income tax; or rather, since he took renewal for granted, on the period for which it would be renewed. With typical caution he advised renewal for three years from 1845 to carry it safely past the hazards of the general election due in 1847; and as an additional precaution, a limitation of further tariff reductions to a figure below £210,000 in order to avoid undue reliance on the income tax revenue. Peel's reaction to this sketch of future financial policy was illuminating. Writing from Drayton at Easter he laid down as an axiom that there would be great difficulty in renewing the income tax unless they proposed reductions in taxation which clearly benefited the mass of the population. Sugar, for example, on which Goulburn confessed himself at a loss to know how to proceed, would have to be included in any tariff revision, despite the political difficulties. On the period of renewal he argued strongly for two years instead of three; partly because they had never concealed their view that a total of five years was desirable to secure the full advantage of tariff reductions; partly because a second period of three years would look remarkably like a permanent arrangement. The difference of approach was characteristic. Goulburn, looking at the problem from an orthodox Treasury point of view, was concerned to keep the national balance-sheet straight, to retain as large a surplus as possible, and not to rely too heavily on the politically vulnerable income tax. Peel, on the other hand, was more fluid in his thinking, more drawn towards the possibility of another large tariff experiment, but more alive to the political factors involved in their budgetary decisions.

During the remainder of the year the accumulating evidence of a handsome surplus for 1844 strengthened the case for a massive tariff reform in 1845; but since this would entail a large and immediate loss of revenue, it also strengthened the case for another long-term renewal of the income tax. The problem for the ministers was that there would be an excess of revenue in 1845 and, without the income tax, a deficit in the two following years. Peel accepted Goulburn's calculations but within this financial framework he was prepared to discard Goulburn's cautious reservations about the amount of tariff reform they could undertake and the size of the surplus revenue they should hold in reserve. To Goulburn's solidity in finance Peel added ruthlessness and imagination. In its perfected form the budget of 1845 was a phenomenon more often seen in war than in finance, a bold stroke of policy secured by thorough organisation of resources. As a piece of administrative planning it was one of Peel's masterpieces. In the end the government found themselves with a working surplus of £3½ million. Peel proposed to return almost all this to the public in the form of a remission of those taxes which, he told the Commons, 'press more onerously on the community than the income tax'. His plan included another drastic reduction in sugar duties, the abolition of all export duties on British goods, and the abolition of import duties on more than half of the remaining items in the book of tariffs, including cotton and other raw materials of industry. The total loss to the revenue he estimated at £3.3 million, a third of which was on sugar. In return he asked for a renewal of the income tax for three years.

In 1842 Peel had asked for the income tax as a desperate expedient to meet a crisis. His budget then had been a courageous but limited experiment. In 1845 it was a grander but infinitely safer operation. What was new was the assurance born of experience. No decrease in the yield from other sources of revenue had been detectable as a result of imposing the income tax; and everything seemed to indicate that the free trade theory of lower tariffs yielding higher revenue was in the long run, though only in the long run, correct. What Peel invited the Commons to do was accept a further period of income tax to make possible a further and even more comprehensive demonstration of that theory. With the Whigs denouncing the tax but signifying their intention to vote for it, Peel had no fear of the outcome. His confidence was more than justified. By Easter income tax, sugar duties and tariff were all safely through the Commons. The success strengthened his assurance and confirmed his tactics.

> I would not admit any alteration [he wrote somewhat jauntily to Hardinge during the recess]. This was thought very obstinate and very presumptuous; but the fact is, people like a certain degree of obstinacy and presumption in a minister. They abuse him for dictation and arrogance, but they like being governed.

The only sour note came from the agriculturalists. Nothing had been done for them; agriculture had not even been mentioned in Peel's budget speech. All that the silent country squires had heard was one more panegyric on free trade. All that they were invited to undertake was one more long stride towards economic liberalism. The omission did not go unquestioned. Bankes, Miles, Palmer and Tyrell all voiced their resentment that agriculture, alone among the great national interests, was to receive no compensation for the continued burden of the income tax.

Throughout the early part of the session questions of free trade and protection continued to rasp at the nerves of the country party. In a debate on agricultural distress in March Cobden in a skilful and temperate speech asked for proof that protection had done anything to satisfy the farmers' grievances. The story has often been told how Peel, after making a few notes, crumpled his paper and whispered to Sidney Herbert sitting next to him, 'You must answer this, for I cannot'. It is not impossible that something like this actually happened. Herbert did reply and in an unhappy phrase said it was distasteful to him, as an agricultural representative, to be always coming to parliament, whining for protection. A few nights later, in a planned attack on the government's free trade policy headed in the Commons by W. Miles and supported outside by the Central Agricultural Protection Society, Disraeli made an ironic speech on the prime minister's altered behaviour since coming to office. Once he had been the fond wooer of the agriculturalists. Now he 'sends down his valet who says in the genteelest manner, "We can have no whining here" '. If free trade was to come, he said acidly, he would rather have it from Cobden than from a leader who had betrayed the confidence of his party; and he ended with his memorable line about a Conservative government being an organised hypocrisy. It was a brilliant speech which evoked applause and laughter from the House. They did not like or trust Disraeli. But they enjoyed listening to him and what he said was balm to many of the inarticulate men around him.

As Peel realised, Disraeli in himself constituted no great threat; the danger was in the situation he was trying to exploit. Miles's motion attracted only eighty votes and probably a number of motives prompted them: genuine protectionism in some, a desire to placate constituents in others. Nevertheless it was an uncomfortable overture to the great parliamentary debate on Maynooth.

By March the bill was in its final shape and John Young, chief whip in succession to Fremantle, reported that there was no danger of defeat in the Commons where Liberal and Irish votes would more than make up for Conservative defections. The real opposition was outside the House. Already hostile petitions were pouring in; public protest meetings were being held up and down the country; even by-elections were beginning to be affected. On 3 April the prime minister expounded the details of the long-awaited measure to the House of Commons: an annual subvention of £26,000, a special grant of £30,000 for new buildings, and a system of annual visitations. Tactically the main danger was that ultra-protestants moved by anti-Catholic feeling and Radicals opposed in principle to any state endowment would combine to defeat the bill on some technical point. There was a general feeling that the government might in such circumstances resign, and Peel did nothing to discourage that salutary feeling. Nevertheless the long debate on the second reading uncovered all the cross-currents in the House, Whigs and Irish joining liberal Conservatives to make common cause against Tory Anglicans and doctrinaire Radicals. Peel showed himself unusually gentle and considerate; it was as if he was concentrating all his energies on the one purpose of piloting the measure through.

Yet the longer the controversy dragged on, the deeper became the issues thrown up by it. Already much of the argument had turned not so much on the merits of the bill as on the record of the man who brought it forward. As the inquest continued, the more sharply Peel began to define his position in the storm of criticism which swept round him. On the third reading he was driven, not for the first time, to expound his basic view of the duty of ministers as against the claims of party interest and personal consistency. Any government, he said, must have the right, without too much regard for past actions or party considerations, to do what it thought best in the existing circumstances. Proud as he was of the confidence placed in him by a great party, he still could not admit that a minister of the Crown 'owes any personal obligation to those members who have placed him in a certain position'. He would rather retire to the obscurity of a private member than hold office

> by the servile tenure of the advice I gave to my sovereign upon every subject, being exactly in conformity with every opinion which every member of that party might hold. . . . I claim for myself the right to give my sovereign, at any time, that advice which I believe the interests of the country require.

Maynooth went through, with larger majorities and less technical damage to the government than might have been expected. But the damage to the party had been immense. Of all Peel's measures it came closest to a repudiation of the constitutional doctrines of Church and State on which the Conservative party had been built up in the 1830s; and it had been carried only with the aid of the opposition. On the second reading of the bill the Conservatives divided 159 to 147 in favour of the bill; on the third reading 148 to 149 against. Following the session of 1844 in which Peel had strained party discipline to the limit, this fresh division was shattering. He had won his bill, but in the process had finally destroyed the morale of the Conservative Party.

Thomas Raikes, the West End clubman and political gossip, believed that the real reason for the revolt of the Tories was their grievance about protection and free trade and their feeling that sooner or later Peel would repeal the Corn Laws themselves. This was probably at least a half-truth. The Maynooth contest had been over something bigger than Maynooth. The split in the party was a symptom as well as an effect. Peel was not unaware of the diversity of motives among his rebellious followers. 'Tariffs, drought, 46s a quarter for wheat, quicken the religious apprehensions of some,' he wrote scornfully to Croker, 'disappointed ambition, and the rejection of applications for office of others.' What angered him was that his four years' achievement apparently counted for nothing as far as his own party was concerned. Trade and industry were flourishing, the working classes better off, Chartism extinguished, the Church stronger than ever, demands for radical reform no longer heard, the financial system on a sound footing, the revenue buoyant. 'But', he wrote ironically to Hardinge at the end of the Maynooth struggle, 'we have reduced protection to agriculture, and tried to lay the foundation of peace in Ireland; and these are offences for which nothing can atone.'

Nevertheless, though Maynooth had scraped bare the relationship between Peel and his party, the end of the session came with the administration looking as immovable as ever. To both Aberdeen and Graham there had been an ominous parallel between Maynooth in 1845 and Catholic emancipation in 1829, with the ultimate consequences likely to be the same. If so, it would need another crisis to demonstrate that Peel had lost his hold on the party. Until then it was doubtful whether the bulk of the Conservatives would be ready to overthrow a minister for whom they had no substitute and whose standing in parliament, in the country, and with the Crown was never higher. For all his unpopularity with his followers the prime minister like an inscrutable colossus still bestrode the political world. 'Everybody expects that he means to go on, and in the end to knock the Corn Laws on the head, and endow the Roman Catholic Church,' ruminated Greville in August, 'but nobody knows how or when he will do these things.'

Chapter 19

The responsibilities of empire

'It is very curious', wrote Wellington in 1841, 'that Sir Robert Peel should have the reputation of being entirely ignorant on foreign Affairs.' It was curious but not surprising. Most people either did not know or had forgotten his support for Canning's policy in the 1820s. His utterances on foreign affairs as leader of the House of Commons under Wellington or as head of the opposition had never been taken as indicating any particular interest. Nevertheless as prime minister he was ultimately responsible for the foreign policy of a state which possessed the prestige of victor in the Napoleonic Wars, wielded the greatest sea power in the world, and had commitments in every quarter of the globe. His detailed supervision of all the departments of his administration ensured that the affairs of four continents came to his desk; and in India, America and Europe issues arose between 1841 and 1846 which needed more than purely departmental attention.

One immediate problem was India, where the Afghan crisis was an inescapable legacy from the previous government. The administration of Indian affairs was unusually complicated; partly because of the division of responsibility between the government and the East India Company; partly because the slowness of communications meant that the government only learned of decisions long after they had been taken by the men on the spot and knew that any instructions they might send out would usually be overtaken by events long before they arrived. To a large extent, therefore, the ministers were confined to the role of spectators, though Peel from his wider experience was more conscious than Fitzgerald, the president of the Board of Control, of the need to be chary of criticism which would arrive too late to affect action, to state the government's view in only general terms, and to avoid instant approval for policies which the next Indian mail might announce had already been abandoned. Nevertheless, six months' experience of Ellenborough's rule in India filled Peel with concern. He thought the new Governor-General had misjudged the position in Afghanistan and by the inconsistency of his orders had created a dangerous situation from which he had only been rescued by the initiative and pluck of his soldiers. Simultaneously, however, Ellenborough was making life difficult for Fitzgerald, his nominal superior. Much of the prime minister's early involvement in Indian affairs arose from Fitzgerald's need for support and advice in the difficult task of controlling his flamboyant, tactless and erratic Governor-General.

The ultimate success of British arms in Afghanistan made it

easy to blunt the attack launched on Ellenborough by the Whigs in the spring of 1843; but hard on the termination of the Afghan crisis came the annexation of Scinde. In a despatch of the previous November Ellenborough had given notice of what he was about and hinted at resignation if not adequately supported from home. This was little more than political blackmail. Relations between the Governor-General and the Court of Directors of the East India Company were already strained, and the receipt of this last message made the unhappy Fitzgerald, standing uncomfortably between the Company and its autocratic servant in India, half inclined to resign himself. Peel emphatically rejected such a counsel of despair. 'Instead of thinking of retiring, maintain your own ground,' he told him in January.

Fitzgerald was not the only sufferer. Peel himself had to undergo trials of patience. When Ellenborough left for India in 1841 he had obtained the queen's incautious leave to write to her directly. Though the ministers gradually became aware of this palace correspondence, they made no remonstrance until April 1843, when Victoria showed Peel a letter she had received from Ellenborough suggesting that many political difficulties might be removed if the queen became Empress of India. In the face of this imaginative but improper suggestion Peel sent to the Governor-General a measured rebuke. 'Direct communications between the Governor-General of India and the Sovereign . . .' he observed, 'are open to considerable objection in point of constitutional principle.' The objection was even weightier if 'they tender opinions or advice to the Sovereign on political questions'. Though he clearly disapproved of the actual proposal, his main purpose was to instil into his distant subordinate the rudiments of constitutional propriety. Ellenborough dutifully accepted the rebuke and promised in future to send all communications for the queen through the prime minister. He was always more ready to accept plain speaking from Peel than from his departmental chief; and when Fitzgerald removed himself from further Indian complications by dying in May 1843, his replacement by the easy-going Ripon meant that the prime minister became even more involved in the continuous narrative of strained relations between the Governor-General and the authorities at home.

By August 1843 Ellenborough's actions in Scinde brought the patience of the Court of Directors to breaking-point. What they wanted was for the government itself to recall Ellenborough. This the prime minister refused to do until the cabinet was in a position to make a considered judgement on the Scinde affair. At the end of October fuller information arrived from India, including an able vindication by the Governor-General of his general policy, obviously designed for publication. With some reluctance but bowing to the compulsion of logistics—'time, distance, the course of events' as Peel expressed it—the cabinet finally decided to accept the annexation of Scinde. Peel's doubts had not entirely been removed, however, and he took care to convey his concern to Ellenborough and at the same time reject his complaints of lack of support from the cabinet. The end came in April 1844 when the news of the incorporation of Gwalior showed that there was no predictable end to Ellenborough's expansionist policy. When the court finally decided to dismiss Ellenborough, Peel instructed Ripon to make no admission which would justify their criticisms and to disassociate the government from their action. Over the appointment of a new Governor-General he told the Directors that he would only intervene if they promised in advance to give their full confidence to his nominee. He handled them peremptorily but what was uppermost in his mind was the need to restore to the office of Governor-General the status without which no public man worth his salt would ever accept it. The guarantee given, he then nominated Hardinge. For Peel it was both an official and a personal loss. Between the prime minister and Hardinge, the cool professional soldier who had been with Moore at Corunna, with Wellington at Vittoria, and with Blücher at Ligny, a warm and affectionate friendship had grown up in the years that had passed since they were colleagues in Wellington's administration. To fill the vacancy left by his departure Granville Somerset was at last promoted to the cabinet though he declined the vacant Secretaryship at War. That office was taken by Fremantle. It meant the loss of an efficient and popular Chief Whip, but six years in that demanding role had clearly earned him further promotion.

There remained the problem of maintaining good relations with the Company and avoiding public controversy. A parliamentary inquest was refused and when Ellenborough, sunburnt and angry, arrived home in the autumn, meditating vengeance on Ripon and the Board of Directors, he was firmly kept in check. The whole affair had demonstrated the weakness of what a year earlier Peel had called 'the anomalous and absurd principle on which the government of India is conducted'. But as long as ministers had to work with the East India Company within the antiquated system of dual control, it was essential that internal friction should not be allowed to degenerate into public controversy. The episode was also an illustration of Peel's management of men and affairs. The defence, against criticisms he often felt to be justified, of a wayward subordinate too far away to be controlled but for whom the government had to take constitutional responsibility, was an exercise in balanced judgement which made it an illuminating passage in Peel's record as prime minister.

It was the more noteworthy since Peel was in fundamental disagreement with Ellenborough's ideas. The prime minister was opposed to unnecessary expansion of British rule in India and disbelieved that there was any danger there from Russian aggression. When the Tsar Nicholas came over in 1844 Peel had a long conversation which convinced him that the rumours of Russian intrigues on the Indian frontier were largely an invention of the French press. Nicholas, who had his own public to consider, was equally sensitive about the British advance in the Punjab. While there was Russophobia in England, there was also Anglophobia in Russia. In a frank talk with Nesselrode, the Russian minister, in October, Peel tried to convince him that, as he reported to Hardinge, 'the consolidation and improvement of the vast domains we possess in India were objects much nearer your heart than the extension of our empire, or the gratification of the cravings of our army for more conquests and more glory'. He attributed the sentiments to Hardinge; they were also his own. The road of imperial expansion had few attractions for Peel.

II

Peel's handling of Aberdeen was an instructive contrast to that of Ellenborough. While in his correspondence with the Governor-General he seemed invariably liberal and pacific, with his Foreign Secretary he often appeared hard and sometimes aggressive. Partly this was due to the difference of character between the dashing, opinionated Governor-General and the gentle, tolerant Foreign Secretary. To be an Ellenborough to Aberdeen, an Aberdeen to Ellenborough, was part of his prime minister's function. Even so, it is clear that there were marked differences also between Peel and his Foreign Secretary. They were differences of temperament rather than policy. Peel was less trusting, less optimistic, more inclined to deploy all the resources open to him to arrive at a given end. Aberdeen was more sanguine, more conciliatory, more ready to announce openly his intentions and rely on the goodwill of others. When Peel once observed rather tartly that one needed 'that charity which believeth all things' to trust the French government, the Foreign Secretary retorted that 'charity should not only *believe all things* but should *never fail*'. This to Peel was merely unrealistic.

Both men were agreed that the maxim for British foreign relations must be to walk softly, but Peel was considerably more inclined to carry a big stick. Since he exercised as close a supervision over the Foreign Office as over any other department of state, Aberdeen had to argue his case more often than he would have preferred. Peel on the other hand had to impart some of his own energy to the curiously devitalised figure of the Foreign Secretary. A reluctant candidate in 1841 Aberdeen continued in office with an absence of zeal or ambition which in a less conscientious man might have had more serious consequences. As it was, any passing physical depression was enough to turn his thoughts to resignation. There was certainly no question of allowing the Foreign Secretary the same independent and almost private conduct of foreign affairs as Palmerston had enjoyed under Melbourne. The prime minister not only discussed general policy but scrutinised all levels of diplomatic activity. He amended draft despatches and instructions, suggested new points for consideration, and proffered his own views on diplomatic appointments. He even showed

a Palmerstonian tendency to criticise style. 'I wish', he wrote to
Aberdeen in November 1842, 'you would require your foreign ministers
and Ambassadors to write *English*. I read some despatches yesterday
from Lord Stuart and I think Mr Mandeville or Mr Hamilton or I
believe both, which are too slovenly for endurance.' Or again, 'surely
it would be better to pay Mr Goldsmith his accustomed salary and
tell him to do nothing—at any rate, not to write such abominable
stuff as the enclosed.' If he rarely tried to overrule the Foreign Secretary
he frequently sought to influence him; and he was capable of taking a
firm line when the occasion seemed to justify it. Yet with all their
contrast of style and temperament, and occasional disagreement over
policy, nothing ever shook the personal confidence between them.

When the ministry took office one of the most pressing and
dangerous foreign problems was the strained relationship with the
United States over boundary disputes and the claim to right of search
at sea by British anti-slavery patrols. The situation seemed serious
enough for Peel, among all his other preoccupations in October 1841,
to circulate a cabinet memorandum stressing the need for precautions
in case war was suddenly forced on them. In an early effort to ease the
tension Lord Ashburton was sent to Washington as special envoy to
solve all outstanding disputes. Throughout the negotiations Peel
showed himself eager to reach a settlement. Agreement on the maritime
question was not enough. 'I think we *must* come to an agreement on the
boundary,' he wrote to Aberdeen in May 1842. The new north-east
frontier fixed by Ashburton and Webster, the American Secretary of
State, while embodying substantial concessions to the U.S.A., satisfied
both the Foreign Secretary and the prime minister; and though
savagely attacked by Palmerston, the treaty was approved by the
orthodox Whigs and their Radical allies. The country as a whole, more
interested in good commercial relations with its best customer, shared
Peel's view that barren lands in the North American continent were
unimportant compared with the risk of war with the United States.

The one outstanding issue left untouched by the 1842 treaty was
the Oregon question. Though an Anglo-American agreement in 1818
had fixed the 49th parallel as the frontier as far as the Rockies, the
future of the Oregon territory on the Pacific coast beyond was still
undetermined. As a temporary measure both powers had assumed
common ownership of that undefined and largely uncolonised area.
Peel and Aberdeen were anxious to come to a permanent agreement,
but the hostility of the American public and President Tyler's difficulties with Congress prevented any progress. Time was on the
American side since once the tide of emigration to the Pacific coast
began to flow, the American settlers were likely to outnumber the
British. The original American claim was for all the territory up to the
parallel 54°40′ and at the best reckoning would hardly be reduced to
less than a continuation of the 49th parallel. This would exclude from
British control the entrance to Puget Sound and Vancouver harbour,

which was the most valuable part of the territory. Aberdeen's proposal was to negotiate for an extension of the 49th parallel frontier to the mainland coast only, leaving Vancouver Island in British hands and the entrance to the Columbia River free to both countries. Peel endorsed this policy in language considerably stronger than Aberdeen was in the habit of using. He suggested that they should get the views of the British settlers in Oregon and resort to arbitration rather than accept any settlement that fell short of Aberdeen's proposal. 'I should not be afraid of a good deal of preliminary bluster on the part of the Americans,' he wrote. 'The best answer would be direct the *Collingwood* to make a friendly visit when she has leisure, to the mouth of the Columbia.'

President Polk's inaugural address in March 1845, asserting a 'clear and unquestionable' claim to Oregon, came close to Peel's definition of bluster and aroused some comment in parliament. Peel took the opportunity to declare that the British claim was no less clear. He hoped the issue would be settled amicably, but if their rights were infringed, they were 'resolved and prepared to maintain them'. This was something more than counterbluster. In February he had questioned Aberdeen's assumption that the balance of power on the banks of the Columbia was, or would remain, in Britain's favour, and suggested that a frigate with marines and artillery should be sent under sealed orders to the mouth of the river. The refusal of the British government to concede anything on the vital issue of the Puget Sound and Peel's strong words in the Commons inevitably produced an angry reaction in America. Nevertheless once matters were brought to a head, it was clear that Congress had no desire for a rupture with Britain at a time when they were moving towards war with Mexico. Outside the matter at issue, Peel for his part took care to do nothing that might ruffle American susceptibilities. At the end of 1845 there was every prospect that the new year would see a final solution to the Oregon question. A conciliatory passage was inserted in the queen's speech and by the early summer of 1846 it was clear that Peel's firm tactics had succeeded.

III

India and Canada were problems of the imperial frontier. Foreign policy proper, to Peel's ministry as to most nineteenth-century British governments, was basically European policy; and there the dominant consideration was the relationship with France. It was a relationship shaped by past conflicts, present distrusts, and future fears. Apart from Russia, France was the only military state capable of upsetting the balance of power on the continent. Alone in Europe she offered a challenge to British sea power. Alone among the great powers she appeared a revolutionary and unstable society. The Orléans monarchy of Louis Philippe, only ten years old and itself the product of a revolution, showed all the insecurity and restlessness of an upstart power. On the surface, with the replacement of Palmerston by Aberdeen and of Thiers by the pacific Soult-Guizot ministry, the years 1840-41 seemed to herald a new era in Anglo-French relations after the strain of the Syrian crisis. Peel impressed the public on both sides of the Channel by the soothing words he uttered about France in August 1842 when replying to Palmerston's attack on the government's foreign policy. Underneath, however, the prime minister represented a tougher strand of continuity in foreign policy than was realised at the time.

Even before he took office he had expressed the discouraging view that Guizot's policy of armed peace was more dangerous than the crackbrained projects of Thiers and he was made profoundly suspicious by French activity in Spain. The tortuous and sordid history of the Spanish marriages which dragged on throughout his ministry provided ample justification for British distrust of French aims and methods. In 1840, in the course of the endemic Spanish civil conflicts of the period, Christina the queen-mother had been forced to leave the country. She took up residence at Paris and Espartero became regent on behalf of the young queen Isabella. Though she was only twelve, her marriage soon developed into an international issue and remained so for the next six years. The restoration of French influence became a primary aim of Guizot and Louis Philippe; and though their official attitude was that Isabella should marry one of the Spanish or Neapolitan Bourbons, there was a lively suspicion that they were assisting Christina and the anti-Espartero faction in return for a promise of marriage between Isabella and one of Louis Philippe's sons.

Peel placed no trust in Guizot's assurances of disinterested neutrality and in November 1841 he suggested to Aberdeen the advisability of a formal communication to the Spanish government supporting their right to be sole arbiter of the marriage of Isabella and assuring them that Britain would not be party to any agreement to settle the matter over the heads of the Spanish people. When, however, in June 1843 a military *coup d'etat* forced the regent into exile, Aberdeen began to waver. What he feared was that the victorious party in Spain would marry Isabella to a French prince in return for a French alliance. To circumvent this he proposed a joint intervention by France and Britain to restore peace in Spain. This also implied an abandonment of the British principle that Spain alone should decide on the royal marriage. To that extent it was a significant concession to French diplomacy and both Guizot and Louis Philippe hastened to welcome the overture.

The visit of Victoria and Albert to the Château d'Eu near Le Tréport in September 1843 allowed the French king and his foreign minister to cement the new diplomatic alliance by showering Aberdeen with protestations of the unselfish nature of their intentions. Reacting

ir Robert Peel, aetat. 56. From the painting by F. X. Winterhalter.

Sir Robert Peel. From H.B's political sketches No.831 (April 1845).

rather differently Peel regarded the meeting as an opportunity to deliver a warning to the French government.

> I hope you will let Louis Philippe understand [he wrote to Aberdeen on the eve of his departure] that we cannot conceive it possible—which of course means that we shrewdly suspect—that he may contemplate, by various cunning devices, under the pretence of friendly concert with us, rendering the marriage of the Queen of Spain with the duc d'Aumale inevitable.

The king disclaimed any wish for an alliance of one of his sons with the Spanish royal house and Aberdeen for his part consented to recommend to the Spanish government the choice of a Bourbon descendant of Philip V. On this happy note of agreement the *Entente Cordiale* was announced to the world. The phrase, coined by Aberdeen, was taken up with alacrity by Louis Philippe and Guizot, and was constantly used by them to advertise the allegedly close relationship between the two western powers. Peel was less convinced than Aberdeen that there was much reality behind the phrase, but he was sufficiently politic to insert in the queen's speech at the start of the 1844 session a reference to the 'good understanding happily established' with the French government.

The year 1844 demonstrated how fragile in fact the *Entente* was and how deep-rooted were Peel's suspicions. In July the news reached London of the arrest and deportation of a former Methodist missionary and British consul called Pritchard following a somewhat fortuitous French naval occupation and subsequent annexation of Tahiti. Roused by the simultaneous news of a French expedition to Morocco and the bombardment of Tangiers, bellicose national feeling ran high on both sides of the Channel. Questioned in the House Peel made it clear that the action against Pritchard had been taken without the authority of the French government but added forcefully that, presuming the reports were true, 'I do not hesitate to say that a gross outrage accompanied with gross indignity has been committed'. Despite warnings from Jarnac, the French *chargé d'affaires*, of the strong feeling in Britain, Guizot was disposed to temporise. Peel, however, was not prepared to wait on the convenience of the French government. The Tahiti and Moroccan events together had undoubtedly incensed him. He thought they demonstrated at best Guizot's loss of control over French policy and at worst complete lack of good faith. Following a cabinet meeting on 13 August Aberdeen warned Jarnac that unless satisfaction was soon offered, he would have to send a formal request for redress. To drive home the seriousness of the situation he read out a confidential letter from Peel in which the prime minister pinned the blame for everything on Guizot.

> If he chooses to send out expeditions to occupy every place where

they can find the pretence for occupation and if the commanders of those expeditions occupy other places not contemplated by their Government, and if M. Guizot has not the power or courage to disavow them, *he* is responsible for whatever may occur in consequence of such proceedings.

The original annexation of Algiers, he continued sharply, had been a violation of French engagements towards Europe. It now seemed likely that Tunis and Morocco would share the same fate. 'I do not', he finished crushingly, 'attach the slightest weight to the disclaimers of M. Guizot and the King.' At half a dozen ports along the Channel naval preparations were going forward, and the only conclusion could be that France was preparing for a war against Britain.

A different sort of importance would have to be attached to this letter had it not been written expressly for Aberdeen to read to Jarnac. Nevertheless the Pritchard case was only the latest of a long series of unsatisfactory episodes in the history of Anglo-French relations since 1841. In itself, as Peel admitted privately to Hardinge, it was a trumpery cause of quarrel. But he had to take into consideration the feelings of the British public. It had become a point both of national honour and of political necessity to extract an immediate promise of reparation from the French government; and if it needed strong language to shake Guizot from his passivity, he was ready to supply it. Aberdeen's advice was to recognise Guizot's domestic difficulties, avoid a public confrontation, and accept in due course any suitable compensation the French might offer. There was no rational ground, he argued, for a quarrel. French naval preparations had been going on for some time, and though no trust could be placed in French assurances, rearmament by Britain would only make war more probable.

His arguments elicited little sympathy. If Guizot could not control French policy, the prime minister replied, he should not be surprised if Britain looked to its own security rather than to 'the delicacies and difficulties of his position as minister'. The Pritchard case was of minor importance compared with the accumulated proofs of hostile naval preparations by France. The real question was whether they could place any confidence in French assurances. If they could not,

> I do most earnestly advise that we should without delay consider the state of our naval preparation as compared with that of France. Matters are in that state that the interval of twenty-four hours— some act of violence for which the French ministry is not strong enough to make reparation or disavowal—may not only dissipate the shadow of the *Entente Cordiale* but change our relations from Peace to War. Let us be prepared for War. Some may think the preparations for it will diminish the chance of peace. . . . My belief is, from all I have seen of the French people and their Government, that they are much more likely to presume upon our weakness than to take offence at our strength.

The Tahiti affair was little more than a nine-days wonder, though while it lasted there was an undoubted war scare on both sides of the Channel. Early in September, when parliament was prorogued, the speech from the throne announced a satisfactory end to the dispute and the return visit of Louis Philippe to England in October symbolised the resumption of the sorely tried *Entente*.

Nevertheless all the old fears and distrusts had been revived and there was always new material on which they could feed. The Spanish marriages still dominated the dynastic thoughts of Louis Philippe and the return of Christina to Spain in the spring of 1844 enabled the Neapolitan Bourbon Count Trapani to be put forward as their joint candidate for the hand of Queen Isabella. Before the end of the year there were well-founded reports that the French government was pressing for a marriage between Isabella's younger sister and one of the king's sons. This 'underhand and dishonest' scheme, as Peel described it, was regarded by him as one more example of French perfidy.

> It is not an actual breach of honourable engagement to this country [he wrote to Aberdeen in December], but considering the state of health of the queen of Spain, the effect will not probably be very different from an alliance with the Queen herself—and there is but little prospect of a *bona fide entente cordiale* between England and France if we are constantly on the look out for being cleverly over-reached. *Entente Cordiale* implies at least frank and honest declarations of intentions.

It was not until seven months later that Guizot admitted the truth of the report. He added soothingly that it was not an immediate event and in any case would not take place until the queen herself had married. This belated disclosure met with an understandably cool reception. When in September 1845 Victoria and Albert paid a second visit to the Château d'Eu, the king and Guizot did all they could to quieten British suspicions. They said positively that until Isabella had married and had had children, they would regard any marriage between her sister and a French prince as out of the question. Aberdeen thought this an ample guarantee and was prepared to leave the matter in abeyance. With this the prime minister, more guardedly, acquiesced.

The war scare of 1844 had undoubtedly given greater urgency to the long-standing problem of national defence. Expenditure on the armed forces had fallen to a dangerously low level in the 1830s and though the Whig administration had made a belated effort to repair the damage of a whole generation of neglect since Waterloo, it was still insufficient. The new Conservative ministry, preoccupied in its early years by financial and social problems, made no attempt to continue even this limited policy of rearmament. But by the spring of 1844 Peel was sufficiently impressed by the argument for defensive maritime bases along the Channel coast to appoint a commission of enquiry. The case rested primarily on the sudden acceleration of French naval preparations and the unpredictable effect of steam navigation on naval strategy in home waters. It was these long-term considerations rather than the sudden war scare with France which blew up later in the year that prompted the first cautious move towards a Conservative rearmament programme. Nevertheless the Anglo-French crisis rubbed home the painful lesson of British naval unpreparedness. In the summer of 1844 there were only nine capital ships in commission, three as guardships in home waters, one off Ireland, one in the Mediterranean, one in Indian waters, one in the Pacific, and two returning home to be paid off. It was scarcely an impressive front-line strength for what purported to be the greatest seapower in the world.

After subjecting the Admiralty staff to a searching inquisition Peel in the end was satisfied of the technical soundness of their case. There remained the diplomatic opposition of Aberdeen, who argued that even the commissioning of one additional battleship would be inconsistent with his assurances to the French government. At the end of the year the Admiralty produced its plans for floating defences and the Ordnance its report on harbour fortification. To the prime minister, immersed in the details of the next budget, they made anything but cheerful reading. He accepted, however, that a great effort would have to be made in 1845. Between the service chiefs, the Exchequer and the Foreign Office, the way was not easy. As he observed to Wellington at Christmas, there were two considerations which inevitably conditioned any policy of rearmament: the state of national finances and the effect on other powers. Financially the plain fact was that, excluding the income tax, the ordinary revenue of the country was insufficient even for normal peacetime expenditure. Diplomatically they must neither appear to threaten other states by hostile preparations nor appear so weak as to invite aggression. Nevertheless in the spring of 1845 the government publicly committed itself to a million-pound naval rearmament programme and the summer found the prime minister carrying on a massive correspondence about naval defence, recruitment, reserves, and harbours of refuge.

In public he sensibly refrained from alarmist statements. When at the end of the 1845 session Palmerston delivered a slashing attack on the country's inadequate coastal fortifications and the danger to British security from the new element of steam navigation, Peel made a cautious and noncommittal reply. He repudiated Palmerston's more pessimistic statements, made friendly references to France, and deprecated any arms race between the great powers. As for the future, he said firmly, he hoped that 'this country will never depart from that policy, which has secured its safety, namely, that of being strong as a naval power, and at the same time not attempting to enter into competition with the great military powers of Europe'. To Wellington, indifferent to the political considerations present in Peel's mind, his speech seemed dangerously optimistic if not actually misleading; and he sent him privately a caustic memorandum describing the utter inability of the army to defend the British Isles against invasion. What weighed profoundly on the duke was that, in his own phrase reported by the faithful Arbuthnot to the prime minister, 'steam makes a bridge for the French and not for us, they having an army of near 400,000 men and we not having one thousand for any sudden emergency'. Peel coolly returned the paper with the advice to send it to Stanley, the Secretary of State for War and Colonies. Next day he sent the duke a memorandum on his own account. 'Whatever be the real state of our defences,' he began dryly, 'I presume even the strictest regard for truth does not compel a Minister of the Crown publicly to proclaim that the country is in a defenceless state.' In the succeeding pages he demonstrated that though there were many deficiencies, the general situation was not as bad as alarmists had painted it, and that he was ensuring that much was being done to improve it even beyond the strict limits of the financial programme sanctioned by parliament. But he ended on a friendly note by welcoming Wellington's cooperation and promising to keep him informed of all new developments.

While soothing the old duke's susceptibilities Peel had to face Aberdeen's growing apprehensions of the effect abroad of the re-armament programme. At the end of 1844 the Foreign Secretary had, in unusually strong language, criticised the new coastal defence plans as 'a system which would virtually stultify our whole policy for the last three years'. Disquiet on this fundamental question complicated relations between Peel and Aberdeen all through 1845. At the Château d'Eu in September Guizot had laughed at British anxieties and Aberdeen returned home full of gloom at what he believed to be the mistaken policy of his own country. He found to his alarm a bustle of preparation in all the service departments and most of his leading colleagues apparently preoccupied with defence matters. A week later he sent Peel what was in effect a conditional letter of resignation. He recorded his conviction that there was less reason to distrust the French government or fear the end of peace than there had been in the four previous years; though he substantially qualified this declaration of faith by admitting that 'it is possible that war may suddenly, and when least expected, take place'. But, he added, at the moment both countries were acting under the influence of panic and ignorance, and he felt completely isolated in the cabinet. He suggested therefore that he should resign quietly as though by prearrangement before any open disagreement on policy could take place or even be suspected.

Peel refused to connive at such an arrangement. It would be improper and useless, he replied energetically on 20 September, to try to conceal the true reasons for Aberdeen's retirement; and quite apart from public considerations, the loss to himself would be irrepar-able. He showed the correspondence only to Graham and Wellington; but to the duke he made it clear that they must attempt a compromise between taking reasonable military precautions and maintaining their declared policy of friendly relations with France. His own personal opinion, he confided to Wellington, was that Louis Philippe and Guizot, so far as it rested with them, were bent on preserving peace. He was equally convinced that the security of the country should not be allowed to depend on the personal attitudes of individual and perhaps temporary rulers of France. Precautions they must take, but they should be gradual and unostentatious.

In this way the personal crisis was averted and the correspondence between prime minister and Foreign Secretary fell back into the more familiar channels of argument over policy. To the end the differences between them were on emphasis rather than objective; and at no time was there any withholding of views and information. Peel's concern, like that of Aberdeen, was peace; but peace without abandoning British interests or foregoing the advantage of power and influence. His pacifism was tempered by a regard for national security and scepticism towards the professions of foreign states. He believed in plain dealing, plain speaking, and occasionally firm action. More important, he looked to the lessons of the past and the hazards of the future; and in the long run would not trust Britain's safety to anything but her own resources. Less diplomatic than his Foreign Secretary, he had perhaps a more realistic conception of national security. The end of his ministry saw the country not only on more peaceful terms with her two great maritime rivals, France and the U.S.A., but better prepared for war.

Chapter 20

The repeal of the Corn Laws

By the summer of 1845 Peel was clearly feeling the accumulated strains
of office. He told the queen in July that the habit of debating everything in parliament and the increase of business in all departments
made it difficult for a minister 'to perform in a satisfactory manner his
duty towards Your Majesty and the Country'. A couple of days afterwards Gladstone, dining with his former chief, congratulated him on
bearing up well under the labours of the session. Peel made a gesture of
dissent, complained of a feeling of tiredness in his head, and spoke
again of the strain on ministers of attendance in parliament. It had
even occurred to him, he said, that it might be best for a prime minister
to be in the House of Lords. To Arbuthnot a month later he wrote even
more strongly that the state of public business during the session was
becoming a matter of serious concern and that he defied any prime
minister to carry out properly the duties of his office and at the same
time sit in the House of Commons eight hours a day for over a hundred
days in the year.

The detailed scrutiny which Peel gave to the work of all departments, while immeasurably improving and tightening the administration as a whole, imposed a degree of labour on the prime minister
which, as he was beginning to perceive, was scarcely sustainable even
over the lifetime of one parliament. There was no immediate prospect
of escape; nor did he seriously contemplate a retreat to the Lords. But
the problem remained and would have to be solved sooner or later.
'The failure of the mind', he added grimly in his letter to Arbuthnot, 'is
the usual way as we know from sad experience.' From a man who
remembered Castlereagh's suicide and Liverpool's stroke, it was not an
extravagant remark.

It was an additional affliction in these circumstances that his one
permanent physical disability affected his head. Since taking office his
old trouble from the shooting accident in the twenties had recurred
with increasing intensity. The symptoms, as he once described them,
resembled the noise of boiling water in his ear. He was rarely free from
some inconvenience and under the strain of prolonged work he suffered
actual pain. His doctor, Brodie, told him that he was simply over-
working his brain. This diagnosis offered neither comfort nor cure; and
it would have taken a less imaginative man than Peel to ignore the
possibility that abnormal symptoms in his head might be the forerunner
of mental collapse. The trouble was never more than the effects of
purely physical damage to the ear; but it had never been adequately

265

diagnosed or treated and not until he went to an ear specialist in 1846 did he obtain some relief. From the summer of 1845 to the spring of 1846 the condition was probably at its worst. As late as the end of June 1846, when discussing his position with Graham and Aberdeen, he suddenly said, putting his hand to the side of his head, 'Ah, you do not know what I suffer here'. The unexpected crisis of the Irish famine had to be faced by a prime minister whom tiredness, anxiety and pain had made more than usually inflexible.

The potato blight which struck central and western Europe in 1845 was a fungus disease which in a suitable atmospheric environment could assume epidemic proportions. The late summer of 1845 was a textbook example of the appropriate conditions. After a cold, foggy winter the spring was chilly and wet. In mid-July the rain returned once more. For over a month the sky was overcast with repeated showers, high winds and low day temperatures. Immersed though he was in defence, foreign policy and Irish education, Peel from early August was already beginning to be apprehensive; and his correspondence contained an increasing number of allusions to the weather and the prospects for the harvest. 'I know not that the state of affairs is really sound,' observed Graham sombrely to Peel in a letter of 15 August, 'when Ministers are driven to study the Barometer with so much anxiety.' The first reports of the potato disease in England came early in August; but for Peel and Graham the real anxiety lay elsewhere. In England the failure of the potato crop would be a hardship for the poor; in Ireland it would be a disaster. By the third week of August they knew that the disease had made its appearance in the sister island and before the middle of October it was beyond all doubt that a crisis was looming in that afflicted country. On 17 October the Lord-Lieutenant confirmed that the Irish potato crop had failed almost everywhere.

By that date Peel was already considering what measures would be necessary to relieve the now almost certain famine. It was clear that the government would have to be prepared for almost immediate decisions. The first need was for reliable information on the extent of the disease and authoritative advice on means of preserving sound tubers. In the second half of October two distinguished scientists, Lyon Playfair and Professor Lindley, were despatched to Ireland to assist the local authorities. Their final report on 15 November stated that at the lowest estimate half the potato crop was useless and that, if the seed potatoes were deducted, only three-eighths of the harvest would be available as food. Lindley, who saw Peel and Graham on 10 November, warned them that even the sound part of the crop might become infected and he feared that the disease would return the following year. With reports from England, Scotland and the Continent indicating a general European failure of the potato crop only marginally less severe than in Ireland, the government was clearly facing a great crisis. Pressure was mounting in Ireland for official action and in the larger island the Anti-

Corn Law League was already demanding that the ports should be opened for the free entry of corn.

What seemed self-evident to Peel and Graham was that any government intervention in Ireland to prevent famine would make the whole position of the Corn Laws untenable. To suspend duties on foreign grain would confirm the contention of the League that the Corn Laws aggravated scarcity and their abolition would secure plenty. A suspension of duties would be unpredictable in its duration; their reimposition only conceivable at the cost of a violent political controversy. Already in the view of those two ministers the Corn Laws had been undermined to the point of being simply a political and economic expedient. That expedient was now suddenly swallowed up by the Irish crisis. In an outspoken letter to the Lord-Lieutenant on 15 October Peel gave it as his opinion that the only real practicable remedy for famine in Ireland was 'the removal of all impediments to the import of all kinds of human food—that is, the total and absolute repeal for ever of all duties on all articles of subsistence'. It is not surprising that he wanted confirmation of the certainty of famine before taking action; but it is equally significant that he was already prepared to think in those absolute and uncompromising terms. Even before the scientists left for Ireland, he felt bound to act on the assumption that government intervention would be needed. On 21 October he took his first important step by recalling the cabinet.

The first of what was to prove a crucial series of autumn cabinets was held on 31 October and for the next five weeks Peel wrestled with the doubts and scruples of his colleagues. At the first two meetings they examined the evidence for a threatened famine in Ireland and listened to a long memorandum from the prime minister. His initial proposal was for the immediate appointment of a relief commission under the Lord-Lieutenant. Since this would cost public money, it would have to be sanctioned by parliament. Could they ask for this and at the same time retain the Corn Laws in full operation? His own conclusion was that 'it will be dangerous for the Government, having assembled Parliament, to resist with all its energies any material modification of the Corn Law'. To some of the cabinet it seemed even at this early stage that Peel was embarking on a course that was both disastrous and unjustifiable. Not only did they think it was wrong for a Conservative ministry to tamper any further with the Corn Laws but they could not bring themselves to believe that the crisis was serious enough to make such a step inevitable. In the minds of all of them was the feeling that to suspend the Corn Laws even for a limited period was to sign their death-warrant; and Stanley wrote a private letter to Peel saying bluntly that to repeal the Corn Laws would be to break up the cabinet.

The third meeting on 6 November brought all their disagreements into the open. What Peel now proposed was to open the ports to foreign grain at a reduced rate, meet parliament at the end of November, and announce their intention to introduce a new corn bill. But when a vote was taken only three of his colleagues supported him: Graham, Aberdeen and Herbert. The rest either objected in principle or thought the necessity had not yet been proved. The final report from Playfair and Lindley had not yet arrived and Peel agreed therefore to give his colleagues further time to consider the question while fresh evidence accumulated. It was settled that they should reassemble at the end of the month and Peel made up his mind that if support was not then forthcoming he would resign. Meanwhile the inexorable chain of events set in motion by the crisis continued to unwind. The Lord-Lieutenant had already been instructed, with cabinet assent, to set up an emergency relief organisation. On their side Peel, Graham and Goulburn instituted enquiries into possible food supplies from Europe and placed a large order through the firm of Baring for £100,000 worth of maize and meal from the U.S.A. It was not only the authorities who were active. With the realisation that the potato crop had failed all over the British Isles the Anti-Corn Law League had redoubled its exertions; and public anxiety was steadily mounting. The unusual series of ministerial meetings had aroused intense speculation and three days before the cabinet reassembled Lord John Russell dexterously exploited the situation by publishing his famous *Edinburgh Letter* calling on the public 'by petition, by address, by remonstrance' to force the government into abandoning the Corn Laws.

It was a deeply troubled group of politicians who gathered at Downing Street on 25 November. Their earlier delay in reaching agreement had meant that even before the famine started, they were being overtaken by its political consequences. Conscious that the initiative was rapidly slipping from their hands, Peel tried once more to secure a decision. Approval of the instructions for the Lord-Lieutenant was a tacit recognition of the reality of the crisis and he pressed this point home to his reluctant colleagues. 'I cannot consent', he observed in a paper he read to them on 26 November, 'to the issue of these instructions, and undertake at the same time to maintain the existing Corn Law.' He admitted that it would have been better if it had fallen to another ministry to carry out a revision of the 1842 act, but he said he was prepared to take responsibility for this if his colleagues would support him. This however was something from which they still flinched. All their old doubts and scruples remained; the lapse of time had merely altered the mechanical aspects of the dilemma. The only step on which they could agree was to call parliament together early in January; and there was a gloomy feeling that the queen would have to be warned beforehand of an irreconcilable difference of opinion among her ministers.

For Peel this was to admit defeat before the parliamentary battle even started. For the last time therefore he marshalled all his arguments on paper in an attempt to convert his doubting colleagues. In this, the longest of the five memoranda he placed before the cabinet that autumn, he still ignored the question of party unity and personal

consistency. Instead he emphasised the danger of further procrastination and the overriding need for an immediate decision. Once more
he posed the inexorable question he had put to them four weeks earlier.
Were they to maintain, modify, or suspend the existing Corn Law? His
paper elicited a variety of replies. Ripon raised the question of compensation for farmers; Wharncliffe wished to wait a little longer before
admitting their inability to agree; Goulburn spoke of the damage to
their reputation as public men and the certain disruption of the party;
Wellington, though still unconvinced, repaid the debt of loyalty over
Catholic Emancipation in 1829 by saying that he would support a
suspension of the Corn Laws if Peel thought the national interest
required it. What was common to them was their respect for Peel, their
wish that he should continue at the head of the nation's affairs, and
their regret at the course he was taking; what they did not do was to
answer his simple question. In a sense that question had been too
simple. If suspension implied revision, what form was that revision to
take? It was an achievement perhaps to have brought them to the
point at which they could even consider such a possibility. The prime
minister therefore took his final step and in a fifth paper read to the
cabinet on 2 December he outlined a practical plan of action. The
famine, he argued, by forcing a suspension of the Corn Laws merely
compelled immediate consideration of a problem which otherwise
might have been postponed to another session. The choice was between
the 1842 act and a new law involving the ultimate abolition of protective duties. What he proposed therefore was a bill which would
bring about a gradual extinction of all duties on foreign corn over a
period of eight years.

In the discussion which followed it seemed to Peel there was a
chance that his scheme would receive the support, however grudging,
of a united cabinet. But no decision was taken and when they reassembled on 4 December Stanley and Buccleuch announced that they
would prefer to resign rather than endorse such policy. That decided
the issue. Faced with the resignation of two of his colleagues and the
reluctance of nearly all the rest, Peel at last acknowledged defeat.
Success even with a united cabinet would have been difficult; without
it, impossible. All that was left for him was to hand over responsibility
to the man who had publicly declared that the Corn Laws must be
repealed. On 5 December he informed the cabinet of his decision to
resign. It was failure; but it had been a near thing. Starting with only
three on his side in a cabinet of fourteen, he had ended with only two
positively against him. Indeed, the most revealing feature of the cabinet
discussions had been the comparative lack of any robust belief in the
Corn Laws themselves. What Peel had to overcome were the more
imponderable factors of inertia, scruple, concern for consistency, and
fears of the political consequences.

What was striking, on the other hand, was the spontaneous reaction of Peel and Graham to the news from Ireland. When they

realised in mid-October that the failure of the potato crop would entail massive government intervention, they took it for granted that the repeal of the Corn Laws must follow. So instant a conviction could only have been possible in men who had long since ceased to believe in either the desirability or value of the Corn Laws. As early as May 1843 Peel had expressed doubts to Gladstone whether he could in future undertake to defend them. The considerations which drove him in the end to a positive determination to repeal them were many: the success of the 1842 budget experiment, the practical demonstration that, contrary to much economic teaching, the level of wages did not vary with the price of food, the belief that agricultural prosperity depended not on legislative protection but on more efficient techniques, greater productivity, and expanding markets; and finally, the conviction that the growing public hostility to the Corn Laws was compromising the position of the landowning aristocracy and in consequence the whole governing structure of the country.

These considerations had operated not as a single irrefutable proof but by a process of continual erosion. Not Ireland but the condition of England provided the underlying motive for repealing the Corn Laws. It was this which made it impossible for Peel to approach the question of Irish famine with impartiality. It was not that the famine was a pretext, but there was no sign that he envisaged any method of dealing with the famine that did not involve the end of protection. So far as he was concerned the Corn Laws by 1845 were living on borrowed time; the Irish famine merely foreclosed the mortgage.

II

In a sympathetic and emotional interview with Victoria and Albert on 6 December it was agreed that Russell should be asked to form a government. A couple of days later Peel composed a letter for the queen to show to the Whig leader, promising his personal support for legislation on the lines indicated in the *Edinburgh Letter*. Though reassured, Russell remained understandably hesitant before the totally unexpected situation which confronted him. To soothe his anxieties Peel secured from Stanley and Buccleuch an assurance that the formation of a protectionist ministry was in their opinion neither practicable nor desirable; but he rebuffed Russell's attempts to involve him personally in the Whig plan of repeal. Any prior commitment of this kind, he wrote to the queen, would be 'distasteful to the House of Commons and embarrassing to all parties'. Although the frigidity of his reply disappointed the Whigs there was no real doubt in the minds of Russell and most of his colleagues that Peel would support them, and on 18 December Russell finally announced that he was ready to form an administration.

Peel breathed more freely at the news. He had been slightly

conscious-stricken at the thought that his last communication might have impeded the construction of a new government and he had already tried to smooth away any unfavourable impression in a letter to the prince. He now prepared to hand over his caretaker commission. After the strain of the past two months he was in a noticeably elevated mood. He had made up his mind that the Corn Laws must be repealed, even if he was not the suitable man to do it. He was now spared the odium of another 1829. Loss of office hardly seemed to trouble him. Perhaps he even welcomed it; or persuaded himself that he did.

But he had not finished yet with the unpredictabilities of Lord John Russell. On 19 December a note from the prince warned him that Russell was not certain after all of being able to form a ministry. Next day he learned from Graham that the Whig leader was going to throw up his commission. The whole situation was transformed once more. Peel's response was immediate and characteristic. His final audience to take leave of the queen had been fixed for that afternoon. He summoned the cabinet to meet him in the evening and wrote a brief line to Wellington. 'I am going to the Queen. I shall tell her at once and without hesitation that I will not abandon her. Whatever may happen, I shall return from Windsor as her Minister.'

When he saw the queen at two o'clock she explained that Russell had encountered objections by Lord Grey to Palmerston's return to the Foreign Office and that though Peel was there to take his leave, she was still without a minister or a government. Russell's half-hearted resolution had in fact crumbled at the first obstacle. His difficulties were obvious; he was conscious of the pessimism of many of his colleagues; and he accepted Grey's cantankerous protests as justification for abandoning his embarrassing task without making any serious attempt to get round them. Peel was stirred and excited at the news. He blamed Russell's procrastination, compared it unfavourably with his own prompt acceptance of office in 1834, and said emotionally that he would stand by the queen regardless of the consequences. If necessary he would meet parliament alone and lay his proposals before it. Staying only to concoct a draft letter for the queen to send to Russell, he left the Castle at four o'clock. In his exalted mood the events of the past fortnight seemed like a dream. He felt, as he wrote later to the Princess Lieven, like a man restored to life after his funeral service had been read. Ahead was the most formidable task of his career. That alone was enough to make him forget the strains and tiredness of the previous summer. His ministry was not over yet.

To his cabinet that evening he said bluntly that he had summoned them not to ask what was to be done but to announce that he was once again the queen's minister. The question now was not one of the Corn Laws but of the government itself. The choice was himself or Lord Grey and Cobden. After a dead silence Stanley repeated that he would still have to resign. Buccleuch, troubled and upset, asked for time to reflect. The rest, led by Wellington, warmly approved of Peel's action.

With that the first obstacle was overcome. Protectionism in the cabinet had been killed stone-dead by the hapless Lord John Russell. The loss of Stanley, which had seemed so formidable a month earlier, was now almost irrelevant. The vacancy was filled after a day's hesitation by Gladstone; and Peel scored another quick success by persuading Buccleuch to stay on and take the Presidency of the Council made vacant by Wharncliffe's recent death.

At the Privy Council on 23 December Peel was obviously elated at the rapidity with which he had reformed his administration and showed it by the freedom with which he talked to Victoria and Albert afterwards. He confided to them that his intention had been to inform his party, sometime during the 1846 session, that the Corn Laws could not be maintained any longer and that he would make a public announcement to that effect before the general election. That decision had been overtaken by events. What he now wanted was to remove the whole question from the dangerous position into which it had drifted: a battle with manufacturers, the working classes and the poor which could only end in the defeat of the aristocracy. His plan was to deal with the Corn Laws as part of a general policy designed to end all restrictions and monopolies; not to favour one class and triumph over another but in the interest of all. There would be compensation for agriculture, not as a bribe but in the form of justifiable social improvement. This wide vista evoked the admiration of the prince. Though many details remained to be settled, it was clear that Peel had already mapped out his strategy for the coming parliamentary struggle.

Before the end of the month this general sketch was being translated into more positive directions to the Exchequer and the Board of Trade. 'My wish', Peel wrote to Goulburn on 27 December, 'would be not to give undue prominence to corn, but to cover corn by continued operation on the Customs tariff.' By abolishing all duties not worth retention and reducing all protection, they would simply be applying to agriculture laws of general application. 'Let us leave the tariff as nearly perfect as we can. . . . I attach great importance to *our doing*, and doing now, what yet remains to be done.' In essence the new policy was to wrap up the repeal of the Corn Laws in one last great tariff reconstruction. Out of the crisis of the Irish famine would be created the crowning achievement of his whole administration. The assent of the cabinet was obtained without difficulty and he was confident of securing a majority in parliament. Russell had promised the queen he would give his support for a final settlement of the corn issue, and for a free trade policy in general there was overwhelming backing in the Commons. The ultimate fate of the government was a different matter. There was no member of the cabinet who did not realise that what they proposed to do would produce a party crisis worse than Maynooth. Peel himself had no illusions on that score. When accepting a seat in the cabinet St Germans asked the prime minister whether he expected to be able to continue in office; Peel replied no. 'It was therefore under no impression', wrote St Germans later, 'that I was joining a durable administration that I accepted.' But this for Peel was a secondary consideration.

Parliament opened on 22 January in an atmosphere of intense excitement. In a firm speech Peel defended his change of view and repeated his conviction that the essence of true conservatism was to advance the national interest, impose the weight of taxation on those best able to bear it, and by so doing discourage agitation and allay discontent. The men sitting behind him listened in an ominous silence broken only once when he mentioned Stanley's view that the crisis was exaggerated and the repeal of the Corn Laws unnecessary. Then all the Conservative benches seemed to break out in cheers. If further proof was needed of the sullen feeling in the party it came in the applause which greeted a characteristic speech from Disraeli full, as Greville described it, of 'gibes and bitterness', and in a warning from Miles that every means would be used to prevent his measure from passing into law. Five days later, in a speech that was somewhat dull and factual, and perhaps designed to be, Peel laid before the House his specific tariff proposals: the reduction or abolition of duties on a long list of articles from soap to sugar and from timber to tobacco in which his audience perhaps was only interested in one item. On corn, when he finally arrived at it, Peel announced that he did not propose an immediate abolition but a progressive reduction until in 1849 the duties would finally expire along with those on all other cereals.

The cheers at the end, like the applause which punctuated his statement, came from the Liberal opposition. On the Conservative side there was gloomy silence. When the House broke up the extreme protectionists were clearly angry, the moderate Conservatives disappointed, and not many of his party happy at his speech. Peel had briefly outlined various forms of compensation for farmers; but neither these nor the three-year delay before complete abolition was enough even for those half-hearted protectionists who had been hoping for something which they could recommend to their angry constituents. Though the Whigs gave cool approval, only a few ultra-Liberals were disposed to recognise the largeness of the policy he had outlined. To many indeed his speech seemed something of an anticlimax.

Nevertheless Peel at the end of January was in good heart. Though there had been a crop of resignations, voluntary or enforced, from the middle and lower ranks of the government, and some free trade Conservative M.P.s sitting for agricultural constituencies had given up their seats, all the rumours reaching him from the Whig camp suggested that there was doubt and division among the opposition also. Some of Russell's followers were pressing him to demand total and immediate repeal; others wanted him to unseat the government. It was unlikely, however, that either the intransigence of the Leaguers or the jealousies of the Whigs would prevent the mass of free-traders in the House from voting for the government. There were signs too that in the country opinion was rallying to the ministers in quarters that would never have embraced the doctrines of the League. Many moderate unpolitical men who had watched the progress of the country since 1841 and admired the skill and success of Peel's policy were disposed to continue their trust in his judgement and integrity. The real danger came from the intensive organisation of protectionist feeling which had taken place in the previous two years. For this the Anti-Corn Law League itself had been largely responsible. The spread of their activities into the rural areas after 1843 had produced a natural but ominous reaction among farmers and landlords. It took the form of a great increase in the number of local agricultural protection societies and in 1844 these had been given national leadership by the formation of a Central Agricultural Protection Society under the chairmanship of the Duke of Richmond. The 1845 annual meeting of the society, held during the alarms and excitements of December, had taken up the challenge, and in the weeks preceding the opening of parliament local branch meetings were held all over England to promote petitions and exert pressure on their county M.P.s.

Anger and despair, in fact, were making the protectionists a more formidable force than they had ever been before; and it was not the League but Peel who was now the enemy. All they needed was a leader. From the League itself on the other hand there was little to fear. All the information coming to Peel confirmed that there was no encouragement nationally for a renewed repeal campaign. The great mass of manufacturers approved the prime minister's policy and were tired of agitation. Cobden's savage and exultant language at the fall of the cabinet in December earned him the rebukes of some of his closest friends. Out of this paradoxically came reconciliation. Peel had been astounded to learn through indirect sources that much of Cobden's rancour was due to what had happened in 1843. When Harriet Martineau, that adroit bluestocking, wrote to both men in an effort to heal the breach, Peel's response was not long in coming. Taking advantage of a reference to the 1843 incident by Disraeli in a debate at the end of February, Peel promptly rose to withdraw unequivocally 'an imputation on the hon. member for Stockport which was thrown out in the heat of debate under an erroneous impression'. Cobden got on his feet in turn to express satisfaction at the prime minister's words and regret for the terms in which he had alluded to Peel on that earlier occasion. It was the end of an unhappy episode in Cobden's life and the start of a new relationship between Peel and one of his ablest opponents in public life.

III

Meanwhile battle had been joined in earnest in the House of Commons. The twelve-day debate on the tariff proposals in the middle of February not only vindicated Miles's warning but threw up a new leader for the protectionists in the unexpected person of Lord George Bentinck. A younger son of the Duke of Portland, close friend of the Duke of Richmond, foxhunter, race-horse owner and prominent member of the Jockey Club, he added energy and prestige to the already half-organised Protectionist Party. He had sat for twenty years as a silent backbencher, but from the end of November the growing speculation about Peel's intentions had aroused in him a passionate and obsessive interest. He now brought to the Protectionist cause the ruthless determination and singlemindedness which he had formerly shown in hunting down dishonest trainers and crooked jockeys on the Turf. Violent and unscrupulous by temperament, he made up for his political inexperience by tenacity and force. As the end of the debate drew near, speculation on the result intensified. At the start the government whips had calculated on a majority of a hundred; but as man after man declared himself in the debate, it was realised that in the minority would be found the larger portion of the Conservative Party. When the House divided in the early hours of 28 February the worst ministerial fears were confirmed. There was a majority of only 97 for the government motion. Of the Conservatives present, 112 voted with their leader; 231 against. The dividing line had been drawn at last and two-thirds of Peel's party had turned against him.

Despite the relative ease with which the tariff measures went through committee, there was no slackening either in the fierceness of protectionist opposition or in their personal animosity towards Peel. On the second reading of the corn bill the government majority dropped to 88; and though this was due to a decrease in the number of those voting rather than to any real shift of opinion, the result encouraged protectionist hopes of defeating the measure in the House of Lords. This in fact was Peel's chief anxiety. The peers, less amenable to party discipline and less exposed to public pressure, were more evenly divided and incalculable. Though an outright rejection of the bill was unlikely, an amendment in committee would be easier to secure and as effective in its consequences, since the corn bill was a money bill and had either to be accepted or rejected in its entirety. Some Whig peers were canvassing for the old Whig device of a fixed duty and an alliance of Whig and Tory protectionists on that basis would probably produce an anti-government majority. April saw a hum of activity in the upper chamber as both sides collected proxies and tried to organise the somewhat amorphous mass of peers.

Meanwhile it was clear to everyone that Peel was merely holding office by courtesy of the Whigs until he had repealed the Corn Laws. Though his ultimate position was untenable, however, he was too good a tactician not to see the immediate strength he derived from the divisions among his rivals. In the Commons the protectionists could neither form a government, nor force a dissolution, nor defeat the corn bill. Their only hope was to beat the government in conjunction with the Whigs on some other issue. Revenge in fact was rapidly becoming Bentinck's sole political objective. Peel had little doubt that sooner or later a suitable opportunity would be provided for him.

> Of the 230 or 240 Conservatives—or whatever was their number— who voted against us [he wrote to his trusted friend Hardinge on 4 April] many will return to their old standard. But suppose a hundred of them remain inveterate and disposed to mischief, they may find the means of placing us in a minority, by a union with the Whigs and Radicals.

The means in fact, like a slow fuse smouldering away in the recesses of the government's legislative programme, was already present.

The wave of violence and disorder which marked the onset of the first famine winter in Ireland had induced the government to prepare a bill, on traditional lines, to strengthen the executive powers of the Lord-Lieutenant for dealing with disturbed districts and to stiffen the legal penalties for breaking the law. To save time it was introduced in the House of Lords in February and met with general approval. Though the Whig peers, especially those with estates in Ireland, had reservations about the corn bill, they had none at this stage about the need for stronger measures to protect life and property in Ireland. When the bill came down to the Commons at the end of March, however, it met with considerable obstruction from the Irish Liberals who attacked the whole principle of the 'coercion bill', as they promptly dubbed it, and from the Whigs who took the more moderate but equally damaging line that it should not take precedence over the corn bill. The protectionists on the other hand for obvious reasons were prepared to support it provided it was given precedence over corn. In the event little progress was made with either measure and in the course of April an explicit understanding was reached between Bentinck and the Irish nationalists to waste as much debating time as possible on the Irish bill. Equally ominous was the news reaching Peel that some of the Irish Whig peers like Clanricarde and Bessborough had changed their minds over the coercion bill and were trying to persuade Russell to oppose it in the Commons. The delay affected the whole government timetable. All that could be done was to sit it out patiently. Not until the second week of May did the House return to the corn bill.

The long frustrating grind of April robbed Peel of much of his energy and elasticity; and the final committee stage of the corn bill brought a renewal of the bitter personal onslaughts launched on him by Disraeli and others. On 15 May, the last evening of the debate, Disraeli returned to the attack in a speech of sustained and studied invective. For thirty years, declaimed the orator with his sallow un- moved countenance and passionless voice, Peel had traded on the ideas and intelligence of others. His life was one long appropriation clause; he was the burglar of others' intellects. No statesman had committed larceny on so great a scale. As phrase followed polished phrase the men round him laughed and cheered and laughed again. When Peel rose after midnight to wind up the debate he was met with screaming and hooting from the protectionist benches and for the first quarter of an hour he was struggling to get a hearing. The personal attack he dismissed in a few sentences. In taking the course he had, he observed contemptuously, 'the smallest of all the penalties which I anticipated were the continued venomous attacks of the member for Shrewsbury'. If Disraeli held the view of him in 1841 which he now professed, the only surprise was that he had been ready to take office under him in that year. Then, turning to his main theme, he reviewed once more his reasons for believing that it was in the national interest to make a final settlement of the Corn Laws. So far as his own career and ambitions were concerned, he started to say—and was at once overwhelmed by the storm of jeers which this personal reference evoked. He stopped, tried to resume, stopped once more. His voice failed him, his eyes filled with tears, and for a moment the embarrassed and half-sympathetic Whigs across the gangway thought he was going to break down. No one had ever seen Peel beaten in the House of Commons before; but he was not beaten now. With an enormous effort he pulled himself together and carried through to the end his fifth and last great speech in the memorable Corn Law debates of 1846.

Fighting now with his back to the wall, he spoke more sharply and revealingly than he had ever done before. A continuance of the Corn Laws, he said, would only have been possible at the cost of a desperate class struggle. The Irish crisis made necessary a review of those laws. What made necessary their repeal was a wider consideration. 'The real question at issue is the improvement of the social and moral condition of the masses of the population.' Though he had changed his mind over protection for corn, in his general advocacy of free trade he was acting consistently with his whole public career. Then, in his peroration, he said something which came from the heart of his political philosophy.

> If I look to the prerogative of the Crown, if I look to the position of the Church, if I look to the influence of the aristocracy, I cannot charge myself with having taken any course inconsistent with conservative principles. . . . My earnest wish has been, during my tenure of power, to impress the people of this country with a belief that the legislature was animated with a sincere desire to frame its legislation upon the principles of equity and justice. . . . The greatest object which we or any other government can contemplate should be to elevate the social condition of that class of people with whom we are brought into no direct relationship by the exercise of the elective franchise.

Deprive him of power tomorrow, he finished defiantly, they could never persuade him that he used that power except for those ends. When he sat down Disraeli rose to deny, in rather uneasy and obscure language, that he had ever asked for office or solicited any favour from the government. It was a curious lie, indeed a double lie. He had both solicited Peel for office in 1841 and twice subsequently applied for patronage. All that the prime minister did was to repeat significantly that if Disraeli held the opinions about him in 1841 that he had uttered that night, he was wrong to have told Peel he would be glad to take office under him.

With the corn and tariff bills safely through the Commons Peel now concentrated on the House of Lords. The danger was not defeat on the second reading, where the government could use its battery of proxies, but a hostile amendment in committee. There were reports that Lord Bessborough had said he would challenge any attempt to use proxy votes to reverse a decision reached in committee; and Peel circulated a cabinet memorandum asking for his colleagues' opinions on the constitutional issue involved. All agreed that on past precedent and by present necessity the use of proxies would be justified. Nevertheless the fate of the bill depended on others; the Peelites no more commanded a majority in the Lords than they did in the Commons. Peel's last fears vanished, however, with the news of a meeting of Whig peers on 23 May when Russell told them that he would be no party to any alteration in the bill and that if the government were forced to resign on that issue the Whig peers must look elsewhere for a leader. With that the repeal of the Corn Laws was virtually accomplished. It was almost an anticlimax when a few days later the bill passed its second reading in the Lords by a majority of nearly fifty.

The charmed life which the government had been leading was now almost over. At the end of May Peel told the prince that even if they escaped defeat on the Irish bill, they would be confronted with a second hazard in the shape of the postponed sugar duties on which the Whigs had threatened opposition. His own view was that a great effort would be made to defeat the government on the Irish protection of life bill. When that long-delayed measure resumed its limping progress after Whitsun, surmise soon became certainty. Peel's assessment was that there would be a clear majority against the government and that at least sixty protectionists would vote with the Whigs and Liberals. Before the inevitable end came there was one last violent personal attack by Bentinck on the prime minister. In the debate on the second reading of the Irish bill on 8 June, he accused Peel of having 'chased and hunted' Canning to death in 1827, although he had subsequently admitted to being convinced by that date of the necessity for Catholic emancipation. He was therefore convicted on his own confession of 'base and dishonest conduct'. The effect of this charge, dug up from the past of nearly twenty years earlier, was to disgust many even of Bentinck's own supporters. Yet there had always been something of a legend about Peel's breach with Canning in 1827 and it was regarded as odd that he did not make an instant denial. In fact he had been so angered at the insult that he felt there was only one fitting reply. Walking back with Lincoln to Whitehall Gardens in the small hours of the morning he asked him to act as his second. Only after much remonstrance and argument from the younger man did Peel reluctantly agree on the following day to abandon his intention of challenging Bentinck.

Instead, a few days later, he made a studiously moderate reply, clearing himself before a sympathetic House but making no attempt to retort in kind on the protectionist leader. Disraeli returned to the subject later in the debate. The evidence on which Bentinck had based his accusation were words which appeared in a report of a speech by Peel in 1829 given in *The Times*, though not included in the versions printed in *Hansard* or any other independent publication. On this slender foundation Disraeli renewed the accusation on behalf of his leader who by the rules of debate was precluded from speaking again. Peel rose in a considerable temper, promised a full explanation, and asked the House to suspend judgement. Though hampered by the inaccessibility of his old correspondence, which was stored at Drayton, he was able with the help of friends and colleagues to make a detailed refutation of the charges on 19 June, demolishing Disraeli's argument point by point, but disdaining to take issue with the man himself. He was cheered all round the House and the whole prolonged incident merely degraded the protectionists and added to the moral authority of the prime minister. 'Like every unjust and malignant attack,' he wrote to the queen, 'this, according to Sir Robert Peel's impressions, recoiled upon its authors. He thinks the House was completely satisfied.'

So far he had been content to let events take their course, but the time had come when the final question had to be settled. In a circular to the cabinet on 21 June he argued that it was in the interests of neither the Crown, the country nor themselves to stay in office once the corn and tariff bills were passed. Even if they gained a technical victory on the Irish bill, they would still be beaten by obstruction and delay. The alternative to resignation was a dissolution of parliament. But what justification could they put forward for such an act? To dissolve on the specific issue of the Irish bill would be a hazardous step. If 'No Popery' was a dangerous cry for a general election, 'coercion for Ireland' would be even worse. To dissolve on any other ground would, or at least should, imply that they hoped to succeed in an appeal to the electorate. To go to the country on the repeal of the Corn Laws was too personal and retrospective. A wider platform of 'free trade and the destruction of Protection' pointed to an alliance with free-traders of all kinds, irrespective of party allegiance: logical in theory but impossible in practice. His conclusion was that they should neither remain in office when they had lost power nor precipitate a general election which they could not win.

Though there were divided views among his colleagues on his

general attitude, there was complete agreement that if defeated on the Irish bill they would have to resign. Their dilemma was soon solved. On 25 June the corn bill received its third reading in the Lords and a few hours later the government was defeated in the Commons on the second reading of the Irish crimes bill. A majority of some twenty against the bill had been expected and Peel had discouraged sympathetic free-traders and radicals who had thought of abstaining rather than vote against him by pointing out that nothing they could do would save the ministry. In the event it was a majority of seventy-three. Of Bentinck's protectionists less than a third followed him into the opposition lobby. Nearly half of them, refusing to allow their feelings on corn to dictate a factious vote on coercion, supported the government. Only some fifty who abstained made the difference between the actual and estimated margin of defeat. But added to the solid mass of Liberal votes, Bentinck's seventy-four were more than enough. Along with Whigs, Leaguers, Irish and Radicals trooped a hard knot of revengeful Tory members to vote a Peelite cabinet out of office and the Conservative Party out of power for the next thirty years.

The following Monday, 29 June, Peel announced the resignation of the government. It was an occasion few could forget. Great crowds lined the route between Whitehall Gardens and Westminster; and when Peel came out of his house he was cheered all the way down to the House of Commons. Inside, the chamber was packed with M.P.s, peers, and ambassadors When Peel arrived soon after six, a little breathless from the exertion of walking, he placed his box containing the news of the Oregon treaty on the table and sat down for a while until he had recovered himself His manner was colder and dryer than ever, though any sympathetic observer could see that this was only a mask for the emotion underneath Then he rose before a hushed House and began to speak in a quiet voice as if already a detached spectator of the political scene In what was almost a series of bequests to his successors he commended the broad continuation of his Irish and commercial policies. He then made a brief reference to Hardinge's military successes in India and a longer one to Aberdeen's work as Foreign Secretary. This led him to the Oregon settlement which he explained in detail. Returning to the repeal of the Corn Laws he said it had been carried by a combination of parties, yet neither he nor the Whigs were really entitled to the credit for that measure. The name which ought to be associated with it was that of Richard Cobden. Then came the famous and controversial peroration. He would leave office, he said, censured by those who on public grounds valued party loyalty and party connection, censured by those who genuinely believed in the principles of protection, and execrated by every selfish monopolist.

But it may be that I shall leave a name sometimes remembered with expressions of goodwill in the abodes of those whose lot it is to labour, and to earn their daily bread by the sweat of their brow, when they shall recruit their exhausted strength with abundant and untaxed food, the sweeter because it is no longer leavened by a sense of injustice

He sat down; it was all over. As soon as the cheering stopped and the formalities of adjournment completed, he left by a side door to escape the crowds at the main entrance. Once in the street, however, he was immediately recognised. The hats came off and the spectators made a lane along which he passed to continuous cheering which did not cease until long after he entered his house.

IV

'No living soul could have done this but Peel,' wrote Hobhouse. It was a just compliment from one who rarely gave compliments in that quarter. The repeal of the Corn Laws was in a special sense Peel's personal achievement. Not only would it have been impossible without the alliance of Peelite Conservatives and Liberal Whigs in parliament; but without Peel's leadership and influence it could not even have been attempted. Once he had announced his decision, his immense prestige allowed him to dominate the national scene. One of the remarkable features of the repeal of the Corn Laws was that it took place with the Anti-Corn Law League standing by as almost silent spectators. Nobody in 1845 would have thought that possible; but Peel was able to enlist a body of support in the country which outweighed the League. The veteran free-trader Charles Villiers testified in June that 'no other Minister but Sir Robert Peel could have carried the repeal of the Corn Laws; that half the commercial men in the City would have been against it, had it been attempted by Lord John Russell or anyone else'.

Yet for all that, perhaps because of that, it was the most controversial act in the career of a man who almost seemed to invite controversy. At the time, and long afterwards, it was argued that repeal was unnecessary; that the Irish disaster was exaggerated; that Peel used it merely as a pretext. The facts of the Irish famine scarcely need recapitulation; it was the greatest social disaster experienced by any European state in the nineteenth century. There can be little doubt either of the genuineness of Peel's concern. Behind his reasoned arguments in cabinet and in parliament was an emotional force. 'Are you to hesitate in averting famine which may come, because it possibly may not come?' he broke out savagely once in the Commons. 'Or, Good God, are you to sit in cabinet, and consider and calculate how much diarrhoea, and bloody flux, and dysentery, a people can bear before it becomes necessary for you to provide them with food?' To Croker, who expressed cynical doubts about Peel's motives, Wellington made a remark which would have been arresting from anyone, and was doubly so from a man so hard and matter-of-fact as the duke. 'I cannot doubt', he wrote back, 'that which passed under my own view and frequent observation day after day. I mean the alarms of the consequences in Ireland of the potato disease. I never witnessed in any case such agony.'

It was true, as Goulburn and others pointed out, that the repeal of the Corn Laws would not in itself feed a single Irish peasant. The real question, however, was whether the government could embark on a great public relief operation and still keep the Corn Laws in force; or if they suspended them, whether they could ever be reimposed. Peel, and after his own fashion Lord John Russell, judged not. Politicians are often accused of acting at the last moment and under the pressure of events. But successful preventive action can always be criticised as unnecessary since it can never be proved what would have happened had the action not been taken. Yet some facts stand out. The Irish famine, as Peel and his advisers suspected, lasted some three years. Suspension of the Corn Laws would probably therefore have continued until 1849 or 1850. Meanwhile a general election would have come and gone; and during the whole of that period the Corn Laws would have been the target of incessant attack. The relative quiescence of the League in 1846 was only secured because Peel offered a final settlement. It would have been a different matter had he shown no sign of repealing as distinct from merely suspending the law.

Yet, when all the arguments are weighed, it is also true that for Peel the abolition of the Corn Laws had become only a question of time: the declaration of his inability to defend them a question of timing. It was this which is the real basis for the charge that he 'betrayed' his party. That word is perhaps misleading. Peel could claim with justice that in repealing the Corn Laws he was acting in the best interest of the landed gentry and that what he did was the most conservative action of his life. His followers could reasonably complain of desertion, but not of betrayal. He warned them, before and after taking office, that he would be guided only by his sense of national interest. Yet the fact remained that in the thirties he had defended the Corn Laws; in 1842 he had passed another, if lower, protective tariff. He had come into power at the head of a party based on the landed interest; and that party expected protection to continue. What he did in 1846 was to sacrifice both his own consistency and the views and interests of those who had put him into office. It was here that he showed little consideration and not much sympathy for his party. This was something which even his most loyal supporters found it hard to bear. The 'betrayal' was not merely of the protectionists but of the Peelites too. He not only alienated those who did not agree with him, but wrecked the political careers of some who did. In private relations Peel was loyal almost to a fault; but on public issues he was capable of the hardness without which perhaps no statesman can succeed.

The disruption of 1846 moreover was only the culmination of a growing divergence within the party. Given his underlying physical tiredness and the increasingly strained relationship with his followers, there could have been little value or attraction for him in the prolongation of his ministry. In such circumstances there must have been a powerful subconscious appeal in the prospect of one last memorable act with which to crown his five years of power. It was the achievement which mattered; not the price that had to be paid for it. Over almost a decade he had seen the Corn Laws grow into a bitter social issue. His own mind had hardened towards a solution and fate had thrown in his way a great and imperative opportunity for ending the conflict. His sense of timing, which was one of his superlative qualities as a politician, was still faultless. The striking feature of the repeal of the Corn Laws was the calmness and control with which it was carried through. Without a dissolution, without a general election, without a class struggle or threat of physical force, the issue was finally set at rest. The aristocratic constitution had shown its resilience and statesmanship; and in so doing had strengthened its claims to the confidence of the nation. It was this, in the last analysis, for which Peel had been working; and in which, at great personal cost, he had succeeded.

Chapter 21

Peelites, Whigs, and protectionists

'I do not know how other men are constituted,' wrote Peel to Aberdeen in the August following his resignation, 'but I can say with truth that I find the day too short for my present occupations, which chiefly consist in lounging in my library, directing improvements, riding with the boys and my daughter, and pitying Lord John and his colleagues.' It was a peaceful picture and to his friends the ex-prime minister made it excessively clear that he had no intention of returning to office or ever leading a party again. The savagery of protectionist attacks had even made him consider at one point retiring from parliament altogether. Though he had drawn back from that extreme decision, he was determined to maintain a completely independent position in future. The arguments of younger colleagues like Herbert and Gladstone that this would be impossible left him unmoved. Tiredness, pain and resentment all helped to create this stubborn mood. Writing to Graham on 3 July to thank him for his aid in their last successful campaign together, he said that he could not have gone on much longer. 'Few know what I have been suffering from noises and pains in the head.' Nevertheless, as the months passed his attitude showed no signs of softening. The following February he was still writing to the sympathetic Hardinge of his satisfaction in being able to enjoy not only the leisure of family life but also political independence and 'freedom from the base servitude to which a minister must submit who is content to sacrifice the interests of a great empire to those of a party'.

For the younger Peelites this was a daunting prospect and despite the studied neutrality of their chief they did what they could to keep his party in being. They at least agreed with Peel in not wanting an alliance with the Whigs. Lincoln, Herbert and Dalhousie had refused almost contemptuously invitations to join Russell's cabinet and in general Peel's followers were disposed to be more openly critical of the ministers than their reluctant leader. Nevertheless, when Goulburn explained at the end of the year their plans for organising what he called a party of observation, Peel was discouraging. Political adherents could not be kept together, he observed, merely from a highminded and disinterested desire to promote national interests. A party needed the stimulus of competition for place and power, and a determination to take every advantage of its opponents. 'As I am not prepared to enter into that competition, as from feelings I cannot control the necessity of resuming power would be perfectly odious to me, I am wholly disqualified for the reorganisation of a party.' And he flatly forbade the use of his name in the circulars they proposed to send out at the start of session.

Talk of 'Conservative reunion' had started almost before the Whigs were warm in office. Goulburn himself in the spring of 1847 tentatively raised the question of some communication on tactics between the two wings of the Conservative opposition. This suggestion had an even stonier reception from his chief. Though he did not wish to be an impediment, Peel replied on 3 April, he could not be a party to any attempt at reunion. Quite apart from disagreement on principle with the protectionists,

> it would be repugnant to my feelings and indeed inconsistent with my sense of Honour to enter into a Protectionist Confederacy with such of the leaders of that Party as during the last session of Parliament either openly preferred or covertly sanctioned accusations against me that were equally injurious to my Character and devoid of Truth.

It was something that he recognised how much his attitude was conditioned by a purely emotional reaction. But he still thought Goulburn optimistic and he still found it easy to conclude, when brooding over the history of his ministry, that the roots of disunity went back to a period long before 1845.

What was more important to Peel was the plight of the Whig administration still wallowing in the trough of the Irish famine, and the clear readiness of at least some of its members to look to him for assistance and advice. By May 1847 wheat had doubled in price since the previous summer and despite the surplus he had inherited from the Conservative government Charles Wood, the Whig Chancellor of the Exchequer, had to ask for a loan of £8 million to meet distress in Ireland. On this he had already taken private soundings with the former prime minister. After discreet overtures through John Young, the Peelite whip, and Edward Ellice, the Whigs' general man of business, Wood paid an inconspicuous visit to Peel in February to discuss a plan that had been put forward to raise the income tax to one shilling and extend it to Ireland. Peel assured him of his readiness to support the government in any bold attempt to meet the revenue deficit by direct taxation. But it was important, he emphasised, to be sure beforehand that they could carry their proposals. Since the income tax was due to expire in any case in 1848, he favoured a postponement of any new proposals until that year. His words could hardly have failed to carry weight; and no heroics were attempted when Wood brought forward his budget a fortnight later. Though he had no high opinion either of Russell's ability as prime minister or of his methods of famine relief, Peel did what he could in the Commons to defend the Whigs against criticism from both Radicals and protectionists.

The general election of 1847 did little to diminish the government's need for Peel's assistance. Though the nominal strength of the Liberal Party increased, many independent radical members were returned who disagreed with ministers on several crucial matters of policy. In a House of Commons with at least four discernible groupings, it was clear that the ministers would be able to count for regular support on less than half the total number of members. 'To no party except the extreme Radicals is there any real cause for triumph', was Bonham's comment on the result. Nevertheless, the Peelites had done well, maintaining their numbers at about ninety, with no losses of any consequence. Peel himself had received invitations to sit for North Lancashire, for the City, and for other large towns; but loyalty to his own constituency, and a prudent reluctance to abandon the freedom of Tamworth for the onerous responsibilities of a large constituency, made him deaf to all solicitation. His only personal contribution to the general election was a published *Letter to the Electors of Tamworth*, designed for a general audience rather than his loyal Staffordshire constituents, 'some of whom', he remarked lightly to Aberdeen, 'will, I fear, have hardly patience to read it through. I rather wished to have a decent opportunity for putting some things upon record.' But since the *Letter*, in addition to giving a concise explanation of his reasons for repealing the Corn Laws, also contained an unequivocal statement that he had no desire to return to office or lead a party, it afforded little encouragement or assistance to his followers.

Yet to others it seemed that the election had created a situation in which the ministers would either have to become more radical in their policies or rest uneasily on the casual support of Peelites and Protectionists. In either case Peel's position would be crucial. Victoria in September tried to elicit from Aberdeen some clear information on the state of the Commons and the strength of Peel's party. Aberdeen made the bleak reply that as the basis of party was either the possession or pursuit of office, and Peel was interested in neither, it could hardly be said that he had a party at all. This evidently surprised and discomfited the queen. Why it should, Peel wrote back, when he had lost no opportunity of saying to her exactly the same thing, he could not imagine. But, he added with a tartness that suggested a certain sensitivity on the subject, 'I suppose Sovereigns are equally incredulous as to the unwillingness of Laymen and Churchmen for preferment, and give no more credit to the professions of a retired minister than to the *nolo episcopari* of an aspiring Dean'.

The financial crisis in the autumn of 1847 could only have strengthened his conviction that the most useful part he could play in politics was to prop up the faltering Whig administration. At the height of the panic during the weekend of 22–23 October the Chancellor of the Exchequer descended on him in a series of hasty interviews to describe the situation and receive advice. At Windsor, where Peel had been invited for the weekend, with the assent of the ministers he explained the nature of the crisis to the uncomprehending Prince

Albert and wrote an impromptu memorandum for him on the technicalities of the Bank Charter Act and the extent to which the government wished to modify it. The official papers conveying the cabinet's final decision were shown to Peel at Russell's request while he was still at the Castle. In the parliamentary inquest which followed in November most of the discussions tended to revolve round the financial and commercial policy not of the Whigs but of the preceding administration, and Peel found himself in the peculiar position for an opposition member of virtually winding up the debate for the government. In this delicate role he achieved the ambidextrous feat of vindicating his 1844 act, approving its suspension by the cabinet, and supporting a commission of enquiry. The government was pleased; the crisis soon passed; and the more partisan controversy over the 1844 act was relegated, as the Whigs had hoped, to the safe obscurity of a select commission.

II

Gratifying as it was for his opinion to be sought in time of crisis, the confidential relationship established with Wood in 1847 could only have circumscribed still further Peel's parliamentary freedom of action. Even though he was disposed to think that in many respects the Whigs were not up to their work, this in itself was a reason for giving them his assistance, which in turn meant subordinating his own views to the overriding necessity for keeping the ministers in office. The session of 1848 demonstrated more forcefully than ever that Peel was rapidly becoming a captive of Whig policy. Faced with an industrial depression, the need for continued Irish famine relief, and higher service expenditure, the cabinet finally braced itself for an increase in the income tax from sevenpence to one shilling and its renewal for five years. The storm of opposition which this proposal encountered, however, made them retreat in the end to the safer ground of sevenpence for three years. In effect, what Russell attempted to do was to apply Peel's fiscal principles without Peel's political tact. When the budget was first introduced Peel expressed his opinion privately to Goulburn, Cardwell and Gladstone that had he been responsible, he would have absorbed the extraordinary expenses into the Exchequer, renewed the income tax at sevenpence, and pledged the government to bring expenditure into line with revenue. This in the end was exactly what the cabinet decided to do; and they must have known, through Graham and Greville, that it was Peel's advice.

In February and March, when the unhappy Wood was caught in a crossfire from Cobden and Disraeli, Peel came time and again to the government's rescue. Later in the session, when the Whigs tried to fulfil their pledge of repealing the Navigation Laws, he virtually took over the debate from Russell and cut the protectionist arguments of

Herries and Disraeli to ribbons. Even after he had departed to Drayton for the summer he was recalled by an urgent note from Charles Wood to help defeat a motion by Herries on the currency question. It was a degrading session for the Whigs. Russell's floundering exhibition on the budget and his notorious ill-health had even raised the possibility of his early retirement. Some ministers thought that if that happened Peel's return to office would be a national necessity. No encouragement came from either Peel or his closest associate Graham for that line of thought. Yet other circumstances seemed to point in the same direction. With the eviction of Bentinck from the titular leadership of the party in the winter of 1847 the protectionists seemed weaker and more disorganised than ever. A party patronised rather than led by Stanley, with a ducal nonentity, Lord Granby, as his lieutenant in the Commons, and its one man of talent distrusted and disliked, appeared to have neither present strength nor future prospects. At the start of the 1848 session there had even been tentative approaches to Goulburn, Graham, Gladstone and Lincoln by individual protectionists to discuss reunion.

Yet, as any observer of the parliamentary scene could see for himself, what divided Peelites from protectionists was not only policy but personalities. The old hatred of Peel was still alive among some of the country members. When he rose to speak in the Navigation Laws debate a section of the protectionist party exceeded even the normal inelegance of House of Commons manners by setting up a great hooting and bellowing in an effort to close the debate before he could be heard. Leaderless or not, moreover, the protectionists held together and on any issue where they could enlist support from other dissident groups they were capable of running the government close to defeat. The younger Peelites had no wish to enter into a permanent alliance with the protectionists, but they were growing restless at Peel's perpetual readiness to let Whig necessities take precedence over his private opinions. They did not think that the weak and blundering administration of Lord John Russell could continue much longer; and they calculated that the only possible successor would be a central coalition under Peel. If their reluctant leader needed to be impelled into office, they were ready to give him an unsolicited push. Over the Whig relief programme for the West Indies, for instance, which attracted criticism from all over the House, Gladstone, Herbert, Lincoln, Cardwell, even Goulburn, voted in support of a hostile protectionist amendment. With the help of a judicious speech by Peel, which may have helped to decide the votes of a few wavering Peelites, the government scraped through by fifteen votes; but it had been a near thing.

What the 1848 session demonstrated in fact was that firm government was almost impossible as long as the party system was dislocated; and that as long as Peel and the Peelites remained an incalculable floating element, the party system could not be repaired. What remained obscure was whether Peel could be induced to realise this. The continental revolutions of that year underlined the need for strength and stability at home; the efforts of Cobden and Bright to revive the old League as the basis of a new radical party held out the prospect of yet another fissure in the political system; and to these public considerations had been added one more marginal factor, the death of Bentinck in September. To both Goulburn and Bonham, who visited Drayton later that autumn, it seemed that there had been a slight softening of Peel's attitude, not so much from anything specific he said as from his general criticisms of the government and some friendly references to his former followers. But whatever Peel's thoughts were on a possible or even probable return to office, he kept them to himself. It was not obvious, in fact, that he had any ultimate views about his future. Everything he said and did indicated that he was content to assist the Whigs as long as they could provide an administration which protected the essentials of Peelite policy.

The unanswered, perhaps unanswerable, question was how long an administration could last that was so patently lacking in ideas, leadership and parliamentary strength. Russell's persistent efforts to recruit individual Peelites, culminating in his invitation to Graham in January 1849 to enter the cabinet as First Lord of the Admiralty, had all dispiritingly failed. The credibility of the Whig government had almost disappeared; more than ever they presented the appearance of a caretaker cabinet administering the country until they could be replaced by a more permanent political combination. As long as Wood was at the Exchequer there was some guarantee to Peel of financial orthodoxy but over Irish administration and foreign policy there were irreconcilable differences between Peelite and ministerial attitudes. There was hardly a feature of Russell's handling of the Irish situation, for example, which Peel wholeheartedly approved. In the enforcement of law and order he thought the Whigs too timid; in their larger policy too unimaginative. The political and economic paralysis caused by the famine provided in his view an unprecedented opportunity for carrying out fundamental reforms in Ireland which would have been unthinkable a few years earlier. He wanted land legislation on the lines recommended by the Devon Commission; and it was an open secret that on religious questions his mind had travelled far beyond Maynooth. At a house-party at Vernon Harcourt's home in Nuneham Courtenay in July 1848 he had talked freely of the need to make a final adjustment of the relations between the state and the Catholic Church. He told Sheil, the veteran Irish politician who was one of the guests, that what he favoured was direct endowment of the clergy by the government.

Though Russell clearly thought that as long as Ireland was peaceful it would be folly to raise controversial issues, Peel continued to urge the importance of taking the unique opportunity provided by the famine to introduce basic reforms. Something of what he had in mind emerged in a debate in March 1849. Starting with the proposition that the famine had not created but merely exposed the realities of the Irish situation, he argued that what was fundamentally wrong with Ireland was its social and economic structure. Government intervention and assistance would always be ineffective unless landed estates could be improved and until there was a shift from a subsistence potato economy to large-scale cattle and arable farming. Why, he asked, should they not appoint a government commission to assist distressed areas and take over encumbered and insolvent estates? Why should they not, he enquired even more daringly, make such a commission 'instrumental in forwarding the transfer of property from one class of proprietors to another'? What was done for the good of Ireland was in the end done for the good of Great Britain. 'It is in the growing conviction that its weakness will be our weakness, its disease our disease, that I see the faint hope of a decisive remedy.'

It was a speech of great courage and imagination; but the ideas it contained were a generation before their time. Nevertheless, Clarendon the Lord-Lieutenant, who was in London at the time, was sufficiently impressed to seek an interview with Peel the following week. Peel gave him a memorandum on his proposals but assured him that he would willingly abandon them if Clarendon would take up the question of encumbered estates himself. Even though the bill which Clarendon brought forward later in the session fell short of the policy which he advocated, he gave it support. Between Clarendon and Peel there proved to be a sympathy on the Irish problem which the Lord-Lieutenant was unable to detect among the grandees of his own party; and there was further consultation between the two men during the next few months. Though there seemed little likelihood of persuading Russell's cabinet to take up a programme of radical reform for Ireland, it was something that Peel could influence individual members of the administration.

Inevitably, therefore, the 1849 session saw no change in his steady determination to assist the government and damp down any threat of opposition from his own followers. His support was all the more valuable since the renewed depression in agriculture, coinciding with the legal expiry of the Corn Laws, provided the protectionists with both excuse and incentive to continue their attacks on the government's economic policy. One of these occasions, a debate in July on a motion by Disraeli for a committee on the state of the nation, enabled Peel to give one of the most comprehensive explanations of his free trade philosophy that the House of Commons had yet heard.

It is a question which affects the happiness of the people, which affects their social progress, their progress in morals, in the enjoyment of life, in refinement of taste and civilisation of manners—it concerns these things at least as much as it concerns the accumulation of wealth.

It was the confidence in parliament inspired by the repeal of the Corn

"The Drill" – Cabinet discipline (December 1845). Peel first dismisses and then recalls his squad. The Duke of Wellington is left-hand man in the front rank with corporals stripes and Waterloo medals. Stanley is seen breaking away from the rear ranks.

(Top) The room in which Sir Robert Peel died. (Bottom) The crowd waiting outside Peel's house in Whitehall Gardens, 30th June to 2nd July, 1850.

Laws, he went on to argue, which had contributed to the decline of Chartism and the absence in Britain of those revolutionary storms which had convulsed other European nations in 1848. A policy which had borne such fruits should not lightly be thrown away.

Disraeli's motion was defeated by 140 votes and a few weeks later the session ended. All the same the old problem of Whig political weakness and uncertainty of policy still remained. Between protectionist demands for agricultural concessions and radical demands for cheaper government, the ministers' path seemed as faltering as ever. With the coming of winter there was increasing talk in ministerial circles of a move to restore a fixed duty of five shillings on foreign corn. Ellice mentioned the possibility in a letter to Graham which could be interpreted as fishing for a reaction from the Peelites. Thinking that there could be no harm in dropping a warning shot across the cabinet's bows, Peel composed a letter for Graham, ostensibly private but designed to be shown to Ellice, who could be relied on to pass the contents to the ministry. In this, while professing a diplomatic disbelief that Russell would go back on a policy to which he had so often pledged himself, Peel spoke in significant terms of the 'fearful struggle' and 'disastrous' consequences of any attempt to reimpose duties on food. The cabinet were clearly conscious of a sudden cold draught of Peelite distrust. A friendly letter from Russell's elder brother, the Duke of Bedford, in November allowed Peel to speak out freely on the danger of any move, under any pretext, to revive protectionism. Bedford's reassuring reply, quoting an extract from a recent letter from Russell, convinced even the sceptical Graham. A few days later, Charles Wood, meeting Peel's son-in-law Villiers by accident on a train journey, pointedly said to him, 'Tell Sir Robert that we had six cabinets and the Corn Laws never once mentioned in any of them.'

Even among the Peelites agriculture was a potent source of division. Of the eighty or ninety men who nominally followed Peel, many represented rural constituencies, many had agricultural connections, many had ties of sympathy with the other half of the old Conservative Party. The farming depression made some of them look with favour on protectionist schemes for agricultural compensation who would have rejected a crude return to a corn tariff. Disraeli, fishing for support in any quarter that could be turned against the government, was not blind to the possibilities of this situation. A motion he put forward on relief for agriculture early in 1850 attracted thirty-five Peelite votes as against the twenty-eight headed by Peel who narrowly saved the ministry from defeat. To John Young, the Peelite whip who had himself parted company from his leader on the issue, it seemed that this sort of disagreement could not go on indefinitely. In a strongly worded letter written the next day he pointed out to Peel that the Peelites as a body had no confidence in the Whig government. Probably as many as 160 M.P.s would be found to rally round Peel personally, but they would not go on night after night, session after session, risking their seats in order to keep in office those whom they regarded as political opponents. If a protectionist administration was to be avoided and Peel's commercial policy given fair play over the next few years, Peel would have to provide the lead himself. It was the sharpest warning Peel had yet received that if he did not take the initiative, a solution of a more unwelcome sort might emerge from sheer pressure of political forces. Young may have exaggerated the weakness of the government and the strength of the potential support for Peel, but his fundamental diagnosis was clearly right.

The situation was the more dangerous since the 1850 session brought into the open the long-standing discontent with Palmerston's handling of foreign policy that was felt by Peelites of all shades of opinion. To Aberdeen and Peel, as to many other British politicians, it seemed that Palmerston, by his encouragement of democratic nationalism abroad, was deliberately increasing the tension in a Europe which after the 1848 revolutions was facing an era of both internal and external strain. Their dislike of Palmerston was embittered by his popularity with the radicals and the widespread conviction that his colleagues only put up with his bellicose behaviour because they were afraid of the trouble he would cause them if he were dismissed. Though Peel had been extremely circumspect in his public comments on foreign affairs, he was well aware of the strong feeling against Palmerston at Court and in the House of Lords. He shared the common opinion that Palmerston was the one positively harmful and dangerous element in the government. Where he differed was in his view that Palmerston's iniquities were not enough to justify overthrowing the whole Whig administration. Early in 1850 the campaign against Palmerston blazed up once more with the anti-Russian naval demonstration in the Dardanelles and the British blockade of the Piraeus in pursuit of the dubious claims against the Greek government of the somewhat disreputable British subject Don Pacifico. But though Peel expressed himself strongly in private about the Greek incident and the naval insult to Russia, which he thought even more irresponsible, he sharply rebuffed pressure from Aberdeen to join in a formal parliamentary attack. Action of that nature, he replied, suited neither his isolated position in politics nor his view of the political consequences of forcing the government into resignation. If he had to choose between a concerted party attack on the Whigs and retirement from political life, he added ominously, he knew what he would do.

Events, however, were not to be stayed by private argument between senior members of the Peelite connection. When in June the successful censure motion by Stanley and Aberdeen in the House of Lords was answered in the Commons by Roebuck's motion of sweeping approval for Palmerston's foreign policy, Peel reluctantly concluded that it was impossible for him to keep silence any longer. He had not sought a challenge but being challenged, he could not with self-respect evade the issue. In a grand parliamentary set-piece there was little likelihood that the government would be defeated; the only question was the size of the majority. In the event the four-day debate at the end of June was a parliamentary triumph for Palmerston; even oratorically he took the honours with his great *civis Romanus sum* speech on the second night. Peel spoke on the last evening. It was the speech of an elder statesman: quiet, reflective, unpartisan, not designed to win votes but the more impressive because of its restraint. He repudiated any desire to overthrow the ministry or condemn its general conduct of affairs. But when asked whether the foreign policy they had pursued was best calculated to maintain the honour of Britain and peace with other countries, he felt bound to express his opinion that the great and costly engine of diplomacy devised by civilised nations to prevent war had been perverted into a source of irritation and hostility. He abstained from any controversy on the various matters raised by Palmerston 'in that most able and most temperate speech, which made us proud of the man who delivered it'. But he took issue with Roebuck's argument that the moral influence of Britain must be used to support any men, anywhere in the world, who were struggling to achieve self-government against their legitimate rulers. The classic policy of Britain, he reminded the House, was one of non-intervention in the affairs of other countries. No lasting good could come from attempts to dictate to other nations. 'Constitutional liberty will be best worked out by those who aspire to freedom by their own efforts.'

As he left the chamber to walk home in the early dawn of 29 June Peel was a tired but contented man. He had been able to speak his mind, but the government was still safe. One M.P. who saw him moving up Whitehall observed that he must be one of the happiest men in England, having voted with his party and yet in accordance with his own feelings and opinions. It was an irony of history that Peel's last act in the House of Commons was to go into the lobby with a united Conservative opposition.

Chapter 22

Peel and his contemporaries

Peel in his prime was one of the more conspicuous members of the House of Commons. Even apart from his air of authority and the deference with which he was treated, his physical appearance was striking: the big figure in the long blue frockcoat, white waistcoat and drab trousers, the florid complexion and legs which always seemed slightly out of proportion to the rest of his body. One of the first things strangers noticed was his peculiar gait—his 'two left legs' as O'Connell satirised it—the stately forward movement, the arms hanging down, the feet almost sliding over the floor. Next people noticed the broad countenance, the curved nose and intelligent blue eyes. When not abstracted in thought his look was direct and expressive, sometimes beaming with humour but equally capable of cold austerity. He was fastidious over his personal appearance and was one of the best dressed men in public life. The ample white waistcoat was usually adorned with a gold chain and bunch of seals with which he would play as he leaned back with legs crossed and hat tipped over his eyes listening to debates in the House. When he spoke he usually began quietly, with his hands clasped behind him. Then, as he warmed to his theme, he would lean his left hand upon the table and point an admonitory finger at his critics. During significant passages in his speech he would thump the box in front of him at regular intervals. When he made some deft sally or party point, he would turn and look at his supporters for the expected laughter and cheers.

As a speaker he had the asset of a strong, flexible voice. He could range from soft persuasiveness to sonorous defiance, from sly banter to grave solemnity. Though, like most of his contemporaries, he had some provincialisms of accent, he was clear and precise in his diction. Temperamentally unfitted for oratory in the grand manner, he had no gift for the sublime passage or polished phrase. What he had done was to weld his voice and intellect into a superb instrument for work in the House of Commons. He never forgot that the purpose of speaking was not to delight posterity or the readers of morning newspapers but to make an immediate effect on the men around him. For this what was essential was knowledge of the business in hand, ability to seize on weaknesses in the opposing case, skill in marshalling every argument in support of his own, and an awareness of the interests and prejudices of his audience. The House of Commons had dozens of members who, given due notice, could come down and deliver a glittering speech on a set theme. But these isolated displays of verbal brilliance were of little parliamentary value compared with Peel's professional qualities: the sense of the ebb and flow of debate, the retentive memory, the practised skill in incorporating new matter into a prepared speech, the timing and choice of argument. At his best there were few people who could influence the House as expertly as Peel could in the period after 1832. Lord John Russell once said that the three best parliamentary speakers he had ever known were Plunket, Canning and Peel. Plunket was the most persuasive, Canning the most charming, and Peel the most formidable in debate.

In advancing his views it was as though he were addressing himself to the neutral and waverers. Measured and reasonable in his arguments he was rarely aggressive, never ungenerous. He appealed to the minds of his audience rather than their hearts. His aim was to convince rather than to captivate; his method a process of intellectual proof. A characteristic speech would begin with a definition of the issues involved, followed by an enunciation of the various actions open to the House. Each would be analysed and discarded until only one remained. He was himself aware of the extent to which this had become a Peelite gambit. 'I have more than once excited a smile', he confessed good-naturedly in a debate in 1847, 'when as first minister of the Crown I have said that there were three courses which it was open to me to adopt.' This technique of proof by elimination had the advantage of bringing all aspects and arguments under consideration, forestalling subsequent speakers, and seeming to point to one irresistible conclusion. Peel was one of the best special pleaders in parliamentary history. To his opponents he had no equal in the gentle art of dressing up a case. Had he been at the Bar, G. C. Lewis once observed, he would have got more verdicts than Scarlett, the greatest professional advocate of the day.

If he rarely entranced, he usually interested his audience and though he hardly ever attempted elaborate witticisms or ironies, he began about 1828, with growing confidence in his mastery of the House, to display a taste for quiet fun. Peel's humour was of the mild variety which consists in goodnatured amusement at the foibles of others and a conscious enjoyment of an occasional verbal pleasantry. To his family and friends this development came as no surprise. From an early age he had a quizzical eye for the absurdities of human nature; and residence in Ireland had provided him with an inexhaustible fund of anecdotes with which in later life when in the mood he would delight an intimate circle. This characteristic he preserved to the end of his life. Carlyle left a description of him at a dinner in 1848 when he sat next to the great man.

He is towards sixty and, though not broken at all, carries especially in his complexion, when you are *near* him, marks of that age: clear, strong blue eyes which kindle on occasions, voice extremely good, low-toned, something of *cooing* in it, rustic, affectionate, honest, mildly persuasive. . . . Reserved seemingly by nature, obtrudes nothing of *diplomatic* reserve. On the contrary, a vein of mild fun in him, real sensibility to the ludicrous, which feature I liked best of all.

Not everyone encountered this lighter side to Peel's nature, however, particularly on first acquaintance.

In large assemblies he was apt by his reticence and formality to confirm his reputation for coldness. At Drayton, during the autumn round of parties, it was a matter of common observation how Peel became more talkative whenever the guests diminished to a small circle of old friends and grew more impersonal and ceremonious when the company was swelled by strangers. This reserve which often went further than he realised, was the result partly of shyness, partly of an innate distaste for saying more than he felt or believed. Gladstone noted Peel's strict use of words, even in small matters. He would not, for example, tell a colleague he had found a paper valuable unless he had really done so. Years of official life, acting on a temperament that was naturally self-conscious, made it easier for Peel to deal with problems rather than people. Even when giving his attention to others, his mental absorption could easily be misunderstood. Hawes, the Radical M.P., once went to him with a request from a committee of which he was chairman. When he had finished stating his case, Peel gazed at him without uttering a word. Finally Hawes, growing embarrassed, picked up his hat and apologised stiffly for having taken too great a liberty in coming to him. At that Peel started up and exclaimed 'Good gracious, you are quite mistaken. I was only thinking how best I could comply with your request.' And he added a disarming remark about his unfortunate manner which so often gave the wrong impression.

In contrast to this were his friendly relations with some of his younger followers. They included not only Lincoln, Herbert, Eliot, Cardwell and Gladstone, but lesser figures like George Smythe and William Gregory, the grandson of Peel's old Irish under-secretary. Gregory, who entered the Commons in 1842 at the age of twenty-five, was at once taken up by Peel who introduced him to the Speaker and gave him the run of his house in Whitehall Gardens. If the prime minister was busy, he would silently raise a hand and his young visitor would close the door again. If not, he would call Gregory in for a chat, discuss the political news, and frequently end with some racy story 'which he told', recounted Gregory, 'extremely well and with fits of laughter'. With Lincoln and Herbert his relations were even closer. For Lincoln, estranged from his stiff, melancholy father, he almost took the place of a parent, watching over his political career and advising him on the unhappy personal problems caused by his wife's adultery. Writing to Lincoln after Peel's death Herbert recalled that the very last time he had been with Peel, they had been talking about Lincoln and his affairs, 'and he gave the attention and the anxious advice which a Father would have given for a son. God knows, we two owe him much.'

The kindness that was one of Peel's basic characteristics came out in other ways. In the fact, for example, that with few exceptions he never bore a grudge against past opponents and in his practical sympathy with misfortune and unhappiness. When Maginn, an Irish Tory journalist who had virulently attacked him over Catholic emancipation, fell on evil days, Peel anonymously subscribed £100 to a fund raised on his behalf. When Sydney Smith, who had lampooned him on many occasions, self-consciously refused an invitation to dinner in 1842, Peel got one of their common friends to overcome his resistance and greeted him on arrival with unusual warmth. Macaulay, whose studied personal attacks on Peel during his last ministry were second only to those of Disraeli, found himself getting on wonderfully well with Peel on the Board of the British Museum four years later. Their acquaintance ripened and in June 1850 he dined at Peel's house. 'How odd!' he reflected in his diary. Before the end of his life Peel was reconciled even with the man whom he had challenged to a duel in 1837, Captain Townshend. Writing to Lady Peel in 1850 Townshend expressed his thankfulness that all past differences had been buried before her husband's death. 'Of this I am amply satisfied by the kind— the more than kind—manner in which both you and he received me. *There was much to be forgiven.*' To the importunate, egoistic, debt-ridden painter Haydon he showed a tolerance, sympathy and practical generosity that did not diminish throughout the long years of their sometimes difficult acquaintanceship. Obstinate and cantankerous as Haydon often was, even he in his more candid moments could admit that Peel 'had a tender heart' and had shown patience and kindness in the face of the 'bitter things' Haydon had often said to him. At the height of the savage Canning controversy in June 1846 Peel found time to answer Haydon's last, despairing appeal for financial assistance and almost his last act as prime minister was to grant a pension to his widow.

II

There were other acquaintances of a more elevated nature than poor, suicidal Haydon. Loss of office did not bring to end, for example, Peel's close friendship with the royal couple. He was a frequent visitor at Windsor and Buckingham Palace; and the flattering attention paid to him by Victoria and Albert left spectators in no doubt as to his continuing popularity at court. Albert indeed could almost be included in Peel's band of young men as far as affection and deference were concerned. 'He feels', wrote Victoria when Peel died, 'he has lost a second father.' Sometimes this filial deference had been excessive. Having talked freely with Albert in the spring of 1846 on the danger for the monarchy of getting involved in religious questions, the prime

minister was taken aback to be presented a few days later with a voluminous Albertine memorandum recording everything he had said.
He told the prince that he had done what he often did in cabinet: that
was to say, advance various lines of argument to ensure that all aspects
of the problem were taken into consideration. But he could not, he
added seriously, allow this record of his uninhibited conversation to
stand as a formal statement of his opinions, especially as it might look
as if he had tried to dissuade the queen from a policy which his successors might recommend to her. At this, to Peel's obvious relief,
Albert threw the offending document on the fire. In its place the
prince fell back on the blameless reading-list in constitutional history
which Peel had prepared for him: pamphlets, parliamentary debates, a
chapter of Blackstone, and an extract from a letter of Burke's, the whole
of which, Peel added encouragingly, was well worth perusal, 'as indeed
is every line which Mr Burke ever wrote on any subject'.

After his resignation the only other embarrassing incident that
occurred between them was when Albert sent him a paper on the state
of parties resulting from the general election of 1847 and asked for his
comments. Peel evaded the direct question and confined himself to a
largely retrospective account of his relations with the Conservative
Party and some general comments on the likely future development of
British politics. What his reply did reveal, however, was his own
attitude to the disruption of 1846. It was a bleak, unforgiving analysis.
Though the Conservative Party had been born in the reconstruction
of politics after 1832, he wrote, 'the seeds of its final Dissolution were
probably sown at its Birth'. It had gathered strength because of the
wisdom and moderation with which it at first behaved; but once it had
attained power it began to resent control and in both civil and religious
matters tended to revert to principles which were incompatible with
the changed political situation created by the Reform Act. Even before
1841 he had often experienced great difficulty in imposing his leadership without creating an open conflict. But, he added defiantly,

> I made as few Concessions to Party as it was possible to make,
> consistently with the maintenance of Party Connection, and how-
> ever much I have been blamed for not showing more deference to
> a great Party, and for not acting more steadily on Party Principles,
> all I have to regret is that I shewed so much.

As for the future, he continued, there were certainly signs of growing
democratic tendencies in some of the larger towns and the next great
popular movement would probably be for parliamentary reform. But
only a very stupid protectionist could fail to see that the repeal of the
Corn Laws had removed the one immediate issue on which such a
campaign could be launched. What he hoped, he concluded optimistically, was that the demagogues would weaken themselves by
internal dissensions and that 'the quiet good sense and good feeling' of

the country would sustain the executive government in demonstrating that the best way of carrying on the business of the country and making rational improvements was to follow 'less turbulent, less noisy but more sagacious Leaders'.

The subject on which the prince more frequently sought and more readily obtained Peel's advice was foreign policy. This for Peel was a more congenial because less partisan aspect of politics. The issue of the Spanish marriages in particular drew together Englishmen of all shades of opinion. In the autumn of 1846 the British government was officially informed that simultaneous marriages would take place between Queen Isabella and the reputedly impotent Duke of Cadiz, and between her sister and the duc de Montpensier, younger son of Louis Philippe. Public opinion in Britain, shared by both Peel and the royal couple, was shocked at the news. At Albert's request Peel undertook a prolonged historical investigation into the legal aspect of the affair, beginning with the Treaty of Utrecht in 1713 and the renunciation by Philip V for himself and his successors of the crown of France. Though in the end Peel had to confess that 'the whole transaction is to me unintelligible', his views were sought by many parties to the dispute, including Albert, Palmerston, Aberdeen and Guizot. His advice, however, brought little comfort to Windsor. While he agreed that the simultaneous marriages represented a clear breach of faith on the part of the French government, he counselled protest only against the manner and not the matter of the double ceremony. It would be dangerous, he suggested, to take any formal stand which might preclude a future British government from recognising a possible succession to the Spanish throne of a Montpensier claimant. Some of Palmerston's despatches on the subject, shown to him privately, were in his opinion unnecessarily angry; but he observed the constitutional proprieties by refraining from comment except on factual matters. Apart from Aberdeen, no one knew of his correspondence with the Palace on the subject.

The revolutions of 1848, which destroyed the dynastic schemes of the Orléans family, also ended the brief honeymoon of sympathy between Windsor and the Foreign Office. Though Albert grew increasingly alarmed and despondent at Palmerston's headstrong foreign policy, it was impossible for Peel to be more than a sympathetic but discreet listener to the prince's complaints. Fortunately there were less controversial matters on which he could act as friend and counsellor. He strongly advised the prince to accept an invitation to stand for the Chancellorship of Cambridge University in 1847 and when the contested election only yielded Albert a narrow and unsatisfactory victory, drew up a cogent memorandum listing six reasons why the prince should swallow his pride and accept office. When less than six months later the industrious Albert took up the thorny question of educational reform at Cambridge, Peel gave him both encouragement and practical advice on the best way to proceed. On his side Peel was drawn into the project for holding a great national trade exhibition which the prince, as President of the Society of Arts, brought forward in 1849. Indeed he ultimately became one of the more active members of the royal commission appointed in 1850 to superintend the execution of the project. His support in parliament seemed to the prince so essential to the success of the project that his first thought on hearing of Peel's death was that it might have to be abandoned.

One of Peel's many services to the Great Exhibition of 1851 which he never lived to see was to enlist the aid of Lyon Playfair, the famous chemist. His relationship with Playfair was an example, in fact, of his general encouragement of the small but growing band of scientists and technologists who were beginning to make their mark on early-Victorian society. Of all the leading politicians of the period Peel was probably most sympathetic to the progress of scientific thought. It was this which brought him in 1848 the offer of the presidency of the Royal Society, an honour he declined on the ground that it should be confined to professional scientists. It was on the advice of scientific friends that he had persuaded Playfair not to leave Britain in 1842 to take up a chair in Toronto. He appointed him the following year to the commission on large towns, and when that employment came to an end found another post for him in the government geological survey. He also frequently invited him down to the scientific parties which were becoming a feature of Drayton hospitality. Along with men like Buckland the geologist, Stephenson the railway engineer, Smith of Deanston the agricultural drainage expert, and Wheatstone the physicist, Playfair was a regular member of the panel of speakers whom Peel organised at various times between 1842 and 1850 to preach the virtues and expound the techniques of scientific farming to his tenants.

Peel's interest in agricultural reform was longstanding. As far back as 1836 he had warned the House of Commons that agricultural-ists must look to self-improvement rather than external aid and argued that unless farmers made their land more productive they would never be able to compete with the products of virgin territories overseas which steamships were beginning to bring into the world markets. He was an original member of the Royal Agricultural Society founded in 1838, and after the passage of the Corn Law of 1842 did all he could to spread the doctrine of scientific farming on which he believed the future of British agriculture depended. His correspondence with political friends like Arbuthnot and Graham often strayed into such rural topics as turnips, fertilisers, and stock-breeding; and they in turn sometimes acted for him in the purchase of pedigree bulls and heifers from Scotland and the north of England. One of his special interests was drainage, perhaps the greatest need of contemporary British agriculture for both arable and pasture land. With the advice of Smith of Deanston and Josiah Parkes, the consulting engineer of the Royal Agricultural Society, Peel embarked from 1844 onwards on a large drainage scheme for his own estates which absorbed a great deal of his private budget. Before the end of his life he had made himself one of the model landlords of his time. By 1850 most of his draining schemes had been completed, in some cases with spectacularly profitable results. A survey undertaken in that year by the agricultural expert James Caird on behalf of *The Times* singled out the Peel property as an outstanding example of enlightened farming policy. From other witnesses, with no reason for partiality, came similar testimony. The League journalist, Somerville, writing under the pseudonym of the 'Whistler at the Plough', interviewed cottagers at Drayton in 1844 and confirmed Peel's reputation as a humane and generous landlord.

III

In 1848, when revolutions swept over Europe from the Pyrenees to the Carpathians, Britain presented a spectacle of order and tranquillity. The contrast, underlined by the fiasco of the Chartist demonstration in April, made many Englishmen ponder on the reasons for their immunity. Peel, calling at the French Embassy to offer his condolences on the collapse of the Orléans monarchy, interrogated Jarnac, the *chargé d'affaires*, on the real nature of the Paris uprising. When he took his leave he observed pensively that Louis Philippe and Guizot had been in a position not dissimilar to his own in 1846. They had the choice of either parting with their most devoted political supporters or facing revolution. The course he himself had taken had been painful but he still believed it to have been the right one.

Jarnac, like Guizot, knew Peel well and had even been invited to Drayton. Both had talked over the problems of their times with their host and both were left with the enduring impression that Peel's fundamental concern as a statesman was with the social condition of England. 'What struck me above all in the conversation of Sir Robert Peel', wrote Guizot later, 'was his constant and passionate pre-occupation with the state of the working classes in England.' To Guizot he described them as 'a disgrace as well as a danger to our civilisation'. The younger and more imaginative Jarnac recalled many years afterwards in more romantic language a similar impression. Sitting after dinner one day at Peel's house in Whitehall Gardens, they began to talk about the troubled internal state of France. Peel asked Jarnac about the writings of the French socialist, Louis Blanc, which he had obviously read very carefully, and cross-examined the young French-man about the extent of their influence. Jarnac expressed the opti-mistic belief that such protests against the inevitable conditions of modern society could never have much success in a nation as intelligent as the French. Peel was unconvinced; he put it to Jarnac that such writings had to be judged by their influence not on the wealthy and educated but on the countless masses born to toil, ignorance and undeserved suffering. In their uneducated minds and cankered hearts what upheaval might not be produced by such appeals to their hopes, their greed and their vengeance? The old fabric of Europe was undermined and he could not feel that even England was safe. Who was to measure the envy, resentment and revolutionary feelings at work below the splendid surface of their civilisation? To the startled French diplomat these were new and disturbing questions. But there was no mistaking the seriousness with which his host had put them. 'I understood then for the first time both the precipitate abolition of the Corn Laws and the dominant characteristic of Sir Robert Peel's peculiar genius.'

Not all Peel's after-dinner conversations, however, turned on such uncomfortable topics. Freedom from office allowed him leisure for the lighter side of life. Besides entertaining at Drayton and being guest at other country house parties which enlivened the parliamentary vacation, he was constantly seen on public and private occasions in London during the season, breakfasting with Hallam the historian, for example, and arguing with Mahon and Macaulay on points of classical history, or attending the private viewing days at the Royal Academy. He still kept up his interest in painting, involving himself in the controversy over cleaning old canvasses that agitated the National Gallery in 1847, assisting in the choice of pictures for the Royal Gallery, and adding to his own collection. From 1841 he was commissioning portraits of colleagues like Graham, Stanley, Hardinge and Gladstone and by 1844 was building an extension of the gallery at Drayton to house them. He himself submitted less readily to the artist's brush. He sat at the queen's request for the Winterhalter painting of himself and the Duke of Wellington in 1844. Otherwise he refused to lend himself for any more likenesses, influenced possibly by his disappointment at Linnell's poorish portrait of 1838. Critics in general agreed that though Winterhalter had caught Peel's superficial expression and attitude, his best portrait remained the one which Lawrence had painted in 1825. What the *Examiner* unflatteringly called the 'portly fullness of person' which Peel had in later life was missing, but Lawrence had captured, as no other painter had done, a suggestion of the amused and amusing side of Peel which was an essential part of the man. For the actual appearance of Peel in the 1830s and 1840s, as he was seen daily walking between Whitehall and Westminster, the most lifelike impression was recorded not in any painting but in the innumerable sketches by the cartoonist H.B.

The mixture of pride and self-consciousness which deterred Peel from exposing himself to brush and canvas, operated even more puritanically in the matter of personal awards. Other than the Privy Councillorship that inevitably came with high office, he accepted no political mark of distinction from the Crown throughout his long career. In a sensible, persuasive letter Wellington asked Peel in October 1842 to allow him to propose to the queen the award of the

Garter, instancing the precedents of Walpole, North and Castlereagh. Peel replied courteously that his letter was more gratifying than the distinction could ever be. 'So far as private feelings are concerned, I do not desire the Garter. I might indeed say, with perfect truth, I would rather not have it.' How strongly he felt on the point was shown by the note he left behind at his death, desiring that no member of his family should accept any reward or title on behalf of his own services in public life. What from pride he rejected for himself, on public principle he distributed only sparingly to others. In his five years as prime minister he created only five peerages, a record of parsimony unequalled before or since. With baronetcies he was only a shade less frugal. 'There would not be a simple squire in the land,' he observed dryly to Graham in 1841, 'if the fever for honours were not checked'; and to Richard Monckton Milnes, who sought that honour for his father, he replied discouragingly, 'I advise him to retain the distinction of not being a Baronet'. In his civil awards the outstanding feature was his disinterested promotion of the arts and sciences. Wordsworth was given a pension in 1842; Tennyson one in 1845. Among the scientists Forbes the physicist, Richard Owen the naturalist, Robert Brown the botanist, William Hamilton the astronomer, and J. Curtis the agricultural entomologist, all had their researches assisted by a judicious grant of pensions.

Though in his awards to scientists Peel took advice from the leaders of the profession, his literary pensions were backed by his own knowledge and taste. He was surprisingly well read in the lighter literature of the day. Tennyson's works he knew well enough by 1845 to have formed a high opinion of them; and he told the poet Hood in 1844 that there was little he had written which Peel had not read. It had become his habit when returning from the Commons at night to read for a short time before going to bed to ease his mind from the distractions and irritations of the day; and his London library had the miscellaneous character that marks the omnivorous reader rather than the bibliophile. Literature apart, his bookshelves revealed a man interested in the practical side of life—history, law, administration, economics, and science—rather than philosophy or religion. Even literature mainly impressed him for the mirror it held up to life. Shakespeare he admired less for the poetry of the language than for his 'lessons of practical wisdom'. Among the political writers his ideal, not surprisingly, was Burke—'that illustrious man who in comprehensive and philosophical views of all public affairs, and of the great principles of social government, surpassed all the statesmen who preceded him, or have followed'.

This practical outlook explains Peel's love of history, a subject in which he was more knowledgeable than commonly supposed. His interest in the French Revolution is well known; there were more than two hundred volumes at Whitehall Gardens on that subject alone. But his correspondence with Mahon in 1833 on the latter's *History of the Reign of George I* showed that he was well acquainted, for example, with British eighteenth-century politics and personalities. Mahon was so impressed with his acute observations on Walpole that he sent him the draft character sketch he intended for his *History*. In his long critical reply Peel effectively quoted against the young historian such authorities as Pulteney, Bishop Newton, Hardwicke, Onslow and Coxe. Intellectually, moreover, his assessment of Walpole was in another class to the conventional rhetoric of condemnation which Mahon had inserted in his draft. Perhaps even at that midway point in his career Peel felt an affinity with the great eighteenth-century statesman.

> There must surely have been something very extraordinary [he wrote to Mahon] in the character and powers of that man who, being the son of a private gentleman, without any advantage from a distinguished name, or services of illustrious ancestors, was Prime Minister of England amid great public difficulties for a period of twenty years. . . . Of what public man can it be said with any assurance of certainty that, placed in the situation of Walpole, he would in the course of an administration of twenty years have committed so few errors, and would have left at the close of it the House of Hanover in equal security, and the finances in equal order?

Whatever comparisons may be made between Walpole and Peel, it is difficult to escape the impression that Peel had a keener interest in the great domestic minister of the first two Georges than in Pitt, the conventional idol of the Tory party. His innate sympathy, born of professional understanding, is in illuminating contrast to the superficial literary portrait drawn a few years later by Disraeli of the 'Venetian oligarchy' which ruled England in the eighteenth-century.

He used the leisure of retirement, moreover, to make a contribution to the record of his own times. He was the last person to write personal memoirs; but the same qualities which saved him from the vanity of autobiography impelled him with almost painful self-consciousness to set down a justificatory account of the two great controversial episodes of his career—Catholic emancipation in 1829 and the repeal of the Corn Laws in 1846. Though he provided a connecting commentary, the bulk of both papers was made up of contemporary letters and memoranda. It was an appeal from politics to history; and the evidence was assembled with as much integrity as any man can bring to his own case. Though the material was necessarily a selection, nothing remained in his correspondence, or indeed in any other collection, to contradict or modify on any essential point the account he gave. In 1849 he added a codicil to his will, designating Cardwell and Mahon as his literary executors; and in private he indicated to them a wish that they should after his death publish these two papers.

The completion of his memoirs and the codicil of 1849 was a curiously valedictory act for a man who had only just completed his sixty-first year, whose health was good, and whose ultimate return to office was thought to be inevitable. But Peel in 1849 was in a nostalgic mood. In August he, Julia, and their youngest daughter Eliza went up to the Highlands where Peel had rented a house from Lord Lovat called Eileann Aigas: a picturesque stonebuilt residence romantically situated on a rocky island in the River Beauly about fifteen miles west of Inverness. Despite the dull weather which greeted them, Peel was deeply attracted by their island eyrie, perched on a rocky, birch-covered cliff, and accessible only by a winding track through the woods and a single timber bridge spanning the torrent beneath a foaming cataract. The game was sparse but his interest in shooting had waned in recent years and he was more than content to while away his days in that lovely, lonely countryside, far from the haunts of tourists and the gossip of politicians. With September the weather set fine and they lingered on in the tranquillity and sunshine as though loth to fix a date for their departure. Lady Peel wrote to Bonham that she had never seen her husband so happy. Not until nearly the middle of October did they finally leave, calling on Aberdeen and Graham on the way back. In writing to Aberdeen to thank him for his hospitality Peel spoke with unusual affection of his Scottish visit. 'I am sure that there is no one, not a Scotchman, who feels a stronger attachment to that country than I do. I know not exactly why and on that very account, the attachment is sincere and lasting.' Then he added an odd sentence. 'It would be painful for me to think, what is very probable, that I shall never see the Highlands again.'

Epilogue

On Saturday 29 June 1850, the day following the great Don Pacifico debate, Peel rose after a short night to attend a meeting of the Commission on the 1851 Exhibition at eleven. Returning home in the afternoon he worked for a short time in his study and then went out for his customary ride at about five. His horse was a recent acquisition, purchased at Tattersalls the previous April by a friend, Becket Denison, who had ridden it in the London traffic for a time before recommending it to Peel. Lord Villiers had also tried the horse and thought it suitable for his father-in-law. Only afterwards did it transpire that it had been discarded by Sir Henry Peyton, one of the best riders of the day, because of its trick of kicking and bucking, and sent to Tattersalls for disposal. Peel's own coachman had doubts about the animal and advised him not to ride it; but Peel found it hard to disbelieve Denison's assurances and had ridden the horse regularly for about eight weeks without incident.

At the top of Constitution Hill, within sight of St George's Hospital, he met two daughters of Lady Dover, escorted by a groom on a rather skittish horse. He had barely exchanged greetings before his own horse began to plunge and rear. It then swerved violently and threw Peel over its head. He fell face downward still holding the reins and the horse stumbled on top of him, striking his back with its knees. In the light of what was later discovered, this second impact was probably critical. Bystanders ran to his assistance and aid was summoned from St George's Hospital. Dr Foucart, a Glasgow surgeon who saw the accident, came up and was presently joined by Sir James Clark, the royal physician. In great pain and almost unconscious Peel was lifted into a carriage and taken back to Whitehall Gardens where Julia and the other members of the family were anxiously waiting. When they arrived he recovered consciousness and walked with assistance to the front door. Then, overcome by the pain of the effort, he fainted once more. They carried him into the dining-room on the ground-floor and placed him on a sofa. There, in front of the tall windows overlooking the Thames, the muted activity of the sickroom began.

A distinguished company of medical men quickly assembled: Hodgson, Peel's family doctor, Sir Benjamin Brodie, the leading surgeon of the day, Dr Seymour and Mr Hawkins, physician and surgeon respectively at St George's Hospital. They found on examination a comminuted fracture of the left collar-bone and a large swelling of the tissues below the bone and under the pectoral muscles which suggested that one or more ribs at the back were also broken. A patent water-mattress was obtained and with some difficulty Peel was placed on a table with his arms supported by pillows. During the evening he was allowed to see Lady Peel but he was in such a state of shock that all other visitors were forbidden. Next day there was no improvement. The swelling below the shoulder-blade had enlarged and was pulsating with the action of the heart. It was clear that there was not only a severe internal haemorrhage but also intense pain caused by the pressure of the haemotoma on the large nerves passing through the armpit. Application of leeches to allay the inflammation was tried but affected the patient so much that he had to be given an immediate stimulant. All Sunday night and Monday Peel remained in the same precarious state. During the night of Monday he was delirious, frequently tried to raise himself, and became so exhausted that the doctors thought that he would not survive till dawn. While unconscious he frequently muttered the names of Hardinge and Graham. On Monday evening Hardinge was sent for, came at once, and stayed at Peel's bedside all night.

Outside the sickroom there was a constant stream of visitors and enquiries. Albert and Wellington came on the first evening and when the news spread over London during the weekend, the carriages began to arrive and a crowd gathered in the street. On Monday there was a constant procession of callers from early morning until late at night and as the day wore on the crowd at the gate, mainly poor people, began to thicken. They came and went, the men in their working clothes and the women in their shawls, passing on the latest reports to each other and peering through the railings at the darkened windows: but the numbers never diminished. All night long and all through Tuesday the whispering crowd filled Whitehall Gardens. When a fresh bulletin was put up about two o'clock there was such a rush to the gate to see it that a policeman had to read it aloud to the crowd. No doubt in this intense popular interest there was an element of morbid curiosity, intensified by the Victorian love of deathbed pathos. But it was not this which impressed observers as the dominant feeling among these humble watchers in the street. They found the spectacle striking not because it was a conventional but because it was such an unusual and unexpected tribute from the ordinary people of London. 'Unknowing the significance of their own appearance,' wrote one of the journalists reporting the scene, 'these poor folk were, in reality, the guard of honour accorded to the last hours of Sir Robert Peel—by the People.'

On Tuesday morning 2 July there was a gleam of hope. At four o'clock Peel had fallen into a deep sleep which lasted until eight. When he awoke he said he was in less pain. His pulse had dropped and he took a little nourishment. Afterwards he walked round the room supported on each side. At noon his condition was still better and Hawkins expressed confidence in his recovery. But two hours later there was a sudden deterioration. His breathing became stertorous and he gradually sank into a coma. The pulse was weaker and more rapid; and stimulants had no effect. At half-past six the doctors abandoned hope and advised the family that it was unlikely he would live another twenty-four hours. The Bishop of Gibraltar, Dr Tomlinson, an old friend, administered the sacrament and the members of his family were admitted one by one. Julia who had remained kneeling by his side was by this time so overcome that she had to be led away. Hardinge was already present and Graham arrived soon after. By nine o'clock Peel lapsed into unconsciousness once more. For another two hours the silent circle in the room listened to the painful breathing of the dying man. It ceased at nine minutes past eleven.

II

In deference to the feelings of the family there was no post mortem; but the accounts provided by Hodgson and Brodie leave no doubt on the salient features of the case. Victorian doctors were well accustomed to simple bone fractures and would have had little difficulty in treating them. The cardinal aspect of Peel's accident was the comminuted, that is to say, the fragmented fracture of the collar-bone accompanied by fracture of the ribs. Fragments of bone undoubtedly pierced a major blood vessel and may have introduced infection through the skin. The doctors believed that it was an injury to the subclavian vein which produced the haemorrhage and it is possible that the subclavian artery also was pierced. The surgical shock caused by these injuries, resulting not only from loss of blood but from excessive pain, could in itself have produced death. The subsequent symptoms however point to the development of broncho-pneumonia caused either by stasis in the left lung or direct injury and infection from broken bones. Given the state of medical techniques at the time, nothing could have saved Peel's life. Chloroform was already being employed by Simpson of Edinburgh, but its use in this case would have been of no value in allowing a more detailed clinical examination of the injuries; it would merely have killed the patient. Even a century later the exploration of such injuries as Peel sustained would be a hazardous surgical undertaking. The doctors did what their not inconsiderable knowledge and experience suggested. If they failed to save their patient, it is unlikely that they made his condition worse. From the moment he was picked up on Constitution Hill, Peel was a mortally injured man. Not the fall perhaps but the knees of a stumbled horse did the irreparable damage.

On Wednesday, as the news spread all over the country, shops closed and flags were flown at half-mast. The House of Commons immediately adjourned and when they reassembled the following evening Russell paid the formal tribute of the House, followed by several others. Many members were in black and some took off their hats when Russell began to speak. Graham, incapable of speech, sat there in tears. Goulburn confined himself to a dry statement on behalf of the family rejecting a burial in Westminster Abbey. In the Lords Lansdowne broke with precedent by a formal reference to the loss sustained by the other House. The Duke of Wellington, though he could hardly speak for tears, talked of Peel's passion for truth as though it were a quality he had not usually encountered among politicians. Throughout their long connection, he told the peers, he had never known Peel say anything which he did not firmly believe to be true. He was thinking perhaps of the slanders levelled at Peel in 1846; but it was left ironically for Stanley to make the most eloquent and touching tribute to 'a great man and a great statesman'. Though they had differed in opinion, he said significantly, there had never been any personal hostility between them; and he had never attached any unworthy motive to Peel's political conduct.

> To promote the welfare of his country he was prepared to make, and did actually make, every sacrifice. In some cases those sacrifices were so extensive that I hardly know whether the great and paramount object of his country's good was a sufficient reason to exact them from any public man.

During the next few days the newspapers vied in laudatory comment on what *The Times* called 'the greatest statesman of his time'. What observers noted was the common mood of all classes, from the queen to the humblest labourer. 'Great expressions of national sorrow', wrote Carlyle. 'Really a serious expression of regret in the public; an affectionate appreciation of this man which he himself was far from being sure of, or aware of, while he lived.' When older men searched their memories they could find nothing to equal it since the death of Pitt, though Aberdeen who could remember that event, thought the feeling for Peel more genuine and widespread. Some were surprised at the outburst of national sentiment. 'I thought he had a great hold on the country,' observed Greville, 'but had no idea it was so deep and strong and general as now appears.' Some surprised even themselves. 'Once', wrote Macaulay on 4 July, 'I little thought that I should have cried for his death.'

For ordinary people, indifferent to party politics, there had already been a sacrificial element in his resignation in 1846. The tragic nature of his death four years later irrationally reinforced this popular sense of a great statesman who had deliberately renounced the highest reward of politics for the good of his country. The justification which Peel had hoped to earn from posterity he received from his contemporaries while his body still lay at Whitehall Gardens. Nor did those feelings disappear immediately. The statues and monuments that began to appear in parks and public places all over Britain during the next few years; the cheap prints of his portraits to be found hanging up for the rest of the century in the cottages of country labourers and the backstreet homes of working-class families: these were mute evidence of the effect of his life on the popular traditions of the nation.

Yet equally permanent and more prominent, as Peel's generation died out, was the recollection of his inconsistencies and betrayals. To make a sudden change of opinion on a fundamental issue, to desert one's followers in a crisis, is something which many great statesmen may have to face. But to have done it twice, as Peel did over Catholic emancipation and the Corn Laws, seemed to indicate something deeper than the chance necessity of events. To those who put political consistency or party loyalty above all other public virtues, his offence was unforgiveable. Even the more dispassionate could conclude that he had been either very unfortunate or very careless. Perhaps Peel was in fact prone to political accident. His pride was too stiff, his temper too authoritative, his readiness to take responsibility too overpowering. His sense of duty drove him to face great issues; his intelligence provided him with radical solutions; his integrity denied him ordinary safeguards. He was always strong-willed, sometimes stubborn. He rarely admitted having made a mistake, never on anything important. He piqued himself on never having introduced a measure which he did not pass. It was a recipe for triumph, but also for disaster. Though in the last eighteen years of his life he had no equal as a parliamentarian, his skill was in dealing with the House of Commons as an assembly. He was less happy in dealing with its members as individuals. For that reason he can scarcely be said to be a great House of Commons man. With the party system he never really came to terms. His fundamental outlook was executive and governmental; his approach to politics, whether in office or opposition, was that of a potential minister of the Crown.

Yet against the somewhat slipshod generalisation that Peel was not good at handling men must be placed his outstanding qualities as head of an administration. The aloofness, the arrogance, the impatience he sometimes displayed in his dealings with his backbenchers, were singularly absent in his handling of colleagues. In the cabinet and towards younger men he showed a tact, kindliness and loyalty which made his administration one of the most harmonious of the century. No other prime minister left such a devoted band of followers. It was this which made the split in the Conservative Party so significant for the future of Victorian party politics. Most of the rank and file went over to Stanley; the brains and experience of the party stayed with Peel. The same difficulty of assessment is present when judging Peel as a party leader. Between his attitude as minister and his position as leader of the Conservative Party there remained a contradiction which he never resolved. Though in securing supreme power in 1841 he owed everything to party and nothing to the Crown, he conducted himself in office as though the old-fashioned theory of royal confidence and ministerial responsibility to the Crown was a reality of political life. While he recognised his indebtedness to his party followers, the obligations which that debt imposed he was prepared to ignore. His allegiance was to an older concept than party loyalty; it was to the service of the state. Yet what Peel did for the Conservative Party after

EPILOGUE

1832 was fundamental. He revived and reshaped the scattered forces of the opposition, provided them with a fresh philosophy, found new sources of support, and led them to ultimate victory. His place as the founder of modern Conservatism is unchallengeable. Disraeli's 're-education' of the party a generation later was inevitably a return to Peelite principles since only on those principles could a party of the right in the conditions of Victorian politics obtain power.

At the time of his death the party disruption of 1846 seemed of little consequence compared with his impressive catalogue of achievements: the Royal Irish Constabulary, the Bullion Committee and the return to gold, legal and criminal reform, repeal of the Test and Corporation Acts, Catholic emancipation, the Metropolitan Police, the Ecclesiastical Commission, tariff reform and free trade, the income tax, the Bank Charter Act, Maynooth and the Irish Colleges, the Devon Commission, and the repeal of the Corn Laws. It testified to his master passion in politics; the desire to get things done. It was said of him by Disraeli and others that he lacked originality; that he merely appropriated other men's ideas. It was a curious misconception of the role of politicians. The statesman is not a mother but a midwife. Original ideas are of little consequence in themselves until the time is ripe for putting them into practice. The test of political skill is in choice, timing and execution. Politics is the art of the possible; yet to determine what is possible often takes judgement and courage. The measure of Peel's quality is that he did what other politicians thought could not be done. 'A great doer of the impossible', Harriet Martineau called him; and Goldwin Smith, who was so nearly Peel's first real biographer, summed it up in one stately sentence: 'For a quarter of a century, at least, he was without question the first public servant of England.' The combination of intellectual power, governmental experience and parliamentary ability, put Peel in the last twenty years of his life in a class of his own. In mental capacity alone he was one of the ablest prime ministers in British history.

Yet he was not solely an intellectual; there were other more intuitive and imaginative qualities. The fundamental feature he exhibited after 1841 was a desire to reunite the country. The events of 1846 were only a supreme example of an attitude which underlay his whole conduct as minister. The significance of the action he took over the Corn Laws was symbolic; and as a symbol it was rivalled only by the Reform Act of 1832 as the decisive event in domestic politics in the first half of the nineteenth century. By 1846 the Corn Laws had been elevated into a test of governmental integrity. Peel's response, and the sacrifice it entailed, did more than anything else to heal the social breach and restore public confidence in a political system that was still aristocratic and oligarchic. By 1850, though Peel could not have known it as he lay dying at Whitehall Gardens, the larger problems of his time had been met and solved. The age of revolt was giving way to an age of stability, and of that age Peel had been the chief architect.

III

He was buried beside his father and mother in the little parish church of Drayton Bassett on Tuesday 9 July. It was a family ceremony to which only his closest and oldest friends had been invited. But all over the country on that day, in towns like Manchester, Birmingham, Liverpool, Bristol, Leeds, Wolverhampton and Bury, mills stopped work, shops closed, and in the sea-ports the flags of the vessels in harbour were lowered to half-mast. At Drayton crowds of workmen and country labourers with their wives and children came in from the surrounding towns and agricultural districts, from Sutton, Coleshill, Tamworth, Lichfield, Stafford and Birmingham, spreading over the wooded expanse of the park and gathering round the churchyard. Some were in mourning, the men in their Sunday velveteens with scraps of crape, the women in bonnets and shawls. Shortly before the time of the funeral the sky was overcast and there was a drenching storm of rain. When it stopped the funeral procession, followed by a long line of coaches and horsemen, moved slowly from Drayton Park along the narrow lanes. As they neared the churchyard the sky darkened and it began to pour down once more. In the pelting rain the heavy crimson-palled coffin was taken out of the hearse and carried inside.

A Short Bibliography

1. The basic sources in print are:
Sir Robert Peel from His Private Papers, ed. C. S. Parker. 3 vols, 1891–99: a selection of the more important letters and papers from the mass of Peel Papers now in the British Museum.
Memoirs by the Rt. Hon. Sir Robert Peel, ed. Lord Mahon and E. Cardwell. 2 vols, 1856–57: Peel's own account of the three major crises of his career, incorporating much original material.

The Private Letters of Sir Robert Peel, ed. G. Peel, 1920: mainly correspondence between Peel and his wife.
Speeches of the late Rt. Hon. Sir Robert Peel delivered in the House of Commons, 4 vols, 1853.

2. Of the many nineteenth-century books on Peel the following are of permanent interest:
M. Guizot, *Sir Robert Peel, Étude d'histoire contemporaine*, Paris 1856: an account by a contemporary French statesman and historian who knew Peel personally.
Lawrence Peel, *Sketch of the Life and Character of Sir Peel*, 1860: a character sketch by a cousin and contemporary.
Lord Rosebery, *Sir Robert Peel*, 1899: a reprint of the review of Parker's three volumes which appeared in the *Anglo-Saxon Review*. A brilliant and perceptive essay by an outstanding late-Victorian politician and man of letters.

3. More modern books on Peel are:
A. A. W. Ramsay, *Sir Robert Peel*, Constable, 1928: the first scholarly biography, based partly on manuscript sources (for the 1822–32 period).
Tresham Lever, *The Life and Times of Sir Robert Peel*, Allen & Unwin, 1942: a readable popular life.
G. Kitson Clark, *Peel and the Conservative Party: a study in party politics*, 1832–1841, end edn Cass, 1964: a large and detailed monograph based on deep knowledge and meticulous research.
Norman Gash, *Mr Secretary Peel, The Life of Sir Robert Peel to* 1830, and
Sir Robert Peel, The Life of Sir Robert Peel after 1830, Longman, 1961, 1972.

4.   For recent essays on Peel see Asa Briggs, 'Sir Robert Peel', in
The Prime Ministers, ed. Herbert van Thal, vol. 1, Allen and Unwin
1974, ch. 24.
Norman Gash, 'Wellington and Peel 1832–1846', in *The Conservative
Leadership* 1832–1932, ed. Donald Southgate, Macmillan, 1974.

INDEX